Flatbush Odyssey

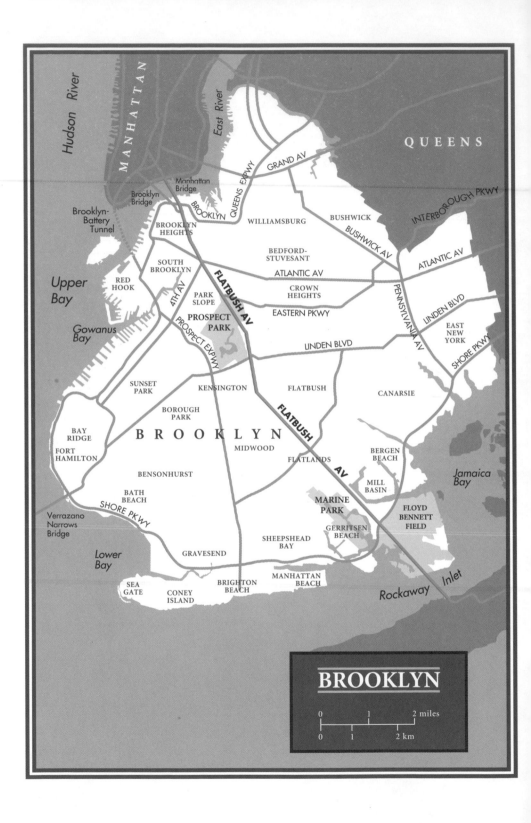

BROOKLYN

Flatbush Odyssey

A Journey Through the Heart of Brooklyn

ALLEN ABEL

M&S

Excerpt from "Nesting Time in Flatbush" from the show *Oh, Boy!* by P. G. Wodehouse reprinted by permission of A. P. Watt Ltd. on behalf of the Trustees of the Wodehouse Estate.

Canadian Cataloguing in Publication Data

Abel, Allen J., 1950-
Flatbush odyssey

Includes bibliographical references.

ISBN 0-7710-0703-5

1. Abel, Allen J., 1950-　　– Homes and haunts – New York (State) – New York. 2. Brooklyn (New York, N.Y.) – Description and travel.　3. Brooklyn (New York, N.Y.) – Social life and customs.　4. Flatbush Avenue (New York, N.Y.).　5. New York (N.Y.) – Description and travel.　6. New York (N.Y.) – Social life and customs.　I. Title.

F129.B7A55　1995　974.7'23　C95-930552-1

Typesetting by M&S, Toronto
Maps by Visutronx
Printed and bound in Canada on acid-free stock.

McClelland & Stewart Inc.
The Canadian Publishers
481 University Avenue
Toronto, Ontario
M5G 2E9

1　2　3　4　5　　99　98　97　96　95

For my mother

CONTENTS

INTRODUCTION

There is a deceptively simple air about Brooklyn, for Brooklyn, like love, cooking and other basic needs of man, is more complicated than most people imagine. . . . it is something as ageless and elusive as a woman's charm.

John Richmond and Abril Lamarque

Brooklyn, U.S.A., 1946

At ten o'clock on Thanksgiving morning 1992, my wife, Linda, decided it was time to tell my mother about this book. We were eating breakfast at the Golden Krust Bakery in Cohoes, New York, just across the Hudson River from historic Troy, where Linda and I had once lived. My mother had ordered scrambled eggs and bacon, with no intention of eating any of it, and "half a cup of light, light, light coffee" that she expected, after decades of similar requests, to arrive full to the brim and black. And it did.

"What if Al came to live with you for three months?" Linda posed.

"Not a chance," my mother replied, picking indifferently at her plate. The thunderbolt sailed right past her. She'd been hoping for nineteen years that, when I came home from my brief fling with Linda, it would be forever. Now my wife was offering her a mere crumb.

"It's true," I asserted. "Three months in Brooklyn."

My mother, Hennie Lucci, formerly Hennie Abel, formerly Henrietta Jacobson of New Utrecht Avenue, Brooklyn, was wearing a pants suit in orange velour with matching Peter Pan booties and a burnt-umber felt peaked cap, on which she had pinned a small walrus-bone brooch I had bought for her in the Northwest Territories. She had her sunglasses on. (Outside, it was pouring rain.) Around her neck, among other millstones, was a pendant with two tiny crowned heads with jeweled eyes, representing me and my sister, Deborah, who was sitting next to my mother, making a total of four Abels, current and former, here at the Golden Krust.

We were enduring what, in our family, passes for a family reunion, in the guise of a nostalgic return to Troy.

"He's going to do a book about Flatbush Avenue," Linda continued. "And he'll stay with you while he's researching it."

"I heard you the first time," my mother replied. "My heart turned over."

Linda explained the basic plan. I'd spend a couple of months traversing Brooklyn, campaigning down Flatbush Avenue, the main street of my childhood, meeting the various residents and describing the sights. I'd begin at the rusting blue towers of the Manhattan Bridge and conclude, more than ten miles later, at the estuarine bird sanctuary at Jamaica Bay.

I had left home at seventeen to attempt astrophysics at Rensselaer Polytechnic Institute in the Hudson Valley, where the holiday assemblage at the Golden Krust was now becoming fascinated with the alien quartet in our booth. During my migrations upstate to college and a newspaper sportswriting job and, later, to Canada, my mother had remained in the same apartment on the same dead-end Flatbush street she had moved into, newlywed and pregnant, in the summer of 1949.

"Will you let him write about you?" Linda asked. "Because when he was going to write a story about his born-again cousins in Texas and he asked Ben, Ben said, 'Wait 'til I'm dead.'"

Ben is my father. The marriage had broken up in 1968, though Ben now called Hen daily from Century Village in Florida and regularly mailed her packages of air freshener and Ritz crackers as tokens of his unyielding ardor. Nothing delighted him more, at the age of eighty, than spending three dollars on postage to demonstrate to his sixty-nine-year-old ex-wife that he had been sharp enough to save thirty cents on biscuits. It was my father's penurious tendencies that had helped sever the connubial bonds in the first place, back in the Johnson administration.

I outlined the proposal and delineated some potential scenes: the merry Flatbush Terrace banquet hall, scene of the Allen Joel Abel bar-mitzvah soirée that nearly bankrupted Hennie and Ben in 1963, now a Haitian kindergarten; the Chinese restaurant where a teenaged Barbra Streisand worked as a cashier; the Irish funeral home where the completely non-Irish Fred Lucci, my mother's second husband, lay in his coffin for two days in 1986 before any of his innumerable relatives deigned to venture by. What had become of these places? How had my homeland changed so utterly? How had parts of it remained so achingly unaltered? I tried to make the journey down Flatbush sound warm and nostalgic. But Linda scared my mother nearly to death with tales of my foreign correspondent's courage.

"He's going to ride the Flatbush Avenue bus *at two o'clock in the morning*?" my mother gasped, turning to Debbie, an unemployed nursery-school warden, who was watching the scene unfold with dumb horror. "Why does he want to go where two men got shot the other night?"

My mother turned to me.

"You'll come home at two in the morning and it will be like the night I came in from a dance and in the lobby was this big, big fellow. And I was giving him a very careful look-over and he said to me, 'Why are you looking at me like that?' And I said, 'I look at everybody like that.'

"Then somebody buzzed him into the building and he glared at me and he said, 'See? I have somebody to see here.' He held the elevator for me, but I pretended to have to tie my shoelace and let him go up alone. I seem to have loose shoelaces very, very often."

I pictured the lobby of my mother's apartment building on East 31st Street, a half-block off Flatbush, wedged between a jumble of other six-story tenements and the Long Island Rail Road right-of-way. Once, freight trains stampeded regularly under our fourth-floor window – one would appear each Saturday night, drowning out the denouement of "Perry Mason" – but now the line had been long neglected and the timbers ripped up, leaving an ugly scar across the Borough of Churches, filled with garbage and milkweed.

I wondered if, inside, the stone lobby floor was still shinily polished, the long, dim hallways and the entombing elevator the same as in the years when I and my best friend, Brucie, forbidden to parade outside in costume, would trick-or-treat from door to door, until some older boy would squirt us with a water gun filled with vinegar and, crying, we would dart home. My mother had lived in this same building for forty-three years, through two marriages, the birth and growth of two children, the better and worse hemispheres of her life.

But outside, East 31st had become an urban catastrophe, its shrubs and hedges uprooted lest they serve as hiding places for muggers. (In the fifties, they were our "jungle"; the slope to the railway tracks was our Olympic toboggan run.) Now abandoned cars lay, burned out and hellish, against the curbside; car alarms punctured the uneasy nights with their screams, the new lullaby of Flatbush. Immigrants in apartment D6 blasted carnival music all night. Upstairs, in E5, someone trundled heavy carts up and down the corridor at one a.m., in tasks we were too terrified to query. Now I was proposing to return there from my nest of comfort in much-praised Toronto. Linda, of course, would stay behind in her native Canada.

"I think it's an excellent idea," I heard my mother saying to my wife, snapping me back to reality at the Golden Krust. "But I don't think he'll want to come and live with me."

"Then could he live with Doris?" Linda suggested. Doris had been my mother's closest friend for more than forty years, give or take intermittent decades of complete, bitter estrangement. Doris dwelled on the second floor of an apartment building right on Flatbush and hadn't been robbed in her entranceway for more than a year.

"If you stay with Doris," my mother told me, "don't go barefoot. She hasn't got any rugs."

She brightened. Thoughts of Doris's thriftiness made her greatly pleased.

"She hasn't got any *floors*."

Sister Debbie heard this and, convulsing, spit up her bagel.

"Like the ham said," my mother stated, noticing our improving mood, "I'm on a roll."

I asked my mother if she would be willing to do some research for me. She emitted a congested rattle from deep in her throat that I took as a signal of approbation.

"Could you go to the main library at Grand Army Plaza every day for two months and look stuff up?" I asked.

"Every day *for two months*?" my mother responded, and tumbled into one of her apoplectic coughing fits. Venturing to Grand Army Plaza at the far end of sylvan Prospect Park, a thirty-minute bus ride from East 31st through the largest Caribbean community north of Paradise Island, required an act of courage it could take days for her to muster.

The coughing continued. Finally, my mother gasped her compromise: "How about twice a week?"

We began to reminisce about Prospect Park and its squalid little zoo, about the New China Inn and the goldfish pond at Brooklyn College and

Fairyland and various other personal landmarks along Flatbush's long, swerving course from the East River to the Atlantic tidewater. I recalled taking Debbie regularly to her orthodontist in Brooklyn's tallest edifice, the Williamsburgh Savings Bank tower at Flatbush and Atlantic Avenue. We'd take breakfast at Bickford's pancake house across the street; by 1980, this same Bickford's was a boarded-up, vandalized shell, a symbol of Brooklyn's decay. And Little Debbie, nicknamed for a local brand of baked goods, was now thirty-seven, a full-grown, as-yet-unmarried woman of Dolly Partonesque proportions, crowned by her latest attempt at hair coloring, a russet dye that was receding from the crown downward, as if obeying Newton's Law of Universal Gravitation, leaving bare gray threads at the peak.

Recovering from her cough, my mother brought forth a plan of her own.

"I could have my cataract operation and you could take care of me," she proposed. It sounded like a good idea. After her last cataract operation, she was beholden to my sister's aid, putting the proverbial fox in charge of the literal Hen-house.

(Debbie still lived in Brooklyn, in a basement apartment in the neighborhood called Canarsie, after the thoroughly extirpated tribe of local Indians. She was fastidious about her dining habits, yet her living quarters were piled waist-high with old newspapers, Willie Nelson albums, and hockey-team sweatshirts. Little Debbie was a one-woman Odd Couple.)

I mentioned a starting date in the spring of 1993. I'd ask for a leave of absence from my television job. It was settled. My mother sighed in a curious mixture of delight and resignation.

"Finally," she said, "I have a reason to get a paint job."

∾

The visit to Troy proceeded. We drove to the brownstone row house where Linda and I were married on a sun-kissed April Saturday in 1974. (That day was the first time my parents had seen each other since their separation six years earlier. Fred Lucci, my mother's second husband, was there also, appearing in photographs of the rather uncomfortable affair with one hand in his jacket pocket, as if fingering a gun.) Now, Little Debbie took a few snapshots of Linda and me at the front steps, and a few more on the splintering back porch, where we newlyweds once swatted horseflies and barbecued inexpensive cuts of meat. But my mother never got out of the car.

Troy in 1992 was a city of rusted old factories whose prosperity had peaked at the time of the Civil War. But to me, it represented the break with Brooklyn that my mother and my sister had never made. Troy was where I "earned" my college degree – aided by a pass-fail grading system forced on the Rensselaer administration during the anti-Vietnam War upheavals of my junior year. There I managed the school's hockey team, got married to a sweet Canadian infidel, and sold bowling shoes at Andy's Sporting Goods until I was fired for rudeness to customers. The *Troy Record* was my first newspaper; I started as a part-timer in the sports department, taking Little League linescores over the phone at fifty-four dollars a week. Mornings and afternoons on WTRY, I was "Al Abel on Sports," wild-haired and idealistic.

Nine years in Troy had blanched the Brooklyn out of me. Returning there in autumn made me all weepy and moist. But I realized what my mother must have felt, sitting alone in the car, puffing her Parliaments, while Linda and I drowned in dopey nostalgia: this drear little burg was where she lost her son.

∾

Early in the spring of 1993, two days after the third "Storm of the Century" in five months, the snowplows had yet to reach East 31st at the dead end by the railway tracks. Some melting had taken place in the days following the thirteen-inch burial. Now, huge boulders of slush buckled and heaved in the street like the balsa-wood ice floes in *Alexander Nevsky*.

The district looked awful. The famous green canopy at the front door of our building was gone, removed after forty years (at least) because a new generation of uninhibited inhabitants had taken to swinging from its supporting poles. Trash bags and flash-frozen dog droppings stained the snowbanks.

When the windowless elevator door closed and the ancient machine began reluctantly to rouse itself to motion, I felt as I had when my documentary crew and I flew into Kuwait and saw the first hellish billows of poisonous smoke from seven hundred blazing oil wells. I thought: I'm coming here to *live*?

"You're feeling well?" I asked my mother as she unlocked the two deadbolts and slid the chain off the door to admit me.

"I'm not emaciated," she said. (She often forecast her death from willful starvation.)

"Oh," I replied. "Then I'm not seeing you at your worst."

She was wearing faded blue jeans and a black T-shirt decorated with a rampant imperial dragon that my father had bought for her when Linda and I took him around Hong Kong during our China years. She looked pretty good for sixty-nine going on seventy going on a pack and a half a day.

"There's nothing wrong with my respiratory," she said. "And when the doctor said there's nothing wrong with my circulation, I told him I don't get around much any more."

Fifteen minutes later, we were sitting on the couch and she was laughing and force-feeding me halvah. In a burst of parental paleontology, she laddered into the hall closet and extricated a carton of family memorabilia from the top shelf. In the box, crammed with ejecta, was the doctor's prescription for the treatment of my circumcision ("apply Vaseline dressing until healed"), the invoices and seating arrangements for my bar mitzvah at the Flatbush Terrace ($20 for skull caps, $10 for satin-covered matchbooks, $650 for 100 dinners of roast chicken, rissole potato, and "Vivid" peas), and another doctor's note from 1959, on which she had written this poem:

> Though you upset me
> and I upset *you*, too
> We know we love each other
> And Dad & Debbie too

Then Little Debbie blew in from Canarsie for dinner. We sat in the living room and listened to the car alarms and the chain-saw screaming of spinning tires as lost and snowbound Trinidadians tried to U-turn at the dead end. My mother put on a Crystal Gayle tape. She had us where she wanted us.

She stalked theatrically into the doorway and turned and said, *"Don't,* under *any* circumstances, have a seventieth birthday party for me." The date was still three months off, late June.

"Done!" I cheered. Inwardly, I took it as a direct order for a full-scale Roman bacchanal.

∾

In the carton of old photographs and papers was another souvenir. It was a letter from Troy, written by a bewildered eighteen-year-old in the first weeks of a disassembled family. Dated September 26, 1968, it read:

Dear Mom,

I have spent many sleepless nights over what I should say to you. I certainly wanted, after the initial shock wore off, to act as an adult in this situation, and decided to act with a completely open mind. But I felt obligated to alienate myself from you until you stopped refusing to let Debbie see her father. . . .

I am sure you have suffered enough in the past year. My greatest hope at the present time is that the shouting and the crying is over. . . .

I hope that this letter clears up any doubts about me you may have had, that now you are in a more optimistic frame of mind than the last time I saw you, and that our next letters will be on a more congenial level.

Love,
AJA
Dorm B, Room 208

I hadn't remembered my six-month boycott of my mother; I'm sure my mother never passed an hour without it stabbing her again and again. In June 1968, on the last day I would call this flat my residence, my father and I had walked over from his candy store on Avenue D – we were sleeping on army cots in the back room; we'd watched the news of Robert Kennedy's assassination there – and we found my mother in the kitchen, and my mother was screaming, "Don't touch me! Don't touch me!" Now I was coming home again, to live with her for part of a year, explore the boulevard along which all this, and so much more, had been played out over the decades and centuries of renowned, hilarious, homely, devastated, bucolic, seething Brooklyn.

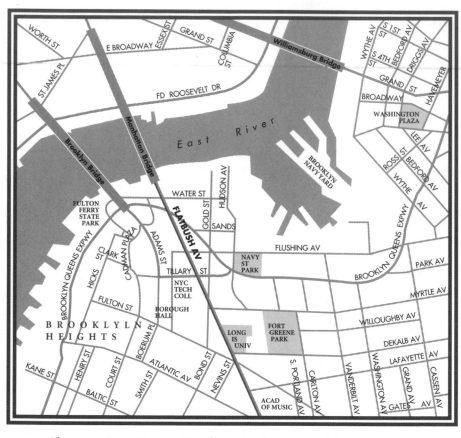

Chapter One: Down Under Manhattan Bridge Overpass

Down Under Manhattan
Bridge Overpass

1

This was the morning Brooklyn had craved in the most private of its prayers. I stood at the river's edge and marveled at the mystery, closed my eyes, opened them to the same mad corroboration. It was true. Manhattan had disappeared.

For ninety-five years, since its misstep into the agglomeration of so-called Greater New York, the borough at whose coastline I was now balancing on a hillock of smashed auto glass and splintered dock pilings had regretted the whole affair. Now, it seemed, the parties finally had divorced. A separate city again, Brooklyn had seceded so enthusiastically, it was floating toward Portugal.

But it was only fog.

I was trying to get as close to the actual waters of the East River as I could without getting drowned or arrested. Little Debbie and I were violating the "No Trespassing" signs on an abandoned pier at the foot of Pearl Street, Brooklyn, directly under the roadway of the blue Manhattan Bridge. This was to be the ceremonial inauguration of my lamebrained intention, a slow meandering toward the other shore of Brooklyn, ten miles to the southeast, by way of Flatbush Avenue, whose traffic flow, honking and snarling and shuddering, began on the bridge a hundred-odd feet above our heads.

Coming down off the span, a driver would proceed arrow-straight along Flatbush into downtown Brooklyn, climb up the renascent hillside district known as Park Slope, wend around disarmingly bucolic Prospect Park, then lock the doors and roll up the windows for the nervous transit of the much-less-affluent core of the borough, where my mother and I lived (she permanently and I as a three-month guest). Finally, one would rocket through the Flatlands towards the opposite watershed and the end of the avenue, which happened to conclude in a National Recreation Area full of marsh-grass and ibises. It would take me all spring to make the journey, on foot and alone, except when accompanied by Little Debbie, who was accepting work as a substitute kindergarten teacher in Harlem as often as one day every two weeks.

As luck would have it, she was free this morning for the kickoff. Neither of us had ever been down here by the river before, though Debbie had lived all of her life in the borough, and I had been a brave explorer of my native streets until departing for university in 1967, which was just about the time it became inadvisable to go happy-wandering in Brooklyn without full body armor and an elephant gun. With commendable eagerness, Sis had tried to scout a route to the riverbank a couple of days earlier, but she got lost under the Brooklyn Queens Expressway and had to use her urban survival skills to backtrack to familiar precincts where she knew she could find pizza and Evian.

We were scrambling at the very lip of the gelatinous river, cut off from the living world by abandoned warehouses and a big hydroelectric sub-station, on whose wires deranged wine-headed finches were burbling the first come-on songs of spring. There didn't seem to be anybody else alive. Huge brick buildings stood abandoned, Troy-like, their windows bricked up or knocked out completely, old paper-bag factories and storage houses now obsolete, forgotten, and dead. The piers that once pulsed with riverborne trading had been turned into parking lots, enclosed by coils of concertina wire, or left to crumble like glaciers calving into the East River scum.

The fog was belligerent. It obliterated Gotham, rendered the Brooklyn Bridge, an eighth of a mile away, vague and ethereal, surrendered a Circle Line tour boat for an instant (what could they possibly see?) then ate it again. Even the towers of the Manhattan Bridge, right over us, dissolved into conjecture.

The morning had begun with two fierce thunderstorms, rare for so early in spring. Now it was dripping again, from the sky and the bridge itself, so that not even standing under the span gave shelter. Sodden, and satisfied that I had made at least a perfunctory show of beginning my trek at the river,

I was telling Debbie we should be heading back to East 31st Street, before our mother assumed we had been waylaid, tortured, and killed, which usually took her about twenty minutes.

Then, while making one last obeisance towards the water, I saw a dark shape floating in the stream. It was a loon, a wild bird, impossible of cities, wintering in this least pristine of channels. Soon this primeval fisherman would depart for the north, perhaps to echo his Tyrolean yodel across the lake where Linda, my wife, would pass some of my absence at her mother's lovely mid-Ontario cottage. Quickly, with great excitement, I called Debbie.

Debbie thought it was a duck.

The pier where we were standing was a recking wreck of torn-up concrete, old truck tires, twisted cables, and kitchen trash. Even the street names down here were throwaways – Dock, John, Water, Front, Jay – as if it would be wasteful to bestow more lyric titles on such brief and untraveled lanes. But the loon transported me. I watched him dive, disappear, then surface with a flapping, silver six-inch catch. Above us, the grinding grey snake of the Brighton Beach subway inched across the Manhattan Bridge, metal on metal, burrowing for Brooklyn. The noise was infernal. But the loon heard only the tide.

∾

We didn't go home. We walked west along cobblestone streets, swathed in mist and light rain, tripping over ancient railway tracks that no one had thought it profitable to disinter. We crossed Main Street, whose name might once have been apt, when this forgotten fluvial zone was all the Brooklyn there was.

That would have been in Walt Whitman's time, the eighteen-teens and twenties, when the first of Robert Fulton's steam ferries replaced the sailboats and horse-drawn powerhouses that propelled commerce and commuters across the tidal strait. It took a leap of imagination now to hear what the poet–boy heard, "the heave'e'yo of stevedores unlading ships by the wharves – the refrain of the anchor-lifters," because the dockland in which we walked was empty and menacing and New York across the water was still nonexistent in this morning's delicious gloom.

Part of the shoreline between the Brooklyn and Manhattan bridges had been designated a New York State Park. This initially seemed to be a hoax – the first sign we saw for it was on a wire fence, behind which was a yard full of garbage and diseased machinery. But then, rounding the corner of New Dock and Water streets, we found a gate, and that led into a grassy area with picnic tables, pale lemon daffodils, and a boardwalk right at the water's edge.

I was a bit nervous (as usual) because there was only one open entrance to Fulton Ferry State Park and, once we moved away from the gateway, anyone could come in behind us and block our route of escape. But Debbie had brought her tools of self-preservation with her – a whistle and a miniature folding knife – and so we moved farther and farther along the walkway, though I kept thinking that, if she blew that whistle while being carved up by some felon with her own picayune switchblade, anyone within earshot would assume it was merely the mating call of the East River loon.

There were some explanatory historical signs posted at the riverfront, but these had been completely covered with artful graffiti, and it was the same when, having survived the State Park, we crossed under the Brooklyn Bridge itself and stood beside its mighty Gothic anchorage, which had been scrawled on and defiled. We leaned over the water, and I spotted a pair of swooping, black-headed laughing gulls and a double-crested cormorant furiously flapping upriver, towards Bellevue Hospital and the United Nations. So there was at least some life here.

"Just as you are refreshed by the gladness of the river, and the bright flow, I was refreshed," Whitman wrote in "Crossing Brooklyn Ferry," anticipating everything save the construction of the bridges and the abandonment of the wharves and passageways beneath them. From this bank, in 1776, George Washington's Massachusetts ferrymen scurried a decimated army of rebels to safety under a fog as thick as this morning's. A century later, fifty million people a year would cross between the largest city in America and the third-largest, a muscular, independent Brooklyn.

Today, on the Manhattan shore, I knew, there was a wonderfully vibrant recreated seaport, with high-masted schooners and high-priced saloons. But on our side of the grey oilcloth, the East River bank had become a place of desolation and dark alleys, and the last thing I wanted was to get shanghaied in the first two hours of my trip. Down here, the river was glad to be left alone.

∾

We backtracked east along Plymouth Street, and again passed under the Manhattan Bridge, which was splashing both water and torrents of reconstruction noise at us, as riveters, hidden from view behind webs of orange mesh, went at the old blue-rinsed dowager hammer and tongs, trying to keep it from collapsing like Tinkertoys. The Brooklyn Bridge was a symbol of New York – an identifying icon, like bagels or Leona Helmsley. But nobody even *liked* the Manhattan Bridge.

When it opened, on December 31, 1909, the fourth great suspension across the East River, the best the Brooklyn *Daily Eagle* could say about it was that it cost twenty-six million dollars and that it could carry a load of eight tons per linear foot. Its construction, the newspaper reported, had been delayed for more than a decade by two changes in the mayoralty, Brooklyn's subsuming into New York City in 1898, architects' disputes, bid-rigging, patronage, lawsuits, and injunctions, "a history of delay and controversy during which the foundations stood on either side of the river as monuments to official longwindedness."

Hardly anyone was killed building it. One of the unfortunate exceptions was a worker named McShane, who was blown 120 feet into the air when the hose of his compressed-air drill came loose. McShane snapped an inch-thick plank in half as he descended and was still alive when he landed here on Plymouth Street. Moments later, he was gone.

That was in April 1909. Three months later, two ironmen named Gilchrist and McGillis – almost all the workers were Irish – fell towards the river from the Brooklyn tower 135 feet in the sky. Gilchrist landed on a wooden platform after a fall of 40 feet and lived. However, the corpus of William Herbert McGillis, a Canadian from Toronto, "describing a great arc, shot into the water with tremendous force and was not recovered."

When McGillis hit the water, the four hundred other laborers, adhering to custom, claimed the rest of the day off.

"Compared to other work of this kind, accidents have been few," the *New*

York Times said. "Not half a dozen men have been killed since the work started. According to the Chief Engineer, from twenty to forty men are usually sacrificed to the building of a large bridge."

Only three hundred automobiles crossed on the first day, paying a ten-cent toll that has long since been abolished, an insane municipal policy that daily grants tens of thousands of cars and trucks free passage into Manhattan, where they idle, gridlocked and fulminating, until their drivers die of asphyxia or the homeward rush hour begins.

When the Brooklyn Bridge was inaugurated in the spring of 1883, designed and built by the Roebling family and other men of Troy who went a lot further with their Rensselaer degrees than I had, the clergyman who delivered the benediction thought the suspension cables were "almost like blossoming festooned vines along the perfumed Italian lanes." A couple of days later, twelve people were crushed to death in a stampede on a stairway when a woman slipped and dozens fell on top of her and someone screamed "The bridge is falling!"

The Manhattan was neither as hexed nor as idealized. When it opened, even though its arches were copied from the Porte St. Denis in Paris and the colonnade was supposed to have been inspired by the Piazza of St. Peter's in Rome, the *Eagle* had allowed that the Manhattan Bridge was "perhaps outclassed for beauty." Thirty years later, the Federal Writers' Project dismissed it as "just-matter-of-fact."

LeCorbusier thought the Brooklyn Bridge "as strong and rugged as a gladiator." Of the George Washington Bridge from Manhattan to New Jersey he wrote, "here, finally, steel architecture seems to laugh." LeCorbusier found the Manhattan Bridge "pedestrian." But no pedestrians crossed it now.

∾

At the corner of John and Pearl, this first exploratory morning, was a parking lot, and this was regulated by a fellow named Pete, an Italo-American in a sodden leather cap, who was the first live Brooklynite we encountered on the excursion. I was so happy to see someone else down here under the bridges that I overcame my natural self-possession and started a blithe conversation with this total stranger, an act that in New York is as automatic as blinking, but one that in Canada is grounds for summary arrest and censure by Parliament.

Pete came out of the shelter where he kept the cashbox and a television set and encouragingly substantiated all my worst suspicions about the lonely streets Debbie and I had been prowling for two hours.

"It's got so bad around here," Pete said, "so *bad*-bad, you gotta be bad to keep up with it."

He motioned to one of the old warehouses and told us not to go near it, because it was a marshaling yard for drug fiends, but of course we had just sniffed around the uninhabited loading dock there, and I had paused to urinate against the wall.

"The crackheads," Pete said. "The crackheads come down here, they hand you a can of shaving cream, they say, 'Gimme fifty cents.' Stupid. I mean, you're gonna be a thief, rob some big jewelry store. But down here, they rob your umbrella, they rob your chain, just so's they can say, 'Hey! I robbed somebody!'"

I held tighter to my umbrella.

"I got a knife," Debbie said hopefully, manipulating her miniature weapon.

"A knife won't help," Pete replied, sober faced.

∾

Other signs of life began to emerge as the rain abated. As we wandered among the old factory buildings, ignoring Pete's warnings, we saw that some of them were taking in truckloads of scrap cardboard and shredded paper. Wire-bound, compacted bundles the size of refrigerators were standing in groups on the dark, cavernous work floors, as if conversing among themselves. On Adams Street, right beside the stained concrete anchorage of the Manhattan Bridge, we stopped for grape juice at a tiny lunch counter run by immigrants from the Dominican Republic, and the owner said he had plans to punch holes in the brickwork of his café to serve more expeditiously the hard-hatted workmen who were repairing the ninety-year-old latticework over our heads. There were even some small row houses next to the restaurant, making it evident that many people worked – and quite a few actually lived – full-time within earshot of the bridge's awful din.

Proceeding down Front Street, I saw a dazzling, pure-white glow coming from the second-story windows of one of the warehouses. Immediately, my years of broadcasting experience kicked in and I told Debbie, "Those are TV lights!" So we tried to find an entrance to the building to see what was going on.

I fumbled in my pockets for some documentation to prove that I was a bona-fide television journalist – my face and voice would never give it away – but then I realized that I had jettisoned all forms of ID, along with credit cards, driver's license, Ontario health-care certificates, and photographs of Linda, back at my mother's, lest they be found on my carcass in this sinister wasteland and used to perpetrate further misdeeds. All my cash had been divided into four small amounts, each kept in a separate pocket, though I planned to surrender happily every dollar and dime should any crackhead come at me with a pistol or a can of shaving cream.

The building was 75 Front Street, and it turned out to my astonishment to be the current home of Gleason's Gym, the Sorbonne of boxing. I had covered a lot of big fights in my time – Ali versus Frazier, Leonard versus Duran, George Chuvalo versus "Pretty Boy" Felstein – but I had never been to Gleason's, which was renowned as the cradle of champions in the Sweet Science, as fist-fighting was often called by smug columnists like me who never had their neurons scientifically rewired in the ring.

Nobody was getting lobotomized at Gleason's Gym today. The huge training room had been given over to a film crew, just as I had suspected, and in one ring were two splendidly conditioned young men in singlets and headgear, daintily sparring. And leaning on the ropes in front of them was big old bald George Foreman.

They were making a commercial for automobile parts. (On U.S. television, it had become difficult to watch any station for thirty minutes without seeing Foreman's defoliated cranium nodding and smiling in some endorsement or other, usually in mocking reference to his Brobdingnagian appetite. When not fighting or huckstering, he was in rehearsals for his own situation-comedy show.) When he mutilated "Smokin' Joe" Frazier, knocking him down six times and out once, to become heavyweight champion in 1973, Foreman was assailed as a brutish monster, but he had subsequently metamorphosed twice: first into a humble Texas preacher in retreat from a world of vanity and evil, and then, returning to the prize ring, into a comic-book Palooka, wildly popular, a tender-hearted, sumo-sized assassin in a cruel ghetto game.

"Roll sound!" a voice screamed, and then, "Action!" The specimens in the ring began their light-gloved engagement as background to the famous heavyweight's spiel. Whole squadrons of lighting technicians, slate-clappers, producers, directors, camera operators, and caterers snapped to rapt attention.

George Foreman, forty-whatever and still active in the paid destruction of his fellow man, hollered eight words: "THAT'S WHY I TRUST MY BRAKES TO MEINEKE!"

Debbie and I were watching the taping on a video monitor, having moved into the midst of the production team unmolested by any of the muscular behemoths – Gleason's regulars, apparently – who were hanging around the loft. Foreman took a short breather, pacing the floor in a gray hooded sweatshirt, stage-whispering to himself, over and over, the script he was to perform next. Then he went back to his station under the light-standards, the sparring began anew, the crew's designated Aquarius squirted water on the fighters to simulate perspiration, and the giant who had been champion of the world when I was still covering high-school football for the *Troy Record* was heard bellowing his praise of Meineke's low prices: "I COULD USE THAT EXTRA MONEY . . . FOR FOOD!"

The stage manager called a break, and the old warrior started walking directly toward us. Daydreaming, half-dissolved in recollections of interviewing this man after an easy knockout in Utica, New York, in 1975, and wondering if I should ask for an autograph, I suddenly realized that Debbie and I were standing directly between George Foreman and a table laden with cold cuts and doughnuts.

There was no time to think, but somehow, with seconds to spare, I grabbed my baby sister and hustled her safely down the stairs and back into the colorless spring day.

∾

Now we had to find our way up and out of the riverside laneways.

Closer to the Manhattan Bridge anchorage, all routes seemed to lose themselves in various on-ramps and off-ramps of the river crossings and the notorious Brooklyn Queens Expressway, or BQE, a *vena cava* of Brooklyn's aging, over-taxed Circumferential Parkway ("The Belt"), which down here in the industrial zone was a noxious, listless serpentine of tractor-trailers lined up nose to tail like elephants in a circus parade. Pearl Street dead-ended, Adams rammed into a concrete wall, Anchorage Place led into a construction yard. But we made our way up little Washington Street, found a tunnel under the highways, and twenty minutes later I was sitting in a wing chair in the Estée Lauder boutique in the Abraham and Strauss department store in the Fulton Street Mall, and Little Debbie, who hadn't had a steady paycheck in two years, was skating towards me delightedly with four silk blouses, a steal at $103.

Coming downtown for the ceremonial First Steps, just after breakfast, we had tried taking the Flatbush Avenue bus, but when the driver's-side defroster went tits-up at Grand Army Plaza and the windows clouded over, we were all thrown off into the rain and had to walk the rest of the way to the riverbank, two long miles on my *Geographia Street Map of Brooklyn with Bus Routes*. So we decided to eschew the bus and take the subway back to our mother's apartment, just for kicks.

I remembered that the Flatbush Avenue branch of the IRT subway had a station right in the basement of Abraham and Strauss, but that proved to have been bricked up for at least twenty years, and we had to venture back out into traffic and then locate a stairway for the Hoyt Street station, which, to welcome me back to Brooklyn, was on fire.

As we made our way down the steps toward the turnstiles – I had my token all ready, of course – pink-faced firefighters ("New York's Bravest"), in long heavy coats and wearing tanks of oxygen, were just emerging from the hole. The southbound Number 2 Flatbush train was standing at the platform, doors open. It had been held while what turned out to be an inconsequential blaze in some inconsequential refuse on the track, more smoke than flame, was extinguished. (Garbage above ground was the province of the Department of Sanitation, "New York's Strongest.") Soon we were ready to depart, and the last thing I saw as the doors closed at Hoyt Street was a young Irish fireman standing on the platform in black rubber boots, holding a double-hooked wooden pole taller than his helmet-top, and absently whistling. It took a moment for it to sink in that he was whistling "This Old Man," the tune of the theme song of Barney the Dinosaur.

It was only my second trip on the subway in Brooklyn in about fifteen years. I had abandoned it at the climax of its systematic demolition at the hands of time and bankruptcy and schoolchildren, at about the same moment that the rail-mad Paul Theroux, committed to a full week's wanderings in the cold hell of the tunnels, detailed "a nightmare . . . manifest suffocation . . . a sense of disgust and horror" in the *New York Times Magazine*. The trains – and especially our IRT line, known popularly as "The Beast" – were the setting for so much mayhem and savagery, real and reputed, that even I, the son of Ben Abel, had been known take a yellow taxi to my mother's from assignments in Manhattan, willingly paying fifteen dollars for what could have been a one-dollar ride.

When Debbie and Linda and I had gone a couple of years ago to visit Ellis Island, the landing-place at which ancestors named Jacobson and Abelowitz had entered the New World at the turn of the century, our trip concluded at the Manhattan ferry dock in a greasy rainstorm that melted taxis on contact and, as a last resort, we had taken the Number 2 to Flatbush, without physical injury. Now, I had noticed, the subway was said to be enjoying some sort of rebirth – *New York Magazine* had recently hailed it as one of ten things about the decaying metropole that had actually improved – and so I settled in for the twenty-five-minute underground haul to Hennie's, remembering to not so much as glance into the eyes of anyone else on board and not even flinching when, at Eastern Parkway–Brooklyn Museum, a teenaged male in the purple-and-yellow harlequin pants currently in fashion held the doors open and pounded on the windows and called out to the high-school girls in our car, "I like your poo-see!"

At Franklin Avenue, there was a man playing a steel drum on the platform. At Sterling Street, a worker was erasing thick red spray paint from the white tiles of the station. At Winthrop, where I once staggered from a train and unloaded the Mexican supper my best pal Brucie had encouraged me to eat before a Yankees baseball game, absolutely nothing happened this time.

Our car was delightfully devoid of painted initials and calls to destroy the white, black, or brown race. Even the route maps were visible. In fact, although all the door panels and windows had been so vigorously scraped and carved by knives and screwdrivers that you couldn't see where you were until the doors opened at a station, the system could veritably be described, as it was now proudly hailed by the Transit Authority, as "graffiti-free," at least in comparison to the late seventies. This militated against some of the claustrophobia and abject terror – especially on a short trip such as this on a familiar route at mid-afternoon – but it still was edifying to surreptitiously scan the faces of one's fellow travelers and to try to separate the slashers and contract killers from the honor students and remittance men.

The train was crowded but not crammed. Debbie and I were the only whites in our car, pioneers at our own birthplace. (Above us was a neighborhood totally Jewish and Irish until 1970, now the nucleus of a new Carib-America, principally Haitian, but also Jamaican, Trinidadian, Vincentian, Bajan, Grenadian, Bahamian, Guyanese.) Advertisements were intimate and interrogatory. "TORN EARLOBE?" the billboards asked. "FOOT PAIN?" Cures were promised for secret, hidden burdens: spider leg veins, fungus nails, sebaceous cysts.

"STOP SUFFERING NEEDLESSLY!"

Franklin, President, Sterling, Winthrop, Church, Beverly, Newkirk, Flatbush. The names flooded back in immutable sequence, imprinted forever on rides to hockey games and Broadway shows and the planetarium, on Saturday-morning commutation to my eye doctor and my sister's orthodontist when Debbie was even littler, two children alone together on The Beast.

It seemed ludicrous to contemplate – it made me feel, at forty-three, as antique as the first American Abelowitz – but I had grown up at a time when it was common to ride the New York subway for pleasure. Some of my schoolmates once tried to see if they could visit all 458 stations in less than twenty-four hours. (They could.) Brucie and I rode for hours on school nights to play ice hockey in Queens; to haunt the World's Fair and the old baseball stadium known as the Polo Grounds; to see the Mona Lisa at the Metropolitan Museum. Later, working collegiate summers as a mailman in steam-bath Manhattan, idling home to my father and our army cots, I would explore as many routes as I could, braced against the front window of the first car as the trains leapt out of river tunnels, cantilevered over toy trestles, plunged back into the bowels of the great city. Astoria, Rockaway, Forest Hills. The Sea Beach line, the West End, the wooden cars of the Culver Shuttle.

Today, day one of a springtime in Flatbush, a quick and uneventful trip through a different universe ended where a thousand boyhood travels had begun. (Or maybe it was I that had changed more than my borough.) At the end of the line at Flatbush Avenue, exiting relieved and rather pleased with myself a slight two blocks from home, I noticed a flyer on the window of the token booth. It said:

REWARD $10,000
for anyone with information regarding the homicide of a Transit Authority token booth clerk at the Euclid Avenue subway station on Wednesday, November 25, 1992, at 10:20 p.m.

Under this was a separate poster detailing the killing of another token clerk at Van Siclen Avenue – both were IRT stations in the vast slums of eastern Brooklyn – but I thought: I'm not a cashier. I don't ride at 10:20 at night. I don't go to Euclid or Van Siclen, so this does not frighten me. It does not frighten me.

I was home.

2

"Having yaw compwex cah-bo-high-dwates, yaw pwo-teen, and yaw fwoot?" my sister asked me at breakfast. "Good boy!"

I was enjoying a Muenster cheese sandwich on an onion-poppy-sesame bagel, a glass of skim milk, and a banana. Deborah was enjoying preadolescence; she'd taught four-year-olds for so many years, she had finally become one.

We were preparing for another day's exploration. I ate a full morning meal and carried only a pen, a notebook, and several small caches of one-dollar bills. Debbie consumed nothing before elevenses and portaged a shoulder bag filled with enough fruit-and-nut bars, water bottles, guidebooks, rain gear, Eddie Bauer catalogs, and organically grown feminine-hygiene products to outfit a hike to Surinam.

This was East 31st Street on one of the first mornings of the tour: Deb brawling with her luggage, me assiduously flossing my teeth and putting on my Baltimore Orioles cap (the O's meant nothing to me personally, but I thought the avian emblem would register politically neutral in districts where the colors of the Chicago Bulls or Los Angeles Raiders might, unbeknownst to me, convey some deadly gang affiliation); then our mother, awakened preternaturally by our movements, shuffling in her pink slippers and nightgown, cigarette in place, bound for the apartment's only bathroom, attempting a movement of her own.

"May the Force be with you!" I called out, encouragingly, as she went by the kitchen.

"If I use force," she answered, trailing smoke and ashes, "my hemorrhoids pop out."

The apartment consisted of a living room, a bedroom, and a small kitchen, with a rather long hallway and a small entrance foyer. The Abels had arrived in the summer of 1949 – my father and his twin brother were operating a luncheonette a block away – and here we still were. The resident population had peaked at four, declined to two when my father and I relocated, hovered at three for nearly fifteen years when Fred Lucci entered the picture, and had been reduced to a singleton after Debbie found her own subterranean accommodation in Canarsie and Freddie died of heart failure at the age of sixty-two. The front door directly faced the old, slow elevator; that made it easier to haul up groceries and for the ambulance attendants to locate Freddie when he'd suffered one of the many coronary and blood-sugar crises that led to his early demise.

I was awarded the bedroom, one dresser drawer, and a fraction of the particle-board wardrobe. I hadn't brought much down from Toronto, just some old jeans and denim shirts, nothing to mark me as affluent or even worth bothering with. I was going to melt invisibly into the pavement, as Whitman had – "myself effusing and fluid, a phantom curiously floating" – and in Brooklyn in 1993 it was best to effuse without any necklaces, bracelets, watches, or other signs of obvious solvency.

("You're going out *with your wedding ring on?*" my mother had gasped on the very first day. So I took it off and left it for safekeeping in a leather jewel box I bought for her in Zagreb during the Yugoslav civil wars.)

During my visit, my mother adjourned to the fold-out sofa in the living room, watched by a set of long-faced Modigliani reproductions and a huge, expensive R. C. Gorman print my increasingly insolvent sister had bought for her in Santa Fe. Slumbering on the hide-a-bed was no great sacrifice: she and Ben had slept on a couch for more than a decade while Little Debbie and I dwelled on opposite sides of a wooden partition that was installed to bifurcate the boudoir. That wall had long since been Gorbacheved, so that now, when Debbie spent a night at the apartment, she had to curl up on a small love seat in the living room.

The building itself was six stories of red brickwork, built in the early nineteen-thirties, when these remote precincts, once the hereditary estates of the original Dutch burghers, were being sold to developers and made available to the lower-middle classes. (The IRT subway had been extended to the Flatbush terminus in 1920, placing this section of Brooklyn a quick, safe forty minutes from Times Square.) I could just barely recollect a vacant lot across the street – once there had been tennis courts, a skating rink, and a miniature golf course – but by 1954 all of East 31st between Avenue I and the Long Island Rail Road cut under Flatbush Avenue was taken up by similar six-story buildings. The nearest park with ball diamonds and football fields was some three miles away. So we played football between the parked cars and hockey on screeching metal roller skates, raced up and down the elevators, held jousting tournaments on bicycles with stickball-bat lances and garbage-can lids for shields, sledded down the railway embankment, and gently placed the area's pestilential tent caterpillars on the wings of model airplanes and then blew them to hell with firecrackers.

Life here was thoroughly urban; we'd never had a car, a lawn, or a dog. My father and his identical twin worked seven-day weeks in long white aprons, selling Lady Borden ice cream, pipe tobacco, magazines, Name Day cards, cherry Cokes, egg creams, model airplanes, crepe paper, pipe cleaners, malted milk, typewriter ribbons, and as many as ten daily newspapers. When I was three, my father, having sold the store around the corner on Avenue I and having spent a year or so as a longshoreman on the Manhattan docks, joined his brother again in a candy store on Avenue D in a fifty-fifty Irish–Italian neighborhood about a mile from our apartment. It was there that I eagerly went to work as soon as I could see over the counter, vending bubble gum and two-cent pretzels and other wonderful cah-bo-high-dwates.

My mother had blossomed during the war, a black-haired, plaid-skirted Bensonhurst bookkeeper, doing her part for Victory, dancing with doomed soldiers and sailors at the 42nd Street USO, the flesh of foxhole dreams. By then, she was already motherless and often fatherless as well, having got through the Great Depression "on relief," reduced to picking through second-hand clothing at the welfare offices, given a job by the make-work National Youth Association, until, on exactly her seventh day of employment, her boss put his hand on her breast and she quit. She married Ben Abel in 1948. He was eleven and a half years her senior, small and blue-eyed, an infantry sergeant with a Purple Heart who had seen house-to-house fighting in the Rhineland. She wouldn't go out to work again until Fred Lucci and his string of unsuccessful restaurants and variety stores.

She was still gorgeous, olive-skinned, fond of extravagant jewelry – Indian beads, cockatoo feathers – a flirt, and an off-price fashion plate. She kept her hair gray and very short, like Jane Powell in the Polident ads on television, but she still had her own teeth.

"Never had to shave my legs," she announced to me one day without being asked. "Women *abhor* me for that. Went to a podiatrist once, thirty years ago. Never had a manicure. Never had a pedicure. Never had a massage. Never had a perm."

She paused for effect.

"Natural beauty," she said.

Ten weeks from her seventieth birthday, it was concussive for her to grasp that she had outlived two sisters and a brother; she'd slip into the bedroom when I was collating my notes and say, "I'm the only one left." I didn't know whether she was seeking praise or commiseration. I'd sit quietly and then, a moment later, she would brighten and look all dewy-eyed at me and sing out, "My son! My son!" like a mad mama Zero Mostel.

I told friends before I left Canada, "Every son should go home to live with his mother once every twenty-five years." I thought a long sojourn would depressurize the compacted joy and guilt and recrimination and dismissal and remorse; I figured it might help to balance the books for all the trips I had taken with my father, to Poland and China and ball games and National Parks. By the fifth day, I was telling my mother how I believed this had become my longest stretch in Brooklyn since 1968. Even for Fred's funeral I had stayed only half a week.

"Most of the others were three or four days," I said.

"Yes," she replied. "But Linda was here."

∾

I strove to transplant to Brooklyn the exemplary eating habits of my Toronto yuppie life. (Linda was a dietician.) I went out to Waldbaum's and brought back Great Grains cereal, grapefruit, zero-per-cent milk, and fat-free yogurt that tasted like the paste we used to make in the kitchen sink from flour and water to hold together papier-mâché. My mother countered with sour cream, cottage cheese, Mallomars, frozen blintzes, corn muffins, chocolate-covered graham crackers and Sugar Wafers. She looked at my shopping list and said, "I've never made fresh broccoli *in my life*, and I'm not going to start now."

I took the kitchen radio that was set to "easy listening" and tuned it to all-news WINS. I plugged in my Interplak electric toothbrush and esta blished my special shaving cream For Sensitive Skin in the medicine cabinet. I exercised regularly with my rubber-hose chest expander. I went to bed at 9:30 at night.

For a few days each spring and autumn, the morning sun would just peek over the building across the street and cast its golden rays on our kitchen. This happened soon after I arrived, and afforded me the chance to demonstrate my new environmental awareness, which by now had thoroughly overtaken my innate desire to blow up caterpillars.

My mother was sitting by the kitchen window, as she always did in the early mornings. ("Early" to her meant before 11:15.) She set the window fan to "exhaust" and went at her first Parliament of the day, flicking the ashes and casting the butt into a Planters peanut can half-filled with water and already the grave of a pack of coffin nails or more.

I heard a sound: "hoo AHH-oo . . . hoo AHH-oo." A mourning dove was perched on the fire escape, tame and iridescent, tan and pink and flecked, in the sunlight, with blue.

"It matches my living room," my mother said.

I explained that this was not a feral pigeon but a lovely little messenger of spring. The lesson was absorbed: that even in this concrete cul-de-sac, Nature could find ingress and be observed. My mother thanked me.

"If you weren't here," she said, "I would have thrown water on it."

～

On Sunday nights, my mother went dancing at a chapter of Parents Without

Partners that she liked to call People Without Promise. This left me alone to play solitaire, scream along with the "Doo-Wop Shop" oldies show on WCBS-FM, recline on the couch in the room where Little Allen had lain with the chicken pox and measles, made dinosaurs from Play-Doh, watched Sputnik and Superman and the World Series. Free of witnesses, pretzels were mine.

The first time this happened, I stayed up until nearly ten o'clock, then glided to sleep in serene contentment.

At 12:30 a man down on East 31st Street started chanting: "PHOK DA MOTHA-PHOKAH! IF I HAD DA PHO-KIN' MONEY I'D BUY A PHO-KIN' GUN AND SHOOT DA MOTHA-PHOKAH ..."

Then I heard a woman's voice yelling, and the man gave it up. I waited a few minutes for gunshots, heard none, and slept until 1:15, when the car alarms began.

These were standard equipment for a borough where automobile theft supported hundreds of families with thousands of hungry children, and where it was a source of joyful surprise to emerge from one's home in the morning to discover that one's vehicle had *not* been stolen overnight. It had even become common practice to *request* that your car be swiped, as Hennie and Freddie once had done, using Fred's alleged underworld contacts.

Lately, it had become routine to install some sort of automatic cater-waul so that, although the car might be stolen anyhow, the thieves would enjoy it less. A device called "The Club" that locked the steering wheel with a thick metal bar was also popular – I counted nine of twenty-four cars on our block equipped with it – but Caribbean Brooklyn, where we lived, seemed especially delighted with the musical possibilities of mechanical screaming.

So now I was bolt upright in bed and one of the vehicles directly below the window was emitting an amazing variety of complaints, all at nuclear-test volume. First it was a Paris police car – *bee*-boop! *bee*-boop! – then a circus pennywhistle going up the scale, then a pack of barking soprano dogs, then a standard fire engine, the all-done signal of Satan's microwave oven, and, last but not least, what sounded like the first eight notes of the "Moon-light Sonata" played on an air-raid siren.

As it was usual on this block to gently expand an insufficiently long park-ing space by ramming the cars in front and behind, and since these alarms were set to a hair trigger, another concerto began just down the street as someone else came home, setting off an anvil chorus of slamming doors, cursing, squealing tires, and, when yet another alarm was touched off, seventy-six more trombones.

A few minutes after this calmed down, my mother came home from her evening out and began some of her doomsday coughing.

At 2:12 a.m., one of her dance partners rang twice ("Signal me when you get home!") to indicate that he hadn't been murdered in the past half-hour. The telephone was on a shelf fifteen inches from my pillow.

Presently, someone called to order a taxi.

We got a lot of those.

Then everything was copacetic until five minutes to six, when my mother emerged from her couchette, hacking violently, and sat down by the kitchen window where we had seen the mourning dove and swallowed a Bufferin and coughed, I wrote in my notebook, "like a madwoman."

"Maybe you should take your temperature," I ventured, interrupting my morning routine with the chest expander.

"I don't want to know if I'm sick," she said, phlegmatically.

∽

We compromised at frozen broccoli. My mother made chicken cutlets and egg noodles and this was dinner for Friday, the twenty-third of April, and on the twenty-third of June, she'd turn seventy.

I didn't have to remind her. She said, "If Cel were alive, she'd be calling and saying 'Two months! Two months!'" But Cel, the older sister who had raised her after their mother died a young, young woman, was not alive. Fay, the other sister, was not alive, and Louie, the brother, was not alive. Only Hennie was alive, the last of the Jacobsons.

Debbie had work today. She was always on the roster to substitute-teach, but somehow she had been made eligible only for districts in Harlem and the Lower East Side of Manhattan, an enormous trek on the "graffiti-free" subways from her airless King Tut's tomb in seaside Canarsie. Sometimes the Board of Education would computer-dial her in the evening, and she would leave Brooklyn before 6:30 the next morning and make it to school on time. But more often the call would come at 8:15 to be present at 8:40, and since the journey took more than an hour, she would have to decline.

Tonight, she burst in just in time for the cutlets. She unburdened herself of an Everest of baggage – in addition to Debbie's usual role as a traveling branch of the New York Public Library, our mother had given her thirty-four dollars with which to buy breads, rolls, almond horns, bagels, and cakes. Then she called her Canarsie number to check for messages and learned that the Board of Ed. had already requested that she return on Monday to the same Harlem school where she'd worked that day.

"I'm not going back to them," Debbie announced, angry and defeated, which was rare for her. She was a game little cowgirl with a master's degree in Elementary Education, tough and self-sufficient and generous and loyal.

"You'll spend my thirty-four dollars but you don't want to work," our mother snapped back.

"Do *you* want to do it?" My sister began to scream full-throated at our mother, who was smoking at the fan by the window. "Have YOU ever done it? HAVE YOU EVER DONE IT?"

I cringed and played with my soggy broccoli.

"YOU do it!" Debbie thundered, and stormed away, but in this apartment, no one could storm very far.

Soon she came back to the kitchen and said that she had had a bad day on 120th Street with a room full of first-graders throwing books and calling each other "Fuck." Then there was Duke Ellington's famous A Train homeward, and although the subways were getting better, the A Train from Harlem in 1993 was still not the Orient Express.

Until two years ago, Deb had directed a private pre-school at a mixed-income housing development on the East Side of Manhattan. (She took the subway every day and often stayed late for Rangers hockey games and, except for the fatal shooting of a policewoman on the Canarsie line and a few chain snatchings, nothing terrible ever happened at all.) Then the school went out of business, and now, after two years on the dole and off it, she was in a tough spot. She was expecting to be offered a full-time job in the city schools in the fall, but this was almost certain to throw her in with much larger children in a dangerous, devastated neighborhood. If she accepted, the best that she could hope for would be two hundred days like the one she had just had.

∾

At nine o'clock the next morning, the storm had passed and we were getting ready to leave the apartment when my mother corralled me in the kitchen and said, "Sit down and talk to me. I *beseech* you."

It wasn't a crisis; she was just overflowing. She wanted to tell me about the old tennis courts across the street, about disappeared taverns on Flatbush Avenue and the slights of long-dead neighbors. I sat. We remembered the days when the only alarms on East 31st Street were bitter old men who, when one of us kids would brush against a vehicle while stretching for a touchdown pass, would storm into the gutter and bellow, "Get the hell off my car!"

Thirty-five-year-old tiffs and insults consumed her. She still fumed that Little Debbie had once been falsely accused of shoplifting; a schoolmate stole a hair ribbon and, when caught, gave my sister's name. I told her how one of the boys on the block had swiped a copy of *Tropic of Cancer*, and how we all had clustered around him in an alley between buildings while he pointed out astonishing words like "cunt."

"You broke a window," my mother said. (I had lost the memory.) "A group of kids was throwing rocks and one of the rocks went through a man's window. You went back and gave the man two dollars. All the other kids ran away. You were the only one who paid."

But her idol had feet of clay. One night, the older boys commanded that everyone go into the local candy shop and walk out with something stolen. They took magazines, baseball cards, candy. I grabbed a pack of Doublemint and then, as everyone strutted out of the store, laughing, I darted back in and returned it. The shopkeeper saw me place the gum on the counter and he looked down at me and said softly, "Allen? *You?*"

Debbie was putting on her Yankees cap. It was time to go. There was a brief skirmish over umbrellas. I declined to trade my Gore-Tex rain jacket for a less-valuable "Sesame Street" poncho with Bert and Ernie on the back.

"Then let me at least cut the sleeve of your coat," my mother said, reaching for a pair of shears.

We walked down the hall past the Modiglianis, the Mary Cassatt posters, and the embroidered folk-art wall hangings I had bought for her in Ecuador and Bangladesh. We undid the two locks and the chain.

We kissed the mezuzah (but not our mother) for luck, opened the door, and started down the long, shiny corridor toward the stairway, avoiding the elevator, for fitness's sake.

"Be careful!" our mother called out.

"No!" I replied, already on the third floor. "We'll be reckless and foolhardy!"

We continued the downward climb.

"Need tissues?" came a faint voice from the fourth floor.

3

Down on Plymouth Street, when I returned two days later to the forgotten waterside beneath the Manhattan Bridge, there was a 1993 Bonneville sedan parked with two wheels on the cobblestones and two wheels up on the curb. The car had been burned so thoroughly that only the seat-belt buckles remained intact. Here was the archeological evidence of a masterfully performed "torch job," left to be dragged away by New York's Strongest. I couldn't even tell what color the body paint had been. Or the color of the seat covers: there were no longer any seats.

I was wandering the region on a spectacularly brilliant morning that rendered the Manhattan skyline not only visible, but imminent. The World Trade Center, repaired from its recent terrorist bombing, stretched toward an unlimited sky. The river sparkled. Its gladness refreshed me. But my loon was gone.

Right at the river's edge was a Puerto Rican gentleman, picking through a pile of household refuse someone had taken the trouble to haul all the way down here, then heave onto the pier. He had already found a handsaw and some paintbrushes by the time I encountered him, and he was deciding whether he could use a jaunty party hat covered in gold-colored foil.

He was carrying a couple of fishing rods and, when I asked whether he had found them here also, he said that, no, he had been casting for flounder under the Manhattan Bridge.

"You mean you would *eat* fish you caught in the East River?" I said disbelievingly.

"Look at a map," the Puerto Rican answered. "You eat fish from the ocean. Is the same water."

As I walked back towards the corpse of the Bonneville, from a distance I could see that two men were standing in front of it and one had pulled out a camera. I assumed that these were insurance investigators working on the inevitable stolen-car claim.

They were tourists from Belgium.

"We came over on the Metro," one of the Belgians said. "We have only a little time in Brooklyn." His shoulder bag bore the address of a travel agency in Ghent. His friend backed up and backed up with the camera, trying to get the immolated car and the Twin Towers of the World Trade Center and the choiring strings of the Brooklyn Bridge in the same frame. He snapped off a few shots.

"New York in a nutshell," the second Belgian announced, delighted with his assessment. I imagined them back in their medieval city, eating French fries with mayonnaise and showing off the photos and boasting how they had descended into the netherworld of Brooklyn's lawless streets.

The Manhattan Bridge was directly above them, but of course they took no photographs of that.

ରେ

"You are in a kind of urban dell, fringed with old buildings instead of trees," the *Brooklyn Daily Eagle* rhapsodized, after sending a reporter down here in 1954. "Carpeted with cobblestones instead of grass, with a wide horizon straight ahead where the river and Manhattan's startling jagged skyline on the other side are open to view. You feel – perhaps because you know – that history has been made here, and it is still being made."

By this the *Eagle* meant the construction of the Brooklyn Queens Expressway, which had required the demolition of dozens of buildings from Walt Whitman's time and later. These were saloons, boarding houses, brothels, factories.

History was still being made in 1993, or at least planned. Adjoining Fulton Ferry State Park was a long, heavy row of nineteenth-century ware-house buildings, deep red and stolid, with arched windows and heavy iron shutters. These were the Empire Stores, once the repository of coffee beans, animal hides, molasses, cereals, and sugar, witness to an age when there were so many of these colossi along this waterfront, Brooklyn was known as "the walled city." There had been a proposal to rehabilitate the Empire Stores and install a museum of maritime commerce. But the proposal had been written in 1977 and, sixteen years later, the buildings remained boarded up and mute.

Only one hand was actively working to build this part of Brooklyn, to put up mighty towers and turn out products, and that was the hand of God. For this district between the bridges and astride the congested expressway was the world headquarters of the Jehovah's Witnesses. Anyone who had ever driven across the Brooklyn Bridge had seen the huge green signs: "Read the WATCHTOWER," "Announcing, JEHOVAH'S KINGDOM."

I had never made the connection – that the messages pertained exactly to the factories on which they were painted. Wandering around at ground level with Debbie on the first morning, I hadn't realized where we were. The printing plants of the Jehovah's Witnesses on Adams and Sands and Pearl streets turned out millions of tracts and testaments every year, but they were so hermetic and insulated at ground level – clean bare walls and closed green doors – you could walk right by them, never guessing you were in the fields of the Lord.

∾

Tours of the Watchtower factory complex began in a luxurious waiting room on Adams Street. It was just after one p.m. when I arrived. Moments later, I was joined by busloads and busloads and busloads of people from Cleveland. Children carried disposable cameras and one man was cheerfully studying a New York subway map as if it were a schedule for the monorail at Disneyland.

Small groups of sun-flushed, fit young men bounded through the small doorway, carrying softball gloves or basketballs, and disappeared into a tiny elevator. Workers in clean white hard-hats strode purposefully through the room.

My personal guide appeared. He was a slim, confident man in his thirties named Art Almquist, possessed of the religion's self-assurance and an excellent set of initials.

Art Almquist was a small-town fellow out of Idaho, whose father was a Lutheran and whose mother was a Presbyterian. He had five sisters who were, as he put it, "of the Witness faith," and three brothers who weren't. His religiosity piqued by the Witnesses that came to his home, Almquist had traveled to Brooklyn at the age of sixteen to climb the Watchtower for himself. He immersed himself in the tenets by going door to door.

"Like Jesus," he explained.

Like everyone else who worked in these buildings and the many others the Witnesses owned across Brooklyn's formerly important downtown, Almquist was a volunteer. He was paid no salary, dined at a communal table with nine Brothers and Sisters, worked five and a half days a week, began each morning with a Bible lesson, and lived with his wife in a dormitory in exquisite Brooklyn Heights, where the Witnesses maintained twenty-three refurbished old hotels and residences as Bethel, their House of God.

We went up to the twelfth floor of one of the five factory buildings and, at the window, he pointed out the Witnesses' garage, where his wife worked to service the vehicles that transported the people who printed the Bibles that carried the Word. Beyond was the river and the bridges and Manhattan's "startling jagged" skyline. From the other side of the building, we could look far into central Brooklyn and the borough's immense zones of dereliction and urban despair.

The Witnesses went out into that doomed and sinful world bolstered by the certainty that "He that does the will of God remains forever" (1 John 2:17). Almquist preached at meetings and worked with the Latino community. He was not a hermit. He understood that, in some of those neighborhoods, you could turn the wrong corner at the wrong time and suddenly find yourself knocking on Heaven's door.

"One of the Brothers got mugged last night," he told me. "They got the three dollars he had on him."

As the tour continued, superlatives were punted about like footballs. A hundred thousand items were printed each day. Computers could speak 240 languages. Seventy thousand visitors toured the complex each year; almost all, I suspected, were Witnesses from out of town. The Brothers were nearly self-sufficient. They made their own windows, machine tools, furniture. A new thirty-story residence was going up across the Brooklyn Queens Expressway. It seemed to be the only building currently under construction in all of economically moribund Brooklyn. City codes required that union men do the structural steel- and brickwork and the roofing. The Witnesses, self-trained, did the rest.

All around us, sturdy young men hauled bales of paper and ran drill presses. Young women fed sheets of pigskin for book covers through cutting machines. In another part of the complex, not included on my tour, wizened wise men in their eighties and nineties directed an empire that extended from Adams Street to Iceland. They had no archbishops, ayatollahs, or popes. There were three thousand of them, diligent and committed, down here in Whitman's walled city. And yet they anticipated that these earthly enterprises were to be swept away, perhaps before dinner.

"Sometimes we're labeled 'calamity howlers,'" Almquist admitted.

"In New York," I replied, "you're not alone."

I got serious for a moment. I said, "You believe that all of this will disappear, don't you?"

"That remains to be seen," Almquist responded. "The original purpose seemed to be for us to lead a simpler kind of life in Paradise. Cultivating the earth, small villages and the like."

"If it's all going to be blown away," I asked, "then why bother building these factories?"

"To spread the Word," Art Almquist said.

∾

One of the things Art and I could see from the twelfth floor of the Watchtower was the reconstruction activity on the Manhattan Bridge. A couple of years earlier, much had been made of the calamitous disintegration of the Williamsburg Bridge further upriver. Harry Reasoner went out in a rowboat with a city engineer, and they were shown on "60 Minutes," tearing away pieces of rotted concrete from the bridge foundation *with their hands*. Now it appeared that the pretty blue Manhattan was in equal need of salvation. I wanted to watch. It was my bridge.

One morning a few days later, I stepped determinedly into a trailer in the construction yard and walked out with a helmet, a red-and-yellow safety vest (so they could find me when I fell in the river), and a union man named Tommy Cush, small and friendly and crimson-faced, shop steward for Local 361 of the International Association of Bridge, Structural and Ornamental Iron Workers. A waiver I signed stated that my heirs and assigns would make no claim should a compressor hose work loose and blow me 120 feet in the air like poor McShane, air-freighted to heaven here in 1909.

Tommy Cush – it rhymed with bush – had been a high-altitude iron worker for twenty-five years and had fallen only once, a mere two stories, breaking only his leg and shoulder. He had been engaged as many as fifty-two floors above street level, and he said that working at such heights was "easy, once you get used to it." But he had watched as a union brother next to him fell off the Queensboro Bridge and, as he put it, "I seen many men die."

Still, he said, it wasn't that ridiculous a profession. "On the big buildings, the beams are so wide, you'd have to commit suicide to fall off."

Time and traffic and acid rain had given the city's infrastructure a bad case of gangrene, and this meant money in the pockets of the men of the union. The Manhattan Bridge was a choice example – virtually every one of its rivets, cables, and pinions would have to be replaced, and that could take dozens of workers five or more years of five-day weeks at fifty dollars an hour, plus overtime. Tommy Cush pointed up to where the Brighton Beach train was clawing its way along, and he reported that, without urgent retooling, the rusted span soon would have trembled and shuddered itself to the point of nervous collapse.

"It's deteriating," the union man observed.

To get to the platform where the work was going on, we were going to climb a temporary stairway that the iron workers had installed beside the mammoth concrete anchorage on Adams Street in Brooklyn. It was possible to grab a pickup truck and drive over to the beginning of Flatbush Avenue and then onto the bridge itself – one traffic lane had been closed off during the reconstruction to permit access to the work site – but it wasn't every day I was offered the chance to make a hundred-foot ascent on a steep, narrow, slippery, swaying metal ladder, so I declined the offer of a ride.

Moments later, I was two flights up (out of twenty) and Tommy Cush, having pranced ahead like a Dall sheep, was calling back down to me, "Take your time!"

The stairway led to a secret world I would gladly have climbed a hundred flights to see. We were *inside* the anchorage. From below, it had appeared to be a solid concrete massif, but now we entered cave-like rooms and passageways and great hollow shafts, a vast Egyptian mystery pyramid stained brown and black and rusty red by ninety years of New York time. Vaults of yellow stone arched above our heads, and the thudding of the traffic resounded down the corridors.

Tommy Cush showed me the chamber where the suspension cables, thick as trees, were fixed to Olympian iron bolts. And another long, narrow hallway that was the worker's locker room, an untidy, masculine litter-box of newspaper sports sections, Macanudo cigar wrappers, and Playmates of the Month. Then farther on, we climbed hand-over-hand up a rough wooden ladder to the platform, big as a football field, on which the iron men were saving the bridge from death.

The platform hung from the bottom of the bridge like a koala on a eucalyptus tree, mounted on wheels that enabled it to be moved along when one section of the girders had been removed and replaced. Every few weeks, all hands would gather on the deck and, using ropes wound around pulleys at each end of the platform, would heave'e'yo the hundred-ton assemblage down the track to the next work station. Eventually, they would be blocked by the bridge tower that stood in the river itself, and the whole wood-and-steel platform would have to be quartered, lowered by crane, trucked to the waterline, mounted on barges, floated to mid-river, hoisted, and reassembled.

The work was laborious, repetitive, hazardous, possibly toxic, and almost mortally loud. A torch was used to slice off the head of each bolt. Then a heavyweight puncher – a mechanical George Foreman – battered the old rivet out of its hole. When all the rivets in a beam had been taken care of, the girder itself was walloped out of position and a new one was lowered by crane from the roadway to replace it.

The men seemed jovial and as brotherly as Witnesses. There were blacks and Latinos, but mostly they were Irish, as they had been in 1909. Tommy Cush brought me over to meet a fellow named McSomething – it was much too noisy to hear every word – and told me that his buddy was worth three million dollars.

"Lottery?" I screamed.

"Real estate," he bellowed back at me. "Florida."

"Then why are you working?" I hollered, putting my mouth right against his ear.

"It's under water," McSomething replied, laughing and full of beans.

High, high above us, at the very summit of the tower, men were working on the blue iron balls through which the cables passed on their flight from borough to borough. You got up there by walking up the parabolic cable itself with nothing to hold on to but a couple of single-strand wires and nothing below you but eternity. I asked my escort if he had ever made such an ascent. This too, he said, was "easy, once you get used to it." I could even make it up in sneakers, he vowed.

I looked up at the tower and down at my Rockports. My heart was knocking out old rivets. We made a date for some other time.

∾

It was well-known in New York that most of the most insanely acrobatic aerial ironwork was done by Mohawks. Not Cherokees or Chickasaws or Creek or Blood or Sioux; only the Mohawks from up at the Canadian border were fearless enough to walk celestial steel. On the Manhattan Bridge, one Mohawk still did.

Russell Rice was the name I was given when I asked Local 361 about the fate of the celebrated sky-dancers. At lunch hour, still exultant at having survived my morning's climb of the scaffolding and my peek into the interior of the monumental anchorage, I sat on a tool trunk in one of the crew's equipment trailers and talked with him, safely on the Brooklyn ground.

Rice was forty-two, broad-faced and heavyset, with unexpected blue-green eyes and soft, pink features. He called himself "full-blooded," and this seemed a matter of pride as much as genetics. Four generations of Rices had been high-altitude iron workers. A distant cousin owned Rice–Mohawk, the contracting company that was re-riveting the bridge. Russell had three brothers in the trade, and their father, of course, had been an iron worker also, until he fell off the approach to the Verrazano Bridge in 1963 and broke his neck. But he survived.

In 1949, there were eighty-three Mohawks in Local 361 of the Association of Iron Workers. They lived in a compact community, a mile up Flatbush Avenue, in a part of Brooklyn called North Gowanus, and they shopped and socialized along Atlantic Avenue, near their union hall. Italian grocers in their neighborhood stocked the Quaker Enriched and Degerminated Corn

Meal that the Mohawk women used to make a boiled bread called *ka-na-ta-rok*. A tavern called the Spar served *o-nen-tso*, a corn soup. A sign over the entrance to a saloon known popularly as The Wigwam said, "The Greatest Iron Workers in the World Pass Through These Doors."

A spread in the *National Geographic* in 1953 showed the men working fearlessly in the stratosphere, topping off skyscrapers, constructing the General Assembly Building at the United Nations. That was fitting, the magazine said, because the Mohawks had been part of the multi-national Iroquois Confederacy that predated the European conquest. The *New Yorker* found the Brooklyn Mohawks generally "thick-set, fleshy and broad-faced." They were said to be "agile as goats." Their eyes were "sad, shrewd and dark brown."

But blue-eyed Russell Rice betrayed no legacy of sadness. He was as jolly as a pro wrestler. He viewed his Brooklyn upbringing with equanimity.

"We were never taught about being Indian in school," he said in the tool shed, which muted a little of the thundering from the bridge above us. "Our history wasn't part of their history. They'd only mention that the pioneers came and shot us."

When Russell was in the seventh grade, his father had his terrible accident and, no longer able to work on high steel, he moved his family back to the reserve at Kahnawake, on the Quebec side of the border, on the south St. Lawrence shore. The Brooklyn Mohawks had always kept half their hearts in Canada, and many commuted back and forth as New York's demand for fearless girder-riders waxed and waned. Russell Rice still drove back and forth to Kahnawake on weekends, nine hours each way. He had four of his own children and a foster child in school up there, playing lacrosse and ice hockey, learning their language and their heritage as he never had, in this new era of cultural awareness and tense land-claim stand-offs. It was a reversal of the course of centuries; his kids would be more Indian than their father.

The Mohawks had first come to New York in the thirties to build bridges and apartment buildings and the great Art Deco masterpieces of Manhattan. By 1993, only a few were scattered around the metropolis in the building trades. Most of the families had gone back to Kahnawake. High-rise construction techniques had changed. Cranes now leapfrogged themselves upward as the structure rose, lessening the need for men to ride girders a thousand feet above the pavement. The Spar and The Wigwam were long gone. Local 361 had moved its offices to Queens. North Gowanus grocery stores no longer stocked degerminated corn meal.

The new hazards were more insidious than broken legs and necks. The doctors kept reminding Russell Rice and the other men on the bridge to be aware of the warning signs of lead poisoning from the old paint and rivets: forgetfulness, vomiting, loss of appetite. There was nothing to indicate that Russell's interest in food had been compromised, but the lead count in his blood had risen from seven to twenty-three in only six months, and when it hit thirty or so, the doctors might take him down from the platform for his own good.

"Will your sons become iron workers?" I asked him.

"I hope they stay in school," the Mohawk replied. "But that's what they hoped for me, too."

∾

Of the Native Americans who came to Brooklyn about a thousand years before the Mohawk iron workers, not a lot is known. They were said to have greeted Henry Hudson in 1609 "manifesting all friendship," but not long after that a Dutch sailor named Colman was shot through the neck by a flint-tipped arrow, and what that arrow started was finished within two centuries by diseases and wars with other desperate tribes.

They were known as Canarsees, "people of the enclosed place." They wore furs and lived in longhouses and cultivated maize, squash, beans, pumpkin. Their farmlands were passed down through the women's clans. The Dutch generally saw them as passive agriculturalists and oyster collectors. They paid tribute to the Iroquois Confederacy in shell beads known as *wampum* and were attacked by Mohawks in 1643, with many deaths, when they failed to make a payment. (The Dutch had said they didn't have to.)

Compared to other colonies along the Atlantic coast, raids and massacres by and against the settlers were minor and infrequent. Relations were rather cordial. In 1670, three Canarsee sachems made their marks on an agreement to sell much of what would become central Brooklyn to the Hollanders. The natives received:

10 Fathoms of black wampum
10 Fathoms of white wampum
 5 Match coats
 4 Blankets
 2 Gunners night guns
 2 Pistols
 5 Double handfulls of powder
 5 Bars of Lead
10 Knives
 2 Secret aprons
 1 Half barrell of Strong Beer
 3 Cans of Brandy
 6 Shirts

The Canarsees evaporated rather quietly. No organized extermination was deemed necessary. The last of them was said to have died about 1800. They left piles of oyster shells and the name of my sister's neighborhood. One of their trails through the woods to the ocean is now called Flatbush Avenue.

∾

When Mohawk Indian steelworkers began to assemble in large numbers in Brooklyn in the nineteen-thirties, those whose ancestors had been converted to Protestant Christianity in Canada often came to worship at a downtown church called the Cuyler. A young minister, ordained at the Cuyler in 1926, devoted himself to this new group of "immigrants" and to the study of their language.

The minister was now ninety years old. The Reverend Dr. David Munroe Cory lived in an apartment in the section of Brooklyn called Gravesend, at the opposite coast of the borough from the fantastic commotion of the Manhattan Bridge. (Gravesend was another of the seventeenth-century Brooklyn villages, but it was settled by the English, not the Dutch, and its founder was a woman, Lady Deborah Moody.) He greeted me with ceremony in a sitting room cluttered with church magazines and photographs and a snoring Siamese cat. He told me that he had just recently retired from service at a church on Avenue T.

"Sixty-five consecutive years as an active minister," Dr. Cory said. "I broke the record. All denominations."

Dr. Cory was a man of parts – clergyman, writer, traveler, explorer of unpopular worlds. He wore maroon trousers, a brown jacket, and a plaid tie over a clean white shirt. He apologized for forgetfulness and said, "That's the trouble when you get old. There's so many things you've done." Whenever he spoke, he closed his eyes.

I had found him through a twenty-year-old clipping from the *New York Times*. Dr. Cory was a remarkable man. In 1941, he issued a revised translation into Mohawk of the Gospel of Luke. He had studied among the Navaho and other nations as well, and in 1955 he had written a book called *Within Two Worlds* that went through five printings. It called for understanding and tolerance of the Native American thirty-odd years before *Dances With Wolves*. He wrote:

> There has been a tendency among non-Indians to judge an Indian's progress by the degree to which he has adopted white culture. This is based on the naïve assumption that what we are is the best that can be . . . Indian people do not always share this point of view.

I was given a guest book to sign, the opening pages of which dated back to 1960. I thought: let me possess half of this man's grace when I am ninety. I asked Dr. Cory whether, in all his tracing of his ancestry, he had discovered any Indian blood.

"No," he said softly. "I was hoping that there might be. But there isn't."

4

High in one of the abandoned factories under the Manhattan Bridge, a window was open and star-white flashes from what might have been welding torches were shooting through the air like lizards' tongues.

The building was a tired pile of chianti-colored brick with the words "RACHMAN BAG CO." still visible on the northern wall. Three floors above me, the window where I had seen the flashes on Saturday was open again and on the ledge next to it was a panther or leopard stenciled from rusted iron, caught in mid-stride, pacing the air. The Brighton Beach train rumbled overhead, adding thunder to the artificial lightning.

From around a corner on Plymouth Street came fifteen people carrying big black plastic bags. These were mentally handicapped adults bringing litter they had collected at the riverbank to be added to the bales of paper and cardboard in the bowels of one of the old warehouses. Then they wheeled around and went into another old building that turned out to be the AHRC – the Association for the Help of Retarded Children. From the curtains and painted paper flowers at the upper windows, it seemed that many of them had been brought to live down here in the shadow of the unloved bridge, in a district I had first thought fearsome and vacant in the fog of an early spring morning.

At Rachman Bag, I found a side entrance, which was locked, and a number of jerry-rigged doorbells that were connected to wires hanging like fishing lines from various windows in the edifice. There were listings for designers and woodworkers, painters and sculptors. Unknowingly, I had found DUMBO.

Down Under the Manhattan Bridge Overpass was Brooklyn's answer to Manhattan's acronymic SoHo and TriBeCa, the remains of the nineteenth-century "walled city" put to use as lofts and studios by the borough's starving Rodins and would-be Warhols. This was no Greenwich Village – there were no boutiques, no avant-garde theaters, no bookstores or coffeehouses – but buildings like Rachman Bag offered space and freedom and no shortage of inspirational noise.

I waited outside the big steel door, expecting someone to come out eventually and, unexpectedly, the first to emerge was a woman with a tiny, tiny infant boy. I joked about the maddening racket from the bridge and asked if many artists were at work in the building behind us.

"Not just working," the woman shouted, as Russell Rice and his union brothers pounded away at the big blue girders. "Also *trying* to raise children."

It was suggested that I go up to the fourth floor and spend some time with a man named Steven Singer, creator of the oxidized feline on the window ledge at Rachman Bag. The door was opened, and I climbed up three long flights of gray wooden steps in a silo of white-painted brickwork illuminated by bare yellow bulbs. At the fourth level was a rough-beamed studio, and in the studio was the man of steel.

Steven Singer was a slim, intense magician, who took scrap metal from the geriatric bridge outside his window and turned it into bumblebees, lissome maidens, and potent tribesmen with big hard dicks.

"I have sold pieces of this bridge for a lot of money," he said. "I'm turning shit into gold."

Steven Singer was glib and energetic, self-possessed and cocksure. He danced me toward a shelf of Venus figures, each six inches high and wrought from a single railroad spike shaken from the Brighton Beach tracks.

"These are the sveltest, most elite things I've ever done," he chirruped. (It was true; they were metal made flesh.) "Look at them! They're individually welded. Professionally done. *Nothing* could possibly be more exciting to me than this."

We went around the loft, which had floors of sturdy broad planks that must have withstood the bag-making machinery of the Rachman period. I saw tables piled with junk. Singer saw goddesses.

"If you *knew* you wanted to become an artist," he said, "if you were *always* the best artist in school, *always* the best cartoonist, if people were always telling you, 'Find a real job,' but you *knew* this was what you should do and you grow up and you *do* it and it's your *life*, then you're *really* living. You'll pay any price. You'll do *anything*. It doesn't matter. It's a trip."

From Singer's window, you couldn't see the water or the Manhattan towers or Lady Liberty, the most ennobled sculpture of them all. You looked down at the Rice–Mohawk equipment yard, straight ahead to the bridge roadway, and up to the Watchtower of the Jehovah's Witnesses.

The bridge transported his creativity; its din rattled loose his ideas. "It's like a river to me," he said. "It deposits silt and I mine it."

He held out a rivet for me to caress.

"It's ninety years old. It's corroded. But the steel is so *strong*. It creates such a deep and lasting character."

We went to the open window.

"Beautifully ugly," the sculptor said.

I asked about the price for a lithe, gleaming fetish the artist called the *Venus de Brooklyn*. "Tens? Hundreds? Thousands?" I estimated.

"Thousands," Steven Singer said.

We looked out the window again. Two weeks ago, I didn't even know if it was possible to get down here below the big blue span. Now I had climbed the scaffolding, walked the cobbles, seen a loon. To my right was the bridge and the river and to my left was ten miles of Flatbush Avenue.

Downtown Nowhere

1

Flatbush Avenue came spilling off Manhattan Bridge in a hurtling, honking carnival of trailers and cars and vans, their drivers wending and weaving for lane and position on the downward slope like clumsy novice skiers until the whole anarchic mess came to a halt at Tillary Street. Then, when the light turned green, the stampede started up again, as if spooked by a cannon fired back at the riverbank by Walt Whitman or Tommy Cush. It would be like this, I expected, for ten more manic miles, all the way south to the sea.

There were only a few trucks coming off the bridge whose proprietary markings had not been inundated beyond legibility by graffiti: Chai Sung Oriental Foods; Steelcraft Fluorescent; Mascaro Waste Transport. An empty blue-and-yellow bus marked "Department of Corrections" bounded back from its nesting site, looking for another load of Brooklynites to trundle off to jail. Nobody had spray-painted *it*.

I was standing in a small grassy area on the west side of the roadway at what might be called Flatbush Avenue's first inch. A woman was lying at my feet in the fetal position, gently rocking as she slept, and next to her was an empty can of a popular Caribbean legume called Pigeon Peas. Behind me was an enormous whitewashed factory, with a sign at its top advertising Howard Clothes. This mass-market haberdasher was long out of business – the building had a million square feet of space to let – but Howard Clothes had once been so common in closets around here that my father would joke, "I have my own private tailor," and then, when asked his tailor's name, would delightedly reply, "H. O. Ward."

This was Bridge Plaza, once the setting for two monumental allegorical statues by Daniel Chester French. Worldly *Manhattan* was seated with a

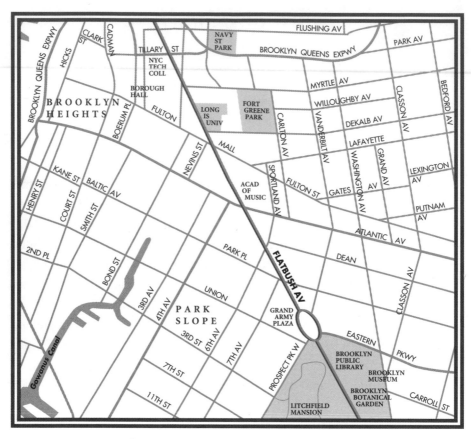

Chapter Two: Downtown Nowhere

winged globe and a peacock, while maternal *Brooklyn* was depicted with a church steeple and a studious child beside her. The vanity of the first statue and the humility of the second made it evident which borough would reign and which would remain a supplicant for civic patronage and favor, a prophecy that came exactly true. The ladies remained seated here for fifty years, until, in 1963, they got up and walked to the front entrance of the Brooklyn Museum, where they remained, stately and indifferent, anchored only yards apart but never exchanging a word.

Technically, the boulevard before me was Flatbush Avenue Extension, built in 1909 as a run-up to the bridge from Fulton Street and now the address of two universities, a major public-health clinic, a cheesecake emporium that billed itself as "Junior's Most Fabulous Restaurant – The Heart and Pulse of Downtown Brooklyn," several major office towers, and the two theaters, one destroyed and one about to be reopened, that gave birth to rock and roll.

To the east, Willoughby Street, boyhood home of Mickey Rooney, led to a public park and the tallest Doric column in America, beneath which were interred the bones of some twelve thousand American prisoners of the murderous British during the Revolutionary War. To the west, just off Flatbush Extension, the Albee Square Mall, an indoor shopping plaza, had been opened. I thought it apt when, early in my wanderings – when I still was expecting to be shot, stabbed, or clubbed as I rounded each corner – I walked into Albee Square and the first merchant I encountered was sitting at his cash register and reading a pamphlet headed "Make Your Hobby Your Career – Become a Gun Pro."

At Junior's Most Fabulous, on the northwest corner of Flatbush and Fulton Street, nothing had changed in forty years, save a photograph of Bill Clinton carrying two candy-striped cartons of cheesecake. (It had been hung on the far side of a pillar near the take-out counter, where almost no one would see it.)

The menu at Junior's was so extensive that it was possible to order Selection 277 – fresh halibut *en casserole*, with macaroni and cheese – and barely reach the middle pages. When the steel baking dish arrived, it turned out to contain an unnaturally orange-red volcano, with the thick, white slab of fish buried at its base, the macaroni heaped on top of it like lava, and some boulders of carrot and a single floret of broccoli implanted at the cone like a plug.

This came with dishes of pickled beets and coleslaw, warm, crumbly corn bread, and tea served New York style, which meant a carafe of tepid grey water, an empty cup, and a lonely paper tea-bag on the side.

Junior's was the Brooklynest joint surviving. The big cafeterias and lady-like tea rooms of my boyhood were long gone from downtown, replaced by hamburger chains and kosher pizzerias and Korean hot-and-cold buffets, and the new immigrants, whose unlicensed street market flourished on the Fulton Mall outside the picture windows, could not know an egg cream from an egg roll. (The latter was a pseudo-Chinese appetizer and the former was chocolate syrup, milk, and carbonated water, stirred with a fork until foamy and gulped before the head collapsed. It was now, in 1993, available in *bottles*, for God's sake.)

But here, the old order held, and the old order was taken by waitresses who must have been here to serve Aunt Cel and her thirteen-year-old nephew, when we lunched here in 1963 after seeing *For Love or Money* at the Albee Theater, now razed in favor of the shopping mall.

"Dessert, hon?" I was asked by one of them one day, having gnawed through seven inches of a turkey sandwich and still not reached the other side. She had her hair cut severely short and dyed severely red, and her eyebrows were plucked and redrawn.

"Am I truly your 'hon'?" I responded, big-eyed.

"No!" she said severely, slaying me, and slapped the check on the counter.

∾

A sign on the bulletin board on the fourth floor of the Board of Health building said: "The Only Stress-Free People Are Dead People."

The Board of Heath building on Flatbush Extension was a First World consulate in a despairing country. Most days, a queue of the ill and ill-served of the borough wound around the five-story structure with grates on its windows, patiently waiting for visas to a fantasyland of healthy babies and strong, clean teeth. Inside, schoolgirls in the "low socio-economic categories" learned how to feed their mewling infants, and teenaged boys waved off positive results in the Sexually Transmitted Disease clinic, saying, "That's not a lesion. It's a zipper cut."

It had been a routine morning: 187 immigrant children from Haiti and

Bangladesh and Nigeria had been brought in for inoculation to comply with the city's straightforward policy: no shots, no school. Most had never seen a doctor before. Dozens of women sat waiting for checks from the State of New York that could be exchanged at participating groceries for eggs, juice, cereal, milk, cheese. The elevator had been defaced by "Night Shift" and "Dark & Lovely."

The affliction of the current hour was tuberculosis. The disease was a specter from an earlier century, called back to see what havoc it could wreak in a modern city. Already, the damage was considerable. New strains were multiplying and mutating in the bodies of the homeless and the immune-deficient, the women who sold their bodies for impure heroin, the men who tore the copper wiring out of fire-alarm boxes and sold it to buy crack cocaine.

Bright red flyers left on street corners and at rooming houses and emergency shelters announced: "TB CAN BE CURED!" But treatment consisted of as many as a dozen pills a day, every day for half a year. It was almost impossible to enforce. The director of the TB clinic, Stan Cutchins, said that nearly every patient gave up on the regimen sooner or later, usually sooner.

Stan Cutchins sent his clinicians out into the streets to make sure that TB patients took their enormous numbers of pills. They sought them in alleys, parks, dumpsters, flophouses, abandoned buildings under the bridge. It was called Directly Observed Therapy. They gave out subway tokens to lure the recalcitrant to the Board of Health for check-ups. Perfect attendance for a week earned a five-dollar certificate, good at McDonald's or Kentucky Fried Chicken. Thus satiated, the patient would conclude that he didn't need his medicine any more, and the cycle would begin again.

There was one room here I was determined to visit. In the bowels of the Board of Health building was a secret library that few people ever entered, but no one, once admitted, ever left. I was let in through a heavy blue steel door and tiptoed down a spiral staircase. At the bottom was a yellow-tiled mausoleum in which were kept the fragile paper birth and death records for the various boroughs of Greater New York going back into the nineteenth century. Hundreds of shelves held thousands of volumes of certificates bound in canvas-covered cardboard. Each book was three inches thick.

Granted only a few moments in this climate-controlled sanctum, I hurried down the galleries to try to find the answer to a minor family mystery:

the correct date of my father's birth, which had been lost for more than eighty years in the broken Yiddish translation of the family's oral traditions. I searched for the Manhattan records for December 1911, but these were manifold – it would have taken hours or days to find the twin Abelowitz boys – and my escort paced impatiently and I had to go, leaving all my anteced-ents, the Jacobsons and Bresses and Quints, to sleep into another century.

As soon as I climbed back up the stairway, I wished I had begged for more time. A weight of sorrow lowered on me like fog. I never met three of my four grandparents. The fourth, my father's father, died when I was only four.

Down there, I thought, I might at least have touched their names and left my fingerprints.

∾

"On May 11," my mother said, "it will be exactly fifty-five years since my mother died."

I was in my bedroom, tidying, cataloging my notes, and placing clip-pings from the New York papers in file folders: Crime, History, Religion, and a dozen more.

"I heard her last breath," she said.

I made no reply. I didn't know if she was leading somewhere, or just marooned in a sweet, sad mood, as I had been at the repository under the Board of Health.

"When a parent dies, you regret all the talks you didn't have," she went on. Now I knew where she was headed.

"Well," I said. "After three months, there shouldn't be anything *we* haven't talked about."

"That's up to you," my mother volleyed.

I returned to my notes.

"I had to do an assignment once in school," she said. "I had to ask my mother when was the happiest time of her life. She said it was when she was a little girl in Russia and she used to go and sit by a lake, all by herself, and just look out at the water."

She waited.

"When was the happiest time of *your* life?" I obliged. I thought I knew the answer. It must have been during the war, her working years as a young, strap-hanging commuter, the nights when she and her sister Fay would dance with the servicemen and "bring home strays." But I was wrong.

"The happiest time of my life," my mother said, "was when you were from one to five years old."

That night she ate a huge bowl of spaghetti with oily, fried ground beef, the breading I had scraped off my pork chops, and a sweet potato. Fortified like a TB patient after a five-dollar McDonald's feast, she proceeded to defeat me at Scrabble, by three points, for the first time in years. Then I recovered my senses and, in the second game of the twilight doubleheader, demolished her by ninety-five.

∾

"A city," wrote Margaret Mead, "is a place where there is no need to wait for next week to get an answer to a question, to taste the food of any country, to find a new voice to listen to and familiar ones to listen to again."

I was reading this on a poster in the window of the clothing boutique operated by the film director Spike Lee, a couple of blocks due east of Junior's, on my way to Fort Greene Park. At Spike's Joint, commerce and homily danced groin to groin. Wisdom echoed from Chief Joseph: "We only ask an even chance to live as other men live." And Goethe: "Treat people as if they were what they ought to be and you help them to become what they are capable of being." And a label on a hat: "Spike Lee caps are a mix of street culture and social awareness that you can wear on your head."

The caps, at nineteen dollars each, bore socially aware code words like "Real" and "Livin'" and "Nubian." (The Malcolm X revival that Lee's film and fashion empire had engendered only a year earlier seemed to have evaporated, having exhausted the attention span of the music-video generation.) Another hat said "Peace Ya-Dig," but this plaint had gone unheeded just a few weeks earlier, four blocks away. In a schoolyard on Adelphi Street, an errantly passed basketball had struck a boy on an adjacent court in the head, leading to an exchange of words that ended when one young man thrust a knife into the subclavian artery of a seventeen-year-old son of Nigerian immigrants and left him to bleed to death on the sidewalk. At the funeral service, the minister said of Christian Abakpa: "He left the African bush to die in the Brooklyn jungle."

I turned north and started to climb up the hill to the park where the Revolutionary War martyrs were interred. It was a steep ascent, made against a current of running, laughing teenagers, making their way from a phys.-ed. period in the playground back to Brooklyn Technical High School at the south side of the hill. Fort Greene had its violent episodes, but it also encompassed this famous yellow-brick seat of science education and long blocks of exquisite brownstone town houses, one of which, 260 Cumberland Street, was for many years the home of the poet Marianne Moore. When I reached the summit and found a bench, I was sitting where Richard Wright wrote parts of *Native Son*.

The view was stupendous. Manhattan and the bridges lay revealed to the north and north-west, while farther to the east was the immense zone of poverty, pride, and hopelessness where Spike Lee had made his masterpiece, *Do the Right Thing*. In that film, a pizzeria in Bedford–Stuyvesant was trashed and burned in the final act of a dispute over the absence of photographs of African-American heroes on the restaurant's Italian wall of fame. The argument seemed as trivial as a mis-thrown basketball, but Lee had caught the dynamic exactly – Fred Lucci, my mother's second husband, was the embodiment of Sal the fictional pizza man – and in the borough to which I had returned, we all were playing in the same giant schoolyard in a dangerous, sudden-death game.

The 145-foot column at the crest of the hill had been erected in 1906 to honor the bones of the anonymous wretches entombed years earlier in sealed brick vaults below. A huge cauldron perched atop the Doric capital was designed to display a perpetual flame, but money to fuel this beacon ran out within a few months. The vessel now served only to tempt Brooklyn's crackheads, since it was the largest item of copper they had not yet stolen and sold to underworld smelters.

The Prison Ship Martyrs, as they were known, were men who died in abominable filth and squalor aboard British vessels in the East River from 1776 to 1783. Although their numbers may have exceeded American casualties from all the land battles of the Revolution *combined*, the Martyrs were virtually unknown to schoolchildren and, for that matter, adults. Few sightseers come to the column. Fort Greene Park, deserted when the kids from Brooklyn Tech departed, was not a place in which I wanted to be by myself for long. In fact, having lingered at the monument for a respectful three minutes or so, I was so relieved at having made it safely back down to DeKalb Avenue that I rushed right into Spike's Joint and bought a couple of postcards.

∾

Few survived the prison ships. For seven years, holding New York and its harbor uncontested following their rout of Washington's army in the Battle of Brooklyn, the British could do as they pleased with the men they had captured. The gospel of the Prison Ship Martyrs tells us they were pleased to let them die.

The vessels were retired gunships, stripped of masts and canvas and moored beyond reach of rescue. Their names were genteel: *Whitby, Chatham, Kitty, Prince of Wales, Clyde, Stromboli, Jersey.* Of these, the *Jersey* was the best-known of a little-known fleet, largely because a man named Thomas Andros lived to write of the months he spent aboard her:

> Utter derangement was a common symptom of yellow fever, and to increase the horror of the darkness that shrouded us (for we were allowed no light betwixt decks), the voice of warning would be heard, "Take heed to yourselves. There is a mad man stalking through the ship with a knife in his hand." I sometimes found the man a corpse in the morning, by whose side I laid myself down at night. . . .
>
> In the morning, the hatch-ways were thrown open and we were allowed to ascend, all at once and remain on the upper deck during the day. But the first object that met our view in the morning was a most appalling spectacle. A boat loaded with dead bodies, conveying them to Long Island shore where they were very slightly covered with sand. I sometimes used to stand to count the number of times the shovel was filled with sand to cover a dead body. And certain I am that a few high tides or torrents of rain must have disinterred them. . . .

General Washington was aware of the maltreatment of the prisoners and he wrote to Lord Richard Howe to complain, to no effect. Reprisals against

Britishers held by the colonials were threatened but not carried out. Mean-while, mornings aboard *Jersey* and the others continued to be heralded by a cry from above: "Damn'd Yankee rebels, turn out your dead."

Thomas Andros had been right – the corpses he watched being hastily interred at Wallabout were soon unearthed by the tides and floated away. Many had washed up at the riverbank where I would see a loon an eon later, and, when construction of Brooklyn's huge Navy Yard began early in the nineteenth century, still more skeletons were uncovered. When Walt Whit-man was a young boy, the bones were kept in a "temporary" ossuary on York Street, and they remained there for decades, long enough for the boy to grow to become editor of the *Eagle* and to continually decry the "strange, rickety, mildewed, tumble-down wooden structure" that was an insult to "the proudest, most precious legacy our city holds, from the past, to pass onward to the patriotism of the future."

Whitman accepted as an article of faith that the number of men who had died on the prison ships was twelve thousand. This figure has been decried by modern scholarship as "gross exaggeration . . . unadulterated propa-ganda," but the myth had him in a hammerlock and he campaigned passionately for a suitable memorial.

But it took another twenty-five years before thirteen coffins representing the rebellious colonies were moved from the old building on York Street to the new tomb at Fort Greene Park. And it took thirty-five more years before the unveiling of the record-setting Doric column and the short-lived per-petual flame. In 1900, new construction at the Navy Yard had exhumed another seven caskets' worth of bones, so that now, on the hill east of Junior's Most Fabulous Restaurant, there were twenty sacred reliquaries in Amer-ica's little-known catacomb. Debbie and I petitioned several times for entrance to the vault itself. But it appeared that the Parks Department had forgotten where they kept the sacred key.

2

Brooklyn was the most famous place in the world. It had delivered itself of Lena Horne, Jackie Gleason, Barry Manilow, Mickey Spillane, Mary Tyler Moore, Mike Tyson, Dom DeLuise, Lou Gossett, Jr., Thelma Ritter, Connie

Francis, Joan Rivers, the Gershwin brothers, the Talmadge sisters, Danny Kaye, Aaron Copland, Arthur Miller, Little Anthony and the Imperials, Norman Mailer, Sandy Koufax, Beverly Sills, Allen Funt, Vince Lombardi, Eddie Murphy, Phil Silvers, three of the four Three Stooges, Lord Haw Haw, and Mae West. Brooklyn had invented Twizzler licorice, Dutch Boy paints, Faber pencils, Detecto scales, and Navy aircraft carriers. It had had its own big-league baseball team, its own language, its own cuisine, and its own Coney Island.

The borough's pinnacle of daffy repute was reached during the Second World War. Three hundred and twenty-seven thousand sons and daughters went into uniform. They were called "the largest number of fighting men and women from any single community at any time in the world's history." Their home town was depicted in cinema as a breeding ground for sentimental lunatics. The merest mention of the word "Brooklyn" threw audiences into convulsions. (When a crowd was composed predominately of Brooklynites, the same effect could be achieved by saying "Canarsie.")

In countless movies, as they prepared to face a human-wave assault by suicidal Japanese on some lost Pacific atoll, leathernecked Marines invariably were heard to sigh something along the lines of, "Jeez, my Moitle back in Bensonhoist soitainly is a poil of a goil."

It was estimated that one out of seven Americans had been born here, or had relatives who had been born here, or knew someone who had relatives who had been born here.

Passenger: "Where are we, cabbie?"
Driver: "Nowhere. This is *Brooklyn*."

The people of the borough were parochial, worldly, innocent, savvy, ignorant, brilliant, refined, rabid, welcoming, illiberal, and almost unanimously mad. They streamed over the bridges and through the tunnels for cocktails and culture in the Babylon that was Manhattan, then returned to their dizzy domicile eager to swallow sausages, venerate slapstick, and kill umpires. Nearly a century after the borough's political amalgamation with Manhattan in 1898, Rod Stewart could still sing of rush-hour trains full of Brooklyn girls, desperate to escape their "little world."

The little world had been subdivided in our minds into neighborhoods as distinct and inimical as Soviet republics. Bushwick knew nothing of Sheepshead Bay; as far as Red Hook was concerned, Brownsville might as well have been on Mars. Subway routes were like trenches at the Somme – it was understood that poking one's head up at the wrong station invited a swift, certain death. Loyalties were intensely localized. On East 31st Street, when I was a boy, we were perpetually afraid of being set upon and massacred by the Mongol hordes from East 29th.

This Balkanization had an historical basis. What was now called Brooklyn had once been six separate towns. Flatbush and Flatlands, the districts through which I was bound on my ten-mile peregrination, had remained politically independent and essentially rural until late in the nineteenth century, untouched by the first avalanches of immigration.

Even in the 1950s, the pastoral remained. I could recall a vegetable farm just north of Coney Island that seemed, to a city child, as expansive as the Ponderosa. Until, at thirteen, I was bussed to Norfolk to spend two weeks with the Virginia side of my mother's family, it was the only farm I had ever seen.

The centrifugal pull of Manhattan was irresistible when I was a boy. Subway entrances were marked "To City," which meant Wall Street and Times Square. Downtown Brooklyn was a zone to be transited underground en route to Yankee Stadium or Radio City Music Hall. There was little reason to squander fifteen cents on the half-hour journey to Downtown, since Macy's department store in humble Flatbush equaled the best of Fulton Street and the regional delicacies now confined to Junior's could then be savored within walking distance at any of a half-dozen delicatessens *du quartier*. Until I wandered into it on this trip, looking for a bathroom, I had never been in Borough Hall, Brooklyn's Reichstag.

By 1993, a Brooklynite's world had been condensed even further, to a padlocked apartment, a familiar street, a row of low-end shops. The slap-happy daffiness of the Danny Kaye years had drained away. In 1989, the Honeymooners' mythic "Bensonhoist" had made headlines as the scene of the summary murder of a black teenager by a pack of white youths. A police precinct in Brownsville reported a homicide every sixty-eight hours. Lovely Moitle most likely had relocated to Florida.

The movie-screen face of Brooklyn now was the unbridgeable racial chasm depicted in *Do the Right Thing*. Its quaint manner of speaking had been bequeathed to the unspeakable Andrew Dice Clay. Instead of a roisterous melting pot, it had become an archipelago of solitudes, Los Angeles without the freeways. Old-timers maintained that Brooklyn had perished in 1957 when the Dodgers baseball team moved to California, but the mighty Yankees had remained in the Bronx, and the Bronx was surely no better.

> *Larry King, returning in 1992 to his childhood home on Howard Avenue in Brooklyn, to the driver of his limousine*: "What do they call this neighborhood now?"
> *Limo Driver*: "Death."

Since few people ever left their immediate territory, my avowed intention to traverse Brooklyn by way of Flatbush Avenue was met everywhere with awe and disbelief. I was warned not to go near Church Avenue; at Church Avenue, they told me to avoid Parkside. A police officer from the 84th Precinct down on Gold Street whispered, "Stay west of Flatbush. It's bad on the other side." Subway riders told me to stay off the buses; bus people said the subway was hell. Only my sister willingly accompanied me up the metaphorical Zambezi. My mother's crowd expected me to disappear like Amelia Earhart: a last phone call, then silence.

∾

I had spent more time in Pittsburgh and Quebec City and New Delhi than I had in Downtown Brooklyn. I was a walking encyclopedia of Istanbul, and Hong Kong held no mystery for me, but coming up out of The Beast at Clark Street or Borough Hall, I had no idea where I was. Blundering about, I made wonderful finds.

On Earth Day in late April, Debbie steered me unerringly towards a new complex of office towers called MetroTech, where children from a private school in moneyed Brooklyn Heights were gingerly liberating Painted Lady butterflies from supermarket bags and placing them on low evergreen shrubs. We listened as the environmentally friendly Tom Chapin stood in the drizzle and sang: "Good garbage breaks down as it goes. / That's why it smells bad to your nose."

At a row of tables staffed by various interest groups, we picked up free copies of recycling hints, guidebooks to the natural history of the region, and a 179-page volume called, somewhat confusingly, *Making Less Garbage*.

MetroTech had sprung up magnificently at the end of Myrtle Avenue, where the elevated train had once clattered and screeched, until it was scrapped in 1970. The gas company and the Chase Manhattan Bank now called its shiny modern towers their home. Phalanxes of smartly dressed office workers spilled from the buildings for lunch. Croissants were eaten. It was said that some of these people actually commuted from Manhattan.

Billboards announced that more construction was to commence at any moment: more corporate headquarters, more government offices, even a Brooklyn Hilton. A new communications center for the borough's police emergency phone line was planned for Tillary Street. (Screaming for help was a growth industry.) But so far, only the signs had been erected.

A Hilton would be welcome, as there were no hotels downtown other than Single Room Occupancy hostels for the indigent. In fact, there were no hotels *anywhere* in a community of more than two million people. According to my guidebooks, Brooklyn offered three motels at the far southern end of the borough, one bed-and-breakfast overlooking Prospect Park, and one converted apartment hotel used mostly by Hasidic Jews. It had no Amtrak service, no inter-city buses – except gamblers' junkets to Atlantic City and Haitian charters to Montreal – no Avis or Hertz agency, not even a ferry service to enthrall latter-day Whitmans. Kennedy and La Guardia airports, of course, were in Queens.

Decades earlier, Downtown Brooklyn had been the capital of a burgeoning hinterland of requited dreams. At Albee Square, a half block from Flatbush, the central branch of the Dime Savings Bank, a heavy, high-domed hexagon built in 1923, was a hushed chapel of fundamental values. Inside, twelve red-marble Corinthian columns rose to capitals inset with giant Mercury-head dimes. More oversized ten-cent pieces were spaced around the rotunda, an allegory of frugality. Solid stone benches were engraved with encouragements to thrift and perseverance. "A pendulum travels much but it only goes one tick at a time." Or "A hundred years of vexation will not pay a farthing of debt."

I sat on one of the benches and looked through the front doors to the discount sneaker stores, the taco stands, and the credit jewelers of my new borough. Outside, on the Fulton pedestrian mall, a young man in a suit and a small bow tie was selling copies of Louis Farrakhan's black-consciousness newspaper, *The Final Call.* A crazy man sat on the sidewalk and sang in a piercing falsetto to the hedges and the traffic and the sun.

Fulton Street met Flatbush at the nexus of a Levantine street bazaar. Vendors squatted on the pavement, sat on folding chairs, stood beside pushcarts. They sold counterfeit perfumes, tropical fruits, candied peanuts, Resurrection plants, Black Soap ("Soap of the Ancients"), bundles of herbs, Muslim tracts, television antennas, leather purses, bootleg videos, and talismanic incense with names like Coco-Mango and "Channel" No. 5. T-shirts bore forgeries of designer monograms and exhortations to legalize marijuana ("Lick It, Roll It, Smoke It"), to drink until catatonic, and to respect the sanctity of The Black Family ("It's a Pride Thing.")

It might have been Sarawak or Panama City. The peddlers were Hispanic, Caribbean, and African; Hindu, Rasta, and Mohammedan; belligerent, indifferent, and shy. They wore dreadlocks, dress shirts, kurta-pyjama, Senegalese robes. They spoke a thousand tongues.

Above and behind the merchants were the forgotten edifices of old Brooklyn – fortresses like the Pioneer Warehouse on Flatbush at Livingston Street with its Romanesque arches and buttressed castle doors. Faded advertisements on the walls of abandoned buildings still spoke of Sheet Metal and Tinners' Supplies, but the local economy had shrunk to curbside peddling, an above-ground underground empire. At the entrances to legitimate stores, uniformed security guards stood with arms crossed, tense and suspicious. Behind them, their elbows on display cases, lonely merchants watched their livelihoods being eaten by squatters, who filed no forms, obtained no licenses, used no utilities, obeyed no regulations, owed no rent, and paid no taxes.

I was standing at the threshold of the new Brooklyn in the spring of the Phillies Blunt. This was a particular brand of cigar, displayed in boxes on the counter of every convenience or variety shop I entered, which was commonly being hollowed out by purchasers and used as a wrapper for enormous joints of dope. Many of the street vendors I was passing sold both the cigar and clothing extolling its euphoric effects.

"Gettin' Blunted," the shirts proudly proclaimed.

It was the year of the Blunt, of Snapple beverages and Arizona Iced Tea and new, powerfully alcoholic, malt liquors with names like Crazy Horse and Midnight Dragon. The *New York Times* reported that it had become common for schoolmates to share forty ounces of Crazy Horse and a Blunt or two before and after classes. One boy called the combination "cookies and milk."

I walked south along Flatbush and came to a bench in a triangle called Temple Square. Behind me was the old red schoolhouse where, at seventeen, I had to line up for hours to apply for "working papers" when I took my first summer job away from the Abel Brothers candy store.

Across Flatbush, the message board outside the Brooklyn Academy of Music announced *Peer Gynt* and Monteverdi's *Return of Ulysses*. A gardening center – here, in the core of the concrete city – maintained pots of impatiens and begonias and Funny Girl roses behind enough barbed wire to fence the Korean DMZ. A parkette at the junction with Fourth Avenue had been planted as a miniature botanic garden, complete with a rustic wooden bridge over a stream forever dry.

The open-air Casbah extended along Flatbush from Fulton Street to Atlantic Avenue, where Downtown petered out into rows of brownstones, some neat and some derelict, and an enormous hole in the ground that extended east for blocks and was someday going to be the locus of yet another Brooklyn renaissance. This pie-in-the-sky Brasilia had been proposed for at least sixty-five years, and the current plans had been tied up in lawsuits since the mid-eighties, but it recently had been announced, triumphantly, that Bradlee's, a discount clothing chain, would be opening a store here by 1995. Visiting corporate executives would stay at the Brooklyn Hilton.

∽

The intersection of Flatbush and Atlantic was one patch of central Brooklyn that was not *terra incognita* on my mental map. Years ago, had it not been for my poor eyesight and Little Debbie's ill-partitioned teeth, we might have gone sailing right past here on the IRT, just as we had burrowed through the rest of Downtown on our way to Manhattan to see the Empire State Building or *Man of La Mancha*. But I was as blind as a referee, and Debbie's smile, our parents were told in 1962 by an orthodontist in the Williamsburgh Savings Bank building, would require three years of intensive retrofitting, an estimate that proved to be four years too low.

Whenever I was scheduled to visit my ophthalmologist on Lafayette Avenue, a couple of blocks east of Flatbush, it was customary for my father and me to enjoy the pancakes at Bickford's, a restaurant in the Long Island Rail Road terminal building that now, along with the building itself, had been replaced by the huge empty pit. And Debbie was hauled into the foundry on the twenty-seventh floor of the Williamsburg Bank tower for regular molar maintenance, bringing us often to this famous corner of the vast Brooklyn world.

Now we had returned, and as my sister and I waited for the start of a guided tour of the bank tower – the borough's tallest building at 512 feet – a man wandered by, stopped, let his jeans drop, and bared his buttocks for us in a traditional Brooklyn gesture of welcome.

Our fellow tourists were somewhat better mannered. They wore Etonic running shoes and T-shirts from the Galapagos Islands. A gay couple rolled up on skates. Old friendships were renewed; people had met before at street fairs and tours of Victorian homes and walkathons in Prospect Park. It was my first glimpse of another side of the new Brooklyn – pro-active, committed, urbane – that could look beyond the shattered glass and the Phillies Blunts to see a future and a past.

The tour was arranged by the Brooklyn Center for the Urban Environment and was called "Williamsburgh Bank Tower: Art Deco Gem," though the hall we would visit was a Romanesque basilica with Byzantine detailing. It had been completed in 1929, just in time for the Crash, as the intended focus of a huge new business district that would rival Manhattan itself. The site seemed a logical choice. A dozen subway and streetcar lines and the Long Island Rail Road from the suburbs converged here. Flatbush, Atlantic, and Fourth avenues flowed henceforth to irrigate the rest of the borough, and the bank tower itself was a jewel of workmanship. But then came Black Tuesday, and almost all the prospective tenants went bankrupt and were replaced, at lower rents, by every orthodontist on earth.

Our guide, a gentleman named John Gallagher, who affected a walrus mustache and a curved Bavarian-looking pipe, was philosophical. He said,

"Brooklyn either lost out to Progress or was *spared* Progress." Similarly, I thought, should Bradlee's renege and Atlantic Center emerge stillborn yet again, the borough would at least be gaining a nice big empty lot.

The Williamsburgh Savings Bank tower was, like the Dime a few blocks back up Flatbush, a purposefully ornamented temple to the god of husbandry. Exterior walls were decorated with symbols of fecundity and diligence from the animal world: rabbits, pelicans, beavers, parrots, squirrels with acorns, lions guarding chests of treasure. An elaborate frieze depicted the Four Races of Man: a European, reading a book; a Mandarin, holding a fan; a Mayan, with bow and arrows; an African, wielding a spear.

To the right of the entrance on Hanson Place, the architects had included a small bas-relief of a grimacing safecracker trying to bust into a vault. But Progress had obscured the felon's unhappy fate. A large electric sign had been installed to the left of the portal, covering nearly all of another carving that showed the unlucky man behind bars. No wonder so many Brooklynites seemed unaware that crime does not pay.

We were taken to the observation deck at the twenty-sixth floor, a rare treat. (This public area was usually closed to the public.) The vista encompassed all of our borough, Manhattan, Lady Liberty and Ellis Island, and beyond to New Jersey and the western states. Placards elucidated the British invasion of 1776, the Battle of Brooklyn that nearly cost Washington the war, the American retreat in the sheltering fog. The monument to the Prison Ship Martyrs poked into the sunlight from Fort Greene hill to our north.

Just above our heads was what used to be the largest four-sided clock in the world. It was twenty-seven feet in diameter and had just been eclipsed by an upstart in Milwaukee or Detroit. (Our guide wasn't sure.) Above the clock, the building peaked in a smooth phallic cupola. Below us, satellite dishes clung to the sides like fungi and the foundation plunged 140 feet beneath street level, so deep that pumps had to work continually to keep the East River out of the safe-deposit boxes.

The banking floor, still in use, had been designed in the form of a church. (The trustees of the Williamsburgh were not subtle about equating wealth with holiness.) It was, we were told, 66 feet high, 120 feet long, and 72 feet wide, with a gilt Zodiacal ceiling and balconies at the north wall where ex-Marines once were stationed as guards at the triggers of surplus First

World War machine guns. Robbery attempts were rare enough that the weapons were never fired, but the ex-Marines were.

A beautiful pictorial map above the gun emplacement showed rays of golden sunlight falling on the corner of Flatbush and Atlantic, while puny, penile Manhattan fairly disappeared beneath the glow. Here was the borough's whispered prayer again: that Gotham would disintegrate, leaving Brooklyn to rule and prosper.

The guided tour ended and we walked back out into the sunshine, a little disappointed. Security guards had denied our group permission to see the mighty pumps down at the water table. Manhattan still existed. And Little Debbie's orthodontist had moved out of the Williamsburgh before we could file a lawsuit.

Her teeth were starting to spread apart again.

∾

The Long Island Rail Road terminal building had been wiped from the landscape, but underground, the trains still ran. Directly across narrow Hanson Place from the bas-relief of the unsuccessful safecracker, two stairways led from street level into a cool, low-roofed waiting room, where sleek day-coaches idled and hummed before starting east for suburban Bellerose or Syosset. Most journeys required a transfer at a major junction in Queens.

Most of the commuters on the LIRR sprinted underground from their suburban train to the adjacent platforms of the IRT subway and their miserable jobs in Manhattan. They never pierced the surface of Flatbush and Atlantic. They never guessed that the heavy blue girders of the station were holding up nothing but sky. And no one up on Flatbush could tell that the floor of the open hole beneath them was the roof of a hidden world.

The station became my oasis. I'd retreat from the compressed humanity of the street markets, buy a Snapple at the snack bar, choose a clean wooden bench, read *Flatbush Life* or the *New York Carib News*, and contentedly watch the drones careering toward their conformist corporate desks. There was no public toilet – in Brooklyn, these were as rare as loons – but one afternoon at 1:35 a security guard let me sprint onto the 1:40 Hempstead Express and use the cabinet and dash off again before the train's departure. I loved that man.

The Long Island Rail Road Station was intensively policed. A lectern at the railhead was usually leaned on by a couple of uniformed officers from the Metropolitan Transportation Authority, and beyond the subway token booth and turnstiles, in a separate bureaucratic jurisdiction, were the city's beleaguered transit cops. These were luckless souls who, after progressing through the same training program as regular patrolmen, had been commanded to spend their working lives in the sunless viaducts, ticketing turnstile jumpers, assisting bewildered tourists, and hunting down the murderers of the token clerks at Euclid and Van Siclen avenues.

I applied to the New York Transit Authority to spend a day with its subterranean commandos, and permission was granted instantly, over the phone, just like that. I'd report for roll call at 7:30 the next morning, which meant rising at six, or about an hour and a half after my mother, who was usually as nocturnal as a whippoorwill, finally put away her Parliaments and her dog-eared solitaire deck and bedded down for the night.

It should not have been surprising that the administration would be eager to show off The Beast. A survey published in *Newsday* reported that 59 per cent of respondents agreed with the statement, "The Transit Authority appears to have a plan in mind for improving the subway system." Two out of five rated the system as "excellent" or "good." And 57 per cent said, "I would tell a friend from out of town that it is okay to take the subway."

Yet exactly the same percentage said that if they had a choice, *they* would never ride it at all.

At our Flatbush Avenue terminus, a woman had been appointed station manager and deputized to solve minor wrangles and to smile incessantly. More than a hundred other locations were being similarly served. Tributes to the efficacy of these public servants were published in leaflets handed to each day's dazed commuters. Riders hailed "great improvement" and "professional leadership." Tales were printed of station managers stanching floods, removing garbage, rescuing a lost, handicapped child. Crime on the subway, it was announced, had decreased for twenty-eight consecutive months.

"We know what some of you think of us," said a Transit Authority spot on WINS all-news radio, "and, *boy*, do we want to change your minds."

～

The evening before I was to join the transit cops, a seventeen-year-old boy, wearing a motorman's uniform, walked into a train yard in Upper Manhattan, gave a false name, cited someone's badge number, climbed behind the controls of the Eighth Avenue Express to Queens, and proceeded to take two thousand passengers, possibly including my sister, up and down the system with estimable precision for three hours until he tripped an automatic brake in Harlem and panicked, afraid to climb down near the high-voltage rail to reset the manual switch.

"HE TOOK THE A TRAIN," the papers exulted.

The next morning, I showed up at the underground police station at Franklin Avenue in Brooklyn just in time to hear the officer of the day inform his troops that some hooligan had stolen a train, to which nearly everyone responded in unison, "Dey caught him awready."

The public-relations man at the Transit Authority described the Franklin Avenue stationhouse as "probably the worst in the whole system." It was located at the northern end of the southbound platform, up a stairway, behind a thick blue door. The first thing I saw when I entered was a plaque honoring twelve officers who had been killed since 1963 while on duty aboard the hurtling trains. Next to it were dozens of Polaroids of pistols and machine guns confiscated by the courageous flatfoots with whom I was to pass a long, dark day.

They asked me if I wanted to wear a bulletproof vest.

I declined. I had been shot at during the Romanian revolution (while cowering stupidly behind cans of petrol in a van in Timișoara) and had survived the killings at Tian'anmen Square (in a room at the Regent Hotel, Hong Kong). I assumed myself to be indestructible, a decision I regretted as soon as I went out on patrol and noticed that one of the officers I was accompanying, a young, bull-necked, muscular, virile former college baseball star, was encased in a flak jacket that looked as if it could withstand a direct hit from Saddam Hussein's Super Gun.

The young man's name was Steve Werner. We were riding to the major interchange at Flatbush and Atlantic, across from the Williamsburgh Savings Bank tower and beneath the empty lot that someday would be Bradlee's Discount Clothing. Officer Werner, chatty and fit, had been three years on the transit force. His partner, Jim Mandes, a more laconic and wearier man, with four medals on his chest, had done ten.

One day when Steve Werner was on the Brighton Beach train in Brooklyn, a report came in that someone was firing a gun from the roof of a building. Steve was the nearest officer to the scene. (In an emergency, transit cops may vault to the streets and city police descend to the tunnels.) He said, "It was just like a movie. Hat off. Gun drawn. Step by step, creeping up the stairs. Heart goin' a mile a minute." The man surrendered.

Another time, there was a call that someone had been robbed at gunpoint on the Flatbush Avenue route. Steve Werner, just out of the academy, stepped from the platform into a car as crowded as the Prison Ship *Jersey*, and there was the description on his radio, come to life.

"I saw that he had the gun in a bag," Werner said. "I drew mine. We were gun to gun. I told him, 'If you touch that gun, I'm going to shoot you.'"

I doubted that Steve Werner would ever shoot anybody. He had played shortstop and the outfield at Long Island University and never thought about anything except hitting the curve ball. Some buddies were going to take the examination for the police academy. Steve went along for a laugh, got the highest score of the bunch, went through basic training, and winced when the word beside his name on the assignment sheet said "Transit." Now he had weathered three years on the force, he was worried about inhaling steel dust day after day, and he said, "When I go on the subway out of uniform, I don't feel safe without my gun."

Jim Mandes said, "I *never* take the subway, but if I had to, I'd take my *three* guns."

We arrived at Atlantic Avenue and walked over to the vestibule where incoming riders from the 2, 3, 4, 5, D, and Q trains could transfer to the B, the M, the N, or the R. Steve and Jim spent part of every workday here, waiting for someone to leap over the turnstile so they could slap him with one of the sixty-dollar fines for fare evasion that amounted to 90 per cent of their summonses. This tedious detail occasionally was enlivened, as it had been on a recent afternoon, by gangs of high-school pupils going at each other with knives and hammers until valiant constables waded into the melee, waving their batons and barking into their portable radios, "Ten-thirteen. Ten-thirteen. Officer needs assistance."

I stood against the wall and watched the patrolmen watch the people watching them. A disheveled, mentally handicapped man wandered through the station, descried a young woman using a pay telephone, and stood just behind her, breathing down her neck, until Jim Mandes shooed him away. A tall, rangy fellow in a blue corduroy cowboy hat strode off the Number 2 local carrying a Clorox jug. He walked down a long, tiled corridor, stopped, poured some liquid out of the container onto the floor, and slowly sidled on.

Then he passed through a gate and into a thick-glassed booth. He was the token clerk.

A man and woman held up a banner near the stairway to the Brighton Beach line and shouted Biblical quotations. Two United States Marines marched by in full dress uniform, in a territory as foreign as Tripoli. There was a man with a bicycle, youths in gangsta regalia, gold medallions swinging, two old fellows – Armenian? Greek? – with a German shepherd pup. Jim corralled them, warned them of the fifty-dollar penalty for unauthorized animals, let them wander sheepishly away.

An old woman skated by on feet encased in plastic bags from the A & P.

"It's getting worse," Jim Mandes, the veteran, said when I asked about the reported drop in crime. "I've had so many people come up to me and say, 'I was just robbed,' and it was on a platform full of people. They don't care. They'll rob you anywhere, anytime. The city police have a tough job, but down here we're elbow to elbow. All day, we're in the crowds."

"Where is it safe?" I asked Steve Werner. He reached for his summons book and unfolded a multicolored map of the 458 stations.

"The Canarsie line is the worst," he said. "The A and the C in Brooklyn are really bad, too."

Those were the two routes that my sister Debbie traveled, every day, when she had work. I wrote this down in my spiral pad and beside it noted: "I won't tell her."

But there were worse things than crime on the subways. On one of his first days on patrol, Steve Werner got the call that everyone who works down here in the dungeons dreads.

"*Man Under.*" It was the code for suicide.

"All the trains were stopped," he recalled. "They shut the power off. I had to take a taxi. When I got there, the conductor was still in shock. I had to go down and find the body. It was in three separate pieces – head, body, and one arm.

"It was my first Man Under. It was very tough for me. I had butterflies in my stomach, and I got dizzy. When I found the head, down under one of the cars, the whole face had been torn off as it got dragged along, so I had to go through the pockets, find some ID. Male white, age fifty-five."

I asked Jim Mandes how many Man Under calls he had answered in his decade on the force.

"I've lost count," he said. Then, thoughtfully, he added, "You know, we're responsible for every piece."

Transit officers in uniform were expected to issue an average of one summons a day. Beside fines for failure to pay the $1.25 fare and the importation of livestock, there was a fifty-dollar levy for smoking or "sleeping where hazardous" and double that for carrying explosives. For plainclothesmen, ten tickets per shift was the recommended amount, if they could restrain themselves to so few.

"I had never thought about being a cop," Steve Werner said during a lull in the human tide. He was earnest, solid; the gang fights and the Man Unders and all the acidity of the new Brooklyn hadn't dissolved him yet.

"Never dreamed I'd say it," he smiled, "but being a cop is the best thing I ever did."

3

Most of the advertisements on all-news WINS were for food stores, airlines, and how safe the subways had become. Only one was different. It announced the redemption of the world.

I heard it on the second night of my return to East 31st Street, in my old room, with a small transistor radio on the pillow next to my head. I burrowed under the comforter and turned the volume down to a whisper, as if a blonde baby sister still slumbered on the other side of the flimsy partition that once split this chamber in two. But Little Debbie was home in Canarsie, watching the Yankees game or listening to Willie Nelson.

Down the hall, my mother was playing her Patsy Cline cassette and softly crooning lyrics that to me were merely country songs but that for her must have awakened personal elegies of passion and loss. She would listen to that tape, and one by Crystal Gayle, every night without exception, until I finally objected to the monotony and was rewarded, spitefully, with *The Best of Trini Lopez,* followed by *Ferrante and Teicher's Golden Hits.*

But now, on WINS, the repetitive parade of weather reports, lottery numbers, traffic advisories, and stock-market summaries was interrupted by a man intoning, "Moshiach is coming . . . *soon.*"

Moshiach is the Jewish concept of a messianic savior whose arrival will clear the worldly table of war and avarice and usher in a perfect age. Predictions of the First Coming were not ordinarily broadcast on commercial radio stations in the middle of the AM dial. But the message on WINS was straightforward: "Your father wanted it to happen. Your father's father wanted it to happen. For three thousand, three hundred years, since the Jews became a people, they have waited. . . . Now, Moshiach is coming."

A telephone number was given, and I scrambled in the dark for some paper and scribbled it down. There was a toll-free line (1-800-MOSHIACH) and a local exchange for Brooklyn, which had long been the nucleus of American Jewry and which was, in 1993, in such obvious need of supernatural assistance that it had to be any right-thinking messiah's first stop.

"Shalom!" said a recorded voice when I dialed the number. "Welcome to the Moshiach Multilingual Information Line. For the very basics, press 1. For the weekly message, press 2."

I pressed 1 and chose English over French, Hebrew, and Russian.

"One of the Thirteen Principles of the Jewish faith is the 'coming of the anointed one,'" I heard. "Moshiach is *and must be* a human being, sent by God to change the world. But first, we must acknowledge that the world is deficient and wanting. . . ."

I pressed 2 for the weekly sermon.

"We were, and still are, like dreamers. . . . When Moshiach comes, we'll know the truth. . . ."

I hung up the telephone and rolled back to the pillow, where WINS was still softly nattering. Ceasefire in Bosnia. Tie-up at the Lincoln Tunnel. Mets lose. Moshiach on his way.

∾

The next noontime, lost in Downtown Brooklyn, after wandering around the pedestrian plazas near Borough Hall and looking at the statues of Christopher Columbus and Robert Kennedy and the abolitionist Henry Ward Beecher, I needed some lunch and bumbled into a kosher pizza and falafel shop and accidentally met a herald of the new Jerusalem.

I was carrying my tray toward a table at the back of the restaurant when I nearly bumped into a heavyset man dressed in the long coat and black felt hat of the Hasidic sect of fervently orthodox Jews. Then he turned around. He was black.

After fifteen minutes of trying to eat, staring at the man over and around my newspaper, sipping my apple juice, and more staring, I took a deep breath and walked over to his table and excused my piggish curiosity.

"It's just that, um," I stammered, "you don't see many black Hasidic Jews."

He smiled beatifically and moved a chair so that I could sit next to him. He was with a bewigged Caucasian woman whom I took, correctly, to be his wife.

"I'm sorry I was staring at you," I said.

"This clothing," he replied, fingering his garment, "is not just for show when people are looking at you. It's for when the light is not on you, too."

His name was Yisroel Francis. He took my business card and began to twist it around his fingers, absently, distracted from his lunch and his Talmudic train of thought by my abrupt intrusion.

Yisroel Francis told me he was forty years old and that his ancestors had been in the New World centuries before my father's father sailed from the Czarist inquisitions. They were Spanish–Dutch from the Netherlands Antilles, intermarried with darker-skinned islanders to produce mulatto offspring whose Hebraic religiosity was in no way diluted. In fact, Yisroel Francis had chosen to commit himself totally to the study of the Torah and the promulgation of the creed of Menachem Schneerson, the great

Lubavitch Rebbe of Crown Heights, Brooklyn, who had paid for the Moshiach Multilingual Information Line and the advertisements on WINS.

Like poor Tevye dreaming of wealth and probity in *Fiddler on the Roof*, Yisroel Francis had retired from this blemished universe to discuss the holy books with the learned men seven hours every day. His singleness of purpose was given an unwanted boost when he was fired by the Chase Manhattan Bank after twenty years of employment, an action he was expecting to challenge in court. A lot of New Yorkers blamed their setbacks on racism or anti-Semitism, but Rabbi Francis was one of the very few who could do both.

"It has not been easy for me," he said. "People have said things that were not too kosher. I've seen a lot of baseless hatred. I have medals. You just don't see them."

What I did see was a round-faced man in rimless spectacles and a bristly, whitening beard. He was the only black Lubavitcher. He wrote articles for the *Jewish Press*. He and the woman at our table, who spoke little, had four children: Enan, Gershom, Tapharah, Rivkah. I thought of the T-shirts at the street market on Flatbush that celebrated The Black Family.

"Don't you feel your African-American side expressing itself?" I asked. "Don't you feel attached to your race?"

"The race is the Jewish race," Yisroel Francis replied. "The ichor is to be a Jew."

He talked about humility and serving God and he crumpled my card without thinking. His eldest daughter, eighteen, was in seminary. His son, a year younger, was at rabbinical school. The two smaller children were receiving a Jewish education, segregated by sex. They didn't watch television.

Two years earlier, in the summer of 1991, the unstable racial fault line that bifurcates Brooklyn had split open, and death was its price. A vehicle in the motorcade of the Lubavitch Rebbe struck and killed a seven-year-old African-American boy. Some blacks – a lot of blacks – tore apart Crown Heights, chanted, "Hitler didn't finish the job," set upon a Hasid visiting from Australia and stabbed him to death.

"During the riots," Yisroel Francis said, "I didn't want the spotlight. But I was stopped on the street by reporters. Taxis halted when I passed. And the cameras followed me everywhere I went. Even into the House of Glatt!"

That was a restaurant that adhered vigorously to the ancient dietary laws. Being an observant Jew involved culinary practices that seemed extreme to pork-eaters like me. Shellfish was proscribed; so were cheeseburgers, burritos, Chinese sea slugs. Salad greens might harbor microscopic insects whose flesh was taboo. Dishes and cookware were alternated for meat and dairy meals, and an entirely separate set was required on the Passover. Hasidim prayed ecstatically three times a day. The Sabbath was sacrosanct: no phone calls, no laundromats, no college football.

"A Jew should live like a Jew," Rabbi Francis said.

"Does he have to be as ultra-orthodox as you are?" I asked, my courage waxing in proportion to his candor.

"I don't think I'm ultra-anything," he answered. "If you want to be a Lubavitcher, that's *your* business."

Crown Heights had settled down. The television cameras were no longer following Yisroel Francis into the House of Glatt. The *Daily News*, he said, hadn't printed a full-page feature story about him for more than four months. The long-running battle with the Chase Manhattan Bank occupied him and made him ashamed of his anger. He said, "I feel like I'm ninety-five years old."

But despair did not linger. Fatigue and human frailty would be swept aside on the arrival of Moshiach, which could occur at any moment. A ram's horn would sound in Heaven. Somalia would bloom like the Garden of Eden. The Chase Manhattan Bank would wither away. Homeless men with tuberculosis would no longer have to visit the Board of Health. The Jew would embrace the black man. The black man would honor the Jew.

"Why must you advertise the messiah on the radio?" I asked.

"We need the media," the Hasid said. "We need people to have a concept of a messiah, a Moshiach mindset. People want an end to killings, an end to wars and hunger. But they don't think of the religious aspect.

"Calling for Moshiach is like a child calling for his daddy. One child with a soft voice can't be heard. But if enough voices call for him, maybe he opens the door.

"Look at New York. Look at the reality of the streets. People want to eliminate drugs and crime. This, too, is a messianic concept. They think our head is in the clouds. But no! Moshiach is even in mundane things."

I said, "You seem comfortable in your religion."

"You should never be comfortable in your religion," said the black Hasidic Jew. "When you say, 'Let's call it a day,' it's all over."

∾

One thing my mother and I had in common, in addition to strong feelings about Trini Lopez, was that we both had married outside the faith. Religiosity never was our strong suit anyway. I had been sent to Hebrew school, three stultifying afternoons a week, so that I could get bar-mitzvahed like all the other boys on East 31st Street, and for a couple of years I dutifully impressed on Hen and Ben the necessity of the Passover *seder*, the Chanukkah candles, the Purim noisemakers, and the Yom Kippur fast. But as soon as I turned thirteen, I dropped all this like a pop fly in Little League and did not look back.

"It's more important to be a good person than a good Jew," my parents would say. Neither of them attended synagogue or subscribed to the *kashruth* dietary laws, though my father would usually take matzoh rather than rye bread during Passover and would light *yahrzeit* candles on the anniversaries of his parents' deaths. I played baseball with the boys from the Church of the Little Flower, hiding in the bullrushes when they gathered before each game to say their Hail Marys, met Linda at a hotel swimming pool in Venezuela when we both were twenty-three, proposed to her on a sultry August night in Montreal while we were watching *Enter Laughing* on television, and when my parents questioned her evident WASPness, I said, "It's more important to be a good person than a good Jew."

Fred Lucci had reappeared in my mother's life in the spring of 1968. As teenagers, he and my mother had been inseparable. Fred also had been on relief; he also had to accept second-hand clothing – and although Jews and Italians then shared a low step on Brooklyn's long multi-ethnic stairway, my mother's older sister had vetoed any possibility of romance that might lead to miscegenation. It was more than twenty years before he reappeared, calling her Baby and remarking on her undiminished beauty, "O, Madonna! What a *braciole*."

In addition to his enormous number of siblings and cousins and his avowed cordiality with assorted Mafiosi, Fred brought to his second marriage a knack for losing money on horses, a reverence for Frank Sinatra and

Joe DiMaggio, and a furiously short-fused jealousy that exploded into passionate rage if my mother so much as looked at another man. She had been through more than ten years of this, and nearly a dozen of Freddie's small, unprofitable luncheonettes, ice-cream parlors, dry-goods shops, and variety stores, before he suffered a tremendous heart attack that barely failed to kill him.

This happened in the fall of 1982. Fred, my mother, and Debbie had gone to Staten Island for dinner. When they came out, instead of starting back to Brooklyn, he sat with the door of the car open and began retching bile.

My mother went to Roy Rogers Roast Beef to get some wet towels. When she returned, he was kneeling at the side of the car. Then he keeled over.

Linda and I were in Brisbane, Australia, for the Commonwealth Games, so while Fred stayed at St. Vincent's Hospital for thirty-eight days, my mother worked their little store in Brooklyn and then took four city buses, crossed the magnificent span across the Narrows, sat with him a while, then took four buses home. She missed one day of the thirty-eight.

"I had to teach him to read and write again," she told me. "Not that he ever could."

∾

My own Christian bride had a faultless heart; it was the rest of her that didn't work very well. Linda was a child of frozen Canada, so that, when she began to complain at age thirteen of winter chills and fatigue, everyone thought she was goldbricking. But when she fell into a coma on the eve of her sixteenth birthday and the doctors invited her parents to the hospital to make their farewell, the mocking ceased.

They thought she had leukemia. If not, maybe something else. A young intern mentioned reading about a little-known disease called systemic lupus erythematosus. A blood sample was sent to the Mayo Clinic. Lupus it was. A course of cortico-steroids was prescribed and begun. A couple of days later, Linda sensed the presence of a favorite aunt at her bedside and thought: "I'd better sit up and say hello." So she did.

Systemic lupus was a wonderful mystery. It roamed Linda's body like the velociraptors of *Jurassic Park*. It stiffened her joints, gnarled her fingers, constricted her lungs, hobbled her feet, tickled her brain, then moved on. She had been on the steroids for more than twenty-five years. She had passed a day here and a day there in hospitals in Beijing, Hong Kong, Taipei, Chillicothe, Ohio, and Troy, New York.

She bruised at a feather's touch, suffered chronic bronchitis, required an afternoon nap, and had shanghaied me into a nightly hour of head-and-leg massage. But she never complained. Most of the time, she felt only slightly awful. And she knew other lupus patients her age who were dead.

∞

Fred Lucci never really recovered from his Staten Island heart attack. The braggadocio was out of him. The worship of Rocky Marciano and Billy Martin remained, but the playful shadow-boxing and the hellacious parkway driving were gone. He suffered from bloating, then dehydration. His blood-sugar levels went haywire. His marinara sauce wasn't the same. He stopped at Stop signs.

He lived for less than four years after his attack. One crisis followed another. He would be wheeled into the hospital, unable to speak, and my mother would pin a note on him: "Do not give antibiotics – highly allergic!!!" When he was ailing, they had to hire friends to run the little luncheonettes, and the friends stole them blind.

"When he died," my mother said, "Debbie and I had just gone down to the cafeteria to get something to eat. When we came back up, a nurse met us in the hallway. I didn't have to ask. I could see her eyes."

She was telling me this as she burrowed in the closet. Then she turned to me and held up a brilliant red dress. The sun was coming up on a fine spring morning.

She asked: "Is it too hot for chenille?"

∞

As soon as Debbie and I boarded the subway on the third Sunday of my homecoming, it was obvious that we were the only ones headed for the Hasidic circus parade. Everyone else on the Flatbush line that Sunday morning was black, and none of the blacks was Yisroel Francis.

The subway took us to Kingston Avenue and Eastern Parkway in Crown

Heights, where all the ugly confrontation had taken place in 1991. But now, when we emerged from the station, we found ourselves immersed in a sea of small boys in *yarmulkes*, yawning Irish police officers on munificent overtime, hundreds of schoolgirls in navy skirts and sky-blue blouses, and two dozen kindergarten tots roped together like mountain climbers and festooned with yellow stickers that read, "Let's Be Ready – MOSHIACH IS ON HIS WAY!"

The headquarters building of the Lubavitcher movement, a handsome brick corner block, was hung with huge banners printed with Mosaic admonitions. ("In every generation, one must look upon himself as if he personally had gone out of Egypt.") Thousands of folding chairs had been set up. Half of the divided boulevard – the world's first urban "Park-Way," a nineteenth-century creation of Frederick Law Olmsted, the designer of Central Park and Prospect Park – had been closed to traffic. This was a prudent measure; according to an article in *Newsday*, five people had been killed by drunk or drugged or speeding drivers while crossing Eastern Parkway in 1992, and, a week before the Hasidic parade, a two-year-old named Federico Santos had become the sixth soul claimed in thirteen months.

There was a stage and a speaker's podium right in front of this Hebraic watchtower. The Rebbe himself, though past ninety and extremely feeble, was scheduled to appear later to address the throng. Children filed toward their assigned seats, carrying portraits of their living prophet attached to sticks, like political conventioneers. Women in wigs pushed double strollers and led wobbly toddlers by the hand.

Above us soared the world's only Moshiach blimp.

An armored personnel-carrier and an Army "Humvee" were stationed along the sidewalk. Soldiers in camouflage fatigues busied themselves around them. But it was just for show; they were two years too late for the riot. Boys with sidelocks like Slinky toys, wearing skull caps and white dress shirts, clambered onto the military vehicles, fought for access to the turret of the A PC, wrestled their way to the mounted (unloaded) machine gun.

Now one fat little fellow grabbed the handles of the weapon and swung it around so that it pointed at a much-more-puny playmate down in the street.

"Hey, Mordecai!" the pudgy one yelped, pressing the trigger. "Hasta la vista, baby!"

Kids came whirling by on roller skates with a banner that said, "WE WANT MOSHIACH NOW."

The band wore purple-and-gold hats with chin straps and cutaway morning coats. Three junior cymbalists sported mock-beaver busbies. There were fourteen snare-drummers and a couple of tympanists. On signal from their leader, they commenced to play, apparently for the first time in their lives. The racket was satanic.

How had this carnival become tied up with the impending arrival of the Messiah? The idea of wholesale redemption through the intercession of a pure and righteous sage was as old as the hills of Judea. In the twelfth century, Rabbi Maimonides had taught: "In the future time, the King Moshiach will arise and renew the Davidic dynasty . . . and gather in the dispersed remnant of Israel." Eight hundred years later, the Lubavitchers were still waiting. They believed – they *knew* – that their King would be a man of supreme wisdom and scholarship, born again after death to purify mankind, a Christ–Confucius.

When all the attributes of a proto-Moshiach were added together with recent world events – the Gulf War, the collapse of the Soviet Union, the Crown Heights riots – the inescapable conclusion was that the hour of redemption was only moments away and that the best candidate was a ninety-one-year-old Brooklynite named Menachem M. Schneerson, the Lubavitcher Rebbe himself.

Five planes went over, skywriting a welcome to the Redeemer in English and Hebrew. By this time, I was so dazed by the spectacle, I wouldn't have been surprised had they written "Surrender Dorothy."

Then the parade started. On a flatbed truck, there was a giant mockup of a fanciful cover of *Time*. The headline said: "SPECIAL REPORT: *The Unbelievable has happened. Moshiach has arrived.*"

I left my ball cap with Debbie lest it be taken as a sign of disrespect and waded into the seating area to ask a teacher if I might interview one or two of her adolescent girls. Instantly, the woman wheeled like a drill sergeant and barked out names: "Gitty! Altie! Rivky!" They were thirteen-year-olds from a single-sex Lubavitcher school. I asked about Moshiach. They erupted in a chorus of unquestioning faith.

"The person that's Moshiach gets a second soul," said Rivky Brenenson.

"Everybody else only gets one soul. We're waiting for the man with the second soul to die and reveal himself."

"Why does it have to be a man?" I wondered.

"Because it says so in books," said Altie Deitsch.

"It says, 'A son of David,'" explained Gitty Goldberger.

"It'll be a better world," Altie added.

"Nations will beat their swords into plowshares," Rivky said. "The sick will be healed. The dead will rise. Not get up and walk out of their graves or anything, but sort-of rise."

"Nobody will have to work," Gitty smiled.

"Just study," Altie said, finishing her friend's sentence. The prospect of poring over texts unto eternity clearly delighted her.

By now, a dozen other schoolgirls had joined our cluster, and they all were shouting out scenarios for the promised paradise.

"It's a blessing to 'Go forth and multiply,'" said one. "Every woman will have six babies at a time."

"Do you think blacks and whites will get along when Moshiach comes?" I posed.

"I guess so," Rivky replied, with the suggestion of doubt in her voice. "The books say there's going to be peace. I guess that means blacks and whites, blacks and Hispanics, everybody."

But the Rebbe had taken the mystical controversies of Talmudic scholarship and turned them into teen-pop culture. To ensure single-mindedness, he commanded his disciples not to watch television or attend movies. Modern cinema was "bad for us," the girls agreed. Regarding those of different backgrounds, Rivky Brenenson said, "We can say they don't believe. They can look at us and say we're *weird*."

The parade passed. Blacks in the apartment buildings across the parkway from Lubavitch Headquarters leaned out their windows in amazement. An announcement was made that the Rebbe was too ill to emerge and speak to us. Certainly, Gitty and Altie and Rivky would not have to hold their breath much longer.

"What if the Rebbe turns out *not* to be the Moshiach," I asked them. I expected they'd be crushed.

"No problem!" said Gitty Goldberger. "He's not looking for another job. When the real Moshiach comes, the Rebbe will be the first to welcome him."

4

On the north side of Montague Street, across from the red Gothic towers of St. Ann and the Holy Trinity, which contained the first stained glass made in America, was a row of magnificent old bank buildings, three more of Downtown Brooklyn's grandiloquent tributes to parsimony and compound interest. There was a Roman temple and an Italian palace; fierce bronze lions and Corinthian columns as massive as redwoods bespoke the gravity of the banker's trade. Two doors east was a more playful colossus, a true Art Deco gem, a riot of angular ornamentation that now contained the Municipal Credit Union.

Montague was one of Brooklyn's most famous and fashionable streets. It led from the plaza in front of Borough Hall upward to the landmark homes and churches of Brooklyn Heights, the exclusive, historic district where Hart Crane had swooned at the sight of Brooklyn Bridge.

And over on the south side was the usual cluster of old men, misfits, fakers, undesirables and losers like me that announced an Off-Track Betting parlor on the afternoon of the 118th running of the Preakness Stakes.

Inside, there were no seats, no live television of the races, no lavatories, no oxygen. It was crowded. Victory in the Kentucky Derby by a mediocre colt named Sea Hero had been so improbable that this second Triple Crown race of 1993 seemed to be wide open and likely to reward a good bet with a handsome payoff. So the joint was stuffed.

I had it in my mind to walk in, throw down my money – *five* whole dollars – and leave. But two things got in my way. First, I had no idea which horse to wager on. And then, I saw the old Turk.

He was sitting on the Siamese standpipe of the Credit Union building across the street from the betting hall, bald and prim and very ancient, caught by the last slanting rays of sunlight as he fiddled with a pencil and the OTB program. He had a horseshoe of snowy hair and a pure white beard that would have made him look exactly like Rembrandt's Jeremiah, except for the fact that the prophet didn't wear New Balance running shoes. I went over to speak with him. Maybe the old man knew who'd win the Preakness.

"I don't want publicity," he pretended, and then he talked for half an hour.

His name was Israel Abolafia. He was born on Valentine's Day, 1900, a subject of the Ottoman sultan. His family still owned a castle in Gallipoli. He had been a businessman, a movie director and actor, a champion ballroom dancer, an advisor to Franklin Delano Roosevelt. He lived in a Single Room Occupancy hostel on Atlantic Avenue. Much of what he told me, I believe he believed.

He was writing a book about horse-playing. He was holding out for a $75,000 advance. He said, "I teach how to pick winners. Not just winners. *Good* winners."

In every rambling old man I met, I glimpsed myself, should I live. It could be a Presbyterian who ministered to Mohawk iron workers, or a horse-player perched on a fire stanchion. I once interviewed a Norwegian skier who was 107 years old. I sat quietly and listened to him breathe. I told him, "You don't look a day over 106." He lived four more years.

"You're a reporter," Abolafia said when I explained myself (the name was accented on the third syllable: ah-bo-LA-fee-ya). "Your life is different from other people's lives. The prestige of being a reporter must be very great, to get information that people don't want told and spread it across the whole world."

He took my business card and gingerly slid it into the breast pocket of his suit jacket, which was black and stained and shiny with wear.

"You want power," he said, spearing me. "Don't rush! Don't rush! You can be a hundred years old and people will still talk to you. Because you have *curiosity*."

He embarked on a long tale about Roosevelt's New Deal and the inauguration of the Works Progress Administration, which he claimed to have invented. He said that there had been thirty businessmen at a meeting with the President and twenty-nine had been opposed to the WPA, but his voice had been strongest and he had prevailed upon FDR – "Delano," he called him – to give it a try. He said, "The others tried to destroy me, but I was too clever."

He saw the United States sliding into another Great Depression and he was willing to advise Bill Clinton as he had counseled his friend Delano. He said that the New Deal was like the Verrazano Bridge – "The engineers built it once, they saved the plans, they could build it again." He pronounced it "Berren-swano."

The sunlight moved off Israel Abolafia's face, so that only his hands and his cane were illuminated. It grew suddenly chilly in the shade. I asked again about the horse race.

"I bet by *hunches*, from *visions*," he said. "I've won a lot of money in the past sixty years. But I lose, too. Win, lose. Win, lose. Horse-racing is like a wheel taking water from a river. It takes the water up, and then it puts the water back in the river.

"I *love* the animal that puts on all that speed and comes from behind. And *my* horses come from *farther* behind and pay fifty to one, *sixty* to one, and those horses that are two to one or three to one, they choke. *They choke.*"

Israel Abolafia went down the entries for the 118th running of the Preakness Stakes and tried to crystallize one of his magic hunches. He settled on a colt called Personal Hope, which was not unreasonable, since Personal Hope had won the Santa Anita Derby in California and had finished a respectable fourth in Louisville.

Now, in Baltimore, Personal Hope, with my five dollars on his nose, led a field of twelve around the first turn, maintained the lead for three-quarters of a mile, clung to the rail down the home stretch, and watched the rest of the field sprint past him to the finish. The wheel put the water back in the river. Lose, lose. Lose, lose.

∽

According to *The New Deal: The Depression Years, 1933-1940* by Anthony J. Badger, the Works Progress Administration was created by a presidential aide named Harry Hopkins. I leafed through more books on the period, biographies of Roosevelt, and every volume of the *New York Times Index* from 1928 through the Second World War.

No Israel Abolafia.

He had given me the name of his residence: the Hotel Nevins at 510 Atlantic Avenue. Now it was a couple of days after the Preakness. I took the subway to the station I had patrolled with Steve Werner and Jim Mandes. There they were, at their post, waiting for fare evaders. I thought about hopping the turnstile, just for laughs. Then I remembered that they might not remember me. I wasn't *that* curious.

The Hotel Nevins still existed, seven stories high. It may once have been an establishment of moderate grandeur, equal to its setting on the broad avenue. Some of the old terra-cotta decorations were still visible in the lobby, and heavy iron lanterns hung above the sidewalk outside. But the cashier's desk was now protected by a metal cage. Beyond the foyer was a large television lounge with a linoleum floor, and some people were sitting in there and staring up at the screen with a look that said they did this every day.

"Are you from Protective Services?" someone asked me as I tried to walk nonchalantly past the lobby staff.

"I'm not from anywhere," I replied, and kept moving.

A small, stooped middle-aged woman appeared beside me, smiling, keeping up my pace. I revealed my reason for coming. She steered me around a corner, down a hallway, into a small kitchen. In the kitchen were two tables, and at one of the tables, with his back to me, was Abolafia.

I greeted him. He turned around and, like a bellowing muskrat, announced my first and last names. He pumped my hand with the grip of a stevedore and produced my business card from the breast pocket of his jacket. He was wearing the same coat, the same vest, the same shirt, the same blue tie. He smiled triumphantly with all of his four remaining teeth.

"I was thinking of you last night," he said. "When I think of something, it *happens*."

It began again: the New Deal, the ballroom dancing, the palace in Gallipoli, the desire to avoid the world's spotlight. He said he had competed in samba, rhumba, and tango on TV on Channel 13. He had been living in the Hotel New Yorker in Manhattan, but then the Hotel New Yorker was purchased by the Reverend Sun Myung Moon and everybody got evicted. That's how he ended up at Hotel Nevins.

The woman spoke. She said, "He's telling the truth."

Her name was Harriet. She wore a red paisley pants suit and black sneakers. She clearly cared a great deal about Israel Abolafia, and the feeling was mutual.

"You like her, don't you?" I asked the old Turk. I was having a wonderful time.

"It's more than *like*," he said. "You can *like* a lot of people."

He turned to her.

"You're a lady and I'm a man," he announced. "It don't make no difference how old you are."

He had a black toque in one hand and his cane in the other. He had places to go, things to do. He bellowed at me: "DON'T LIE! TELL THE TRUTH!"

"Could I see your room some day?" I asked him.

"If you came there," he replied, denying the request, "you'd say, 'How can anyone live like that?' But I live."

Then he was gone.

Harriet was a social worker. She filled in the gaps. At ninety-three, Israel Abolafia was "not delusional." He was "capable of making decisions, including not going to doctors." He had cataracts and a melanoma. He had been declared ineligible for Social Security because he couldn't produce a passport or documentation to show when he entered the United States. Harriet had pulled strings to get him a welfare check. She paid his rent at the Hotel Nevins.

"They said he couldn't prove he was who he said he was," she told me, shaking her head. "I mean, how many Israel Abolafias can there be?"

In the 1940s, Harriet said, Israel Abolafia tried to break up a robbery and was wounded by a gunshot. He was still afraid that the crooks would come back to finish him off. He had not invented the Works Progress Administration. He had operated a small business that made desk blotters. Up in his little room, he still made them. But how many people used desk blotters?

∾

In China, there were Special Economic Zones. In Brooklyn, there were gaping wards of de-industrialization. The empty pit at the Long Island Rail Road terminus extended east from Flatbush Avenue for block after block, and the buildings that were still standing at its perimeter leaned on their girders like Abolafia on his cane. Squadrons of pigeons whirled and dived into the revealed skeletons of old factories; stout trees grew upward through their rotted planks.

On Pacific Street, a block down from Atlantic, I stopped in my tracks as a dozen lacy yellow dresses on hangers came swooshing down a wire from the third-floor window of one red-brick building that still functioned. The cable led to a parked truck. Shippers caught the garments as they reached sidewalk level and packed them into cartons. Some white lettering was legible above me: "A. G. SPALDING & BROTHERS – FOOTBALLS BKTBLS

SHOES CAPS," a name that conjured visions of sport's Golden Age. Babe Ruth would have minced around the basepaths in Spalding's cleats. Red Grange would have taken his pigskins and stiff-armed his way to a million touchdowns. But now the building turned out *ladies'* wear.

I turned the corner onto Flatbush and stood with my back to the wall of Francesco Pizzeria and made some notes. There was a police station opposite me, and the street was filled with cars and the cars were all covered in dust and marked with large chalk numbers and letters in some kind of secret code. Seeing me writing, two men walked up and explained that these were impounded vehicles, but the men weren't cops. They were Mr. Panhelides and Mr. Kaufman.

Mike Panhelides owned the Francesco. He wanted to tell me about the time that a detective from the 78th Precinct on the corner got shot and one bullet came through the restaurant window. He wanted to tell me about how he and Mr. Kaufman had lived around here for more than fifty years and how this used to be a beautiful area for families and how it was coming back from abandonment and destruction. One-bedroom apartments were renting for $750 a month, which was even more than in Bensonhurst, which Mike Panhelides derisively called "a so-called great neighborhood."

He wanted to tell me about his villa on Chios.

He announced proudly that the 78th Precinct had "the lowest crime rate in Brooklyn," but the fact was that it had the seventh-lowest number of reported robberies in 1992, seventh out of twenty-three. And the 78th was a very small precinct.

And he wanted to tell me about the plane crash. On December 16, 1960, two airliners collided over Brooklyn, and one of them, a United DC-8, hit the ground where Flatbush and Seventh Avenue and Sterling Place converged, a block from where I stood with Mr. Panhelides and Mr. Kaufman. More than a hundred people died in the plane and on the ground. Mr. Panhelides had been working at a restaurant a few blocks south of the impact.

"I said, 'That plane's going down,' " he remembered, and down it went.

"I get goosebumps thinking about it," he said, thirty-three years later. He showed me his arm.

Goosebumps.

∽

South of where we stood, Flatbush Avenue began its climb towards the leafy elevations of Prospect Park. These hills marked the terminal moraine of the glaciers of the last Ice Age, the collected detritus of a great blue-white wall that scraped and scoured the continent until global warming halted it about two miles short of my mother's apartment. Then it melted and washed away the rest of Brooklyn to give us names like Flatbush and Flatlands.

"Brooklyn of ample hills was mine," Walt Whitman gushed, though they were hardly the Himalayas. Still, the Canarsee Indian trail through the wooded uplands was so laborious, and the stagecoach route that succeeded it was said to be so "exceedingly stony," the rural isolation of Flatbush village on the other side of the hills was preserved for nearly a century after Downtown Brooklyn's leap toward city-hood. Until Flatbush Avenue became a planked toll road in 1855, not even the United States Mail passed across this cordillera. Letters from Flatbush to Brooklyn were carried, as a favor, by a businessman named Cornelius Duryea, the borough's first long-distance commuter. Horse-drawn trolleys began to ply the route in 1860, bitterly opposed by the burghers of peaceful Flatbush town. They knew that this was the beginning of the end. And it was.

The districts that lay between the hills and New York Bay were horse pasture until the 1880s, when the opening of Brooklyn Bridge and the proximity of the new Prospect Park combined to make them irresistible to the city's upper and middle crusts. I was now on the fringe of genteel Park Slope, described in my American Institute of Architects' *Guide to New York City* as "a somber-hued wonderland of finials, pinnacles, pediments, towers, turrets, bay windows, stoops and porticoes." I was enraptured. Some of the brownstones were truly beautiful. And I was only blocks away from the childhood homes of Al Capone and Howard Cosell.

Flatbush Avenue was macadamized late in the nineteenth century by inmates from the Kings County Penitentiary. Late in the twentieth century, as I browsed in and out of its multifarious shops, gabbing much and buying little, it seemed to be paved with immigrants for whom Brooklyn had become a jail of a different sort. And there were refugees from within the city itself, urban bushwhackers who had reclaimed some of the somber-hued wonderland and turned it into million-dollar homes.

In a health-food store on Flatbush, at the base of the commercial strip, two men from the Caribbean islands yearned for nothing more or less than escape. The shop was owned by a Guyanese named Keith White, who had been born in London and brought to Brooklyn when he was ten years old.

"I came here with my parents," said Keith White, who was now thirty-three. "I was a minor. I didn't have a choice. Now, if they wanted to bring me here, I'd have to be in shackles."

The store was named Genesis 1:29. The relevant Biblical quotation was painted on the store's rear wall: "And God said: Behold, I have given you every herb bearing seed, which is upon the face of all the earth, and every tree, in the which is the fruit of a tree yielding seed; to you it shall be for meat."

The shop sold every herb-bearing seed that was grown from here to Zanzibar: devil's claw and holy thistle; false unicorn and rue. The shelves were lined with dozens of jugs and jars of arcane roots and granulated substances. The shop seemed to have everything but customers. Keith White said that business was "real slack." Feeling sorry for him, I purchased a dollar's worth of roasted, salted green peas that turned out to be as hard as buckshot and about as tasty as sand.

"It is a cold city," White said when I asked about the place to which he had been imported as a non-voting kid. "I can't deny it – there is some opportunity here. I started from the sidewalk and now I have this store. But the drugs and the violence . . . the trivial violence."

"Has the violence injured you?" I asked. White looked as fit as an Olympic hurdler.

"Mentally," he replied.

At the back of Genesis 1:29 was a carpenter, a fellow from Barbados whose plan was to double-deck the cabinets to make room for still more bark and twigs. The Bajan listened to my conversation with Keith White, and when I asked him how he had adjusted to Brooklyn, he lowered his eyes to the floor.

"The sirens," he said. "All night, the sirens. I want to hear the crickets. In Barbados, you hear the crickets. What I want is to hear the crickets, and see the dew on the grass in the morning."

I went into a restaurant further down Flatbush where you could get anything from fried egg on a roll for a buck and a half to paella for twenty-three dollars. It was called El Rey de los Castillos de Jagua, "The King of the Castles of Jagua," which was a town in the Dominican Republic. There were pink tablecloths and on the walls were mounted two enormous snakes that I hoped were plastic. Across Flatbush Avenue was a place called the Castle of Jagua, and there was another King of Jagua restaurant further up the road. So I asked the friendly young man who brought me a plate of disturbingly yellow French toast to explain the significance of the name.

"My uncle started these businesses," he said. "This is the biggest one, the last one. Don't you know about my uncle?"

"Sorry," I replied. "I'm from out of state."

"It was in all the papers, last August," the young man declared. "Big headlines: 'Man, Wife, Killed by Robbers.'"

(Later, I found the clipping. Sergio and Juanita Ramirez had been found dead at their apartment in middle-class Queens. There was no sign of forced entry. They must have answered their doorbell and admitted their assassins. The apartment had been ransacked. They had a daughter who was a police officer, but that wasn't thought to have been the killers' motive. It was just more trivial violence. One headline said, "Drug Gang Suspected in Queens Couple's Slaying.")

I gulped my French toast and walked out.

A big sign beckoned me to Italian Shoe Repair, a few doors away. I didn't own any Italian shoes, but I went in regardless. A gentleman was armed with footwear, standing at a workbench in the front window, nailing a new heel onto a pair of brown brogans. Above him, sitting on a perch that was suspended from a tack in the ceiling, was a small parrot that had been dead for a very long time.

The stuffed (or toy) bird was so covered with bootblack and dust that it was not possible to tell whether it was a genuine Norwegian Blue. Further back in the cramped, narrow recesses of the shoe-repair shop were hundreds and hundreds of pairs of shoes in piles so deep that the bottom layers must have been sandals dropped off just before the sack of Rome. But the cobbler asserted that he cleaned out everything once a year; everything except the parrot.

The shoemaker's name was Cosmo Sorbara and he wanted out of Brooklyn, too. It wasn't the violence; Park Slope had simply grown too posh for him. He said, "They charge a hundred dollars a day rent and I don't make two thousand a month." He was going to stick it out one more year, until his daughter Rosellina finished high school, and then he and she would go back to Italy where you could get free medical care and collect social insurance at fifty-five, which was six years younger than Cosmo Sorbara already was.

"When I come here nineteen sixty-nine," he said, "it was 95 per cent black people around here. Now it's half and half, black and white. Rich people come now."

The thought dismayed him. Rich people made rents go up. Already, there was a restaurant on Flatbush called Le Bistrot, where you could get goat-cheese salad and Cajun blackened-chicken fingers and filet of salmon with capers. Photographs in the window of a real-estate agency showed off a three-story limestone town house with a "to die for" kitchen ($540,000) and a brownstone with "wonderful Victorian detail" for a trifling $850K. And this wasn't even the heart of Park Slope. It was only that tawdry old Flatbush Plank Road.

Where would it end? The unstoppable armies of Thai cuisine had made a beachhead. An old Celtic tavern had surrendered to satay and *pud*, some travel posters and manifestations of the Buddha had been hung on the walls, and it was now the Thai Lagoon. It was managed by a blithe noodlemonger from Phuket named Roger, who talked me into a bowl of *gang*, jumbo shrimps with bamboo shoots in a thin yellow coconut-curry broth, napping on a pillow of sweet rice.

"This is the land of opportunity," Roger said. "In Thailand, there are no jobs. College graduates drive buses. Right here, you work hard for ten years, you open your own restaurant."

"That's what we need," I thrust. "Another Thai restaurant."

"What am I supposed to do?" Roger parried. "Go back to Bangkok and open a whorehouse so poor farm girls can sell their bodies?"

∾

On the pavement in front of a clothing store called Mr. Michael's, someone had painted two giant eyes with arching, inquisitive brows. Next to the eyes, it was written: "FROM HERE IT LOOKS LIKE YOU COULD USE NEW UNDERWEAR."

How did they know? I wondered.

∾

The shop window next to the tasteful Le Bistrot was crammed with candles, incense, plastic figurines of Indian chiefs and Negro Christs, warrior wonder-women wearing Madonna breastplates, Go Away Evil Spray, Seven African Powers Floor Wash, necklaces, amulets, "attractive" bath oils, and books with titles like *The Eighteen Absent Years of Jesus Christ* and *Candle Burning Magic.*

Inside, the air was so thick with smoke that I thought I would fall on the floor in convulsions, which probably would have incited the staff to burn still more noxious votaries in a vain attempt to revive me. I staggered to a folding chair and sat, clawing at the blue-gray fog, until I was able to croak to the person behind the counter that I'd like to meet the boss.

This was a Haitian herb store, La Botanique de Saint Jacques Majeur, the Wal-Mart of voodoo. The statuary and the potions and the books that taught how to convert dreams into lucky lottery numbers had arrived with the Caribbean immigrants. But the botanicas were luring other Brooklyn-ites to explore their exotic mysteries. Little Debbie had picked up a can of Seven Indian Potencies Room Spray, and even my mother the agnostic had somehow acquired one tall, blue High John the Conqueror Alleged Luck, Power, and Strength candle, which sat unused on top of her refrigerator because she was afraid of what her Haitian neighbors would think if they spied her throwing it out.

After I had waited about twenty minutes, a side door opened and I was introduced to a gentleman named Prophète who was in an expensive business suit.

"I'd like to learn about voodoo," I told him.

"Go to Haiti," he advised, turning and going back through the side door. I walked out onto Flatbush Avenue. The air was as sweet as Colorado.

5

The jet airliner that crashed in Park Slope in 1960 and still gave my friend Mr. Panhelides goosebumps was on its way in from Chicago. Approaching New York in a thick, wet mid-December snowstorm, it collided over Staten Island with a propeller-driven Super Constellation that held forty-four pre-holiday travelers. The Connie hit the ground at an old air base called Miller Field, killing everyone on board.

The pilot of the DC-8 tried to make it to the Long Meadow of Prospect Park. He couldn't. The right wing of the plane – the first commercial jet to crash in the United States with passengers aboard – sliced off the roof of 126 Sterling Place, where a woman named Nevin was standing at her dresser, barefoot and in her nightgown, while her two small children slept. It was 10:30 in the morning.

The fuselage of the United plane hit the Pillar of Fire Church and crushed its caretaker, who was ninety years old. The tail section ended up on Seventh Avenue, a few yards off Flatbush, killing two Christmas-tree salesmen, a butcher, a dentist, and a man from the Sanitation Department who was sweeping snow from the bus lanes. Eighty-three of the eighty-four people on board died instantly, or within minutes. Mrs. Nevin and her family were unhurt.

I was ten years old. I remember hearing that some debris had fallen on Bensonhurst and wondering if it had landed on or near a cousin of mine who lived on 20th Avenue. December 16, 1960, was his fifth birthday. But it missed.

Next door to the Nevins lived the family of Alfred G. Marshall. Mrs. Marshall was reading the *Daily News*. Three of her four children were in the apartment, playing. The tip of the wing of the airplane came to rest on her bed. Neither she nor the children were injured. Alfred G. Marshall added up the damage and settled with United Air Lines for twenty-five hundred dollars.

I walked across Sterling and down Seventh and searched for some monument to the dead of that December. At Seventh Avenue and Flatbush today, there was a group of headstones set into a gravel quadrangle, but these had nothing to do with the crash. They were Art. They bore epitaphs such as: "The press can print whatever they like," "What you do in private is your business," "Illegal aliens may share your rights," and "the State may intervene in your affairs."

The elegant brownstone symmetry of the neighborhood was broken by a low orange brick structure at the corner of Sterling and Seventh. It was the Henry McCaddin and Son funeral home, successor to an older, higher building that had been sheared in half by the United jet from Chicago. In Henry McCaddin's office were some framed newspaper clippings and photographs that showed the tail of the plane resting burned and broken in the snow.

Thirty-three years after the disaster, Henry McCaddin was a stocky, graying man in a shirt and tie. He said that people occasionally came around and left flowers on the sidewalk, and once there had been a memorial service at a nearby Catholic church. He seemed willing to reconstruct the event for me. Had he wanted to forget it, I assumed, he wouldn't keep the photographs on the wall above his desk.

"There were six of us in the building," Henry McCaddin began. "My wife, my oldest daughter, Donna, my accountant and his assistant, and me and one of my workers. Back then, we lived on the top floor.

"When it hit, the first thing I thought of was that one of the gas trucks that used a garage down the street had exploded. I was in my office on the second floor. I could see that the entire back of our building was gone. I came out the front and saw the plane lying there.

"When I got outside, there were two people still alive, strapped in their seats. I assisted another guy trying to get them loose. We carried them over to the bowling alley, but they died.

"We were very lucky. My family was all right. Everybody in our building survived. But the accountant's assistant moved to California and had a nervous breakdown – in the hospital and everything."

Henry McCaddin had been in the Air Force. He had flown in combat in Korea. Then came the crash. Ten years later – ten whole years – he and his wife had had urgent family business on the West Coast and they summoned the courage to take a plane for the first time since 1960. They did not enjoy it. They haven't flown since.

"I'm a boater," Henry McCaddin said.

Business in Park Slope was terrible. Formerly, the McCaddins handled 225 corpses a year, but now it was little more than a hundred. Most of the old-timers of the district were already deceased, and the yuppies who patronized the Thai Lagoon were likely to live for some time yet.

"If we hang on for twenty years," said Henry McCaddin, "we may get a shot at 'em."

The night before my visit, McCaddin and Son got a call from the family of a woman whose husband had been laid out here in 1958. Now the old lady was being trundled into the viewing room. The relatives had remembered. Henry was greatly pleased. Even in death, there was no substitute for service.

"What's the best way to go?" I asked Henry McCaddin, who I thought would know.

"In your sleep," he said in response. "Just go off pleasantly. It happens to very few people. But it's the best way."

∾

The eighty-fourth passenger on the United Air Lines plane was an eleven-year-old boy named Stephen Baltz. He was coming to New York to visit relatives for Christmas. Stephen Baltz was pulled alive from the wreckage on Sterling Place. He was taken to the Methodist Hospital in Park Slope. In his pocket was sixty-five cents in change.

Prayers were said for the miracle boy. His father rushed to Brooklyn to be with him. And when Stephen Baltz died, a day and a night after his plane went down in the snow, his father donated the sixty-five cents to the Methodist Hospital.

Henry McCaddin had told me where to look for a marker that the guidebooks didn't mention. I walked south from the funeral home along Seventh Avenue, which now was a fashionable shopping and dining boulevard, and turned at 6th Street and went into the hospital lobby. In front of me was a small chapel, and on a wall of this chapel, nearly invisible in the dim, respectful light, was a plaque that said: "STEPHEN BALTZ MEMORIAL – *Remembering 135 Victims of the Aircraft Disaster* – Our tribute to a brave little boy."

Attached to the plaque were four dimes and five nickels. It was Stephen Baltz's sixty-five cents.

∾

"Where does this obsession with death come from?" my mother asked me when I told her about my day at McCaddin and Son and the plaque in the hospital chapel.

I didn't answer. Instead, I walked into the bedroom and returned with a volume of Whitman and read to her from *Out of the Cradle Endlessly Rocking*:

> Answering, the sea
> Delaying not, hurrying not,
> Whispered me through the night, and very plainly before daybreak,
> Lisped to me constantly the low and delicious word death,
> And again, death – death, death, death, death, death.

"Do you want to hear about Hart Crane's suicide?" I asked.

No reply.

"Did you know that when Alan Freed died, he was exactly the same age that I am now?"

"Stop it," my mother said.

∾

The man who had set Brooklyn endlessly rocking had died in 1965. He was forty-three, a small-town Pennsylvania nobody by birth, and at death a famous, scandalized, shrunken, alcoholic shell. But Alan Freed's embrace of wild Negro "race music" during the mid-fifties had led to everything everyone who was under fifty today had been dancing to ever since. As a radio disk jockey in Cleveland and New York, on stage, on television, and in some of the dopiest movies ever produced, he had institutionalized rock and roll, the Big Beat that, in the words of one commentator, "appeals to morons of all ages, but particularly to young morons."

Now they were planning a reunion of the old bands and a recital of the old songs. The Brooklyn Paramount Theater, once the setting for Freed's marathon pageants of live music, was being prepared for its first doo-wop jamboree in more than thirty years. In the meantime, the building had been sold to Long Island University. The stage had been ripped out and the orchestra pit had been replaced by a basketball court. Freed himself had been shot down in the payola furor of 1959. Charged with accepting as much as a thousand dollars to promote a record as his "Pick of the Week" or "Sleeper of the Week" – *every* week – he pleaded no contest.

Shame destroyed the man, but the music that nourished my generation was immortal. When I heard about the upcoming show, I was the very first reporter to call the promoters to try to scrounge a free ticket.

There was a time when the Big Beat shook Flatbush Avenue so hard that subway trains fell off the Manhattan Bridge and the Prison Ship Martyrs did the Stroll in their crypt. It began in 1955 and launched the epoch of Buddy Holly and Fats Domino and Chuck Berry; the Chuckles and the Dimples and the Solitaires were big, too. Frankie Lymon and the Teenagers, feeling the heat from reactionary grown-ups, protested their wholesomeness in a song entitled "I'm Not a Juvenile Delinquent." Screamin' Jay Hawkins, embodiment of the jungle menace of the new sound, rose from a coffin on stage to warn the terrified, delighted white children at the Brooklyn Paramount Theater: "I Put a Spell on You."

Tony Bennett was booed off the stage.

The Brooklyn Paramount had opened in 1928. It was the first large theater built for talking pictures, a fantastic confection of gilt and gargoyles, the epitome of the rococo-baroque style of entertainment palaces that came to be known as Louis Quelquechose. It stood at the corner of Flatbush and DeKalb, directly across from Junior's Most Fabulous Restaurant, down the hill from the Prison Ship monument, not far from the allegorical statues of *Brooklyn* and *Manhattan* at Bridge Plaza, and a block from the Board of Health.

By 1955, television had nearly killed the big movie houses. Alan Freed and his rock-and-roll spectaculars brought the Paramount back to life and filled its forty-four-hundred seats. Freed had moved from Cleveland to the center of the universe to spin platters on WINS. He brought B. B. King and Little Richard and the Clovers to white audiences. He was hailed as a pioneer who had given the plaintive, rollicking American sound of black rhythm and blues the mainstream exposure it merited. In other circles he was condemned as a nigger-loving communistic corruptor of American youth. The music he relentlessly touted was new, powerful, irresistible, and dangerous. The youth of Brooklyn went crazy. In Memphis, Elvis Presley was still driving a truck.

The first big show at the Brooklyn Paramount was staged in April 1955, during the Easter school recess. The headliners were the Penguins, the Moonglows, and LaVern Baker singing "Tweedly Dee." Even Count Basie took a stab at the Big Beat. The performances were repeated for a week, mornings, matinees, and evenings. Attendance records dating back to the crooner Russ Columbo were shattered. The gross receipts totaled more than a hundred thousand dollars. The manager of the Brooklyn Paramount was overjoyed. He had gambled on the renegade Freed and won. The theater was saved. The manager's daughter went on to become Suzanne Pleshette.

Alan Freed's rock-and-roll conventions became a fixture of every school holiday break. Chuck Berry, a nervous Missouri hairdresser, introduced "Maybellene" and the cats and kittens dug it. Overweight Antoine Domino sang "Blueberry Hill" and was declared "real gone." Harmonizers from Harlem and Queens, black and white, polished and neophyte, were given their lifetime's chance. Young voices soared to the pinnacle of the outlandish architecture. Attendees at early shows refused to evacuate. Crowds waiting outside revolted. Police were called. It must have been fabulous. Unfortunately, I was in kindergarten, still harkening to Burl Ives.

The Golden Age of Rock and Roll at the Brooklyn Paramount lasted four and a half years. In 1958, there was a stabbing at a Freed show in Boston. Violence – any violence – confirmed the theory that the Big Beat was a voodoo death potion in disguise. Back in Brooklyn, manager Pleshette and his employers decided not to stage any more of Freed's extravaganzas. Dick Clark's sanitized "American Bandstand" usurped Freed's throbbing radio and television programs. The House of Representatives Subcommittee on Legislative Oversight tore the payola mess wide open. Freed moved a couple of shows across the street to the Fabian–Fox Theater at Flatbush Avenue and Nevins Street, but by the fall of '59, it was over. Within a few years, the Fabian–Fox had been demolished, the Long Island University Blackbirds were playing basketball at the Paramount, Alan Freed was dead, and WINS, Freed's first New York outlet, had switched to All News, All the Time.

The 1993 Big Beat Show and Tribute to the Golden Age of Rock 'n' Roll was a brainchild of the people who were trying to revivify Atlantic Avenue, home of the Hotel Nevins and Israel Abolafia and the enormous empty hole atop the Long Island Rail Road terminus.

It seemed like a wonderful idea. Old-time rock and roll was one thing the disputatious racial groups of Brooklyn might agree on, although it was unlikely many Lubavitchers would be eager to hear Willie Winfield and the Harptones sing "The Shrine of St. Cecilia." Still, when I visited the offices of the Atlantic Avenue Association to plead for my press pass, I found the organizers of the concert haggard and distraught. This was because a rival promoter in Manhattan had booked a fine collection of geriatric teen idols for a concert at Madison Square Garden on the Saturday *before* the Big Beat Show. The enemy lineup was impressive: the Duprees ("You Belong To Me"), the Skyliners ("Since I Don't Have You"), and even an appearance by Lewis Lymon and the Teenchords ("I'm So Happy") *for the first time in thirty-five years*. And what was worse was that the Manhattan show was being advertised as the *Brooklyn* Paramount Reunion!

No wonder we wished Manhattan would disappear.

∾

As fate would have it, the 1993 Big Beat Show and Tribute to the Golden Age of Rock 'n' Roll was scheduled to begin about ninety minutes after the 118th running of the Preakness Stakes. So, after losing my five-spot on Personal Hope, I glumly descended from Montague Street and passed along the Fulton Mall, where a young African-American man dressed as the Pharaoh Ramses II was passionately haranguing a small crowd and espousing Biblical evidence that proved, he said, that Abraham and Solomon and Jesus and all the Jews of antiquity were, in fact, "colored people."

"When the white man in Hollywood makes a movie about Moses," he bellowed with fury in his arms and eyes, "who do they get to *play* Moses? A *white* man!"

A placard on the sidewalk where the zealot was speaking listed the Twelve Tribes of Israel and their purported twentieth-century progeny:

> Judah . . . Blacks
> Benjamin . . . West Indians
> Levi . . . Haitians
> Simeon . . . Dominican
> Zebulon . . . Panamanian
> Ephraim . . . Puerto Rican
> Manasseh . . . Cubans
> Reuben . . . Seminole Indians
> Gad . . . North American Indians

Asher . . . Brazilians
Napthali . . . Argentinians
Issachar . . . Mexicans

A flyer handed to me by one of the speaker's acolytes said: "Look for us on cable TV."

I got to the Paramount so early that no one was even checking credentials. I slipped through the performers' entrance and met our master of ceremonies, Joe Franklin, who had been hosting a nostalgia program on a New York television station for at least thirty-five years. Franklin estimated that he had interviewed at least three hundred thousand people, boasted that he gave Barbara (not yet Barbra) Joan Streisand her start, claimed (as did many others) that he was the first to televise that truck driver from Memphis, and did not flinch when he was referred to as "the most famous radio and TV personality in America," even though his show did not come on the air these days until 1:30 in the morning.

The Brooklyn Paramount was one of the most amazing buildings I'd ever seen. The installation of the basketball court had barely wounded the fabulous old dame. There was a hardwood floor, of course, and a scoreboard and banners hailing tournaments that the Blackbirds had won, but high above all of this terrestrial renovation soared an astounding pastiche of Turkish fountains, Roman goddesses, Greek columns, and Atlantian mermaids that added up to an enchantingly beautiful eyesore.

A small stage had been set up and blue gym-mats had been spread in front of it to encourage dancing by any patrons who were both old enough to remember the fifties and young enough to still locomote. I took a seat in the front row of the half-filled wooden bleachers and waited for the show to begin, leaning back with my spine against the row behind me, my eyes always being drawn upward and upward to the mad decorations of this Flatbush fantasia.

The first to perform was a bald man from the Bronx named Norman Fox, whose group, the Rob Roys, had had a hit in 1957 with a song called "Tell Me Why." Norman Fox sang this, and a couple of other numbers, with feeling and energy, and when he introduced his twenty-three-year-old daughter to the audience, he announced, "My kids asked me, 'What is Brooklyn?' and I said 'Brooklyn is the cradle of civilization.'"

The hundreds of us in the hoi-polloi stomped and cheered.

Norman Fox and the Rob Roys were followed by the Bobbettes, who had been pupils at P.S. 109 in Manhattan when they wrote and performed a song about their principal, a certain Mister Lee, and watched in amazement as it vaulted the charts. Starved for a sequel, they followed their success with a clone entitled "I Shot Mister Lee," which may have seemed harmless enough in 1958. But this was not 1958. In a few days, three adolescent gang members from the rough Brooklyn district of Red Hook would go on trial for gunning down the principal of *their* neighborhood school, a caring, devoted man named Patrick Daly, whose pointless death had become a symbol of Brooklyn's descent into anarchy.

After the Bobbettes came the Harptones, and the Harptones were my gods. These were the smoothest of chanteurs (and one chanteuse), led by the angelic tenor of Mr. Willie Winfield, climbing to the rafters of doo-wop heaven on "Life Is but a Dream." It was their syrupy lyrics I had written out longhand and mailed to Linda up in Montreal in the months before we were married. It was their songs I had croaked in showers from Troy to Tokyo and screamed on all-night drives to stay awake. It was their records I had spun on my oldies show on the college station back in Troy, New York.

It was 1970. "You gonna play this shit all *night,* man?" callers pleaded. "Play some Vanilla *Fudge,* man," they demanded. But I was unmoved.

Willie Winfield and the Harptones came together in 1953 in Harlem. They owed almost everything to Alan Freed. He played their records on WINS, when no other white deejay in New York would go near them. (This was insane; they sang sweet ballads without a hint of demonic possession.) Freed made them regulars at the Paramount. They were there when Tony Bennett was heckled and resigned. They were there when Chuck Berry did his duck walk. Now they were past sixty, and they were going to come out and sing. I wondered if Madonna would be back at SkyDome in 2028 to reprise "Papa Don't Preach."

They came out in white suits with wide, sequinned lapels. Willie Winfield, tall and rangy with an air of gentleness and a smile I could see from the bleachers, began to sing "The Masquerade Is Over" with such control and evident delight, even after forty years, that I felt my throat get all lumpy. The mood was contagious. In the row behind me, as the Harptones climbed the crescendo toward Winfield's last, ringing notes – we all knew the song by heart – a man in a Cincinnati Reds baseball shirt bellowed out as loud as he could:

"Take it HOME, Willie! Take it HOME!"

And Willie did. We stood and roared. I knew there was a reason I'd come back.

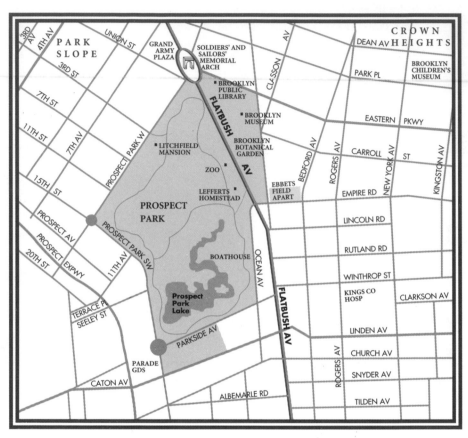

Chapter Three: The Green Heart of Brooklyn

The Green Heart of Brooklyn

1

The masturbating rhinoceros of Prospect Park went by the name of Rudy. Once upon a time, in the smelly little zoo set deep in a hollow of our verdant civic wonderland, Rudy the rhino would extend his spectacular apparatus – it was as long as a softball bat and *flanged* at the tip – and commence to slam it against the floor of his cell, seeking relief. Brooklyn could do that to a guy.

Rudy was more than thirty years old. Twice during his long incarceration at the Prospect Park Zoo on Flatbush Avenue, females had been brought to him, and twice he had gotten carried away with his lovemaking and he *killed* them. Then, some airhead left a gate open and Rudy made his way into the hippopotamus pool and attempted to mate with Betsey. But Betsey had enough troubles of her own. She had given birth to seven little hippos, one at a time, but she had rejected them, and all had died; all, that is, save big little Cleopatra, who was lifted away the day after her birth and driven to the Bronx. The last thing Betsey needed now was some roaming rhino Romeo who wasn't her type, let alone her species.

So, when Rudy started to examine Betsey's pulchritudinous geography, Betsey waxed wroth and likely would have hip-checked Rudy into the pool at the side of the hippo enclosure and drowned him, had a low-ranking zoo assistant not come along and, rattling a dinner bowl, lured Rudy back to solitary.

It was the (former) zoo assistant, Arne Israel, who now, on Pinkster Day at the old Dutch homestead in Prospect Park, was telling me and Little Debbie about Rudy.

Frustrated by his inability to get a leg over a female of *any* genus, order, or phylum, Rudy turned to self-satisfaction. It was only when the thwacking of his fire hose against the cement grew intolerable that our friend would be ordered into the cage to try to calm the old rogue down.

"But I didn't mind getting spermed," the zoo assistant told us. This was not because the young man was a pervert with a preference for large ungulates. It was because the alternative was having Rudy piss on him, and rhino urine has a pH approaching that of sulfuric acid and could be hell on hair, skin, and clothes.

Now, in May 1993, the zoo had been closed for renovations, the animals had been furloughed to various other cities, and our ex-Marlin Perkins had been reassigned to live in a wing of the old Dutch homestead. Arne Israel's job was now to take care of that fragile, two-hundred-year-old structure, one of the last surviving remnants of New Netherland and to ride a power mower across the Long Meadow and the Nethermead, up Lookout Hill, and down the Vale of Cashmere. Those were the man-made natural landmarks of Brooklyn's great public space, constructed in the 1860s by the engine of pure municipal penis envy – despised Manhattan's Central Park had just been completed – and now, in the 1990s, a place of airy relaxation, team sport, environmental activism, senseless murder, nature study, American history, and malicious vandalism.

On a map, Prospect Park bestrides Flatbush Avenue in a polygon of bright green. Approached on foot from the street bazaars of Downtown Brooklyn, it was a sudden Amazonia of natural beauty, dark and jungly, its towering oaks and tulip trees casting their shadows on snarls of forsythia and sumac. This was where Washington's army had fought, and lost, the first battle of the Revolutionary War. It was the home of the Brooklyn Museum, with its matchless collection of Ancient Egyptiana, and the Botanic Garden, with its cherry trees and roses and bonsai. It was the setting for Brooklyn's own Arc de Triomphe, in Grand Army Plaza, the old Dutch manse, the central library, the zoo, and the beautiful Boathouse on a pond, called, charmingly, the "Lullwater." The Laurentide glaciers halted here. The worst railroad wreck in the United States occurred at the south entrance. The Brooklyn Dodgers played a block away.

And it was in Prospect Park that Susie the elephant lived and died.

She had been an immensely popular attraction. Curious and insatiable, she would chew on her keepers' pitchforks for roughage and eat rubber hoses like licorice. Once, she slipped her trunk around the purse strap of an unsuspecting visitor and ate the handbag, whole. The owner of the pocket-book was understandably distraught. It was payday, and she'd just cashed her check.

"Come back tomorrow," the victim was advised. The purse slid through Susie's digestive tract like a hailstone down a drainpipe. The woman got her money back. Also, her credit cards, cosmetics, and keys.

Susie's death was a needless tragedy (our zookeeper related). She had been stricken by a bacterial infection in her colon that soon spread to her lungs. Antibiotics might have saved her, but the administration of giant syringes full of drugs would have required chaining Susie down. Zoo-goers hated to see animals in shackles. Putting the manacles on Susie would have been a public-relations disaster. The decision was made to let the disease run its course. Instead, Susie gave up the ghost.

That was only half of the story. Elephants were observed to mourn their dead with apparent remorse and sorrow. Susie's mate refused to let her body be dragged away by machinery. This made it necessary to cut up the carcass and remove it, piece by piece, through the bars.

The bars were eighteen inches apart. Guess who had to do the slicing.

"We tried chain saws," said the (ex-) low-ranking assistant. Israel was an instantly likable fellow, a farm boy from upstate New York, muscular, round-faced, curly-haired, and ponytailed, perfectly cast in jeans and a green denim shirt and rubber-soled Sorels. Arne – the *e* was silent – was capable of spinning these yarns deadpan, with only the occasional smallish smirk of self-delight. The chain saws, he said, got bogged down in Susie's body fat.

Then they tried long butcher blades, but these fell into Susie's peritoneal cavity and got lost. So Arne Israel had to carve up an elephant with a steak knife.

"She's fertilizer now," he said. He went into his wing of the old Dutch farmhouse – it had been the seat of the Lefferts family, erected in 1687, burned in 1776, rebuilt the next year, and moved here in 1918 from its original site a little further down Flatbush Avenue – and returned with what looked like a large gray stone.

It was one of Susie's molars. He'd been allowed to keep it as a doorstop.

At the other side of the Lefferts Homestead, the Pinkster Day festivities were beginning. This was a spring holiday that dated back to the age of the

Hollanders. Only on Pinkster Day – the Pentecost – were slaves allowed to cavort and carouse and get as shamelessly drunk as their masters. (In the seventeenth century, the Dutchmen here in New Netherland held thousands of African slaves.) So out on the front porch there were some young people clogging with jingle-bells on their shoes, and an entertainer named Abu Shabazz was jumping around and rattling a big yellow gourd.

Arne Israel was married (much to Debbie's disappointment) and he had a ten-month-old son whom he called "Luke, the Prospect Park Baby." We would have been invited into his section of the Lefferts Mansion, he said, but his akita, Moe, was protective of the Prospect Park Baby to the extent that the dog was likely to kill us if we came in. So we stayed outside in the recreated Dutch herb garden.

"When I first came to Brooklyn," Arne Israel said, "I really hated it. I realize now that it was fear, fear of living in a city. In the country, you're isolated. I was shy without being aware of it."

But now he had grown to love the borough. The museum and the Botanic Garden were mere steps away. The shops and restaurants of Park Slope were delightful. He could mingle with us zany, irrepressible Brooklynites – sometimes too closely. (The homeless were attracted to the herb garden, and one disheveled man or woman – Arne couldn't tell which – had taken up residence on the front lawn.) He got to work in the fresh air, smell the flowers, admire the trees, and live in the Lefferts Homestead. And the closure of the zoo meant that he no longer had to scoop out Betsey's prodigious hippo droppings by hand when they got so thick that they clogged the drains.

"They don't make gloves that come up to here," Arne remembered, and pointed to his neck.

But working at the Prospect Park menagerie hadn't always been such unmitigated fun. The grizzly bears – Geronimo, Pocahontas, and Hiawatha – could be extremely dangerous at feeding time. One particular rhesus monkey liked to grab Arne Israel by the ears and smash his head against the bars. Arne took fish hooks, razor blades, and firecrackers out of the mouths and guts of sea lions. He broke six BB guns over the railing of the pool. He pulled a dart from an elephant's forehead.

And it was his job to clean up the carnage when the polar bears ate a little boy named Juan Perez.

It was May 1987. The zoo had closed for the day when, at seven p.m., Juan and two other eleven-year-olds named Tyree and Sammy decided it would be fun to go swimming with the sea lions. It was common for children and teenagers to hang out here in the evenings, blasting their radios and throwing objects at the animals. The zoo was surrounded by a twelve-foot fence, but that was no obstacle.

Juan and Tyree and Sammy removed their sneakers, shirts, and pants and were about to dive in. Instead, they turned their attention to the moat of the polar bear compound. Tyree and Sammy began to have second thoughts, but Juan Perez heaved their clothing and footwear into the bears' enclosure. The boys grew nervous. They were reluctant to return home in their underwear, so Juan climbed into the cage to retrieve the garments. The male bear, Teddy, ambled by, but ignored him. The female, Lucy, scooped the boy up and washed her paws in the moat in preparation for eating.

"We tend to think of bears as a honey-loving creature that is a friend of man," the Parks Commissioner said the next day. "In fact, that's not true."

A passing jogger heard screams and called police. Then all grew quiet. After ten minutes of fruitless reconnaissance among the zebras and kinkajous, officers saw Tyree and Sammy running down a path in panic. One constable reached the polar bear compound and, in the gathering darkness, saw "huge white shadows" and a child's hand and leg. Juan was already dead. Fearing that, if he shot at the bears with his revolver, other, unseen, children might be wounded, he held fire and called for Emergency Services.

Four minutes later, Emergency Services arrived and, dismissing the idea of using a tranquilizer dart – full sedation would take at least twenty minutes, and besides, Emergency Services didn't carry tranquilizer darts – pumped the first of twenty shotgun shells into the two bears, who shook the first slugs off "like mosquitos" before falling dead. Teddy and Lucy were added to the Edgemere landfill in Queens. Arne Israel scrubbed down the compound.

"I really can't blame the animals and I can't blame the police," said an official of the ASPCA.

The saddest irony was that the Prospect Park Zoo had already been scheduled to close for a complete overhaul. The era of big mammals in tiny cages on Flatbush Avenue was over. Fifty years after it opened in 1935, the Prospect Park Zoo had been ranked among the Ten Worst of America's 373 zoos by the Humane Society of the United States. When Juan Perez climbed into their world, the polar bears were about to be shipped, like Cleopatra the baby hippo, to the peerless, modern Bronx Zoo. Geronimo, Pocahontas, and Hiawatha were destined for Central Park. Susie would have been transferred, too, had she lived.

The renovation was nearly complete. The zoo was scheduled to reopen a few months after Pinkster Day as a Wildlife Conservation Center, "child-oriented" and "hands-on." An administrator predicted that it would become known as "the world's greatest children's zoo." There would be wallabies and prairie dogs. There would not be lions, giraffes, polar bears, or hippos. And no rhinoceros.

Where did this leave Rudy? Arne Israel knew where he had been transferred in 1988. But he had heard nothing since. My sister dashed off an urgent inquiry. A few days later, she received this letter from the Registrar of zoological specimens in Royal Oak, Michigan:

Dear Ms. Abel:

I'm happy to tell you that Rudy the black rhino is doing fine at the Detroit Zoo. He arrived here on 13 July 1988. At that time we were told that his estimated age was 36.

We have a female rhino who is now 32 years old, and we have been hoping that Rudy would be able to breed her, but, although he has tried, he has not been able to get the job done. . . .

∾

"No city in the country, of its extent, is better built than Brooklyn," reported Francis's *New Guide* in 1857. "Many of its houses are distinguished for a chaste elegance . . . Brooklyn is sufficiently large to become another London."

But there was one drawback: "The thickly settled parts," said Francis's, "have no public squares or open grounds."

This was intolerable. Even though most of Kings County beyond Downtown Brooklyn remained sparsely populated farmland, Manhattan had its brand-new Central Park and Brooklyn, therefore, required a world-class greensward as well. The city turned its eyes toward the estate of Edwin C.

Litchfield, whose Italianate villa commanded the crest of the glacial moraine. Litchfield's front yard was the decline towards the harbor, and his back forty became Prospect Park.

The excavations, condemnations, elevations, and installations were put in the hands of Calvert Vaux and Frederick Law Olmsted, the men who had fashioned Central Park as a mere warm-up to this, their masterwork. (Olmsted had to be persuaded to return from California, where he was helping to conserve Yosemite.) Prospect Park was intended to encompass three distinct zones: pastures, forests, and waterways. The ninety-acre Long Meadow was, and is, the largest lawn in New York City. The native woodlands were "improved" with the addition of European species. The Ravine was described as "a deep rocky glen, through which a brook gurgles happily." It gurgled still.

The park was completed in the confident years after the Civil War. It transformed Brooklyn. Litchfield sold off his front yard to developers, who created the somber-hued wonderland of Park Slope. (Eventually, his heirs sold the villa to the city, too; it was now the headquarters of the Parks Department.) Real estate to the south of the park, reached by the new Brighton Beach railroad, became the setting for magnificent Queen Anne, Colonial Revival, and neo-Tudor homes. Elegant apartment buildings were erected to the north at Grand Army Plaza and along Olmsted's elm-lined Eastern Park-Way. Old Dutch families surrendered their homesteads to Progress. In Flatbush village, the era of the pig troughs and windmills came to a close.

Generations of Brooklynites partook of Prospect Park's manifold pleasures. My father and his twin brother ice-skated on the lake. My mother, the Ava Gardner of New Utrecht High School, boated with lusting suitors. My kindergarten class was brought to the zoo. We watched the stir-crazy inmates pace their cages for a while, and then I drank my container of milk too fast and threw up on a boy named Shelly Jordan.

But bad Brooklyn burghers flocked parkward also. Even in the 1860s, Olmsted and Vaux had argued against trying to illuminate the interior of the park with gas lamps. They would only attract malefactors and sinister elements. Regarding lights, they wrote: "their use for immoral and criminal purposes more than balances any advantages."

It got a lot worse. The centennial of the park's foundation in 1966 was met with lamentations of a paradise lost to vandalism and crime. Robert Moses, the Parks Commissioner, saw a civic treasure "faced with disorder, destructiveness and defiance of authority which seems worldwide and inexplicable." The wonderful wooden carousel was crumbling; the zoo was one of America's Ten Worst. Muggers haunted the bosky glens. No one in his right mind went to Prospect Park. In Brooklyn, open space meant open season.

Returning to my native soil for a spring of rediscovery, I planned one quick daylight sprint through the greenery for the sake of completeness and prayed not to be preyed upon. I held sour memories of my last visit, circa 1963. Exploring the hills behind the zoo after a picnic lunch of my mother's imaginative lettuce-and-tomato sandwiches, my friend Brucie and I were set upon by a half-dozen miscreant teenagers. I outran them, desperate to protect my very first transistor radio, a rare gift from my Uncle Dave. It wasn't until much later that I learned that Uncle Dave had found the radio on the Sea Beach subway.

My sister, however, saw Prospect Park as a Yellowstone of wonder and delight. Debbie weighed me down with brochures and newsletters. The park had been resurrected. There were bike-a-thons, bird walks, jazz concerts, historical re-enactments, Rollerblade races, sculling lessons, yoga classes, sheep shearing, and the Big Apple Circus. Hundreds of volunteers pulled weeds and planted seeds. The Girl Scouts had made a hundred-year commitment to maintain the Concert Grove. Soon the Wildlife Conservation Center would open. The forsythia, Brooklyn's official flower, was in full lemony bloom. Every day was Pinkster Day.

We decided to join a guided walk entitled "A Tree Still Grows in Brooklyn." (Others on offer included "Wild About Flowers," "Of Twigs and Buds," and "Monumental Celebrities.") We were to meet our Urban Park Ranger at the Boathouse on the Lullwater and then tramp off into the wild interior. I expected a ramshackle shed on a cesspool. Instead, we came to a voluptuous ninety-year-old Venetian palazzo with terra-cotta cladding. Diving for fish in the limpid Lullwater was a little pied-billed grebe.

Inside, even the men's room was clean and wheelchair-accessible. Postcards, T-shirts, and ice cream were available. Exhibits explained the park's history. Donations were solicited. For four hundred dollars, you could have a tree planted in memory of a loved one. For ten thousand dollars you got a private grove of twelve.

A binder held photographs and stories. It was the Brooklyn equivalent of the Cemetery of Martyrs in Tehran, where the high-school boys who had been sacrificed in the medieval war against Iraq slept beneath display cases that held their pictures and wrestling trophies. Here, trees had been dedicated to a victim of Pan Am 103; a girl killed by a car on Seventh Avenue; an undercover drug cop named Joe Galapo, accidentally shot by his partner while frisking a quartet of suspects.

In 1988, a Brooklyn College computer-science student named Jesse Ferreiro, Jr., was shot to death while walking near the Quaker Cemetery at eleven p.m. Someone had climbed up the backstop of one of the Prospect Park baseball diamonds and started firing randomly. There was a newspaper clipping and a photo of Jesse in a light gray suit with a carnation in his lapel. I remembered my driver in Iran as he walked me through the Martyrs' tombs, saying nothing, then stopping at one picture of a handsome young man and turning to me.

"My brother," he said.

❧

The amateur arborists who gathered for the hike they called "A Tree Still Grows in Brooklyn" included an Hispanic woman wearing a button that said, in Spanish, "Jesus is the Answer" and a man who described himself as "a white atheist from Crown Heights" and who announced, without being prompted, "The Rebbe's not the Messiah. All religion is baloney."

This, I thought, cupping my hand over Little Debbie's mouth to keep her from laughing, was going to be fun.

Joe Spano was our Urban Park Ranger. He was a pleasant young fellow whose uniform – Smokey-the-Bear hat, khaki jacket – marked him as a man of authority in matters both botanical and temporal. He led us up a gentle rise and pointed out bald cypress, European larch, red maple, and hornbeam. A local music lover loped by, carrying a tape deck that was emitting Jamaican dancehall music loud enough to be heard on Venus. Joe Spano screamed "LOWER IT!" and, immediately, the man did.

The most famous single tree in Prospect Park was the Camperdown Elm. This was a low, "weeping" anomaly that had somehow not been provided with the gene that made other Scotch elms grow vertically. It had been here since 1872 and was just coming into bud for the 122nd time, spreading its branches like beggars' arms just above the ground.

We walked along a trail that had been scraped clean of vegetation by the five million pairs of feet that trod the Prospect parkways every year. We crossed Lullwater Bridge. Joe Spano showed us sweet gum, box elder, and majestic tulip trees, tall and straight as the Prison Ship monument, and London plane sycamores whose dark, lower bark fell away in patches, revealing mottled areas of pale skin below, à la Michael Jackson.

It was estimated in 1946 that 230,000 trees grew in Brooklyn, including the weedy *Ailanthus* that had provided the title of Betty Smith's famous novel of a girlhood in Williamsburg. Thoughts of the borough's sylvan splendor, it was written (though not by Smith), "warm the homesick heart of a Brooklynite, whether he is basking in Burma or Buffalo."

In 1993, however, a census by the Department of Transportation found only 505,253 trees in the five boroughs of New York City combined and, since the count was conducted in mid-winter, it was not possible to say how many of them actually were alive. A plan was being enacted to plant thousands of Amur maple, Turkish hazel, and thornless osage orange, species that were thought likely to be able to withstand air pollution, soil compaction, oxygen deprivation, and periodic drought, while not growing tall enough to interfere with power lines.

Back in Prospect Park, we were climbing the glacial moraine towards the bank of Olmsted's deep Ravine and dodging the mountain bikes that were coming back down at us like kamikazes, disregarding gravity and the signs that said, "BIKES DESTROY PARKLAND – BIKES MAY BE CON-FISCATED." Snow fences had been set up (and ignored), and Joe Spano told us that the entire area was to be put off-limits to the public for at least five years to give the vegetation a chance to recover from overuse. Beneath us was the famous gurgling stream, which Ranger Spano informed us was fed by a tranquil pond that was fed by a gay waterfall that was fed by a municipal water pump.

"In the sixties," he said, "they cut down all the shrubs. Muggers and rapists were hiding in 'em. Their answer was to tear it all down. There was no enforcement then. The city was in fiscal crisis. The police didn't want to know what was going on in here. Now we're trying to bring the shrub-bery back."

We were seventy-five minutes and barely two hundred yards into the guided tour when, in a copse of red maple saplings, the Urban Park Ranger spotted a small wild black cherry tree and peeled away a section of bark to expose – he exultantly announced his discovery – termites!

The group pressed close. A woman, bored by botany, who had been muttering, "This is bullshit," at each previous stop, leaned in, full of wonder. Joe pointed out the swarm of colorless, harmless-looking workers. Someone asked if he could borrow a few to sabotage a neighbor's house. The Urban Park Ranger shook his head and said, "No. You have to have a queen."

"Can this tree be saved?" a woman asked. Her concern was so sincere that she might have been asking about Brooklyn itself, which was infested with the kind of vermin that climbed baseball backstops and fired guns that killed computer-science students.

Joe Spano explained pruning and tapping and invited everyone to join the Arbor Day Society for only ten dollars a year. The atheist, who had snapped off a twig from the wild black cherry and was holding it tucked under his chin, beamed and said, by way of explaining himself, "I'm a Ranger groupie."

It was time to move on. Joe Spano offered a final tribute to the termites as he led us away.

"They're edible," he said.

∾

For a while, it seemed that the worst that could happen to you at Prospect Park was the theft of your bicycle. In the weeks following my arrival in Brooklyn, there were reports of children as young as seven being accosted at gunpoint and ordered to dismount. The smallest victim was riding his five-hundred-dollar Cross Trainer at noontime when a man lunged at him, pushed him to the ground, and rode off on the machine. A nine-year-old on a Magnet Fugitive had a similar experience. So did a fifteen-year-old on a Huffy Freestyle. A community newspaper referred to the thieves as "pedaling pilferers."

But still it was possible to think of Prospect Park as a place where one might, in the words of the *New York Times,* "wistfully while away the day meandering through its hidden niches."

Then came a rape. One evening at 8:30, a woman jogging just south of the shuttered zoo was grabbed from behind by a man who dragged her into the forest we had explored with Ranger Joe Spano. The incident stunned the park establishment. An administrator named Tupper Thomas said it was the first reported sexual assault in the park in a dozen years. Others tried to explain the attack away. She shouldn't have been alone at dusk, they said; she shouldn't have been wearing headphones; the park was safe. The park was safe.

Two weeks later, a forty-two-year-old drama teacher named Allyn Winslow was murdered while riding his bicycle on the upland trail that led to the Ravine. He often went there, friends told the papers, to puff his pipe and write poetry. Four teenagers ambushed the man and demanded he surrender his Diamondback Traverse. He tried to pedal away. One of the boys shot Allyn Winslow in the back. He managed to ride onward for about a quarter-mile before collapsing in a clearing in front of dozens of witnesses, a few yards from our wild cherry tree and the termites.

Winslow left a wife and children aged ten and eight. Students mourned him as a caring mentor and friend.

The headline in *Newsday* read: "Old Fears About Park Rekindled."

The bike was worth $269.

I told myself again: I'm not a woman who jogs alone in Prospect Park. I'm not a man who rides his bike in the Ravine. This doesn't frighten me. If anyone stops me, whatever he wants, he can have.

2

The boys who killed Allyn Winslow were caught within a few days. The police cut back their low-level helicopter flights over the Ravine. Picnickers returned to the Nethermead. Little Debbie was eager to make another excursion to the parklands. There was no cause for worry. The sun still rose in the east. It was just New York.

My sister was especially enthusiastic about loading up with provisions at Greenmarket. This was a regular Saturday-morning event at Grand Army Plaza at the northern end of Prospect Park. Vendors and producers from nearby states and counties gathered to sell the overpriced gourmet provender of which Debbie was so enamored. As we browsed around the stalls, I wrote down that she appeared to be "apoplectic with joy." She asked me only once for money, and that was to treat me to a nine-grain pretzel sprinkled with sea salt.

Greenmarket was the place where brownstoners from Park Slope, wearing reproduction Brooklyn Dodger uniform shirts, towing blue-eyed husky dogs named Zöe, and pushing Maclaren strollers containing baby boys named Caleb filled their PBS Channel 13 Supporting Member shopping bags with uncooked honey, lamb kielbasa, fresh Mako shark, crimini mushrooms, organic turkey parts, low-fat chocolate milk in glass bottles, Linzer tortes, and wood-fired brick-oven pesto bread.

A sign near the chèvre cheese said: "We Accept Food Stamps."

Just north of the pesticide-free gooseberry preserves was the Soldiers' and Sailors' Memorial Arch, and beyond that was the Bailey Fountain and a monument to John F. Kennedy. In brilliant sunshine, with the World Trade Center seemingly a block, not three miles, away, we walked over to the bust of JFK, whose supporting marble slab had been covered with the rhesus-monkey artwork of creatures named KSPORT and DUSTY. Kennedy faced north, toward Downtown Brooklyn and the Twin Towers, though his likeness had been aligned so that it appeared the thirty-fifth president was staring right into the eyes of another bronze across the street that honored a nineteenth-century gynecologist and educator named Alexander J. C. Skene.

Behind Kennedy was an ornamental splashworks that would not have been out of place among the preposterous statuary of the Brooklyn Paramount Theater. King Neptune, with a coil of rope in his left hand, a frond of seaweed covering his genitals, and the bejowled face of a Bert Lahr, leaned back in unrepentant joy beneath the prow of a cresting sea-raft. Attending him were assorted bronze bullfrogs, cherubs proffering pomegranates, and a Triton blowing a conch shell, while, above decks, life-sized nudes representing stern-jawed Wisdom and firm-breasted Felicity stood back to back, their heads turned northward towards the Manhattan Bridge and El Rey de Los Castillos de Jagua.

The Bailey Fountain – named for the citizen who donated a hundred thousand dollars to have it inflicted on the borough in 1930 – had not yet been turned on for the summer season. The blue reflecting pool was dry and empty except for a windblown carpet of oak leaves and yellowed copies of the New York *Post*, whose headlines screamed of Woody and Mia.

Behind all this, set in the middle of a five-lane traffic roundabout – Brooklyn's Étoile – was the Soldiers' and Sailors' Memorial Arch, the Civil War monument erected in 1892 to the design of J. H. Duncan and renovated in 1902 by Stanford White to allow the placement of three tangled groups of heroic bronze sculpture that made the overloaded Bailey Fountain look like a work of Minimalism. Architect White was also responsible for the gazebos with Tuscan columns and Gustavino vaulting that stood on the other side of the Plaza. These had been attacked so thoroughly by vandals that their solid marble sides had huge gaping holes blasted through them, as if by Sarajevo mortar fire. Stanford White, of course, was shot to death by a jealous husband in the preeminent New York scandal of 1906.

To appreciate the detail of the sculpture groups, it was necessary to cross all five lanes of Flatbush Avenue as it swerved in giant parentheses around the Memorial Arch. The monument predated the motorcar; old photographs showed Grand Army Plaza as a broad, majestic *rond-point*, with the Mount Prospect Reservoir on one side and the new, elegant Eastern Park-Way contributing a few one-horse surreys and Gibson Girls with parasols. But now the reservoir was long dry, Eastern Parkway was where the Lubavitchers clamored for their Messiah, and the traffic around the Memorial Arch was what one would have expected to encounter at Indianapolis if the 500 were driven by blind men.

Surviving a death-defying Ben Johnson sprint across the circle, Debbie and I circumnavigated the arch, noting its intricate embellishments, while all the while trying to contain the terrible knowledge that, to get out of here, we'd have to cross those five lanes again. We had heard that it was possible on certain Sundays to actually climb to the top of the memorial to examine Frederick MacMonnies' Victory Quadriga, which was a two-wheeled, ram's-headed bucket engraved "E PLURIBUS UNUM," pulled by four foaming horses and announced by two trumpet-blowing, broad-winged angels, while Victory herself stood in her chariot like Ben Hur, holding a staff crowned by a small spread-eagled eagle in one hand and, in the other, the sword that Arne Israel should have used to slice up Susie the elephant.

The observation deck, alas, was closed. A sign on the perimeter fence explained: "The steel supporting the sculpture group on the roof is deteriorating and leaks in the roof deck and skylight have caused serious damage."

But the gate in the fence was open, and this permitted Debbie and me to walk under the arch and look at the mounted effigies of Lincoln and Grant. The Great Emancipator sat, hat in hand, on a downcast mare, while, on the opposite wall, his general posed in full uniform on a prancing steed. (The figures were by William O'Donovan and the horses by Thomas Eakins.) Our incursion, however, was short-lived. We were spotted by a Punjabi construction worker with a deep scar on his neck, with whom we had the following conversation:

I (pointing to the Lincoln sculpture): "Do you know who that is?"

Punjabi: "Is Prime Minister of United States."

Debbie: "Abraham Lincoln."

Punjabi: "Yes. Braham Lincoln."

I (veteran foreign correspondent): "That scar on your neck. Were you wounded during the attack on the Golden Temple in Amritsar?"

Punjabi: "No. As child riding bicycle."

∾

Brooklyn's fantasy was that there be no need to go to Manhattan at all. In this scheme, Prospect Park would eclipse Central; the Brooklyn Museum would render the Metropolitan insignificant; the lordly Dodgers would reign forever over New York's minuscule Giants in the standings of the National League. This had not happened. Pavarotti and Paul Simon kept their distance. The only mitigating circumstance in the departure of the Dodgers was that Manhattan lost its ball club, too.

In one category, however, Brooklyn could claim precedence. Debbie and I were making our way to the Botanic Garden for the Japanese Cherry Blossom Festival. We could not have done this in Manhattan. Manhattan's Botanic Garden was in the (ugh) Bronx.

"May your thoughts be as beautiful as what you behold," said a signboard near the entrance. This was an attempt to soften us up for the admission charge, which was pay-as-you-wish. I was figuring on a buck.

"This is a living breathing garden," I read on. "Enter its beauty in awe . . ."

Okay, two bucks.

". . . and let its meaning of life surround you."

I threw in a five for the two of us.

The Botanic Garden, founded in 1910 on the site of a municipal waste dump, was a meticulously groomed oasis, a perfect antidote to the dark and deadly wilderness of the Prospect Park glens on the other side of Flatbush Avenue. Fenced all around and patrolled by uniformed guards, this was one of the few places in the borough where it was possible to feel relaxed and secure in an outdoor, public space.

The cherry blossoms of Brooklyn were not as well known as those of Washington, D.C., but the festival was drawing crowds regardless. We made our way past the Louisa Clark Spencer Lilac Collection, which was just coming into bloom, and the Cranford Rose Garden, which wasn't, and found ourselves in the Cherry Esplanade. A stage had been set up, and Japanese Daiko drummers were preparing to begin their coordinated thunder in an attempt to awaken the fragile pink blooms, which were abundant on some trees and nowhere to be seen on others.

Debbie and I grabbed a quick lunch, then found a place on a bench at the side of the Esplanade, next to an older Jewish couple who were chewing on dried apricots. I was trying to enjoy the spring sunshine and the fragrance of this oasis, but Debbie was still revved up from Greenmarket and the couple to my right was just getting started. I was trapped between:

Little Debbie	*Jewish Couple*
"How much did they charge you for that Japanese lunch? Five dollars? *Six* dollars? I'm surprised they didn't give you *sake* with it. Do you want your strawberry muffin now? Want a peanut butter cracker? I know, 'They're not as good as Linda's.' Did you go over to the Brooklyn Celebrity Walk? I found Ira Gershwin and Mary Tyler Moore. I don't think they have Marisa Tomei yet. See that Looney Tunes sweatshirt on that girl over there? I have the same thing in a T-shirt. A friend gave it to me."	"Phyllis is sitting *shiva* today – maybe we should go over to see her. I want to go to the zoo this year, but first I want to see the aquarium. It's such a sweet breeze, it's cool but not cold. Tomorrow's going to be a big march on Washington. *Time* magazine says only 1 per cent of people are gay – that's *wrong*! They went door-to-door. Only the very self-confident are going to admit it. You know who's against them? Pat Robertson's people. The ones who want prayer in schools. My *God*, school has got to be *secular*."

After about six innings of this palaver, I got up, and Debbie followed. As we walked away, the woman called after us, "Shall we save your seats?"

We moved on to the Conservatory, which contained an exhibit that explained the history of the plant kingdom and a wonderful collection of bonsai, and then to a small garden that claimed to include every plant mentioned in Shakespeare. Farther along one path was a ground-hugging evergreen labeled "Dwarf Serbian Spruce," and as I was crouching down to examine it, I heard a man behind me say, "They shouldn't have *anything* Serbian in here."

Now we were standing (according to a plaque affixed to a large boulder) at the spot where the glacial progress of the last Ice Age had reached its southernmost extremity. We were (said another sign) precisely 115 feet above mean sea level, 3,416.7 miles south of the North Pole, and 2,798.2 miles north of the Equator. A metal bar inlaid in the pavement marked the boundary between the former Village of Flatbush and the defunct City of Brooklyn.

This sort of precision delighted me far more than Debbie's strawberry muffins. It reawakened the Rensselaer physicist. It reminded me that, when I covered baseball, what I enjoyed was not the prancing of the millionaires but the calligraphy of keeping score.

∾

The green polygon at Brooklyn's heart was grace and defilement, cherry trees and pointless shootings, Pinkster dances and utter urban ruin. Directly across Flatbush Avenue from the southern turnstile of the Botanic Garden was the park's Willink Entrance Comfort Station, built in 1912 of limestone and yellow brick with a clay-tile roof and described in a handbook as "a vaulted breezeway . . . that forecasts the expiration of the Classical style." With its double rows of columns and deep overhanging eaves, it was, in other words, the Parthenon of pee.

It now was a reeking, crumbling wreck. Plaster peeled from the exterior. Fallen tiles lay in shards. A gap in the roof had been opened up. Every surface within reach had been spray-painted. A snow fence meant to encircle the building had been trampled into splinters. Scattered around our feet were bone-dry bottles of Richards' Wild Irish Rose; empty six-packs of Guinness and Heineken; a strange, soggy goulash of household goods (water pitcher, oven rack, cable-knit sweater, shoe-polish tin); a long-playing record, broken in pieces and labeled, "An Evening with Diana Ross."

Fearless, Debbie poked her head into the ladies' washroom, while, trembling, I pushed through the door marked "Men." Someone had made a campfire very recently in one of the stalls. The headline on the copy of the *Daily News* he left behind said, "TWO COPS SHOT." But the fire-maker was not home.

I kicked through the rubbish and came outside and heard laughter. Less than a hundred yards away, a queue of children was waiting for a turn on the carousel, and their eager music shut out the darkling city.

The Prospect Park carousel was one of Brooklyn's cherished heirlooms, already a fragile antique when I was a child, and now more than eighty years old. It had been shut for ten years, and I had assumed it to be as abandoned as the Comfort Station, but an array of corporate and private donors had come together to finance its restoration as a gift to the borough's youth. The ride was dismantled and the animals moved to the empty cages of the nearby zoo. There, twelve to fifteen layers of old paint were scraped from the fifty-six hand-crafted, priceless wooden figures. The Wurlitzer band organ was rehabilitated. Electrical connections, cranks, and bearings were replaced. The surrounding shelter, with stained glass in its clerestory windows, was fitted with roll-down iron grates to protect the ride. Lions' manes were lightly brushed with twenty-three-karat gold.

We paid fifty cents each for tickets and joined the line and watched the little Calebs whirl. The band organ played "Georgy Girl," which made me think of Linda in her old bellbottoms, riding a Coney Island carousel with me on her first trip to my Brooklyn.

The music stopped and the riders dismounted. Now it was our turn to saddle up, and my wife was a million miles away and my sister, characteristically, was at the souvenir stand, buying a coloring book.

I chose a bucking stallion with a name plate that said "Ol' Rough & Ready." Debbie straddled "Leopold Prospectus," the King of Beasts. The organ played "Ob-La-Di, Ob-La-Da" and the carousel moved so fast, I nearly got horse-sick. And Debbie had a long history of spit-up on every mode of transport yet invented.

I fixed my gaze at her on the lion, and she concentrated on me and my horse. Around and around we centrifuged like early astronauts. But the childless, childish Abel kids hung on.

∾

The coloring book was for our mother. Antique carousel horses were among her famous passions. They offered the sensual gallop of the wild stallion, tamed and made beautiful by the artist's hand. She had asked me six or seven million times when I was going to buy one for her. But they cost many thousands of dollars, and where, in a one-bedroom apartment on the fourth floor of a dead-end building in Brooklyn, do you put an antique carousel horse?

She had been a painter herself once, but not of equestrian effigies. She took courses at Brooklyn College and came home with thickly brushed still lifes of oranges and eggplant. When it became unwise to walk to the campus after dark, she abandoned the easel and canvas and began painting on blouses and T-shirts: Modigliani women, Degas ballerinas, King Tut's funerary mask. And there were the Mary Cassatts on posters in the living room and bedroom. When Debbie or I traveled we'd send her Mary Cassatt postcards, Mary Cassatt notepaper, Mary Cassatt, Mary Cassatt, Mary Cassatt.

One weekday, after I'd been home for more than a month, I offered to take her on the following Sunday to see the Cassatts and the Egyptian faience and the Rodins at the Brooklyn Museum. "I don't think so," she said. She did not make appointments that far in advance. But I had learned her lexicon. She would be delighted to go. But it was far too early for her to begin to get terrified about riding to Eastern Parkway on The Beast.

At 8:30 on the appointed morning, I was breakfasting on low-fat cottage cheese with canned fruit cocktail, orange juice, and watermelon when she shuffled into the kitchen, threw two cigarettes onto the window sill, turned on the exhaust fan, and sat down to begin the day's smoking. I went to get dressed. She dragged on the stinkweeds and willed her bowels to move.

I retreated into the bedroom and tuned the radio to "American Country Countdown." I was beginning to feel more comfortable with the surroundings and the permanent residents. Only occasionally did the phone ring at midnight with some Pushtu or Amharic speaker trying to book a cab. The young women in C4 still blasted their gospel music, but usually quit by 11:30. The car alarms had become as soothing as Ferrante and Teicher.

My mother was like the press room at the *Troy Record*: dormant by day, roused to life in late afternoon, humming and whirring until well after midnight, and then shut down to rest for the next edition.

Bright sunny mornings were the worst time for her. I'd be up a little after six and the sun would be streaming into the kitchen and the crunching of my whole-grain cereal would wake her up. She'd turn on the exhaust fan and start smoking – Parliament, True, Kent, Doral, Montclair, Basic, Sterling Lights – and the radio would be on and she'd run down the roster:

"I can't *stand* this commercial."

"I can't *stand* anyone being so cheerful in the morning."

"I can't *stand* female announcers."

Then I would depart for the day ("Need tissues?") and when I came home in the evening, she'd be watching "Law and Order" or "Kung Fu" and eating Indian nuts. Everything was wonderful:

"Oh! It's Robert Lansing! I *love* that man."

"Oh! The new De Niro film!"

"Oh! I *love* this commercial!"

On nights when she wasn't out at a dance, her evenings were like a scene from *'Bye 'Bye, Birdie*. I'd be awakened by a car alarm at 11:30 or so, and I'd hear her on the phone in the other room: ". . . and then C—— went over and gave M—— her number . . . she's looking for a younger guy. . . . He didn't *ask* her for her number, she walked over and *gave* it to him. . . . It would be a cold day in Hell before *I'd* go over to a guy and ask if he wanted *my* number . . ."

Her circle included friends from Parents Without Partners, plus assorted neighborhood characters of both sexes. They called her for news and advice. I got to recognize some of the voices: "Hullo. Is Hennie dere?" But rarely did they throw me a how-de-do.

My mother and I had fallen into a routine of genial avoidance. I'd rise hours before she did and have the bathroom vacated by the time her peristalsis kicked in. I'd refrain from calling out all the answers while she was watching "Jeopardy." In the evening, we'd listen to Patsy Cline and play

Scrabble. She took her thrashings with minimal vexation, though the veneer of sportsmanship wore thinner the night I used all my letters three times (FEATURES, ROOSTERS, VACATION), triple-scored the X, quadrupled the Z, and achieved 451 points, a lifetime high, to her 221.

She would write me little poems and leave them on my bed:

> If living alone
> Is what you please,
> Who's to say "God bless you"
> When you sneeze?

Or:

> When there's smoke,
> There's usually a fire there.
> But, here, you know
> It's "*Votre Mère*"

∾

At 10:35 on our museum Sunday, I ventured back toward the kitchen and, when I appeared in the doorway, she barked, "Don't pressure me!"

She was at the table, eating crackers and sorting the coinage she'd need for the subway. It had been so long since she'd ridden the IRT that she did not know the proper senior-citizen fare.

I retreated from the bedroom and she dressed. When next I saw her, she was wearing a dark-blue denim skirt, a white blouse with a band of embroidery across the bosom, and white tennis shoes.

"Security," she said, "is wearing *two* pairs of bloomers."

Just getting my mother up and outfitted was an accomplishment. She knew one woman who never got out of her bed except to feed her cats. She had had a sister-in-law who wouldn't leave home except in her husband's car.

"I'm almost ready," I was told at 11:15. "I'll just go to the bathroom fourteen times, and then we'll go."

The Number 2 line on a Sunday morning was half-filled with church-goers heading for the storefront basilicas and converted synagogues of Caribbean Flatbush. I knew that my mother knew that I knew what she was thinking: there was only one other white passenger, and this was a young Irishman with a New York Jets equipment bag, who had to be an undercover cop. We spoke not at all and stared at the advertisements – "NOSE SUR-GERY"; "FIX YOUR HAIR!" – and when we reached Brooklyn Museum sta-tion at the north end of Prospect Park after the eighteen-minute ride, she climbed out of the darkness with short, gasping breaths and strode *right through* the museum, past African Art and the gift shop and the elevators, and went into the Sculpture Garden to smoke and drink the Thermos of cof-fee she had carried with her in her handbag on the IRT Number 2.

The Frieda Schiff Warburg Memorial Sculpture Garden was a cemetery of perished architecture. Set into the ground, or floating in ivy, or affixed to the rear walls of the museum building, were stone satyrs and cherubs, bronze Minotaurs, sandstone heads of Zeus, dragons, Gorgons, and Lin-colns, all of them rescued remnants of Lost New York. Bareknuckled boxers from the railing of the Police Gazette building. A giant head of Benjamin Franklin. Finials, capitals, scraps.

My mother finished her coffee, and we shuffled back towards the lobby to begin a proper tour, re-entering a museum whose nineteenth-century creators intended it to be nothing less than the greatest in the world.

Here, again, was the familiar theme: the inevitable transcendence of chaste, elegant Brooklyn over Manhattan's decadent isle. The collections of the Brooklyn Museum, designed to be the largest exhibition building on the planet, consecrated to "all departments of art and science," would eclipse not only rival Gotham but Berlin and even London.

The original plans for the building in which we were standing were for a neo-Classical quadrangle on a stupendous scale, with more than 1.5 million square feet of halls and rotundas, an Eighth Wonder to befit America's third-largest metropolis. But Art would be subverted by Politics. In 1898, a year after the West Wing of the new museum was completed, Brooklyn was con-jugated into Greater New York.

The wind went out of the grandiose intentions. Instead of being the cultural center of a proud, independent city, the Brooklyn Museum be-came just another chattel of the Parks Department. Barely a quarter of the

Greco-Roman colossus was built. The total area of gallery space was left at a tenth of the founders' dreams. Eventually, the natural-history exhibits were dismantled and the sciences were abandoned. (In 1935, even the front steps were removed.) In 1992, the Brooklyn Museum drew 290,000 visitors. In Manhattan, the Metropolitan attracted 4.5 million. The Met had twelve times as many members, four times the exhibition space, eighteen times the endowment.

That was fine with us. Our borough did not breed in its children a need to strut and preen. Its autonomy had been surrendered, but it was still able to provide what Marianne Moore called "the kind of tame excitement on which I thrive."

And, anyway, the Brooklyn Museum was hardly a pipsqueak. It soared five stories above the Botanic Garden beside it. Out front were the allegorical statues of *Brooklyn* and *Manhattan* that had strolled over after fifty years at the foot of the Manhattan Bridge. Above them, high on the facade, were more statues in Homeric regalia and the engraved names of great male thought-wreakers: AESCHYLUS, PINDAR, LAOTSE, CONFUCIUS, DAVID, MOSES, ST. PAUL.

Inside the Grand Lobby was a bewildering assortment of junk that turned out to be the current Feature Installation. It was, we learned, a collection of "found and acquired" objects, collated and arranged on a dropcloth the size of a tennis court by an artist named Donald Lipski. The title was *Pieces of String Too Short to Save.* Like the sculptor Stephen Singer, waiting under his bridge for falling chunks of iron, Lipski had come across most of his stuff while promenading around Manhattan.

What stuff? Tires, ropes, gas masks, bomb casings, dentists' chairs, cigar boxes, grappling hooks, ships' propellers, rotary telephones, steel wool, football helmets, missile nose-cones, Sabbath candles, candy tins, boot lasts, test tubes, binder twine, Chinese peasant hats, snare drums, baling wire, and piano keys.

We poked about Lipski's intriguingly incomprehensible concoction for a while and then got down to business. Around a corner and through a doorway, my mother found her Mary Cassatts.

She gasped as she entered the exhibition room. There, amid a treasury of Renoirs, Cézannes, and Picassos in Brooklyn's neglected Quai d'Orsay, was *The Banjo Lesson,* a small aquatint in which two young women, one dressed in blue and one in subtle rose, concentrate on the fingering of their long-necked music box. And nearby were *In the Omnibus* and *Femme debout à sa toilette* and *L'Abat-Jour* and *Young Woman Trying on a Dress*.

"I can't believe that I'm looking at the *originals* of these," my mother said. She was transported. She understood.

She stared at *Femme debout*.

"That's when she started getting her Japanese influence," my mother said. (She was correct, of course. A brochure credited Cassatt's inspiration to the Japanese prints that were in vogue in Paris at the time.)

Scattered around the room – it held a compilation of prints and drawings from the museum's permanent collection – were a Braque, a Matisse, a brace of Manets, Picasso's *Nude Standing in Profile*, nine Toulouse-Lautrecs, and some pretty good stuff by Miró and Gris and Pissarro.

My mother turned to an impression of a finely dressed woman, with hat and folded parasol, captured at a gallery of art. The subject perused a painting – we saw only her back – while another woman, seated, holding a book, turned around to peek at her evident celebrity.

"I know this!" my mother breathed. "It's Degas, *painting* Mary Cassatt at the Louvre. He was supposed to have been her mentor . . ."

She paused in admiration.

". . . and her lover!"

We made our goodbyes to the Cassatts. There was so much more to see. On the fifth floor were the American and European paintings and sculptures that elevated me and the Contemporary Art that made me ill. (In addition to these works, the Egyptian collection, the American Period Rooms, and the Asian porcelain and ancient Peruvian textiles, the Brooklyn Museum was able to scrape together only fifty-eight sculptures by Rodin. And *94 per cent* of its holdings were in storage and not even displayed.) We passed *Head of a Woman* by Alexander Stirling Calder, and my mother ran her hands, probably illegally, over the lissome curves.

"Look at her!" she said. She was swooning. I'd rarely seen her like this, but then I'd rarely been alone with her at art museums. "You say you want the sweetest part of the watermelon. I want a piece of sculpture." Or a carousel horse.

She moved slowly through the galleries in her tennis shoes, missing nothing, her coughing echoing down the stone-floored halls, past the Stuarts and Peales and Copleys, until she came to a halt in front of a late-nineteenth-century portrait of two women by a man named Albert Henderson Thayer. They were *The Sisters*; they wore black crepe dresses; the younger wrapped her left arm around her older sibling's waist.

I moved ahead to study Francis Guy's famous *Winter Scene in Brooklyn* that depicted life along the East River laneways in the winter of 1817. This was a portrait of the district – familiar to young Walt Whitman – that would become the teeming "walled city" of industry and commerce and then decline into the cobblestoned ghost town above which the great bridges roared. But Guy had preserved for us the Dutchmen with their clay pipes, the frame houses and horses and black servants, the sows and the woodpiles and the overarching sky that now was pricked by the bridge towers and MetroTech and the printing plants of the Jehovah's Witnesses.

My mother caught up with me. She pointed back to *The Sisters*.

"It brought tears to my eyes," she said.

We were alone in the long, silent gallery. I listened to my mother's breathing. Aunt Cel was gone. Aunt Fay had taken her own life. Of the Jacobson girls, only Henrietta was left to let her fingers trail the sculptor's touch, to dream into the painter's given world.

3

Ten days after the signing of the Declaration of Independence in Philadelphia on July 4, 1776, Admiral Lord Richard Howe wrote to George Washington to advise him that he had just landed thirty-two thousand British and Hessian troops on Staten Island and to suggest that the colonials might find this an excellent incentive to drop the whole idea of a revolution.

Lord Howe, however, addressed his letter to "George Washington, *Esquire*," omitting his proper title of Commander-in-Chief of the United States of America, and General Washington, quite insulted, sent the letter back.

A week later, Lord Howe forwarded the epistle again, this time indicating the addressee as "George Washington, *et cetera, et cetera, et cetera.*"

Seeing this, the Father of His Country is purported to have said: "It is true the *et ceteras* imply everything. But it is no less true, they imply *any-thing*." And he again marked the envelope "Return To Sender," or the eighteenth-century equivalent.

Lord Howe gave up writing letters. Instead, he invaded Brooklyn.

Brooklyn wasn't much of a prize. All of Kings County comprised merely four thousand inhabitants, most of them Dutch farmers who could not have cared less which faction of English-speaking devils prevailed. The real target, as ever, was Manhattan, where General Washington had nearly twenty thousand soldiers of his own. The British aimed for an early checkmate: to take control of New York, isolate New England from Virginia, tear up Jefferson's mad Declaration, make everyone swear an oath of loyalty to George III, and then go home to make real wars against real countries like France.

Washington endeavored to fortify the heights of Brooklyn with cannon that would fire on the Royal Navy in the East River. The British, therefore, decided to take the forts by land. And that is how thousands of men came to be engaged right on Flatbush Avenue in the first battle ever fought by the United States Army, a battle whose principal action occurred on the future site of the home of Rudy the self-abusing rhino.

Two hundred and seventeen years later, virtually no one in the borough had any idea how much sacred national history had transpired in Prospect Park. There was no soaring Doric column, such as the one that honored the Prison Ship Martyrs, many of whom had been captured in Brooklyn. In the park, there were only a couple of plaques glued to glacial boulders. At Moore's Creek, North Carolina, a swamp where *one* patriot had been killed in a skirmish was made a National Park. But here, nothing.

Some Brooklynites saw this as a reprehensible omission. Organizations were chartered and dedicated to making Brooklyn's multifaceted citizenry aware of its birthright. A broadsheet promulgated by The First Battle Revival Alliance complained:

On August 27, 1776, the fate of American liberty rested solely on what happened in Brooklyn. Never before or since has American history been so focused within the confines of Brooklyn. And never has an event of such magnitude been so ignored . . .

One reason why the Battle of Brooklyn (or the Battle of Long Island, as it was called everywhere else) may not have echoed alongside Bunker Hill and Saratoga as a shining hour in the fight for freedom was that, at Brooklyn, the Americans were outflanked, outfought, outmanned, out-thought, and slaughtered. Washington, who was new at this kind of thing, had the wrong generals in the wrong jobs in the wrong places. Informants secreted among the Dutchmen gave the rebel positions away. Colonial troops were untested militiamen thrown against English and Scottish regulars and mercenary Germans.

Washington's most famous remark during the battle was a lamentation for doomed Marylanders who were being sent on a suicidal charge. His crowning achievement was in getting everyone in boats and rowing hell-bent for Manhattan.

A three-cent stamp issued in 1951 on the 175th anniversary of the rout showed the defeated commandant, bareheaded on a proud white steed, supervising a flotilla of sailboats and barges flying north on a bright, clear day. The stamp announced: "WASHINGTON SAVES HIS ARMY AT BROOKLYN."

But in fact it was night-fog as thick as milk that preserved a shattered army and made the United States of America what it is today.

⌒⌒

The Battle of Brooklyn was a great pincer movement achieved by the British with stealth and numerical strength. They had landed at Gravesend – under the Verrazano Bridge – without opposition, their bateaux and flatboats and gundelows forming what the secretary to the king's admiral-in-chief would call "one of the most picturesque Scenes that the Imagination can fancy or the Eye behold." Then they started up the old Canarsee Indian trail – now Kings Highway – towards Flatbush and the rebel forts and victory.

The Dutch whose homes and farms lay in the path of Europe's most fearsome military body made a quick and rational decision. They ran for their lives.

As the Brooklyn historian Thomas M. Strong would write in 1842:

It was a scene of great confusion, and of no ordinary distress. Compelled to leave their homes and the greater part of their property, and not knowing what might befal their persons or their families, they committed themselves to the good providence of their God. Some had not gone far before they saw the smoke ascending from the neighborhoods of their farms, and knew not but their dwellings were already in flames.

The Lefferts homestead that, two centuries later, would be the residence of the ex-zookeeper Arne Israel was fired by the Americans themselves to keep the British from possessing it. The house was rebuilt within a few months of the hostilities and now, having been moved into Prospect Park and made a museum, exuded a bucolic charm with its gambrel roof, sloping eaves, and double "Dutch" front door.

As the British advance guard hiked its way up Flatbush Avenue from the south, American riflemen set fire to the late-summer wheatfields to deny the grain to their enemy. They prepared to make their stand in the wooded hills, along what now is the East Drive of Prospect Park that winds from the desolate Willink Comfort Station to the carousel to the zoo to Grand Army Plaza.

On the morning of August 27, 1776, five thousand British troops mustered just outside the Wendy's restaurant at Flatbush and Empire Boulevard and began their frontal attack. Meanwhile, another British assault was beginning along the banks of the Gowanus Creek and General William Howe (brother of the admiral who had sent Washington the *et cetera* letter) was sneaking ten thousand men around the left flank of the American lines, undetected and unopposed. At midday, the patriots who had been "valiantly sustaining" themselves in Prospect Park discovered that they were completely surrounded.

To try to delay the closure of the British vise – indeed, to save the cause of American independence – Washington threw a regiment of 250 raw troops from Maryland back *towards* the surging foe. It was at this point that the commander-in-chief allegedly looked down from the safety of Cobble Hill (near Israel Abolafia's Hotel Nevins) and sighed: "Good God, what brave men I must this day lose."

The Marylanders – Brooklyn's Light Brigade – attempted time after time to storm a roughly built farm structure that has come to be known as the Old

Stone House. Each time, they were thrown back, with grievous losses. (They were "young men of the best families," lamented Dr. Strong.) But their sacrifice enabled thousands of their compatriots to escape to the fortified heights and, eventually, to Saratoga and Valley Forge and Yorktown and victory.

The Battle of Brooklyn, by most reckonings, was the costliest blunder of Washington's generalship. Three hundred of his men were killed and about eleven hundred captured, doomed to rot on the Prison Ship *Jersey*, their tumbled bones much later to be strewn in leaden caskets under the extinct perpetual flame at Fort Greene. The British lost sixty-three dead and twenty-three captured. But Howe and Howe declined to pursue their staggering foes. Instead, everyone sat around in the rain for three days, while the rebels slipped away in the mist.

The Old Stone House, predictably, was forgotten. It was used briefly as a baseball clubhouse by the predecessors of the Brooklyn Dodgers. It was buried during a landfill operation in 1890, excavated, rebuilt in 1935, abandoned again, and now, when I walked past on a bright May morning, it was sealed and silent. It stood incongruously in a city playground at Fifth Avenue and Third Street, four blocks from the Methodist Hospital and its memorial plaque to little Stephen Baltz. In one of its pamphlets, the First Battle Revival Alliance, soliciting donations to have the Old Stone House made a museum of the Battle of Brooklyn, cried:

> We are part of history whether we choose to acknowledge it or not. If we acknowledge history we see a rich tapestry before us and our part in its beauty. If we ignore history then we walk forever blind through time.

∾

What the rampaging British had done to the houses of patriots in 1776, so the children of modern Brooklyn wreaked on the flesh and fabric of their city. Just east of the sacrificial hills of Prospect Park – consecrated by the blood of the Maryland regiment, and of Allyn Winslow and Jesse Ferreira – I stood on a subway platform and felt disgust and fear rise in me. This was no place for a traveler to be loitering alone.

It was the godforsaken Botanic Garden station of the Franklin Avenue

Shuttle. The cherry blossoms of the municipal esplanade were barely a block away, but down here was a netherworld of graffiti and trash, of low ceilings and dark, stained walls. Only one track was operational – the Franklin Shuttle line, barely a mile long, was lightly patronized, so a single train went up and back, up and back, up and back. On those rails that were no longer functional, someone had heaved a shopping cart, and truck tires and old shoes and glass. Ivy and weeds grew up through the cracks, reclaiming a landscape that man had profaned and the subway's so-called rebirth clearly had missed.

Two teenaged boys leapt the turnstile and double-stepped down to the platform and hurled a bottle on the tracks. A train rolled in, stopped, departed, but the boys did not board it. Neither did anyone else.

A study of the New York municipal railways called the Franklin Shuttle "the last vestige of old-time transit." The transit cops at Atlantic Avenue called it "The Cooler" and warned me to avoid it like the mange. The Franklin Shuttle dated to 1878. It was only five stops long, linking the A Train that ran along Fulton Street with the Brighton Beach express. Some of the stairways still contained pieces of original metalwork from the nineteenth century. In 1993, the Transit Authority was trying to decide whether to renovate the Franklin Shuttle or scrap it altogether.

The Botanic Garden station was relatively new. It was opened in 1918 to serve the horticultural exhibits and the new baseball grounds at Ebbets Field. The north end was in a short tunnel, but from this point the shuttle traveled in an open cut. In the sunshine at the south end, perched on a bridge above the tracks, was a small ravaged outbuilding, its roof fallen through in places, that had once been a ticket office in the years before the metal token and the automatic turnstile were introduced.

But, this being Brooklyn, someone *lived* in it. And now this person was walking right toward me. He was a tall fellow, fortyish, in dark pants and a yellow hooded sweatshirt and a Mets ball cap, clambering around the barricade at the end of the platform and wobbling back and forth gently as if obeying Satchel Paige's famous advice to "jangle slowly when you walk." Fortunately, I was standing next to a round, muscular, well-armed transit policeman named Serge Pierrelouis.

"I have permission from the police captain to stay there," said the man who lived in the ticket booth.

"Uh huh," said Serge Pierrelouis.

"They said I could stay as long as I don't burn the place down."

"*Who* said that?" asked the officer of the subterranean law.

"The FBI," the squatter replied.

"The FBI?"

"They came around and said I was sellin' drugs."

"The FBI don't investigate that kind of thing," declared Serge Pierrelouis.

"Well, who does, Mister Smart Guy?" asked the man in the baseball cap.

Another constable, a woman, arrived and took the man upstairs to the fortress of the token booth for questioning. That left me alone on the Botanic Garden station platform with Officer Pierrelouis and the two young idlers, who still hadn't boarded a train. Serge knew from experience that the boys hadn't deposited a token upon entry.

"*Nobody* pays their fare here," he admitted.

We looked around the platform at the litter and the spray paint and the sunlight that made my eyes ache.

"The federal government spent so much money to build arms to fight Russia," the transit cop said. "But they neglected the poor people."

This saddened Serge Pierrelouis. He had come to New York from the doleful poverty of Haiti at the age of fourteen and now, after nineteen years in America, a degree in finance and marketing from St. John's University, a job at E. F. Hutton, and three years on the police force, he yearned to return to his country because *his* country, he believed, at least had a *chance* to be saved.

"The calls on the radio – it's always 'Male black.' 'Male black,'" he said. "You arrest them and they say, 'We're your own people, man.' But *they're* the ones who fucked up their neighborhoods. You're hardly *ever* mugged by a white man. The white man does heavy-duty crime, like loan sharking."

Serge Pierrelouis was an educated man who was trying to learn to swagger like the New York cops in movies. He was working on his master's degree. He was defensive about his accent and his bowling-ball physique. He kept saying, "Don't judge a book by its cover." Inside his uniform hat, he kept a small plastic prayer card of St. Michael, "Heaven's Glorious Commissioner of Police."

The Franklin Shuttle rumbled to a halt and Serge Pierrelouis and I climbed on board. It was a short, five-car train, but the first and last cars were dark and not in service. Inside the middle carriages it was bright and clean and there was no graffiti at all. Climbing from the gloom at Botanic Garden station onto a spotless, modern train was dizzying; it was the same feeling I used to get when I'd shove and sweat my way through the airport at Delhi or Dhaka and suddenly find myself splayed in the splendid luxury of a Boeing jet.

A couple of dozen passengers were aboard. Serge and I traveled up the line to Fulton Street and then reversed to Botanic Garden, where we once again met the policewoman and the tall, jangly man who lived in the old ticket shed.

The female officer looked chagrined.

"He *does* have permission," she said. "In fact, he's fixed up that booth real nice. This man has five thousand dollars in the bank. Certificates of Deposit."

"Like I told you," said the man with the Mets cap. "The FBI already checked me out."

We were standing on the platform again when Serge's radio began crackling. Male black with gun in waistband at Fulton Street, where the Franklin Shuttle met the A Train. We had been right there, exactly six minutes earlier. The description was detailed: blue coat, black pants.

Serge listened for a ten-thirteen: Officer Needs Assistance. Nothing. Or a second sighting. Nothing. The man with the gun in his waistband had escaped into the urban undergrowth.

Or it might have been a joke. A desk sergeant at Franklin Avenue had explained the scenario. Punks with radio scanners often phoned in specious alarms just to monitor the police response. This was how they got their laughs – listening to New York's Finest at work, trying to collar a mirage.

❧

South of Botanic Garden, the Franklin Shuttle dived below street level and into a sharply curved tunnel that took it under Empire Boulevard and Flatbush Avenue and into the Prospect Park station of the Brighton Beach line. There was nothing special about this location except for one thing: at this spot, in 1918, a hapless subway motorman turned an autumn evening rush-hour rumble into the worst railway accident in American history.

It was called the Malbone Street Wreck and it was the reason I was so eager to ride the Franklin Shuttle. (Preferably with a police escort.) Unlike the Park Slope plane crash or the American Revolution, it was possible to vicariously relive this great Flatbush Avenue disaster for the price of a subway token. With Serge Pierrelouis a comforting arm's-length away, I pressed myself to the window as our train slid and screeched around Brooklyn's own, authentic, Dead Man's Curve. This time, we survived.

The Malbone Street Wreck, which killed 102 people, was born of a festering labor dispute in the summer of 1918. In August of that year, twenty-nine motormen were fired by the Brooklyn Rapid Transit Company for trying to organize their confreres into the Brotherhood of Locomotive Engineers. The National War Labor Board ordered them reinstated. The BRT management refused. So, on November 1, the union ordered a one-day strike.

The company determined to keep the system running. Dispatchers and motor switchmen, who usually worked behind desks and in the storage yards, were assigned to drive the trains. One of these replacement motormen was Edward Luciano, also known as Edward Lewis or Billy Lewis, age twenty-five. At the trial, the BRT would claim that Edward Luciano had made "a few trips" as motorman before November 1. Eight days before the accident, Edward Luciano's daughter had died of influenza. But neither his inexperience nor the weight of his personal loss could bring back the people he killed.

Luciano's problem was the air brakes. He couldn't get the hang of them. He overshot the stations at Dean Street and Park Place. He went roaring past Botanic Garden at forty miles an hour. Advertising signs, survivors said, "blended into a rainbow." Ahead was the S-curve into Prospect Park, a sharp right, then left. The posted speed limit was six miles an hour.

"Almost at once, leaving Park Place, the train speeded up," a passenger named Reynolds testified. "Some girls about me remarked, 'This is terrible. I'm afraid something will happen.' The cars were swaying and rocking. Everybody was in a marked state of tension and apprehension. . . . I realized there was a terrible lurch. Then everything went blank."

The air brakes failed completely; or, Edward Luciano failed to apply them. The rear wheels of the front car came off the tracks. So did the four cars behind it. The wooden carriages hit the tunnel walls.

Those who were not killed instantly or rendered unconscious staggered from the shredded carriages and tried to walk to safety along the tracks. The Prospect Park platform was only fifty yards away. But at that moment, controllers at the BRT powerhouse noticed that the current had gone off on the Franklin line. They thought it was a prank by the wildcat strikers. The circuit breakers were reset. Twenty men and women were electrocuted, adding to the gruesome toll.

The Brooklyn Women's Motor Corps was the first ambulance team to reach the scene. Many of the women had been nurses with the American Expeditionary Force in France. In the Malbone Street tunnel, they found "heads taken right off the shoulders – brains and other organs spattered against the iron and concrete walls."

But the Women's Motor Corps was said to be "self-possessed and calm."

The dead were laid out at a hospital and in the lobby of the grandstand at Ebbets Field. Men were identified from their draft cards. Many of the women were never identified at all. Mostly, there were Irish, and there were Jews, the burgeoning middle class of the immigrants' paradise: Weinburg, Sullivan, Halloran, Jackowitz, Rubin, McCormack, Maloney. E. E. Porter had been captain of the Williams College Glee Club. W. E. Stephens conducted prayer meetings on the Boardwalk at Brighton Beach. Abe Malamud was found with $620 in cash in his money belt and $200 worth of Liberty Bonds. (The war in Europe would end ten days later.) Sometimes it was reported that 97 people died and sometimes 102. The previous American record, set in Colorado, was 101.

No one was ever convicted. Luciano, indicted for manslaughter, claimed he had never taken a train out of the yard alone before the crash. He said, "I tried to check the speed, but the air brakes wouldn't work." Five members of the BRT executive board were also put on trial. There was a change of venue from Brooklyn to Long Island, a hung jury, a retrial, acquittals, dismissal of charges.

The name of Malbone Street became infamous and was changed to Empire Boulevard.

The Commercial Casualty Insurance Company began to offer policies that covered travel by "subways, trolleys, Rail Roads, ferries, steam, electric and elevated systems." Five dollars bought five thousand dollars in coverage.

After the Malbone wreck, the subway lines of New York City were fitted with devices that could spring up from the track bed and automatically bring a train to a stop in the case of excessive speed. Seventy-five years later, it was one of these "trippers" that halted the A Train that was illicitly commandeered by that seventeen-year-old boy.

The boy hijacker, it was widely reported, had learned to operate a train by spending hours just outside the door of the motorman's cab of the Franklin Avenue Shuttle.

4

At street level on Empire Boulevard, I found no marker or memorial to indicate the scene of the wreck. On one side of the tracks was the Botanic Garden and on the other was a solid, stately replica of Florence's fifteenth-century Foundling Hospital by Brunelleschi that, in Brooklyn, served as a communications center for the Fire Department. Wendy's was on the south side of Empire, and a mural on a blank wall behind the restaurant welcomed everyone – everyone who had survived the transit of Prospect Park – to Flatbush Avenue, Brooklyn's Appian Way.

This was the portal to the erstwhile Village of Flatbush, the core of my long homecoming journey, a settlement as old as Rembrandt and Van Dyck and now as new as gangsta rap and Rude Boy reggae. Once, the boundary between the Dutchmen's placid Flatbush and Whitman's manly Brooklyn had been marked by a prominent tree – a white oak – but in 1776 this had been felled and left in the road to hinder the British invaders. Now the townships were united politically, but the border was still unmistakable. It ran along New York's hair-trigger fault lines of poverty and race and crime.

I walked east along Empire Boulevard. To my right was the dilapidated clock tower of the old Bond Bread bakery, where I had been taken in 1956 on a kindergarten field trip to inhale the unforgettable aroma of loaves that were "Baked While You Sleep." The hands had fallen off the clock, and the building appeared from the outside to be abandoned, but, when I poked my head in a garage door and smelled that glorious perfume again, I learned that the bakery was still in operation, turning out Grossinger's Rye.

Behind the bakery on Washington Avenue was a food warehouse, and on its walls was a collection of giant portraits. Booker T. Washington, Malcolm X, and Marcus Garvey were joined by Bob Marley, Michael Jordan, and Roberto Clemente. I was entering a zone where images of minority success and self-reliance competed with Midnight Dragon malt liquor and Phillies Blunts stuffed with marijuana for the souls of a generation. It was a war of potent symbols. The stern face of Chief Sitting Bull looked out from the painting above me, but one of the most popular of the new super-alcoholic beers that Brooklyn schoolboys were chugging was named for his kinsman, Crazy Horse.

Across Empire Boulevard from this rousing work was the dark megalith of a city housing project, with thick red-brown towers more than twenty stories high. But this was not just another forgotten tenement. On the site of this project once had stood the nucleus of Brooklyn's national myth. I had found Ebbets Field, home of the Dodgers.

"Nowhere but in Brooklyn does baseball arouse such fierce and fantastic frenzies of joy – and gloom," boasted the authors of *Brooklyn, U.S.A.*, enforcing the monotype of the Brooklynite as a diamond-crazed lunatic. "Visitors from other boroughs wisely have kept their critical comments to themselves, while standing inside Brooklyn's boundaries, ever since a 24-carat Dodger fan quietly shot two querulous Giant rooters, killing one and seriously wounding the other, a new high in Dodger passion."

That was in the forties, when the Brooklyn baseball club, known formerly for egregious, buffoon baseball, cozily ensconced at its little brick bandbox, suddenly won a couple of pennants, challenged the despised, patrician Yankees for global horsehide supremacy (but lost), and drove the battiest of its partisans even more berserk.

Then, in the fifties, had come the zenith. The team's roster, once as pink and Protestant as the world beyond Gowanus Creek, came to mirror the borough's sense of self: Robinson and Campanella, the blacks; Furillo and Maglie, the Italians; Koufax, the Jew; Snider and Hodges, the valiant all-Americans. The Dodgers took three National League titles in the space of four years and, finally, after all the losing and the comedy and the excruciating near-misses, a World Series championship was Brooklyn's in 1955. The

Bums beat the Yankees in seven games; Little Red Riding Hood had gobbled the Wolf. Brooklyn's enthusiastic victory parades, it was reported, "had all the horrendous overtones of a maniac's nightmare in Technicolor."

Two years later, the shameless transfer of the franchise to Los Angeles broke two million hearts with one press release. The reasons for the move – management's lust for television dollars, racist fear of a changing borough, or merely shrewd anticipation of California's fabulous potential – have been debated ever since. Gone but not unremembered, the Dodgers had been mythologized in literature and film. They were the eponyms of the elegiac book *Boys of Summer*. Spike Lee wore Jackie Robinson's number 42 in the incendiary *Do the Right Thing* and started a fashion craze. Kids born twenty years after the team's extraction wore Brooklyn Dodger caps, shirts, jackets.

A dwindling legion of bereaved fanatics clung to their youth through the medium of Dodgerdom. There was a Brooklyn Dodger Hall of Fame that enshrined new members every year. (The selectors were running short on heroes; this year's honorees included the team photographer.) "Pee Wee" Reese, the popular shortstop, returned to Grand Army Plaza to sell videos of his life story on "Welcome Back to Brooklyn Day." A tavern in Bensonhurst was sued by the Los Angeles club for calling itself the Brooklyn Dodger Lounge. The tavern won.

I was seven and a half when Walter O'Malley took the Dodgers west in 1957. I had been brought to Ebbets Field only once, during the last home stand of the last season, though no one in the crowd knew of the impending fulfillment of the owner's habitual threats. We took an electric trolley bus, my father and I, to watch the Bums play Philadelphia. I remember little but the green grass and the light towers and the antics of the clown Emmett Kelly at home plate before the game began. I fell asleep in the fourth or fifth inning. I still have the scorecard in my desk in Toronto, and a priceless yearbook autographed that September night by every member of that last Brooklyn team.

Back in '57, owner O'Malley's warning that little Ebbets Field could no longer sustain a big-league franchise was not just doubletalk. The carpet-bagging trend had been well-established. The woebegone A's, Browns, and Braves had all found new pastures. California sang the song of virgin big-league soil. New York City countered with a consultant's study that recommended the construction of a new Dodger stadium above the Long Island

Rail Road terminus at Flatbush and Atlantic avenues. But the Board of Estimate balked at the thirty-million-dollar price tag. Then it was proposed to build a ball park at the site of the 1939 World's Fair in Flushing Meadow, Queens. Walter O'Malley reasoned: "We decided that going to Flushing Meadow was no different, in a sense, from going to Jersey City or Los Angeles. You would not be the Brooklyn Dodgers if you were not in Brooklyn. And as long as you're going to move, what difference does it make if you move five miles or five thousand miles?"

So they moved. In California, the Dodgers won pennant after pennant and attracted more than three million customers a season. The Giants, who departed their Polo Grounds in Upper Manhattan at the same time, prospered in San Francisco at first, fell upon diminished revenues in a blustery ball park, and threatened to uproot for Tampa, Florida. Ebbets Field was demolished in 1960 and was replaced with a housing estate.

The center of the universe was made to suffer only four years without National League ball. By 1993, the Mets, created to fill the void, were in their thirtieth season at Shea Stadium in Flushing Meadow, the home that the Bums declined. (But no one ever called them the Queens Mets.) The Yankees' owner, the voluble George Steinbrenner, was threatening to move his team from the moribund Bronx to suburban New Jersey, but the cry was dismissed as empty O'Malleying. At Flatbush and Atlantic avenues in Brooklyn, where the new Ebbets Field might have stood, was a deep, wide pit, awaiting Bradlee's discount clothier.

After that initiation at the age of seven, I had attended at least a thousand more big-league games, as an adolescent fanatic and then as a dispassionate reporter, often staying awake all the way through. And I had read in a published interview with Duke Snider that, at the height of the team's popularity, one of the Dodgers' equipment attendants had learned to imitate the handwriting of all the coaches and players in order to cope with the requests for autographs. The yearbook I had treasured since second grade, the Duke of Flatbush hinted, might actually have been signed in the clubhouse by a lowly batboy the players called "Charley the Brew."

Da noive a'dat bum!

∾

The low-rise fortress on McKeever Place, across from where Ebbets Field had been, was Intermediate School 320, Jackie Robinson Junior High. Robinson, Number 42, a Brooklyn Dodger from 1947 until the year before O'Malley's lamented evacuation, the first African-American embraced by big-league baseball since the 1880s, was an indomitable battler, fierce and prideful, and a hitter and baserunner of spectacular talent. Even the Southerners on the team who bitterly opposed – and threatened to boycott – his promotion from Montreal were soon brought around to adulation by the force of Robinson's character.

Traded to the Giants in 1957, he chose to retire rather than go over to the enemy. He was the kind of man that schools should be named for. McKeever, on the other hand, was a business partner of Charles Ebbets, owner of the Dodgers, back in 1913. And McKeever, no less than Franklin and Washington and Adams, got a whole street in the Brooklyn gazetteer.

The main entrance of I.S. 320 was decorated with atrociously rendered portraits, not of infielder Robinson, but of three Freedom Riders – James E. Chaney, Michael Schwerner, and Andrew Goodman – murdered in Mississippi in 1964 in the cause of civil rights. I tried to find an entrance to the school – I thought there might be some exhibit on the Dodgers and number 42's career – but the solid metal doors were bolted. Most did not even have handles on the outside. It was easier, I thought, for Jackie Robinson to break into major-league baseball than for me to enter a New York public school.

But I was no novice at being places I didn't belong. I waited outside the center door until someone came out, then bade the man thanks and slipped inside, only to be confronted by a security guard the size of Charles Barkley. Somehow, I bluffed my way to the principal's office, where I made my inquiry about Dodger lore.

There wasn't any. A custodian, I was told, had once operated a tidy little business in Ebbetsiana from his office in the basement, but he had left I.S. 320. There were about a dozen women in the office, managing the school's affairs. One of them was the principal, a tough-loving, soul-mama Muslim, in a green head-scarf, long dress, and penny loafers, named Sister Rasheedah Muhammad. She chortled when I suggested that, at first glance, she came off as a combination of Pearl Bailey and Mussolini.

Sister Rasheedah Muhammad, an aide admitted without whispering, had tried to come on as an autocrat and – the principal nodded as this was said – "this didn't work, with the children or the staff."

The aide's name was Silvia Lavalas. She was a teacher of mathematics to the school's Hispanic minority and chairperson of the Restructuring Committee at Jackie Robinson Intermediate. A lot of restructuring was needed. The school, Ms. Lavalas said, was "a disaster."

"The kids were out of control," she told me. "We had a lot of violent incidents. We were heading toward being one of the worst in this district. In terms of safety, we were one of the most troubled. Academically, we were next-to-lowest out of twenty-six. We believe this can be turned around.

"Sister Rasheedah thought she could just dictate to these children. But kids have to be *reasoned* with today. You have to convince them that they *need* to be educated. You have to make them understand that there is no way they can get around dealing with authority in their lives."

There were seventeen hundred students at Jackie Robinson. The majority, Silvia Lavalas said, lived without a male adult in the home. Many came from the projects across McKeever Place, the Ebbets Field Apartments. They were, she said, growing up with obscenely violent video and rap idols who encouraged them to dust off the cops. Hoop stars hypnotized them into hundred-dollar sneakers. The cocaine industry kidnapped their ambitions, and its attendant mayhem made them hostages in their own homes.

"They grow up with gunfire, twenty-four hours of the day and night and all around them," Ms. Lavalas said, evenly. She did not sound angry. This was just the way it was around Ebbets Field in 1993.

"You don't know the *fear* these kids face, just getting home alive from school," a man interjected. He was a basketball coach named Carlton Screen, Sr. "Three-quarters of them carry weapons, *not* to be the aggressor, but to defend themselves. Every one of them has seen dead people lying in the street."

I was sitting at the guard's table in the main lobby with Coach Screen and now, at three o'clock, waves of dashing, laughing, yelping kids were crashing around us, bursting for the exits with their Jansport backpacks and their oversized jeans and sweatshirts reflecting the current mania for the stylish gold insignia of the designer Karl Kani. (Most of the garments were probably Asian knockoffs, as counterfeit as my '57 Dodger yearbook signed by Charley the Brew. It was the logo, not the quality, that mattered.) I peeked into the day's security register and saw this item: "N—— cut Moktar Aziz with razor then ran out of school."

Carlton Screen, Sr., ran a basketball league on Saturday mornings at a nearby school named for Walt Whitman. He was a member of the basketball Hall of Fame at his high school on Flatbush Avenue. He had won a city championship there in 1965. Carlton Screen, Jr., was playing basketball at Providence College in Rhode Island. The father believed that sport could save the youth of I.S. 320 from themselves and each other. He complained that teachers, struggling much of the time to keep the razor-slashers calm in the classroom, did not have the patience to audit the troubles of marginal, disruptive boys.

"*I* have the patience," he said. "I sit with them six, seven hours and longer. A lot of kids tell me, 'Mister Screen, you're my Dad.' I tell them, 'I love you like a Dad.'"

When Carlton Screen, Sr., was eleven years old, he and his basketball teammates were bundled into a car and driven, without explanation, all the way to Connecticut. He remembered his anguished questions – "Where are we going? Why's it taking so long?" – and his coach's benign silence.

They pulled up at a handsome house in the suburbs and the coach knocked at the door. The man who opened it was Jackie Robinson.

"I was in *shock*," Screen remembered, the awe still evident. The young Bill Clinton had once met JFK; Carlton Screen had touched Jackie Robinson's throwing hand. "His hair was so *white*."

Silvia Lavalas had also met Robinson, here at his school. He would come by occasionally to encourage the children. But the last years of the great second baseman's life had not been happy. His son, a recovering drug addict, died in a single-car crash on the Merritt Parkway at the age of twenty-four. The father's health deteriorated. Jack Roosevelt Robinson passed away in 1972 with the fire still inside him, much too young, at fifty-three. Alive today, he might have made a difference.

We sat a while and watched the kids tumble out into the front yard, to linger beneath the Freedom Riders, watched by two white policemen assigned to see seventeen hundred children safely home. I wondered what would happen to N—— tomorrow and if Moktar Aziz was okay.

"I've been in Flatbush for forty-three years," said Carlton Screen, Sr., when we got to talking about our old neighborhoods.

"Is anything here better than it used to be?" I asked him.

"Nothin," the Hall-of-Famer replied.

∾

From the Jackie Robinson School I wandered south. Behind me on the east side of Flatbush, just north of Lefferts Avenue, next to the old Bond bakery, was a wholesale beverage warehouse. On the wall above it, barely visible, was part of an old advertisement for the livery stables that must have occupied this site. Although a big cloth banner directing drivers to a nearby car wash obscured most of the sign, I could make out: "BUSES, VANS, HORSES FOR HIRE."

But the queue outside this building was not comprised of holidayers planning to go cantering in Prospect Park. Ten men, disheveled and apparently homeless, converged on a small open slot in the wall of the warehouse and pushed through hundreds of empty beer and soda cans and plastic containers. These were the Bottle People; this sidewalk was their Mercantile Exchange. I remembered the exhortations to thrift at the Dime Savings Bank: "Honors come by diligence. Riches spring from economy." Scavenging for empties was the slowest route to wealth I could imagine.

I reversed my route and crossed Empire. Below me was the site of the Malbone Wreck. The wall of the subway overpass had been decorated as a school-art project by the Robinsonians. It was purple and yellow and there were stars and moons and it said "PEACE" and, in Hebrew, "SHALOM," and what I assumed was the Arabic notation for the same general theme.

The southern gate of the Botanic Garden was just a few steps away. I went through the turnstile and strolled until I couldn't hear the Flatbush traffic any more and sat under a Chinese oleaster. A blue jay swooped just inches from my face. Passing me by, enjoying the sunshine, was Brooklyn at leisure: Hasidim, Hispanics, Haitians. A lissome blonde collegian sprawled on the grass with a canvas spread before her, dabbing at a watercolor of yellow irises. A brace of young Cantonese pawed each other on a bench.

A sign over the doorway of the Children's Garden House said: "HE IS HAPPIEST WHO HATH POWER / TO GATHER WISDOM FROM A FLOWER."

I was trying to steel myself for a trek I knew I had to take, once and alone: the mile-long walk up Flatbush Avenue as it sliced through Prospect Park. Taking a deep breath, I slid through the exit of the Botanic Garden and turned right, bound for Grand Army Plaza.

I walked north for a few hundred feet and saw a man coming toward me on the long, little-used sidewalk. He was wearing soiled jeans and a white Navy dress-uniform hat and, as I passed him, he wheeled around and began to follow me. This I did not like.

I was passing the Lefferts Homestead, and then the entrance to the zoo, which was still closed pending its metamorphosis into the Wildlife Conservation Center. The gates were shut and the bas-reliefs above them – scenes from Kipling's *Jungle Book*; Mowgli among the beasts – had been defaced by a creature named SPAR. On my right was the spiked iron fence of the Botanic Garden, which was papered and peppered with copious quantities of garbage hurled, apparently, from passing cars. A city ordinance required that business owners and landlords neaten their pavements regularly, but there were no shops along this empty stretch, and no homes save Arne Israel's Dutch farmhouse, so the trash was left alone to reproduce like rabbits.

I quickened my pace. The man in the Navy hat grew more distant. I relaxed a bit and looked over my shoulder only every thirty seconds instead of every five. After fifteen minutes, the Public Library loomed up on my right. I had made it.

The library was a handsome, welcome refuge. Kings and princes, dinosaurs and dragons danced above the entranceway in gilded silhouette. Inscribed at the cornerstone: "HERE ARE ENSHRINED THE LONGINGS OF GREAT HEARTS / AND NOBLE THINGS THAT TOWER ABOVE THE TIDE / THE MAGIC WORD THAT WINGED WONDER STARTS / THE GARNERED WISDOM THAT HAS NEVER DIED."

I filtered upstairs to a reading room where earnest students pored over books entitled *African Religions and Philosophy, Africa in Modern History, Slavery and Freedom*. Three boys with Whoopi Goldberg hair giggled and taunted a fourth, who, ignoring them, sat down to study.

On a shelf of books about the borough and the city, I learned more about the Malbone Wreck and the Battle of Brooklyn and the world of

Whitman's waterside. And I found a hopeful essay titled "Here Is New York" by E. B. White, from the years before the Bensonhurst murder and the Crown Heights riots:

> The citizens of New York are tolerant not only from disposition but from necessity. The city has to be tolerant, otherwise it would explode in a radioactive cloud of hate and rancor and bigotry. If the people were to depart even briefly from the peace of cosmopolitan intercourse, the town would blow up higher than a kite. In New York smolders every race problem there is, but the noticeable thing is not the problem but the inviolable truce.

Outside the reading room, along the mezzanine hallway, was a row of display cases, and these were dedicated to – what else? – the Brooklyn Dodgers. Books from the library's collection offered "oral history" and "illustrated tribute" to the bygone age. An artist named Alec Gillman had spent an enormous amount of time and energy on a series of scenes from old Ebbets Field. Jackie Robinson stole a base. Red Barber, the radio announcer, called the game from his famous "catbird seat."

It was all true. There really had been a dame named Hilda Chester who clonged a deafening cowbell in the balcony. There had been a Sym-Phony Band, a Knothole Gang for young fans, a woman named Mulvey who didn't miss a home game for thirty-three *years* (she was crowned Brooklyn's Ideal Mother). A perfervid zealot named Frank Gernano really had leapt from the stands to tackle and pummel Umpire Magerkurth.

Now each Brooklynite could choose a world to inhabit: Ebbets Field or Empire Boulevard, the past or the present, E. B. White's or Carlton Screen's. I left the library and crossed the street and waited for the southbound Flatbush Avenue bus.

A few steps away were Stanford White's Tuscan entrance pavilions, which appeared to have been the targets of hand grenades. Behind them was a statue I hadn't noticed before, when Debbie and I had shopped at the yuppie Greenmarket and explored Grand Army Plaza.

It was a likeness of James Stranahan, the man who hired Olmsted and Vaux to build Prospect Park for a young, confident Brooklyn. The statue faced north, toward the Soldiers' and Sailors' Memorial Arch and Lincoln and General Grant. Behind it were the vales where Washington's troops had waited for the British to charge, and the carousel and the Camperdown Elm and the gurgling Ravine where a man was shot in the back for a bicycle.

The inscription at the base of the Stranahan statue came from St. Paul's, London, and the tomb of Christopher Wren.

"Reader," it said to a searching son of Brooklyn, "if you seek my monument, look about you."

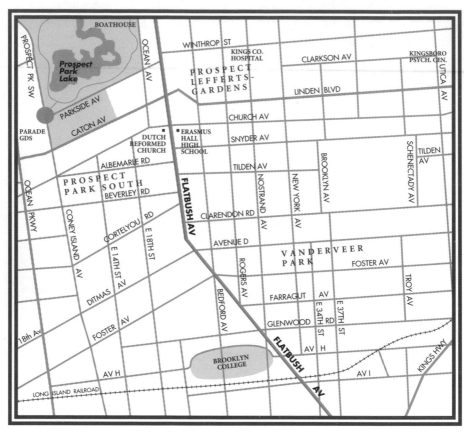

Chapter Four: The Bride of Flatbush Avenue

The Bride of Flatbush Avenue

1

The Bride of Flatbush Avenue examined me and smiled. I was riding home from the library one late afternoon on the B41 bus when I glanced out the window and her eyes met mine. She was standing alone near Martense Street, a stunning brunette, her hair put up and curled. She was wearing a diaphanous veil and a long white gown, and tenderly she held a single rose.

She was two stories tall. Once, the shop below her figure, which was painted on the front of a building, had sold "EVERYTHING FOR THE BRIDE" (I could just make this out from the old, obscured lettering). But now 866 Flatbush Avenue, a block from the center of a seventeenth-century Dutch village, midway between the East River and the ocean, was Two Brothers Electronics, and the brothers' big metal sign had been slapped across the Bride's lower half. Two windows had been cut through the red script name of the old Chéri Bridal shop, and it appeared that someone had fired rusty-brown paintballs at the lady herself, missing twice, then wounding her grievously in the left shoulder and abdomen. But still she smiled.

The corner of Flatbush Avenue and Martense Street was no place for a damsel to stand alone with no protection but a handful of thorns. Below her was the continuation of the frantic sidewalk bazaar that had begun at Fulton Street and had been interrupted by the disquieting tranquility of Prospect Park. Dozens of vendors sold identical T-shirts and sweatshirts, arrayed on blankets on the pavement: Chicago Bulls, New York Knicks, the ubiquitous Karl Kani-Jeans.

Joints and Blunts were being openly and casually sucked, bootleg cassettes and videos were being sold from the open doors of panel trucks, Mexicans were decapitating porgies in Korean seafood markets, and an old white man was pushing a shopping wagon full of shopping wagons, crying softly, "Ten dollars? Ten dollars? Ten dollars?"

A few yards to the south was the intersection of Flatbush and Church Avenue – formerly Cow Lane – which had been the heart of the Hollanders' orderly world. The Reformed Protestant Dutch Church of Flatbush with its perfect white steeple had been erected on the southwest corner in 1796. (There had been a house of Christian worship on this site since the 1650s.) On the southeast side were the neo-Gothic battlements of Erasmus Hall High School, alma mater of a constellation of famous daughters and sons that ran the gamut from Barbra Streisand and Beverly Sills to Bernard Malamud and Bobby Fischer. Enclosed in the Erasmus courtyard was the original wooden Academy, the oldest secondary school in New York State.

The northwest corner of Flatbush and Church was formerly the farm of a prominent old Flatbush family named Zabriskie. A handsome columned mansion had been demolished at the beginning of the twentieth century and replaced twenty-odd years later by the mammoth Kenmore Theater. This had been carved recently into four smaller screening rooms to better display the Technicolor crashes, cops, and carnage that passed for entertainment as the century concluded. To the northeast was a strip of Caribbean bakeries and restaurants, the Guyana Airways office, and a bank that had replaced a delectable landmark of my childhood, Garfield's Cafeteria.

This was the Village of Flatbush in the 1990s: touches of graceful antiquity scarcely noticed amid the wild commotion of the streets. Big blue buses of the Transit Authority huffed and fumed, embedded in the coagulated traffic, while fleet fleets of illicit "dollar cabs" and ten-passenger gypsy vans careened past them in the opposite lanes, then darted in and nipped off waiting riders like barracudas.

Storekeepers specialized in human hair, electronic "beepers," devotional jabberwocky, pseudo-African chemises, cow's-foot soup, or fiberglass fingernails. Everything in one shop cost ninety-seven cents; across the avenue, ninety-six. Old restaurants turned into banks; old banks turned into Lord-praising churches. There was a mosque in the basement of a supermarket. Old warehouses became windowless schools; old people became afraid to go outside.

It had been pastoral New Netherland, then colonial New York, then *haimishe* Brooklyn. Now it was Little Lagos, Petit Port-au-Prince, North

Port of Spain, and my old home town. In 1952, on the three hundredth anniversary of its foundation, Queen Juliana of the Netherlands visited little Flatbush village; shop windows were decorated with toy windmills and paper tulips. Thirty years ago, my friends and I bowled at Spinella's on Church Avenue, trooped to Garfield's for chopped-liver sandwiches, bought our baseball gloves at Friedman's across from Erasmus Hall High and our mohair bar-mitzvah suits at Sid's Pants. Aunt Cel took me to see *Around the World in 80 Days* at the fantabulous Loew's Kings. Classmates' birthday parties meant a stomach-stuffing sundae at an ice-cream parlor called Jahn's. A few of these places remained. Most had vanished into history as surely as the old Zabriskie farm.

The Bride of Flatbush Avenue had watched Schrafft's tea room become a blue-jeans store and the Moadinger Funeral Home turn into the Temple of Salvation. Macy's department store had been abandoned. Ebinger's Bakery was bricked over. The alleys had been ripped up at Spinella's, and now it was a party hall for Jamaican and Haitian Saturday-night saturnalias.

The streets were a frantic emporium by day and a killing zone by night. Businessmen were followed home, tied up, and robbed; or, locked in their own back rooms and cleaned out. Creative burglars bored their way through plaster roofs and walls. Less cerebral stickup men burst right in during office hours, waving machine guns. Taxi drivers, alone and unarmed, were picked off like partridges.

A note in *Brooklyn: Where to Go, What to Do, How to Get There*, published in 1991, said: "This isn't a Caribbean resort, so don't wear your latest mink-lined leather coat."

On a spring evening at 61 Martense Street, right under the eyes of my Bride, someone beat a woman to death and left her husband suffocating in his own blood. Then the building was set on fire as a finishing touch. But this was not remarkable for 1993. *Flatbush Life* gave it a paragraph.

"Come back at ten o'clock tonight," I was told one morning by a man who asked me for a dollar. "You'll get a whole book in one night."

That very night at 10:15 on old Cow Lane, the owner of a furniture store that had grown to be the largest Haitian-owned business outside Port-au-Prince locked his shop, sat down in his Mercedes-Benz, and was preparing to start for home when he was shot dead by a teenaged boy who mumbled a few words, pulled the trigger once, and walked away.

How had the oracle known?

I wasn't a witness. Mornings were my time. For ten weeks, I'd start out from East 31st Street, usually alone, sometimes with Little Debbie, at an hour when hit men dozed and honest shopkeepers primed for commerce. First pedestrian of the day, I kicked aside the chicken bones and negotiated the carpet of smashed beer bottles that made this new Flatbush seem the target of some perpetual Kristallnacht.

Walking, I met a voodoo shaman and the Caribbean Mother of the Year. I told the immigrants: "Imagine if *you* returned to *your* country after twenty-five years and everyone there was white and Jewish!"

No other place on earth could have changed so completely, so fast.

The new possessors of the Village of Flatbush had been here too briefly to shed their loneliness; like the Bajan carpenter at Genesis 1:29, they still dreamed of green fields and crickets. Their opposites, those few of the old residents who had not fled, saw only pillage and decay.

"It is no hyperbole to say that as Flatbush goes, so goes the city," Peter and Dennis Hamill wrote in the *Village Voice* in 1975. "And Flatbush is going."

On Easter Sunday, 1977, the Episcopal Bishop of New York admonished his flock: "Look over your city and weep, for it is dying."

But Flatbush had not gone and it had not died. It was violent but still vital, reconstituted yet recognizable to a native son. It was no paradise, and I could not vouch for the future. After all, I had chosen to make my own life in another place. But the Bride of Flatbush Avenue had kept a vigil. And never did she cry.

∾

South of Prospect Park the avenue made a slight course correction to correspond to the ancient Indian route from the woodlands to the sea. On the west side of Flatbush, right at the curve, sat a woman with a face like a Hindu temple carving and a voice like Ed Norton of "The Honeymooners."

Sister Teresa, Reader and Advisor.

She was sitting in the sun on a folding metal chair outside her storefront, talking into a modular telephone. I could see as I approached that behind her, in a dark little chamber, was a day-bed, and on it was lying an inert little fellow whom I assumed was Husband to the Sister, making him Brother-in-Law.

When Sister Teresa offered to bring out another folding chair, I accepted. We sat together at the door to her mysterious lair and chatted as she waved her flyers at pedestrians. In the shop window was a small collection of candles, statuary, and Go Away Evil ointments that a patron could purchase if the Advisor advised that Satan was on his way over in a dollar cab.

Teresa's mother was an Indian from India and her father was a Greek from Pittsburgh. She had grown up in Brooklyn – hers was no Pennsylvania accent – and she had moved to this location three years ago, after five years of professional prognostication further down Flatbush Avenue. She was rather egg-shaped, and she was wearing a long khaki skirt, bright pink socks, and tennis sneakers. Her confidence in her abilities was manifest.

"We just tell 'em the past, the present, and the future," she said firmly. "Nothing else."

Her little man emerged from the back room, eyed me up and down suspiciously, grunted, and went back in to rest from his exertion.

"What about telling your own fortune?" I asked.

"We don't do dat," she replied.

I could understand why. The past was gone, the present was grim, and her future here was not worth knowing. But she was rarely telling anyone else's fortune, either. Chronic unemployment left people with little disposable income to dispose of on Tarot-card readings. And the threat of violent crime was always present, although I assumed that Sister Teresa would know about any imminent holdup hours in advance.

"It's not the Flatbush Avenue everybody knows anymore," she said. "They got their gunshots. They got their killings. But they don't bother me."

"Why not?" I wondered.

Sister Teresa rapped her knuckles approvingly against a solid iron grate that could be lowered to encase her Little Shop of Auras.

"Dis," the Reader said.

I made my goodbyes and crossed the street. Here was another Haitian religious-goods store, the Midnight Star L'Étoile de Minuit. It appeared to serve a sizable catchment area, being the first such emporium I'd passed on Flatbush Avenue since La Botanique de Saint Jacques la Majeur about two miles back, but when I stopped at Midnight Star to peer into the display window, a man came out and said, "You are from Tax Department, I know, I know. But I cannot pay."

His name was Julio with a French *J*: ZHOO-leo. He was a slim, frenetic man in a dark-blue shirt, who chain-smoked Marlboros as he dragged me around his shop like a rag doll, having accepted my identification card from *la Société Radio-Canada* as proof that I was not a G-man sent to shut him down. Julio complained that business was extremely slow, pointed out water damage to his leaky ceiling that he could not afford to repair, showed me Come To Me Oil and Uncrossing Lotion – "If you feel hot curse, buy this, it take away" – and then he hauled me into a back room and picked up a bottle of magic *eau de toilette* and spritzed me until I smelled like Catherine Deneuve.

"You not Tax Department?" he asked again, just to make sure.

We were in his shrine. A table had been set up with fifteen large candles, all ablaze, and there were more lighted candles on the floor, along with a spindle of kite twine, a ball-peen hammer wrapped in a bolt of black velvet, and ten copper pennies. A small sofa faced a poster of a white woman who pressed her hands to a wound in her chest from which was shining the light of Heaven. This was Ézili Freda, a voodoo *lwa*, a representation of the Sorrowful Mary of Mount Calvary, and she was Julio's personal spirit, his life-guide, his charge, and his wife.

There was a row of photographs on the altar table. Julio picked each one up in turn and explained to me how Ézili Freda, through him, had helped the people in the photograph.

"She wants a man," he said of a dark, lovely client. Then: "This couple want get married." And, "Him t'ief in jail – mother want get him out."

And a Caucasian couple: "These white people in Europe, bridal couple. Wife got boyfriend. Husband come to me. He want her quit the shit."

How had Julio of the Midnight Star come to be possessed by the spirit of Ézili Freda? He had emigrated to the United States in 1984 and had sped directly to Flatbush, which was one of the three capitals of Haitian North America, the others being Miami and Montreal. He worked as a housekeeper, but illness kept knocking him down.

"I called my mother in Haiti," he said. "I told her, 'All time I go to work sick. All time I go to work sick. All time I go to work sick. All time I go to work sick.' She said, 'You have the spirit come from your father.' She told me to make food for the spirit. Make party. My father had the spirit. When he die, I get it.'"

In Brooklyn, Julio made a party for Ézili Freda. This was the means to propitiate the *lwa* and to invite her to speak and act through his flesh.

"After the party," Julio said, "I saw a woman who looked sick. She was too weak to hold her bag. I try my first spiritual job. I go to her home. I tell her, 'Don't be afraid.' I bathe her in some herbs. I do some pray."

"What happened?"

"She fine now."

Voodoo is a healing religion that places heavy responsibilities on those whom the spirits choose. Ézili Freda is a fancy dame; she requires perfumes, powder, and lace to keep her fresh and desirable.

Other spirits are more earthy, less dainty. There are Azaka in his peasant hat and Danbala the serpent. But all require food and drink, daily at the altar and occasionally at big community feasts. If neglected, they grow angry and seek revenge.

"Ézili, my spirit," Julio said, pointing to the poster. He picked up a gourd and began to shake it, and he chanted for a few seconds and said this was on behalf of the white European husband who wanted his wife to quit dipsy-doodling with her boyfriend.

"What's that twine on the floor used for?" I asked Julio.

"That's secret," he replied. "Can't tell you."

As quickly as we had gone into the altar room, we exited, and now I was shoved into another small chamber that was the same but different. Here, the benevolent smile of Ézili Freda was replaced by a skull-and-crossbones wall hanging. Also, there were more statues of various Catholic saints, more pennies were scattered about, and an incense burner was going full tilt.

"This voodoo," Julio explained.

"Why the skull and crossbones?" I wondered.

"Devil spirit. If you no pay, whatever nationality you are, he kill you. Is like any man shoot, shoot, shoot people."

"Like Brooklyn?" I jibed.

"Brooklyn," Julio said, "too many t'iefs."

In 1893, after 240 years in the New World, the Lefferts family decided to dismember its estate and sell it off as building lots. It was a time of flux in Flatbush. The tiny, isolated village, where swine once outnumbered citizens and the Dutch language was spoken in pew and pulpit, had been shaken by the coming of the Brighton Beach railroad and the opening of Prospect Park. The bitterly contentious issue of political union with the City of Brooklyn was being debated; within a year, the village would be absorbed. Already, the New York *Herald* was reporting that Flatbush had "all the necessary improvements," and was describing it as:

> The most beautiful of any suburb of New York or Brooklyn – with grand old trees, shady lanes, and velvety lawns, where almost every old house has a story dating back to the Revolution, the famous battle of Long Island, and sometimes beyond that to the first Dutch settlers and Indians. Flatbush is a lovely place both to the lover of nature and the reader of history. There is a sleepy, comfortable repose about the quaint town, and the street cars and gas lamps on Flatbush Avenue, once the "King's Highway," are modern improvements which seem very much out of place.

Whatever isolationist tendencies the Dutchmen might once have possessed, however, were overwhelmed by the profit to be made by selling land and houses. And so the Leffertses made way for Progress, as did the Bergens and Martenses and Vanderbilts and Zabriskies and all the other landed Flatbush clans whose names now endured only on street signs. The Lefferts mansion, which had stood on the east side of Flatbush Avenue not far from Sister Teresa's studio, was moved a half-mile north into Prospect Park and turned into a museum. The old farmstead was divided into six hundred lots. Small commercial buildings were permitted on the avenue itself, but the rest of the estate was restricted to single-family houses.

Those detached houses remained – owners who attempted to subdivide were sued for breach of covenant – and so did handsome rows of brownstone, brick, and limestone town homes. When these were built, in 1910, advertisements in the *New York Times* noted that they came equipped with burglar alarms and called them "the original no-basement houses – only one flight of stairs for the tired housewife to climb." The whole area had been declared an Historic District called Prospect–Lefferts Gardens.

This zone was now watched over by a community group called the Prospect–Lefferts Gardens Neighborhood Association, or PLEGNA, and it was on my first visit to the PLEGNA office on Flatbush Avenue that I heard a woman brag of the district's livability by saying, "Crime is getting *much* better. We have shootings, but not shooting where death occurs."

The woman, a ball of fire named Gloria Thomas, was the kind of activist who could keep a neighborhood from going to the dogs just by standing with her hands on her considerable hips and shouting, "Cut the crap!" She found apartments for poor people who had been evicted and summer jobs for rootless teens, managed the nightly PLEGNA Civilian Patrol, organized an annual street fair, and, in a candid moment, revealed to me that, despite her dynamic personality, she still, at thirty-five, had "no kids and no man."

Regarding the safety of the streets outside her storefront headquarters, Gloria noted that a whole year had passed since any police officer had been shot in Prospect–Lefferts Gardens.

"We're getting a lot of drug arrests and a lot of dealers evicted," she said. "We used to have shootings *constantly* – every *week*. The kids still have arms, but now they go up on the roofs and fire them off. So you could walk down the street with children and not get shot."

I made the PLEGNA office a regular stop on my long, long walks. One day, Gloria introduced me to an older woman named Mrs. Haynes who had come from Jamaica to Brooklyn in the late sixties and was still here, twelve children, forty grandchildren, and fourteen great-grandchildren later. They and the rest of the staff were trying to decide whether there existed anywhere on the planet a better place to live than Prospect–Lefferts Gardens.

Mrs. Haynes had been to the State of Washington, where one of her sixty-six immediate descendants resided, and she reported that, out there, "You don't hear any fire engines, and if you spread a blanket in a park and have a picnic, white people eat with black people and there's no prejudice."

"I know one place where there's no shootings," I said. (I was thinking of Japan.)

"I do, too," Gloria Thomas interjected. "In your grave."

"In the Dominican Republic," continued Gloria, "you walk out in the sun, have a sunstroke, and fall down and nobody takes the money out of your pocket. They're poor but they live *way* better than us."

"When I lived in North Carolina," said a slim man on a chair in the corner, "nobody ever stole nothing."

"It's all because of drugs," Gloria declared. "Most of the drugs we have here in New York comes in on military planes."

"It comes in on the *President's* plane," said the slim man from Carolina. "They never check it."

"Diplomats," Gloria threw in. "They can't touch *those* suckers. They got immunity. They all bringing in drugs."

I was invited to join the Civilian Patrol, which was supposed to be a senior-junior enterprise with both young and old people touring the Historic District at sundown in PLEGNA's maroon van. But the youth of Lefferts Gardens had lost interest in the project, so I wound up in the van with Horace Smith, who had migrated from Sparta, Georgia, to work in a knitting mill fifty-two years earlier, and Eddie Babb, who came from Philadelphia to see the 1939 World's Fair and never went back home.

They were two benign gentlemen, whose assignment was to roll up and down the narrow, treelined streets of the old Lefferts property, checking for potholes, burned-out streetlights, abandoned cars, and, as Mr. Babb put it, "gangs hangin' around."

The Civilian Patrol was duly deputized by the police department. We were in radio contact with the 71st Precinct, and we had been given a yellow flasher to mount on top of the van. Slowly we serpentined up one block and down the other, passing the splendid residences of Midwood Street, where Beverly Sills grew up, and the basketball courts on Winthrop, which were alive with shouting, leaping men, and Beekman Terrace, where Lainie Kazan's father was a bookie, and a hardware store on Lefferts Avenue that had been held up a couple of nights earlier by a man with a high-powered rifle. There were more murals – Malcolm X, Frederick Douglass, maps of Africa – and everywhere knots of young men drinking Heineken beer from green glass bottles and women sitting on their stoops in the gloaming.

It was what the television people called the "Golden Hour." But soon the sun collapsed behind the sixteen-story apartment towers of Patio Gardens on the west side of Flatbush. When we turned back onto Flatbush Avenue Eddie Babb said, "I just hope we don't drive into a shootout."

Such a fusillade had occurred a couple of nights earlier, on Caton Avenue, which was one of the blocks the maroon van regularly traveled. A Cadillac automobile was noticed by the uniformed police to be weaving erratically. On closer examination, this was explained by the fact that the three men in the vehicle had been shot variously in the eye, back, leg, head, and arm. According to *Flatbush Life*, the men claimed they had been innocently driving down a side street off Caton "when bullets flew through their car."

In Brooklyn, New York, Eddie Babb, who had been a freight shipper on the Baltimore and Ohio Railroad, looked out the window of his van at the clusters of young men on Maple Street and said, "They're wastin' their lives away. They don't seem to have any ambition. They just stand around till the police have to come to move them along. They don't even pick up a book . . ."

2

Not far from the painting of the Bride of Flatbush, I went into a fish store. This was Korean-owned. Most green-groceries and seafood markets were. A Mexican man tended the counter, and two more *campesinos* worked at a sink in the back, cleaning kingfish, parrot fish, butterfish, croakers. Koreans often hired Mexicans, I read in *New York Magazine*. It was a matter of simple economics; Mexicans worked cheapest. The radio was tuned to a country station, and Trisha Yearwood was singing "Walkaway Joe."

The fish store had been subdivided. One side was a kiosk five feet wide and thirty feet deep, lined with the same caps, T-shirts, and Karl Kani sweatshirts that the unlicensed vendors sold from the sidewalk. The Korean stood poised at the front of this chamber. He never let anyone maneuver him to the rear.

"I know what they do," he said. He had been robbed four times already. He said, "Flatbush Avenue a very dangerous place. All the time, every hour, every day, shooting. Brooklyn is a war."

The Korean didn't want his name mentioned. He invited me to feel a lump in his neck. It was shrapnel, lodged too close to the jugular to be removed. He spoke in a Louis Armstrong rattle and said that eight other pieces of steel were scattered throughout his body. A blue shred of metal was working its way out of his left arm.

But that was from Vietnam. South Korea had sent its boys to fight there, too.

"Why do you stay here?" I asked him.

"Two kids in Catholic college," the Korean replied. "One more year. One more year."

There was a clothing store nearby called WHY AND A ½. The name intrigued me. I went inside. The owner was a twenty-four-year-old Syrian Jew named David Esses. The Syrian Jews clustered along Ocean Parkway in a neighborhood that was popularly called Aleppo-in-Flatbush. They were an insular community. They went to the same synagogues, their sons married each other's daughters, they summered at the same resort in New Jersey.

David Esses had been on a buying trip to Hong Kong and had seen a store there with the unusual name. So he borrowed it. He had two other ladies'-wear shops within four blocks on Flatbush. One was called Mona and one was Rich-Rach, which is Hebrew for zipper. He hoped to use these stores as a launching pad for a major chain. But he was not encouraged.

Flatbush, David Esses said, was "a one-way ticket to hell."

He had learned this the hard way.

"I had a person follow me home," he said. Esses was a stocky young fellow, with his hair well-greased and slicked back in the current style, like the actor Steven Seagal. "It was like a movie. He pulled his gun and followed me in the door and held me and my whole family up. My brother was upstairs, and he and my mother heard what was going on and they called 911. By the time the police came, the guy was gathering the money and the jewelry.

"The police were waiting for him at the front door. He ran to the back and shot the glass out of the patio door. They caught him in the back yard.

"Now I take a different route home every night. I make an extra turn here and there. It wasn't so bad for me, really. Some people they follow all the way from Manhattan."

At WHY AND A ½, there was a uniformed security guard for daytime operations and steel plates in the ceiling and side walls to keep the night crawlers at bay. David Esses sold what he described as "moderate junior" dresses, blouses, and slacks, and wrote off 12 per cent of his stock to shoplifting. It wasn't Armani, but it wasn't T-shirts that said "Lick It, Roll It, Smoke It," either.

It seemed a contradiction: to try to nurture a growing business while expecting the district in which it was located to blow up higher than a kite. David Esses was certain of the impending calamity. He called Flatbush "a place ready to burst, in five or ten years, max." He expected "a heavy-duty riot." All it would take was a blackout, a blowup, a Rodney King.

"What could cool it off?" I asked.

"That's not possible," said the clothier.

∾

In the mid seventies, when my mother and Fred Lucci had operated a small convenience shop they called Hennie's on Avenue D in East Flatbush, the neighborhood was said to be "changing." Hennie's was a block from my father's old Abel Brothers soda fountain and newsstand, which by then had been sold off to Koreans. "Changing" meant that black families were moving in. It was a euphemism for "panicking."

Crime had been unheard of. As late as 1968, the precinct closest to our apartment recorded zero homicides. The East 31st Street boys – we called ourselves "the Bombers" – would walk home from Prospect Park after ice-skating on a Friday night, or ride The Beast from Yankee Stadium after an extra-innings night game, without a thought of being set upon and dismembered. But this was no longer possible. The streets along which my father and I walked at dawn on our way to open up Abel Brothers were now the same streets where *Flatbush Life* reported "NO REFUGE FROM GUNFIRE."

It only required one incident to turn a blithe stroller into a petrified stay-at-home. By the time I got back to Brooklyn, that one incident had happened to almost everyone I met. Except me.

Fred Lucci was crossing Avenue I one evening when he heard two men say, "Let's get him!" Luckily, Fred was in the habit of carrying a long iron pipe, hidden in his trouser leg. He went at the men before they could spring, felled one guy with a blow to the neck. They ran away.

One morning at Hennie's, my mother came in to find that the place had been burglarized. She called the police. After they took her deposition and left, she went into the back room to rest on the cot she kept there.

Out from under the bed jumped a male white. He waved a pistol. Instead of screaming, my mother interviewed the thief.

"Why are you doing this?" she asked her potential murderer.

"I got to have money," he said.

Then he demanded cigarettes. My mother asked him which brand he preferred and made sure to give him a book of matches.

After Freddie died, my mother found work at a medical-supply warehouse that was owned by Hasidic Jews. One of the bosses left work one afternoon and was followed to a parking lot on Flatbush Avenue. There, as he walked to his car, someone came up and shot him in the head. He survived. But he's not the same.

∾

In its heyday, Jahn's Ice Cream Parlor on Church Avenue, two doors east of Flatbush, made Abel Brothers look like a child's lemonade stand. At our store, I served up hundreds of egg creams and malted milks and even the occasional two-scoop frappé when a customer was feeling flush enough to spring for forty-five cents. But Jahn's was in another league. It offered a selection of extravagant sundaes that culminated in the world-famous six-dollar "Kitchen Sink," an Annapurna of flavors and toppings that was served in a brass bassinet large enough for Olympic water polo.

History had a way of evening things out. Abel Brothers, it was true, was now the Wing Hing Loon Variety Store. But although there still was a Jahn's on Avenue U in Flatlands, the Church Avenue parlor had become a Guyanese restaurant and bakery called Sybil's.

The first time I ate lunch at Sybil's, I ordered chicken roti – curry wrapped in a sheet of pastry – and a Jamaican Natural Pineapple Soda. Jamaican Natural, the label admitted, was 100 per cent artificially flavored.

The second time, I tried "spinach with shrimp," which was a metal casserole of greens with tiny, chewy, salty prawns, served with a separate steel dish of rice and two pieces of fried plantain.

The third time, I settled for a slice of sponge cake, and finally, I met Sybil. She was a round-faced, sincere woman with perfect copper-colored fingernails, dark Bengali skin, and twenty-three grandchildren, though she looked younger than I did. She had come to the Promised Land in 1969 to study hairdressing, leaving nine children behind in northern South America, and, since then, she had been a housemaid and a jewelry clerk and now she was a tycoon, the owner of a tavern and four bakery-restaurants, the Guyanese Howard Johnson.

"Sybil Bernard-Kerutt," said the *New York Carib News*, "is no ordinary woman."

She had just been named the community newspaper's Caribbean-American Mother of the Year. The accompanying story said: "She is Guyanese-born and is the embodiment of the island's resource. Her character is as sparkling as the island's gold. Her determination – far-reaching as its mudlands. Her enthusiasms – fiery as a bowl of pepper-pot. Her smile – pretty as an island sunset."

Guyana, of course, was not an island, but no one was quibbling. Sybil Bernard-Kerutt was the model immigrant I had been expecting to encounter when I went into the Korean fish store and the clothing shop WHY AND A ½. She had come up with nothing, had worked and studied and saved and sent for her children, and she had prospered. Prospered, that is, until the day her second husband, whom she had met after coming to New York, was kidnapped.

"He went out in back of the restaurant to get his car keys," Sybil remembered. "Three boys kicked him and knocked him down. They took him to our house, tied us all up, and robbed us. Then they took him *back* to the restaurant and took *everything* we had here."

That was in 1985. But Sybil Bernard-Kurett did not abandon Flatbush. She said, "We have to live *somewhere*." Her daughters managed the various establishments. Even after severe arthritis and a hip replacement, she stood for hours beside the ovens in the enervating heat, packaging fresh rolls and buns. But she never walked out the front door of her restaurant on Church Avenue. She drove to a lane behind the bakery and drove back home again at the end of the day.

"I'm not free," she said.

Still, the Bernard-Kuretts, like the others, tied their fate to the Flatbush Plank Road. Yellow banners fluttered from lampposts, promoting "Brooklyn's Biggest Shopping Avenue." Aside from the certainty of armed brigandage and the prospect of violent death, it remained a pretty good place to do business.

Even a Mother of the Year had chosen this as a place to make her fortune.

"With nine kids, and all the grandchildren, it's still a struggle," the tycoon said, with a shrug and an island-sunset smile. "But, you know, I've paid for *nine* weddings. I would have been pretty 'up there,' if I didn't have so many."

3

For the first two hundred years of Flatbush history, except for the collapse of Dutch rule, the Battle of Brooklyn, the British occupation, and the burning of the Town Hall, not a heck of a lot happened. (History, of course, was a European invention. The Canarsees didn't have any.) Farmers farmed, slaves slaved, preachers preached, and, in their spare time, everyone repaired to the village green for a lively game of "Clubbing the Cat."

This was a contest that involved one barrel, several players, and one extremely unfortunate feline. The cat was sealed in the cask, which was suspended from a rope tied between two stakes.

> Then a line was drawn on the ground or a long pole was laid down to show the distance from which the "throwing" was allowed. Now number one stepped forward with his club, which he threw with great force at the barrel. The winner was he who broke the cask and let the cat escape.
>
> Sometimes the cat, too dazed or frightened to jump out of the barrel when it was split open, only fell out.

When that happened, everyone yelled "Bor-ing!" in Old High Dutch and ran off to play "Pulling the Goose."

With pleasures such as these, with bounteous crops of tobacco and barley, and with the Canarsees having sold their land for a few flannel shirts and buckets of seashells and gone obligingly away, it was no wonder that, in 1661, a Dutchman named Jacob Steendam could write of the colony:

> New Netherlands, thou noblest spot of earth,
> Where bounteous Heaven ever poureth forth
> The fullness of his gifts, of greatest worth,
> Mankind to nourish.

It is the land where milk and honey flow;
Where plants distilling perfume grow;
Where Aaron's rod with budding blossoms blow;
A very Eden.

What he did not know was that three years later New Netherland would be defunct, and Governor Peter Stuyvesant, the peg-legged thunderer, would give Eden to the British without a shot being fired. Or, more precisely, only one shot – at the corner of Flatbush and Church.

In the summer of 1664, Governor Stuyvesant learned, to his considerable dismay, that King Charles II of England had awakened one morning with the bright idea of awarding to his brother James, Duke of York, all of Long Island, the Hudson River, and the territory between the Connecticut River and Delaware Bay, even though all of this was Dutch property and had been for fifty-five years. A few weeks later, a flying squadron of English ships appeared in New Amsterdam harbor, and Stuyvesant, playing coy, sent their commander a note that said, in effect, "What's a nice flotilla like you doing in a port like this?"

While the governor tried to stall for time, the English fanned out to tell the inhabitants that the takeover was a done deal. An officer named Scott rode into Flatbush "with colors flying, drums beating and trumpets sounding."

Whereupon, he stepped out, ordered the troop to approach and made a long harangue in the English language, the substance whereof was that the Dutch unjustly occupied this country; that it was his majesty's; if the inhabitants would acknowledge him as their sovereign that they might remain; otherwise leave.

Since nobody in the village had understood a word of what he said, Scott then led his men to the blockhouse, ordered that its only cannon be taken from its mount and thrown to the ground, then had it set up again at a different embrasure – the "King's Port" – and fired once to celebrate the end of the Dutch era.

Then he rode north to Brooklyn and made another speech, this time with Dutch translation, vowing that "I will stick my rapier in the guts of any man who says this is not the King's land." Peter Stuyvesant got the message. The King's land it was.

Under British rule, the Dutchmen kept their farms, their language, their slaves, and their religion. A brewery was opened without opposition because, as Dr. Strong noted in 1842, "the principle of total abstinence from all that can intoxicate was not then known or practiced." Stocks and a whipping post were erected and used principally to discipline slaves. And Flatbush witnessed its first murder.

The victim was an Indian who lived in the cellar of the Martense family farm. This man, it seems, had taken part in a killing or killings on Staten Island before being brought to Flatbush. He, in turn, was done in by a group of Indians from said island who succeeded, Dr. Strong told us, in "glutting their revenge." After that excitement, the burghers settled down and occupied themselves in planting, child-rearing, and "certain difficulties of an ecclesiastical character."

∾

At the nucleus of the village, the corner of Flatbush and Church, then and now and forever, stood the emblem of Flatbush and the testament of the past and the possible. On weekdays, as the bedlam of the new Brooklyn roared and backfired around it, the Reformed Protestant Dutch Church seemed to close its eyes and bury its head, praying the nightmare would pass. Layabouts and dope dealers clogged its steps; Haitian peasant women hung racks of frilly pastel dresses from its fences and squatted on the curb, awaiting trade. The Majik Man ice-cream truck, replacing wonderful Jahn's, installed itself before the locked church doors, and its loudspeaker played "Teddy Bears' Picnic." And once, passing on the B41, I saw the religious zealot I had encountered on the Fulton Street Mall on Preakness Day, sermonizing to the passing parade on the blackness of Solomon and Christ.

But on a Sunday morning, an hour before the call to worship in pews two centuries old, I could almost imagine the corner of Flatbush and Church as the core of a city of hope. It was quiet and still, and the graveyard behind the Sanctuary invited me to enter and disabuse my fears. With my back to the sun and my ears to the silence, I sat for a few minutes on the tomb of a man named Charles Clarkson and waited to go inside the church, to learn what sort of people still knelt here, and what blessings they beseeched.

I moved among the markers and kicked last autumn's oak and ginkgo leaves from paths untrodden and slabs unread. All the founding families were here – Gerritsen, Martense, Ditmars, Schenck, Van Buren, Vanderveer, Bergen. They and their forebears had been pioneers and drunks, slaveholders, washerwomen, hostesses, divines, yeomen, mechanics, gossips, cat-clubbers, and stillborn babes. They had crossed the ocean, heard a cannon announce that their New Netherland was moot, watched their farmsteads burn as the army of the English king advanced on Washington's ragtags. In fading inscriptions on brown Brooklyn stone, I saw how their language had melted away, immersed in the anglophone sea. A stone from 1785 was carved: "Hier Leydt / Begraaven het lichaam / Van Jeremyas Van Der Bilt." But fifteen years later: "Here lieth / all that was mortal / of two lovely promising boys."

The cemetery, which seemed to have been spared vandalism, was bordered on the east by Flatbush Avenue and on the north by Church Avenue, where, two days before I came to Sunday service, a father of two lovely promising girls had been accidentally killed by crossfire during an attempted robbery of a check-cashing store. This was not a good neighborhood. But for now, the street was quiescent; I heard crows in the trees and then the carillon played "Ode to Joy."

I was, of course, neither Reformed, Protestant, nor Dutch. In Stuyvesant's time, that would have been cause for deportation; the governor considered Jews "usurious and covetous" and commanded that they take their "abominable religion" back to Europe. But Amsterdam overruled him. The Jews stayed.

Everyone else in the Wooded Flat (not counting the slaves and Indians) was united in one faith. The first wooden church was erected here in 1654. A stone building went up in 1699. Members of the congregation, if they had paid the proper fee while living, were interred right under the floor. Its steeple bell tolled the approach of the British in 1776. After the Battle of Brooklyn, the dead were dragged from the woods and buried where I now sat.

I left the dear departed and moved to the front steps of the Reformed

Church. Timidly, and ashamed of my Dockers and Rockports – I hadn't brought a jacket or even a tie with me from Toronto – I accepted an Order of Worship from a man at the central pair of white double doors and went inside. The church, which was rather plainly decorated, with an arched ceiling and four stained-glass windows along the north and south walls, was filling nicely. There was an organ loft, and four white choristers appeared in royal blue robes. A plaque memorialized the patriot dead of the Battle of Brooklyn, "buried beneath this church."

Two rows from the rear, I slid into a pew, positioned myself behind a pillar, and tried to stay out of sight.

It was Membership Recognition Sunday, a time for the congregation to commemorate faithful attendance and lifelong service to the church. The list of honorees surprised me – one woman had been coming here for *seventy* years, and several others for thirty or forty – because it testified that not all the descendants of old Flatbush had fled for safer soil. Most of the worshipers filing in were Caribbean immigrants, as I had expected. But scattered here and there were men and women who must have known Church Avenue in the era of the streetcar and the milk wagon, decades before the Phillies Blunts and stray bullets at the check-cashing store.

Two ministers, one white and one black, moved to the pulpit. The latter, Mr. Felix Busby, joined us for the processional hymn – "Saviour, Like a Shepherd Lead Us" – and then excused himself, because he had to pitch a benediction to the Opening Day crowd of the Prospect Park baseball league.

Pastor Daniel D. Ramm remained with us to guide the morning devotions of an earnest, multi-hued flock. He asked us to pray for the people of Haiti and Liberia and to remember a woman named Urania Phillips, who was ill. He reminded us that a certain Wally – everyone seemed to know him – had a date in court in the coming week. We were to pray, the Reverend Ramm said, "that this be the last time."

We were invited to stand and shake the hands of our neighbors. This kind of mandatory fellowship was unnatural to the Abels – my mother would be hissing, "Oh, *brother*" – but I glued on a smile and told each person who came to me how I hoped that Urania would recover and Wally get off with just a small fine.

At the head of the honor roll was a woman named Miss G———. She had been baptized here, seventy years earlier, at the same font on a different planet. She was white-haired, tiny, and bent. Kissing her, Pastor Daniel D. Ramm blushed as red as a strawberry sundae. Younger parishioners followed her and were given plaques and citations.

Inside the Reformed Protestant Dutch Church of Flatbush, an organ played and a hundred voices joined in harmony. Then the service concluded. Dispatching us, the Reverend Ramm asked his Creator: "Send us forth, unto these sometimes mean streets, with hearts that can see beyond the evil, the filth, and the grime."

Behind me as the doors opened, I heard Majik Man roll up to the curb and the tinkle of "Teddy Bears' Picnic." It was Sunday noon at Church and Flatbush. The city was awake.

∾

Miss G—— still lived within a hundred yards of the church where she had been baptized, seventy years before. Behind the graveyard and the parsonage were Kenmore and Albemarle terraces, two elegant lanes lined with handsome row houses that had been designated an Historic District on their own. It was easily possible to travel along Flatbush Avenue without ever guessing that they existed. (I had, a thousand times.) And a side gate tucked at a corner of the cemetery allowed observant residents of the terraces to stroll toward the performance of their weekly oblations without having to enter 1993 at all.

The American Institute of Architects' guide called Albemarle Terrace "a cul-de-sac that says dead end but is far from dead." Another book labeled Kenmore Terrace "charming." The former was a jaunty series of attached houses, their doors and shutters painted a whimsical pink or blue or forest green. The latter was more sober-minded, a row of brick Garden City town homes, built in 1917 and containing some of the earliest built-in garages in New York City. The presence of these houses – and the graceful 1853 parsonage, which was better suited to antebellum New Orleans than anarchic Brooklyn – was as unexpected as a soufflé at Sybil's or a Halston at WHY AND A ½.

I had met Miss G—— after church and had indicated my hope to visit with her behind the leaded bay windows of her home. But each time I telephoned to make an appointment, she was "swamped with company" or "going to New Jersey," and I soon got the message.

"What's it like to live around there for so long and go to the old Dutch church?" I asked her on the phone, conceding that I wouldn't get a face-to-face interview.

"Where else am I going to go to church?" she replied.

I imagined myself at her age, alone in the Wooded Flat, and realized that this was, of course, exactly my mother's situation. But my mother didn't have a Garden City row house or the protection of humble faith.

On a more practical level, she didn't have Freddie's iron pipe any more, either.

∾

A week after my visit to the Reformed Protestant Dutch Church, I again set out along Flatbush Avenue on a Sunday morning, seeking the seekers of grace. I didn't have to go far. Just around the corner from my mother's apartment, I was stopped by an elderly Chinese woman who thrust into my hand a small blue pamphlet inviting me to the Glad Tidings Tabernacle, "A place where God meets man."

Just then, as if on cue, a deep and disturbing rumbling was heard behind me, to the south. It grew louder and louder until the sky was filled with a continuous thunder, booming on a cloudless day. I looked down at the little blue pamphlet – "Forsake all your sin and cry to God for pardon!" – and wondered if this roar was a sign from Heaven, but then I turned and saw the supersonic Concorde, climbing out of Kennedy Airport in Queens to the east, banking steeply southward, bound for London's Heathrow.

I walked on, kicking through the crystal snowflakes of Crazy Horse and Colt .45 bottles that had been shattered in some Saturday-night sidewalk revelry. I passed a woman selling flamboyant gladioli from a supermarket shopping cart, a beckoning "dollar cab" driver in Rajiv Gandhi pyjamas, and vending machines filled with twenty-five-cent trolls with rainbow hair in tiny plastic capsules, the same dolls my baby sister would plead and cry and whine for, when first they hit the marketplace in 1962.

Like a snake asleep on a checkerboard, the avenue imposed itself across the orderly coordinates of Brooklyn, creating weird polygons and angles, and it was at one of these multiple intersections that I truly entered the kingdom of the faithful. Within fifty yards of the junction of Flatbush and Rogers avenues and Farragut Road, I counted five separate houses of worship, opening their doors this one time in the week, and in the next block were at least four more.

None was a church with a steeple and parsonage, or a graveyard to hold the dust of risen souls. These were storefronts and converted restaurants and offices, some decorated and sanctified for worship, others mere empty rooms with folding chairs arranged before a clapboard pulpit. Some had proper signs and stained-glass paneling and neon crucifixes; others one could pass on a Monday and mistake for yet more spray-painted, tumble-down testimony to the death of Flatbush Avenue.

There was an Église de Dieu, a Church of Christ, an Église Baptiste d'Israel, a Liberty Hall Church of God. There was the Église Baptiste Clarté Céleste; "*Fortifie-toi et prends courage,*" its marquee encouraged me.

And more: a Sunday School in the historic old Farragut Theater, which had been erected in 1920, converted in the fifties into a bowling alley, and was now the neighborhood YMCA, still preserving, high on its cherry-red facade, the lyres and lions and mad screaming jester of its randy vaudeville days. Then, the Église de Dieu Bérée and, finally, the Beulah Tabernacle of the Church of God in Christ Jesus of the Apostolic Faith, Inc.

When I had fortified myself and taken courage – wherever I went, I'd be a gate-crasher – I made my decision on which church service to audit. I picked the Trinity New Testament Assembly, on the east side of Flatbush, between Custom Plexiglas and a Haitian men's lodge called L'Alpha et L'Oméga #1. An interloping paleface in disrespectful Levi's, I assumed a metal chair at the back of the whitewashed, unadorned chamber and smiled at everyone, broadcasting my nervous nonchalance. A leaflet at the door averred: "We sincerely want to be your friend." And it was so.

I had arrived during the weekly hour of informal Bible study. Two groups of ten communicants, mostly women and girls impeccably attired, were seated in tight clusters. Straining to catch a phrase here and there, while coyly pretending to read a parochial newspaper called *The Beacon* ("Former Muslims Share Testimonies at Banquet"), I heard a woman in one of the circles saying, "Jesus came for the Jews, but they refused him . . . same for the Jews today – there is a provision that they can come back to God, like the Prodigal Boy . . . there is a path provided, even for the Jews today . . ."

And from other group, a man's deep baritone: ". . . the reason why the Jews never accept the Messiah . . ."

I looked up. "I am from Nigeria," a woman said, standing over me in a gown as white as starlight. She breathed gratitude to God for pointing me to this place. Behind her, the two study groups closed their Bibles and stood up and began to sing without accompaniment: "Jesus, Jesus, Jesus, / Sweetest name I know / Fills my every longing, / Keeps me singing as I go."

"Praise God!" people shouted randomly, like the sudden outbursts of the horseplayers at the littered OTB.

Then a woman came to me and suggested that I go downstairs to meet Floyd Love.

Downstairs was a low-roofed chamber filled with the concentrated exultation of twenty small children whose Sunday School had just concluded. Floyd Love, a twenty-year-old African-American in a black jacket and peach silk shirt, a business major at Medgar Evers College, was their instructor. His mission, he said, was "to grow them up in the church till they get to know right from wrong and Heaven from Hell."

Freed from their catechism, the boys and girls were now screaming like the engines of the British Airways Concorde and bouncing off the chapel walls like quarks in a cyclotron.

"I have to try to save them through love, not condemnation," Brother Love went on, above the din. "There's no point in telling them they're going to burn in Hell." But it was too late to rescue some of the youth of the new Flatbush, at least in the flesh on a Sunday morning at the Trinity New Testament Assembly.

"Many of my friends are dead," Floyd Love said. "One was shot at a party. One was cleaning his own gun. One got shot trying to be the hardest man in Brooklyn."

"Are you the hardest man in Brooklyn?" I asked.

The teacher smiled. "The Devil has made sin very attractive," he admitted.

It wasn't easy being Floyd Love. He said he had suffered a lot of "shame, embarrassment, and persecution" from friends who, like Mae West, when confronted with two evils, always chose the one they hadn't tried.

"Christ said, 'If *I* gotta go through with it, *you* gotta go through with it,'" the young disciple stated of his battle for restraint. I had self-discipline, too – I'd never smoked a joint or fired a gun – but I had grown up in a bygone Brooklyn, where the worst shame was striking out with the bases loaded, or being too queasy to down the last scoop of a Kitchen Sink at Jahn's. Around here, these days, it wasn't easy being *anyone.*

Bowing and beaming to every person I passed, exchanging blessings, the consummate imposter, I made my way back up the stairs and out of the Trinity Assembly. Now, at noon, the streetscape was filled with tinny music that emanated from the open door of the Église de Dieu de Bérée, where three men stood on a tiny stage, plucking guitars before a deep, densely packed crowd. And when these strains ebbed for a second, I heard another melody coming from the Creole church across the street, and people singing, "*Non! Jamais tout seul.*" Never alone. "*Je ne suis jamais tout seul . . .*"

Parked on the west side of Flatbush was an old GM bus with New Jersey plates whose destination sign read, "JESUS IS LORD." It had brought a load of worshipers from Newark to the weekly tabernacle at the Farragut Manor banquet hall in the Borough, formerly the City, of Churches.

I walked closer and basked in the music and the warm, heavy midday light. On Flatbush Avenue, Sunday mornings were the best, the hour when Faith mugged Fear. Lettered on the side of the bus were words to Love by: "YOU DON'T HAVE TO TAKE THE DEVIL'S JUNK."

4

This may or may not count as a religious experience, but a theater down the street from the Reformed Dutch Church was where I once saw the Three Stooges on stage. It was 1962, and my role models were a bit superannuated for their chosen line of work. But they were not nearly as mawkish in person as the motion picture that occasioned their promotional appearance, an astronomical Ishtar entitled *The Three Stooges in Orbit.*

The setting for my remote encounter with the Stooges – I was about fifty rows from the stage, as the pie flies – was the Loew's Kings on Flatbush

Avenue. This was the most splendiferous movie house of all, a "Wonder Theater" built in 1929 to hold nearly four thousand attendees and to dazzle them with so much cuckoo-rococo embellishment that it made the madly ornate Brooklyn Paramount look like a cardboard box. Architecture students could make the Kings' decor sound about as thrilling as the linnean names of plants – "segmental pediment"; "broken entablature"; "terra-cotta archivault" – but it might be easier to visualize the Loew's Kings as Xanadu designed by Kubla Khan on crack.

(The name of the theater rhymed with "Joey's," never with "Moe's." Why Loew's should be two syllables was one of Brooklyn's great mysteries.)

The Kings flourished on Flatbush from the age of *The Jazz Singer*. This was where I saw Phileas Fogg flit around the world and James Stewart confront Liberty Valance. Ben Vereen's mother had been a cleaner at the Kings; after hours, as she did her work, her little son would vault on stage and dance for the empty house. But the neighborhood had "changed." In 1977, the Loew's Kings exhibited *Exorcist II: The Heretic* and then closed up for good. The French baroque lobby, the gilded vaults, the mock-Bayeux tapestries, and the Bernini baldachino were abandoned. Gargoyles gaped in disbelief. The chandeliers fell dark.

Once there had been 14,733 theater seats available *every night* on Flatbush between Church Avenue and Farragut Road. Now, only the Kenmore, sliced into quadrants, remained in business. The Farragut Theater was the YMCA. The Albemarle belonged to the Witnesses. The Flatbush Theater was a furniture store. The Rialto was the grandest of the multiple Églises de Dieu of the Haitian Pentecostals; its 1,500 chairs were intact, but its stage had become a pulpit, and, in place of the silver screen, was a mural of a domed and spired city, set in a peaceable glade, called "The New Jerusalem." And the Loew's Kings, the Versailles of the Wooded Flat, was locked up and dead.

Only the fact that the neighborhood was moribund had kept it from being torn down. In a more economically viable district, a chunk of real estate the size of the Kings would have been scrapped and redeveloped in a flash. But nobody wanted to invest in central Flatbush. So the Kings stood sadly by, its towering marquee rusting, its front doors padlocked like the temple of a god no longer trusted.

More than anything, I wanted to walk its aisles. From the outside, as I strolled past the lobby entrance day after day, I could make out almost nothing in the absence of light. Cool air teased me through holes in the monumental doors, musty and evocative. I had already been inside the anchorage of the Manhattan Bridge and down in the vaults of the Board of Health, where my parents' parents' paperwork slept. Penetrating the Loew's Kings could assuage my regret at not having got in to see the twenty lead coffins of the washed-up Prison Ship Martyrs.

My sister, eternally confident, telephoned the various historical societies and got nowhere. I tried the office of the Borough President and actually had one of my calls returned, a major breakthrough, but the message was that they'd get back to me – and, of course, they never did.

Then I did what any cement-headed Stooge would have done right off the bat. I walked into the storefront that was next door to the theater – it was the office of the Flatbush Development Corporation, a community-service organization – and asked if anyone knew how I might get inside the Loew's Kings.

"Soitainly!" the receptionist curlied. The FDC was temporary custodian of the theater. The man with the key would be in tomorrow morning. It was times like this that made me understand why I was still a second-rate hack while canceled checks signed by the immortal Shemp Howard were being sold in California and snapped up by collectors at $695 *each.*

∽

The man with the key was a Haitian cellist named Ulrick Gaillard. Little Debbie and I showed up at 8:30 on the appointed morning to meet him and to be taken on a tour of the abandoned palace of Ozymandias. Formalities were few. I was asked to get clearance from a Manhattan bureaucrat – the Kings was, technically, city property, awaiting disposition, sale, or demolition – and this was obtained with a quick phone call. Then we signed a waiver, stating that, if the roof chose the moment of our visit to fall in, we would not hold The Greatest City in the World responsible for "claims, actions, suits, judgments, causes of action, demands, losses, damages, liabilities, costs, charges and expenses."

A moment later, Ulrick Gaillard was kneeling on the Flatbush Avenue sidewalk, springing the big Master padlocks and raising the sliding gate that protected the theater from vandals, squatters, and arsonists. He pushed through one of the front portals – the handles had been removed and the door wasn't locked – and we squeezed past the octagonal box office and into the fantastic Carlsbad Cavern of the lobby of the Loew's Kings.

It had been more than fifteen years since the last motion picture rolled credits and faded to black. Now, in a vaulted entrance hall that in itself was bigger than any Cineplex cubicle, there were desks and filing cabinets scattered here and there but nothing else to disturb the daydream that the Kings might re-open in a couple of hours for a kiddie matinee of cartoons, serials, and Fess Parker in *Westward Ho the Wagons*. The lobby was remarkably well preserved. I had expected it to have been savaged like the Botanic Garden subway platform or the Willink Comfort Station in Prospect Park. But this hadn't happened.

"Welcome To The Kings Theater," said a poster in a gilded frame. "Brooklyn's Finest Showplace Presenting First-Run Pictures, Week After Week."

Ulrick Gaillard stood in the dusty light filtering in from Flatbush and said, "Eleven million dollars."

"Eleven million to buy the theater?" I asked. It sounded like a bargain.

"Eleven million just to make the heating and air conditioning work again," he replied.

There had been offers, Gaillard said. Someone wanted to turn the Kings into a giant supermarket. Another developer wanted to partition it into four or five smaller viewing rooms, like the Kenmore on Church Avenue. But the city nixed the deal.

"They want to preserve the Gothic look of this place," Ulrick noted. "I can't believe nobody could just say, 'Okay. Here's eleven million,'" the Haitian shrugged, as we walked across the red carpet and stared up at the plush velvet curtains and the arches that led to the numbered aisles. The curving stairway to the balconies was wide enough for Marlene Dietrich to descend lasciviously in a formal gown – driving a Greyhound bus.

"Donald Trump?" I suggested, nominating saviors. "Ross Perot? George Steinbrenner?"

"I should write a letter to Barbra Streisand," our guide postulated. "I'd tell her, 'Don't forget you come from Brooklyn! Give us eleven million dollars!'"

Ulrick excused himself for a second and, navigating by flashlight, found an electrical control panel and flipped on the few remaining working bulbs of the monumental arcade, the grand, arched inner lobby. Then we followed him, hushed and reverential, into the theater itself.

It was a magical moment. The air was cool, and our footsteps echoed to the dark, dank void. In the blackness, it seemed as vast as SkyDome; the ceiling was so high, and Ulrick's torch so feeble, that only a thin splash of light played on the colors and contours of the hall. And then a pigeon flew, somewhere in the canopy, and we heard its wingtips applauding.

In a 1988 *New Yorker* article, an old man who had been an usher here once described what the Kings had been. It was when they opened *Gone with the Wind*:

> They sprayed the screen silver again, just to make it more reflective, more perfect. The electricians had to take down the red "Exit" signs and change them to blue ones, so that nothing would interfere with the Technicolor effect. It was one of the few reserved-seat pictures. We had to mark out the rows with stencils and paint, and so on. The evening show was O.K. But we began the shows at eight-thirty in the morning. The theater would fill with older women, and there would be the sound of sobbing from one end of the theater to the other.

The tears had dried. The only voice was Ulrick's, a lament for the neglect of so wondrous a public space. His concern seemed heartfelt, even though he had still been a boy in Haiti when the Loew's Kings went dark.

"This neighborhood changed a lot," Ulrick said, in the understatement of the decade.

"Is this area what you thought America would be like?" I asked him.

"I expected Christian good folks, preaching the word of the Gospel like the missionaries in Haiti," he answered. "But I guess missionaries only come to Third World countries."

"Is Flatbush a Third World country?" I posed.

"It can be," said Ulrick Gaillard.

The Loew's Kings was as hermetic and well-preserved as an abandoned castle could be. Its cherubs and goddesses slept undisturbed. When Ulrick's light found a painting on the north wall and caressed the figure of an English maiden in eighteenth-century costume, she looked as surprised to see us as we were to see her.

We followed our guide down the center aisle and climbed onto the stage, where I had seen the Stooges. A skylight tossed down some illumination, and I read the markings on a wall where stagehands once would heave'e'yo the rigging and unfurl the canvas of this landlocked schooner. "MOVIE SCREEN," a label said. "SILVER DOORWAY." "FAKE 3D SCREEN." I recalled a 3D thriller called *13 Ghosts* and how I had struggled to fit those silly red-and-blue plastic glasses over my prescription specs. How long had that memory slumbered? Now it was vivid again – *13 Ghosts* at the Loew's Kings.

Five cans of film lay at the corner of the stage, pelted with pigeon droppings. I was rooting around in the debris, and Debbie had gone prowling down a corridor that led to the old vaudeville dressing rooms, when we were both jolted into gooseflesh by a piercing male voice.

"Ladies and gentlemen!" it wailed. But it was only Ulrick, standing at stage center, ringmaster for a day.

"Ladies and gentlemen!" he bellowed. "The Kings Theater proudly presents . . . Barry Manilow!"

I liked Ulrick. His talents were several. He had learned to play the cello in Haiti – I did not often associate classical music with that benighted country – and, since his immigration, he had performed at the Brooklyn Academy of Music. He also collected antique clocks. But his claim to erudition was invalid. He had never heard of the Three Stooges.

We left the stage and the virtuoso led us downstairs to unimagined wonders. Originally, the Kings was to include a restaurant on the lower level. But the Crash of '29 scuttled this plan, and the empty chamber was turned into a basketball court for the Flatbush Avenue Theater Ushers League. Like a sealed stateroom on a sunken liner, the court had survived in perfect condition, backboards, hoops, and all. Free-throw lines were visible on the floor. In one corner was a poster for a film called *Darling Lili*, starring Julie Andrews and Rock Hudson. Christmas decorations were strewn along a wall. And at the far end were at least a hundred empty water containers marked "Department of Defense – Survival Supplies," artifacts of the fallout-shelter years.

We returned to the lobby and prepared to make our thank-yous and goodbyes. It had been marvelous.

"You should bring your cello here," I told our guide at parting.

"Yes! Yes!" Ulrick Gaillard gasped. The thought was enchanting. Some day, he said, he would haul his instrument into the Loew's Kings and sit on the vast stage, alone. He would play a Mendelssohn concerto for the sobbing wraiths of Flatbush, and the theme from *Gone with the Wind*.

5

Another of the monumental leftovers of central Flatbush was a man named Henry J. Bahnsen. For thirty-five years, Mr. Bahnsen had operated a genteel restaurant and ice-cream parlor on the west side of the avenue, a few hundred yards from the Loew's Kings, and it was still in business, although time had caused some of the letters to fall off his display signs, leaving one to say HENRY' and another to advertise ENRY'S.

When my mother and I were in the neighborhood one day – she was shopping for a new, sturdier lock for her apartment door – we stopped by Henry's. She ordered a chicken-salad sandwich and I went for a chocolate malt, which was presented authentically in a metal mixing can that was left on the counter beside a tall flagon in a metal zarf. A zarf is a holder with a handle, into which a glass is fitted, and a sixteen-point Scrabble word that came in handy whenever I was stuck with the z and unable to make fez or adze or zoa or zing or zenana.

Since it was just a couple of weeks after Easter, my mother asked our server, a woman named Helen, who had worked at Henry's for twenty-three years, if it was time to take the chocolate bunnies out of the display windows and melt them down for resale as candy bars. But Helen said that the Board of Health now forbade this traditional practice, and admitted that the ice cream in my malt had not been made in the basement of the restaurant, as it had been for decades.

In fact, Helen said, Mr. Bahnsen had become too corpulent, and too infirm, to operate the churns in the cellar. Clearly, these were not good times at Henry's. The restaurant was grim and sepulchral on a weekday afternoon. A dozen booths sat unoccupied, apparently permanently, only a handful of dawdling coffee-drinkers slouched at stools along the counter, and the red leatherette covering of the stools themselves had been, like Macduff from his mother's womb, "untimely ripp'd."

Among the graffiti above the men's toilet, some happy husband had scrawled: "Marriage is for wormheads."

"Look at the neighborhood," Helen said, unhappily. "Look at the street and the people on it. It's a mess. Fifteen years ago, Henry said, 'It's going to come back. It's going to come back.' We whispered behind his back: 'He's out of his mind.'

"And he *was!*"

~

I wanted to interview Henry J. Bahnsen, but he wasn't at the restaurant and I was told to come back some other time. Besides, the business of the day was my mother's security. Presently, all that stood between her and home invasion by the neighborhood Visigoths was one deadbolt, a second small springlock, and a chain that had been there when she moved in back in 1949 and that did not appear sturdy enough to hold back a strong breeze. Even though she now had a virile young man about the house to protect her – hoodlums quaked as I passed, brandishing my spiral notebook – she was still in the market for another lock with a long, metal guard-strip that would run nearly the height of the door.

A hardware store called Singer & Singer was, like Henry's and the Loew's Kings, a Flatbush landmark, and it was there that we went to buy the lock. A fellow named Charlie, whose last name was neither Singer nor Singer, was behind the counter, assisted by clerks from four foreign countries: Pakistan, Haiti, Puerto Rico, and Bensonhurst. The staff was friendly and the store well-stocked and apparently thriving. In Brooklyn, anyone who sold locks, bolts; and fences was guaranteed a clientele.

My mother mentioned that I was working on a book about Flatbush Avenue. Her approach was to go right up to someone, point to me like a referee calling a highsticking penalty, and announce, "This is my son. He's working on a book about Flatbush Avenue."

"You're the second writer that's come in here," said Charlie of Singer & Singer.

"Really," I enthused.

"Yeah. A few years ago, some guy comes in and says, 'I'm doing a book about my father. He used to buy chains here.' I say, 'That's nice. Who's your father?'

"'Houdini,' he says."

∽

According to *Death and the Magician: The Mystery of Houdini* by Raymond Fitzsimmons, Harry Houdini, formerly Erich Weiss, the son of a Brooklyn rabbi, didn't have any children.

Sorry, Charlie.

∽

"How's business?" I asked Henry J. Bahnsen.

"It sucks," he responded.

I was back at the restaurant, *sans* my mother, and Henry and I were seated in a vacant booth, which could have been any of them. He was an enormous man in a white apron that might once have been the mainsail of a Nantucket whaler. His face was round, he had a mustache and wire-rimmed glasses, and his heart had given out five times already. Henry J. Bahnsen, confectioner and ice-cream maker and frequent hospital patient, was not a happy camper on the Big Rock Candy Mountain.

"I don't think Flatbush will ever come back," he said, directly. He was not disposed to beat around the bush.

"I don't mean 'come back' as a white area," he went on. "I mean economically viable."

"But it looks busy around here," I offered. "There are people on the street and in the stores."

"They're schlock stores," Henry retorted. "Ninety-nine-cent stores. And the crime rate is phenomenal. I've been robbed twice. They rob with *impunity*. They just come in, gangs of three, wave their guns, and clean you out. The City of New York doesn't give a damn about minority areas. They're more interested in giving out tickets for not keeping the sidewalk clean than in investing to build up the area."

"Why don't you leave?" I asked.

"I wanna leave when *I* wanna leave," Henry said. "I don't wanna be forced out."

Henry J. Bahnsen lived in a flat above his restaurant. So did his elderly mother. The building was typical of every block I walked, starting southward from Lefferts Gardens: a store on street level and two or three floors of apartments above it, most of them built between 1900 and the Crash of '29. A recent study by Columbia University's Graduate School of Architecture, Planning and Preservation called this stretch of Flatbush Avenue "an urban setting with an exciting mixture of commercial and residential uses." The report hailed its "friendly, pedestrian-scaled character."

But closer inspection revealed rot and decay. Shoppers and shoplifters still swarmed the daytime streets, but in central Flatbush, at least a quarter of the apartments above the stores had been abandoned and their windows boarded up. Some of the damage had been disguised with advertising signs, such as the Bride of Flatbush Avenue. At Beverly Road, a long row of upper-story windows were painted over with *trompe l'oeil* draperies to make them look like living homes. One panel showed the silhouette of a woman undressing behind sheer curtains, an attempt at humor in a cheerless locale.

Other buildings were gutted and nude. A convenience store near my mother's place, whose sign said "We Never Close," never opened. The Lin Fong restaurant at Fenimore Street had burned to a crisp and had not been rebuilt.

The second time I went to look for Julio the voodoo man at the Midnight Star L'Étoile de Minuit, the storefront was empty and the gate was locked.

The loss of Macy's in 1992 was a crushing blow. When the modern bronze-and-glass-fronted department store opened in 1948, it was a vanguard of the post-war expansion of Manhattan merchandisers to the suburbs. The arrival of Macy's, and a fully stocked Sears store a couple of blocks away on Bedford Avenue, had ratified the middle-class prosperity of old Dutch Flatbush. Now the big Macy's emporium stood closed and empty, its massive walls plastered with graffiti and signs that said "FOR LEASE." There was a rumor that Bradlee's, the discount-clothing chain that was allegedly going to revivify Atlantic Avenue downtown, might be interested in the Macy's building. In its grief and confusion, Brooklyn looked to Bradlee's as Lubavitchers yearned for Moshiach.

"If we pulled together, we could make it," Henry J. Bahnsen was saying in the booth at the ice-cream shoppe. "But we're not New York any more. It's everybody for himself – 'I've got mine.'"

"What could bring it back?" I asked.

"If they executed enough drug dealers," the big man replied, "eventually, somebody would get the message . . ."

He paused and breathed laboriously the chocolatey air of his sinking restaurant.

". . . theoretically," Henry J. Bahnsen said.

∾

Other businesses seemed to be thriving. Just north of Church Avenue, the Bride looked down on five human-hair salons and three faux-fingernail boutiques in a single block. A big Korean green-grocery had twenty-two different varieties of pepper sauce on a shelf above the yams and plantains. Jansport rucksacks, this spring's essential accoutrement for students and gang members, hung from rack after rack along the avenue, priced at $35.99 and up. The meat markets were always busy.

Two authentic Brooklyn storefront pizzerias, Franco's and Family, were still operated by Italian dough-twirlers in the core of black Flatbush; they were Spike Lee's *Do the Right Thing* come to life. The Korean fishmonger with the shrapnel in his neck was enjoying a steady trade. So was Jamaica Jewelry, at least until noon on May 14, when five young men with Uzi machine guns relieved it of forty-thousand-dollars' worth of necklaces, rings, and bracelets before departing in a grey Toyota.

At a tiny fruit stand called Liu's at the corner of Flatbush and Fenimore, a young Chinese man, two years in America, was sitting with his head in his hands, waiting for customers, when the apparition of a skinny, big-nosed foreigner in flip-up sunglasses and a black baseball cap came up and started talking to him in fractured Mandarin. The clerk beamed like a kid at Mid-Autumn Festival with a sack full of moon cakes, and so did I.

"Meiguo hen hao," he said, and gave thumbs-up. America very good.

It was not a judgment often heard from those who had been around longer. Neil Telsey was fifty-six years old and he had spent thirty-five of them at Neil's Discount Liquors on Flatbush near Caton Avenue. One block east of Telsey's store, Caton Avenue merged with Linden Boulevard, which then, as

New York State Route 27, led eastward through the borough of Queens into suburban Nassau County and then crossed bucolic Suffolk until it concluded, ninety miles from the Bride of Flatbush Avenue, at a loop below the historic lighthouse at Montauk Point.

Neil Telsey drove to work each morning, parked his car as close to his store as possible, passed through two doors made of bulletproof plastic, locked them behind him, and didn't come out again until it was time to drive home. He had grown up here on the streets that were named for the farmers of New Netherlands: Clarkson, Martense, Caton. He had married a woman from Woodruff Avenue, a block from the liquor store. But now he sat at his desk at the back of his shop, smoking Raleighs, eating his brown-bag lunch. He never, ever went to the bank, and I doubted that he shopped at Jamaica Jewelry.

"Everybody puts up bulletproof glass," Neil Telsey was saying. "You've got working people around here, nice people, but with any kind of people, they got their bad ones. Everybody is scared. My customers are scared. They have to *survive* around here."

"Is this stuff really bulletproof?" I asked him, rapping my hand against a transparent material that seemed no sturdier than cardboard.

"Look at this," Telsey said. He peeled back a blue New York Lottery sticker to reveal an asterisk in the plastic. It was the impression a slug had made. He hadn't been at the store when the shooting occurred. When Neil went home each day, black clerks took over and closed up at eleven p.m.

"It was a drug deal gone bad," the shopkeeper explained. "The guy tried to hide in the doorway. He got shot – *boom boom boom* – and died right there.

"I know a woman around the corner, her son got killed. She knows who did it, but she won't tell the police. It's funny; you may not understand it. But she has two daughters. That's how it is around here."

Neil Telsey's store used to be across the road, on the west side, next to a grocery. When somebody succeeded in setting fire to the grocery, Neil's burned with it. That was in 1975. At the time, the white exodus was turning into a torrent. (According to the Columbia University study, central Flatbush was 85 per cent white in 1970 and 15 per cent white in 1980. The Caucasian percentage now was probably less than 2 per cent.) Keeping his balance in the rushing stream, Telsey decided not to flee. He acquired his current property for twenty thousand dollars. He could sell it now, he said, for 350 grand.

He was almost embarrassed to tell me that he hadn't been robbed on the day shift in nearly twenty years. He shrugged and said, "When this neighborhood was white, I got held up all the time."

The most expensive still wines at Neil's Discount Liquors were a 1989 Mouton Cadet Bordeaux for $10.95 and a Soave Bolla for $8.54. At the other end of the spectrum was a tincture called Wild Irish that retailed for $1.80 the pint. Neil Telsey said, "I sell a lot of Moët champagne and Rémy Martin and Bailey's. I'm not a Sneaky Pete store." Sneaky Pete was a wino's wine. Yet the only two customers who came to Neil's Discount while I was there both slid $1.80 through the bulletproof wicket, without having to ask the price, and walked off with chilled Wild Irish.

While the boys with the Uzis frolicked around Flatbush, Neil Telsey was being slapped with a hundred-dollar penalty for maintaining an unlicensed air-conditioner. This made him seethe. It was the same with Henry J. Bahnsen. He had fine after fine for litter on the sidewalk in front of his restaurant.

Neil Telsey paid a thousand dollars a year to something called a Business Improvement District. This money paid for Christmas lights and a private security force, whose official sedan, painted in exactly the same color scheme as a city police cruiser, I often saw parked at the Flatbush Avenue curb, locked and unoccupied.

"It's bullshit," Neil Telsey said.

"Why don't you leave?" I asked him. It was a question I was finding myself asking everyone I met.

"Because I'm fifty-six years old," the liquor man replied. "I'm at the age where nobody wants me."

6

"Rogers Avenue is even more terrible," Pete and Dennis Hamill had reported in 1975 in a *Village Voice* article about Flatbush entitled "A Neighborhood is Dying." "It is a place inhabited by ghosts."

Rogers Avenue was roughly parallel to Flatbush. It ran from the Trinity New Testament Assembly and the Église Baptiste Clarté Céleste up toward Eastern Parkway and riotous Crown Heights, a sea lane of the new North Caribbean. The Hamills had focused on one block as evidence of the district's mortal wounds. Along Rogers, they wrote, between Newkirk Avenue and Avenue D, only two out of eleven storefronts were open for business.

In 1993, that same block was part of a neighborhood that had been cheerfully designated "Clarendon Meadows." I walked there just before ten o'clock one morning to see what had become of the Hamills' distressing arithmetic. I found a barber shop, a laundromat, Danny's Tire Service, the Life-Line Jamaican Restaurant, two groceries, a law office, and the Redemption Gospel Outreach Church. Three other shops were gated at this early hour and may or may not have been functional. At worst, this added to eight alive out of eleven. The ghosts of Rogers Avenue had been replaced by the black immigrant middle class.

Encouraged, I turned west on Beverley Road, trying to get back to Flatbush, and ran smack into the Art Moderne minaret of Sears Roebuck and Company. This building, with its tall, fluted limestone tower, was so distinctive in size and design that it seemed to be a relic of a lost civilization that predated the Canarsees and the Dutch. It stood in an ocean of asphalt, across Bedford Avenue from some unhealthy-looking tenements, one of which, sixty years earlier, had been the childhood residence of the actor Eli Wallach.

The Sears store, I assumed, was as kaput as Macy's Flatbush. The display windows along the Bedford Avenue wall were plastered up and painted over and not a pedestrian could be seen. But I had forgotten the architectural alignments of the automobile age. I turned the corner of the store and came upon a parking lot in which cars were nuzzling chock-a-block, and all sorts of people were climbing out of them and heading for the gateway to the one-stop mega-mall.

I followed them. Inside the faceless monolith, which had been built to a standard pattern sent from headquarters in Chicago, was a full-sized department store. There were Munsingwear work pants and Legtricity stockings, Weedwackers, Bushwackers, and Bugwackers. There was patio furniture. Garden hoses. Lawn mowers. I had found a secret passageway to the United States.

I had to sit down.

It was hot and airless. Customers were speaking Russian, Spanish, Brooklynese. I got up and felt myself being switched into browsing mode, as if by remote control. Mechanically, I walked up and down aisles, fingering knit shirts and dress slacks. I checked the price tags on socks. I hefted a fishing rod and tested its springiness, even though I had gone angling exactly once since I was five years old.

I didn't buy anything. (Carless, I didn't want to walk around carrying a shopping bag.) As I exited, I noticed a large black-and-white photograph, five feet square, half-hidden behind a cashier's counter. It was 1932. A woman was turning a ceremonial key to inaugurate the store I now was leaving.

The woman was Eleanor Roosevelt. That was how important Flatbush had been.

∾

I continued north along Bedford Avenue and soon arrived at the most remarkable block in all of Flatbush town. Snyder Avenue, named for a nineteenth-century architect, offered a bowling alley, a mock-Tudor pub, the capitol of the human-hair trade, a storage warehouse that had been turned into a junior high school, the former municipal courthouse and jail, the butterscotch walls of what had been a famous bakery, the last Flatbush Town Hall from the days of village independence, a defunct funeral parlor, and the only newly built housing units for at least a mile in any direction.

Around the corner was Erasmus Hall High and a dilapidated old public school that was being put to use as an academy for Lubavitcher girls. Then came White Castle hamburgers, the Flatbush Historical Society, Sybil's Guyanese Restaurant, and the spire and cemetery of the Reformed Dutch Church. In theory, one could be baptized, educated, nourished, betrothed, bewigged, incarcerated, eulogized, and buried, all within a few hundred yards.

The Lugo Hair Center was announced *sotto voce* by a small sign flapping above the entrance to what used to be Cook's Funeral Home. From the outside, it didn't look like a wellspring of style and fashion. The building was whitewashed brick, and next to it was an abandoned two-story structure with a fading sign that read "J KURTZ SONS," and I assumed that Mistah Kurtz – he dead.

But Lugo's was intensely alive. It seemed that style-conscious women of color had given up on the Roberta Flack bird's-nest Afros of the seventies and were now piling up enormous amounts of their hair, or someone else's, in fanciful braids and twists and knots, and dying these coils gold and bronze and magenta and aubergine. To achieve this, they patronized any one of the dozens of salons along Flatbush Avenue. And when they were in need of imported raw material, they came to Lugo's.

In big vats in back rooms on Snyder Avenue, straight black hair that had arrived in America in cargo crates was boiled, curled, combed, dyed, and carded like wool. It was the hair of Chinese village maidens and mountain girls from Thailand, cut by mothers with silent tears, sold to grinning, smoking middlemen from the county seat in plastic sandals and stained white shirts, and traded up through a network of facilitators and go-betweens, until it reached Hong Kong or Singapore and the big container ships.

The thought of this commerce, in which one was shorn to beautify another, saddened me. I knew the girl whose long and lustrous pride this hair had been. She had giggled at me as I sat in a barber's chair at Yinchuan on the Yellow River; in Guang'an town in Sichuan Province, she had brought washing water to my room in buckets hung from a shoulder pole.

In Brooklyn, her hair was sold for fifteen dollars an ounce, which made it less expensive than caviar but dearer than the roughest crack cocaine. (In rural China, fifteen dollars was a half-year's wage.) In contrast with Henry's ice-cream parlor and Sister Teresa Reader and Advisor, business here was excellent. Adornment was a basic human need. The man who showed me around Lugo's, John Soto, was philosophic.

"Hair is something you're born with and used to having," Soto said. He was a sturdy fellow with glasses and straight black hair, combed back without curls or artifice. "Hair has to do with individuals and how they perceive themselves. They come in and say they want to look like Diana Ross or Janet Jackson. It's natural. Everybody wants to be Cindy Crawford."

The room where we were talking contained an L-shaped table at which three workers were repeatedly passing long strands of hair over a fine-toothed comb to separate them and make them seem fuller. A palette of ponytails was hung high on the walls, illustrating finished goods with names like "Wet 'n' Wavy" and colors that ranged from ash-blonde to watermelon red. A customer could choose style, tint, and method of attachment. Taken from Lugo's in a plastic bag and brought to the chosen salon, the hair could then be woven, interlocked, or bonded, which meant sticking it on with glue.

For those who craved an even more supple, up-market texture, Lugo's stocked a nice supply of yak.

A large woman named Jones was just getting her credit card back after purchasing $120 worth of Wet 'n' Wavy. She said, "Africans been doing this for centuries. This is culture for us."

"This used to be strictly African-American," John Soto said, talking to me and to Ms. Jones. "Now it has expanded to Caucasians and Hispanics."

"Could it just be a fad that will die?" I asked.

"Only in style," he replied. "The advantage of this is they don't have to color their hair, they don't have to perm their hair, they don't have to chemically alter their hair. All the abuse they'd normally do to themselves, we do here. And our hair will last as long as they do. When they die, it'll be the last thing that remains."

John Soto was manager of the Snyder Avenue facility. Lugo's, a family business and a Puerto Rican success story, had been around for more than thirty years. For most of that time, it had had few rivals. But now it seemed that every other storefront in Flatbush was a human-hair distributor.

"We don't consider them competition," the manager said. "More of a nuisance. The Koreans claim to be selling 100 per cent human hair. But it's really synthetic."

"How can you tell?" I wondered.

"Synthetic melts," John Soto said. And summer was coming. Yuck.

7

It wasn't easy to visualize Flatbush as a separate political entity. Brooklyn had become so populous, with its glacier of settlement covering the entire outwash plain of the Laurentide ice sheet, that, except for the strip of brass in the walkway at the Botanic Garden, there were no remnants of the historic boundaries of the various old Dutch towns. The white oak at the Flatbush–Brooklyn line was long gone, of course, and the big shingled windmill on the Vanderveer farm that watched over the border between Flatbush and Flatlands had burned at the turn of the century.

The original patent of 1685 had set precise demarcations – "from thence with a straight line to the northwest hook or corner of the ditch of John Oakies meadow" – but now the ditches were sewers, the meadows were housing projects, and the straight lines were subway tracks.

Yet it had been less than a century since Flatbush had relinquished its independence and become part of the City of Brooklyn after 242 years as a distinct, corporeal hamlet. (Four years after that, Brooklyn joined Manhattan and "Greater" New York was born.)

From the very beginning, law and order had been a problem. In 1654, a military company was formed to combat "robbers and pirates." Constables were elected and authorized "to whip or punish offenders, raise the hue and cry after murderers, manslayers, thieves, robbers, burglars; and also apprehend without warrant, such as were overtaken with drink, swearing, sabbath-breaking, vagrant persons or night walkers." After the Revolution, a monument erected to honor the fallen patriots of the Battle of Brooklyn was defaced beyond recognition by vandals "who seem to take delight in mutilating every thing."

Because of its central location in the county of Kings, Flatbush village was for many decades the seat of justice and punishment. A sturdy jail was a necessity. However, the first detention center was destroyed by fire during the winter of 1757, a conflagration that continued even after the inmates were let out to try to combat it by throwing snowballs.

The replacement building was famous for being insufficiently secure. On one occasion, a group of prisoners sawed through the bars and all escaped, except for one man.

This unfortunate proved to be so corpulent that he became wedged in the window, and although the sharp points of the iron bars penetrated his clothes, entering his flesh and causing him the keenest

agony, he repressed all outcry until he thought that his late companions were beyond recapture when he made the welkin ring with his
shrieks of pain.

This act of altruism went unrewarded. The fat man was cut loose and
reimprisoned. A few years later, in 1832, the courthouse and jail burned to
the ground. The county seat moved to Brooklyn City.

As Brooklyn City grew and prospered, Flatbush village became even
more insular and self-sufficient, turning its back on the burgeoning commerce and might of Whitman's mid-century Brooklyn. In 1842, the historian
Thomas M. Strong admitted that "it no doubt will appear strange to some,
that a village so contiguous to the great emporium of our country ... should
not have grown with more rapidity." He attributed this to a lack of financial
concupiscence on the part of Dutch landowners, who for generations had
refused to sell a single acre to developers.

Even after the coming of the horse-drawn streetcars and the Brighton
Beach railway, Flatbush repeatedly rejected proposals for annexation. In
1875, feeling robust and defiant, it constructed the elegant High Victorian
Town Hall, with its tall brick tower that still stood on Snyder Avenue, across
the street from the Lugo Hair Center. The dream was to be a little Liechten-
stein in the heart of the metropolis.

The dream lasted less than twenty years. In the end, the people of the village never even got to vote on their absorption into the City of Brooklyn. In
1890, as the wave of immigrant settlement began to wash over the Flatbush
farmlands, delegations favoring and opposing incorporation traveled to
Albany to put their cases before the state senators and assemblymen who
held the power to legislate annexation. Both sides claimed to hold petitions
signed by a majority of Flatbushers.

There was no referendum. In Albany, Progress prevailed. The bill passed.
In 1894, the Village of Flatbush ceased to be. The Leffertses and Zabriskies
subdivided their properties and got rich.

Only the old Town Hall spoke for the No side now. It was set back from
the street and mounted on a thick stone foundation, strikingly red, with
heavy Gothic window frames and metal screens to keep the panes from
being smashed by those who seem to take delight in mutilating every thing.

Flatbush Town Hall, saved from the wrecker's ball by community outcry in the 1970s, had been renovated and turned into a vocational school for teenagers with special needs. Next door was the squat old Magistrates and Municipal Court, dated MCMXXII and engraved at the cornerstones with the words "JUSTICE" and "EQUALITY" but now sealed, empty, and spray-painted. In the alley between the two buildings, enough garbage had been dumped to start a municipal landfill, should Flatbush somehow, someday, recapture its autonomy. Down the block was the former Holden Warehouse, currently Intermediate School 248, and across the street was the defunct bakery called Ebinger's, once as much an element of Brooklyn's iconography as the egg cream or the Dodgers, now bricked over and painted the color of pumpkin pie and converted into U-Store lockers.

It was the morning of my epiphany at Sears. Outside the Town Hall, I stood on the sidewalk, making some notes, and then, eager to visit the historic old building and to see how it had been refurbished, I bounded up the stairway to the entrance and opened the door. I was met by a security guard with arms the size of legs.

"No visitors," he said. He was just doing his job. I didn't want to have to hurt him, so I left.

❧

The architect of the Flatbush Town Hall was a man named John Y. Culyer. At the corner of Church and Bedford avenues, Culyer also contributed a "Flat-bush Common School" that later became Brooklyn Public School 90 and that now, hauntingly tumbledown, its windows broken and its brickwork plastered with posters for reggae concerts, was Beth Rivka, an academy for the female children of the Lubavitcher Jews. Beth Rivka – the House of Rebecca – had been set upon by vandals with unsettling "tags" or nick-names: *Mauser. Sniper. Fury.* Their scrawls were everywhere.

But the school was still very much in use. It was possible to stand on the sidewalk and to look up into classrooms where the Hasidic girls, all in regi-mental blue, sat clutching their pencils in riveted concentration, their hair tied with ribbons, segregated from their brothers by sex, from this neighbor-hood by race, and from this country by the unyielding ferocity of their fathers' faith. (On Memorial Day, I found Beth Rivka in session and thought it a sacrilege.) Gitty, Altie, and Rivky, the girls at the Moshiach cavalcade on Eastern Parkway, had told me that they attended Beth Rivka, but whether that meant they were bused from Crown Heights to John Y. Culyer's crumbling construction on Church Avenue or whether every Lubavitcher girls' school was called by the same name, I did not know.

What I did know was that between Culyer's two masterpieces stood a school more famous in the eyes of Flatbushers than any other on earth. Erasmus Hall High had begun in 1786 as a private academy for boys, funded by patrician subscribers whose rolls included Alexander Hamilton and the man who would later shoot him to death, Aaron Burr. The original building, a two-story hall in the Federal style, set amid flowering dogwood and Balm of Gilead, was now a museum of early American education. Surrounding it on all four sides was a great Collegiate Gothic castle, built in 1906, designed by the Snyder for whom the nearby avenue was named, currently undergoing massive reconstruction and for decades the arch-rival of Midwood High, my alma mater.

When boasting of its roster of famous graduates, Erasmus always led with the usual Streisands and Malamuds and followed with Dorothy Kilgallen, Susan Hayward, and Jeff Chandler.

But this was a mere popgun assault. Snickering at the small-fry Erasmus could muster, Midwood would parry formidably with Woody Allen, Erich Segal, and me.

Visiting Erasmus was only a little less life-threatening than trying to crash the old Town Hall. The wooden academy was open to the public by appointment, so I called and made a date. Well before the designated hour, I arrived at the security desk on the Flatbush Avenue side of the quadrangle and was immediately set upon by four uniformed guards, one of whom, a woman the size of Louisiana, stood up to dam my ingress and bellowed: "ID!"

I unsheathed my CBC press card, which confused and mollified this diligent agent long enough for me to slip inside, just as a dazed and mumbling matriculant, palpably stoned, was being expelled through the same narrow door. All around me, walkie-talkies crackled and spat.

"Go ahead, fourteen."

"Secure exit 1-K."

"One-K secured. Ten-four."

"Unit five, over."

"Go ahead, unit five."

"We have five female students cleared to exit 13."

"Exit 13. Ten-four."

Beyond the portal, glassy-eyed white teachers were leading squadrons of black pupils on expeditionary voyages to unexplored corners of the giant school. The kids had first names such as Brizard, Ronise, Estimable, Ideric, Tislin; they came from Jamaica, Haiti, Guyana, Bedford–Stuyvesant; they wore oversized jeans that bunched like elephant's skin at their ankles, or flamboyantly colored shorts, or overalls with the straps hanging loose and flapping as they walked. Girls piled waxy wavelengths of hair into conical turrets dyed tangerine and maroon; boys wore dreadlocks or had hieroglyphs etched into their close-shaven skulls – peace symbols, the Air Jordan logo, the Nike cuneiform. There were twenty-nine hundred students in all.

I was relegated to a marble bench outside the auditorium to await the start of my tour. Restless, I sneaked away and wandered the halls, waving my visitor's pass like a talisman at the legions of uniformed guards. I looked in a display case and saw baseball trophies dating back to 1901; a plaque donated by the Loew's Kings; a recent photograph of the white track coach, surrounded by thirty-one athletes of color.

By the time I got back to the assembly point, my scheduled group tour had begun without me. I hurried down into the inner courtyard and found thirty black children huddled around the statue of Desiderius Erasmus that stood in front of the old wooden hall. They were junior-high-school boys and girls, who might be coming here in the future, depending on their personal choices and their scores on examinations. If they attended Erasmus, it would be likely that they would complete their entire careers in the city system without ever knowing a white classmate.

New York's high schools varied enormously in expectations and achievement. Scientific and technical "magnet" schools saw nine out of every ten students earn diplomas. Other schools in rougher districts were holding-pens, where barely one pupil in seven saw things through until graduation. In 1990, illustrious Stuyvesant High in Manhattan, named for the peg-legged Dutch governor, awarded 662 of the Regents Diplomas that conferred especial academic excellence. Wingate High in besieged East Flatbush bestowed precisely one. Erasmus stood somewhere in between.

In 1978, Erasmus had registered the second-highest dropout rate in the five boroughs. More recently, it had been designated a magnet school for hotel and restaurant training. Unfortunately, pending the construction of the promised Hilton, Brooklyn didn't *have* any hotels.

Midwood, on the other hand, offered special courses in bio-medical sciences and had one of the lowest dropout rates in New York.

Out in the courtyard, the three Erasmus girls who were guiding our tour wore teal blazers with a Dutch windmill crest that certified them as students of Hospitality. Eager and sincere, they delivered a memorized spiel about the statue of the sixteenth-century Dutchman and invited the younger children to turn their backs to Desiderius and to try to toss pennies over their shoulders and have them land in the scholar's open bronze book.

As this game was being played, three boys with Jansport backpacks walked by, blithely skipping class, and heckled us, yelling, "Hey! Dat's *me* on da statue." This angered our guides, one of whom pleaded with the group, "Don't listen to them. They cut classes. They hang out in the hallways. They do what *they* wanna do. If y'all come to Erasmus, please, *don't be like them.*"

When the hecklers passed, the courtyard grew quiet again, notwithstanding the pounding of the reconstruction workers, whose scaffolding covered much of the superstructure of the tired old school. Bright orange webbing hung down, as it had when I climbed the Manhattan Bridge, creating an unnatural backdrop to the brilliant red azaleas of the plaza, which had inspired the opening phrase of the old Erasmus song, "When the Spring comes back to Flatbush in its garden by the sea."

The sea, of course, was five miles away, but only a Midwood man would know that.

We went up the steps and entered the historic wood-floored academy. On the walls of the foyer were tinted postcards of a ceremony held at Erasmus in 1911 at the 125th anniversary of the founding of the school. Students dressed as New Netherlanders took part in an historical pageant.

Other rooms were fitted as a study hall and a dormitory from the eighteenth century. Not mentioned by our guides was the attic where misbehaving students were once confined and severely punished. (The nineteenth-century Flatbush poet John Oakey recalled "being flogged into learning with rattan and rule.") I wandered away from the group and went upstairs, where one parlor was hung with photographs of noteworthy graduates: Eli Wallach, Beverly Sills, pro football executives Sam Rutigliano and Al Davis. A replica of the United States Constitution rested on a podium covered in baize.

I left the museum and re-crossed the courtyard and went back into the neo-Gothic temple of academe. Turning in my visitor's pass, I nodded to the security staff and headed for the Flatbush Avenue exit. But they didn't notice me. They were attuned to a radio that was nervously warning, "Be advised. Be advised. There is no patrol currently operational. Be advised. Be advised . . ."

❧

I was killing time before my appointment with the man and woman who had saved the Flatbush Town Hall. Eschewing yet another meal at Sybil's, I made a lunch stop at the White Castle on Church Avenue. This was a standard fast-food outlet, but very clean and sanitary, with a well-scrubbed washroom and a uniformed security guard. I ordered fish on a bun and, when this turned out to be the approximate size of an Oreo cookie, I learned that, at White Castle, sandwiches were commonly purchased by the sackful.

"Gimme twelve burgers," a moderately hungry customer might say. But I was a light eater.

(A few midnights later, two men were walking through the parking lot of the same White Castle when they were shot at from a passing car and seriously wounded. This was not necessarily a comment on the insufficiency of the fish sandwiches; drive-by shootings were a Flatbush commonplace. But reports of gunplay by moonlight never scared me. By that hour, I was always in my bed, riding the Dreamland Express.)

The couple with whom I had requested an audience were a lawyer named Irving Choban and his wife, Rosalind. They were holed up in a ground-floor office on the north side of Church Avenue, across from the White Castle. A sign on the door said, "Ring and Wait," and I did, and presently Mrs. Choban, who was bowed with fibrous dysplasia, unlocked the entrance and showed me into a small museum and told me to wait until her husband was available. Padding around the antechamber, I studied antique, hand-tinted postcards of Brooklyn Bridge and the Reformed Dutch Church and maps of the old trolley routes. I had gained the headquarters of the Flatbush Historical Society.

Mr. Choban was an historian and community activist, who had seen his chosen community go to the dogs. This was not his fault. He and his wife had lobbied and labored for years to keep the Flatbush Town Hall from being demolished. They had succeeded; the building looked beautiful from the outside, which was the only side I saw. It would be their monument, their link with the proud Flatbushers who, a century earlier, had lost the battle to keep their village free.

The Chobans were in their seventies. They lived in the tiny historic district of Albemarle and Kenmore terraces, just behind the old Dutch Church. They had had the azaleas stolen from their garden. They had had the copper leaders and gutters stolen *right off their house.* Rosalind Choban had been mugged once at the entrance to the local post office and once on the Flatbush Avenue bus.

Irving Choban had been robbed at gunpoint while walking through the graveyard where the Leffertses and Martenses and Van Der Bilts lay in heedless slumber.

"Then why do you stay?" I asked him, having been admitted to the rear office.

"There's nothing like walking to work," he replied.

He was a forthright man, sunk in a red padded armchair, who had suffered too many fools. Above his cluttered desk were three oils of nautical scenes by "Roz," and over the door was another painting of the Brooklyn Dodgers in action. As I sat with the lawyer and talked, the artist busied herself in the outer office, and when she had to go on a brief errand, she announced her movements on an intercom: "I'm unlocking the door now..."

"I have a heart condition," Mr. Choban said. "I'm not supposed to use the subways. I had an office in Manhattan, but I moved it here."

"Here" was the frantic precinct of the PLEGNA patrol and Neil's

Discount Liquors and the Bride of Flatbush Avenue. It was a place where, Irving Choban said, "children walk on the street and if they see a flower, they root it up." Irving Choban had lived here for sixty-five of his years.

"Why don't you move to Florida?" I asked him.

"I'd be homesick," he replied. "My house, I'd miss it so much. The beautiful wainscotting. The beautiful back yard. Beautiful. Beautiful . . ."

I hoped for an invitation, but none came.

Our interview continued. What troubled the president of the Flatbush Historical Society was not the mugging in the cemetery but the disconnection of the hamlet with its past. What bewildered him was that not one child from the famous high school across the street ever had come in of his or her own volition to look at his museum. (Students sometimes were *assigned* to root through the Chobans' cartons of historical detritus.) America never would be the immigrants' country. But Flatbush could be their village.

Out of 110 members of the Chobans' cultural society, more than 105 were white. Some were shopkeepers who fled for Queens or Nassau by nightfall. Some were from the respectable families who lived in the grand Victorian houses in the area called Prospect Park South. And some were yuppies who had fallen in love with the Garden City row houses of Kenmore Terrace.

I raised a query about the descendants of the original burghers; what had become, I wondered, of the Clarksons, the Bergens, and the Schencks?

"There *was* a Schenck," Irving Choban said. "The last survivor of the family. She got mugged, moved to Long Island, and died."

Carrying on, indefatigably bearing the torch, the Chobans organized jazz concerts at the Reformed Church parish house and slide shows on Flatbush history. The current edition of *The Spirit of Flatbush* – their own newsletter – lauded their dedication. From the *Spirit* I learned that Rosalind Choban's mother had been a music teacher and that two of her students were George and Ira Gershwin.

I left Mr. Choban to his legal work and burrowed into the files. In unsorted middens of donated papers were clippings and albums and shreds of centuries. The Malbone Wreck. The addresses of butcher shops, circa 1909. The visit of Queen Juliana of the Netherlands to the crossroads of her long-lost colony in 1952. An article from the *Eagle*, dated 1946, heralding the coming of Macy's.

Now Macy's had come and gone, flourished and folded, all in the blink of an eye. I made a photocopy of a pamphlet about the Battle of Brooklyn and bought some reproduction postcards. On Church Avenue, the trees were coming into bud. I left the law office, and Rosalind Choban bolted the door behind me. The cruelest time to sense the death of history was when the spring came back to Flatbush in its garden by the sea.

8

Next door to the community-service agency that was next door to the mildewed fantasia of the Loew's Kings Theater was a clothing store that sold "African Village" tunics in bold colors and stripes and umbrellas emblazoned with a map of the so-called Dark Continent. A sign in the display window of the store observed: "No race in the world is so just as to give others for the asking, a square deal in things economic political and social."

As I walked past this shop one afternoon, I heard a scratchy recording of a man giving a speech in a clipped, forceful, staccato cadence. A small loudspeaker had been set up outside the door, and I could make out, through the static, the odd phrase: "Palestine for the Jews . . . Japan for the Japanese . . . time to unite four hundred million Africans . . . unite to build a great nation of our own on the continent of Africa . . ."

It was the voice of Marcus Garvey, the Jamaican-born herald of Negro self-improvement, apostle of the Black Christ ("Forget the white gods!"), pied piper of the Return to Africa.

A man behind the counter of the store, which was identified on a sign above the window as "INFINITY Indigeneous [sic] i-zigns," beamed when I walked in and asked about the recording, which was obviously not of recent making. It was from 1917, the man said, and Garvey had come to New York to inaugurate his Universal Negro Improvement Association, to be followed, within a few years, by his African Orthodox Church and his indictment on charges of mail fraud and his imprisonment and deportation. Marcus Garvey was too early, but he had been granted one eloquent hour, and now his words were ringing out over old Dutch Flatbush, or at least as far as the little loudspeaker could carry them.

"It's the culture-nomic revolution," the man at the cash register said. His name was Anthony Stone, and he was a Jamaican whom I would have taken for a youth just out of Erasmus had there not been a wisp of white in his goatee and had he not told me that he had already served a stretch in the United States Air Force. Anthony Stone was full of complaint, but not anger; irony, but not defeat. He offered me a banana, my first gift from a Flatbush merchant since Julio at the Midnight Star drowned me in a free monsoon of Go Away Evil aftershave.

Stone had been brought to America when he was eighteen and, like nearly every other immigrant's child I talked to, he shook his head at the recollection and said, "It wasn't my decision. I wish they hadn't gone." His father was Jamaican, but his mother was Cuban, which cost him high-security clearance in the USAF. Stationed at Clark Air Force Base in the Philippines, he was, he said, trained as a mechanic but was never allowed to go near the A-bombs.

Now he was behind the counter of one of the only black-owned businesses in a thoroughly black neighborhood, and he could only shrug and smile when I pointed out to him that the umbrellas in his window had been manufactured in Red China and the "African Village" shirts and slacks were marked "Made in Pakistan."

"Why don't you go back to Jamaica?" I asked Anthony Stone. I was getting a little tired of having to ask this all the time.

"I want to be ahead of the guys I went to school with," he answered. "They're all set up. They got jobs. I don't want to be behind when I go back."

I didn't see how clerking on Flatbush Avenue could advance any man toward his dreams, but Stone was enthusiastic about the clothing store, which he said had not been cleaned out by burglars in several weeks. He was not consumed by fear of crime; his attitude was "Take what you want – it's not much."

"Everybody *could* be physically afraid," he said. "But you got to focus on your mission."

"What's your mission?"

"It's economics. It's empowerment. It's building community and family. It's the culture-nomic revolution. It's propagating our culture through clothing. Slowly but surely, our people are waking up."

"This isn't culture. It's just a fad," I said, pointing to a T-shirt that said,

"21th Century – M Garvey – Africans at home and abroad rise and shine with the dawn of a new day."

"It's Africans going back to their traditional way of clothing," Anthony Stone insisted.

"It's Spike Lee," I countered, feeling uncustomarily feisty. "It's just merchandising."

I looked around. Only a couple of leftover caps and T-shirts carried the Malcolmian "X" that Lee's cine-biography had made so banal that even white Republicans sported it. A year ago, a shop like this would have carried very few items that *didn't* have an "X" on them.

"I don't know what Spike Lee's motive was," Stone said, his voice dropping. I had scored a point. "When you commercialize something, you milk it and milk it and milk it until it's dry."

Anthony Stone reiterated the rhetoric I had heard back in Prospect–Lefferts Gardens about half the drugs in New York City coming in on military planes. Crack cocaine, he said, was "a plot against blacks, just as our consciousness was being aroused."

When I asked him where he thought he'd be in ten years, he said, "A free South Africa."

∾

African-ness was in the air. It had started back at the Fulton Street Mall with the fire-breather in the Egyptian robes who claimed that all Brazilians were the lost tribe of Asher and that the Haitians were the house of Levi. Downtown, at the health-food shop named Genesis 1:29, the owner, Keith White, wearing a Tut's-head T-shirt, had told me that "the cat's out of the bag" and that "European doctrine" would no longer hold sway over black men's lives. In many other stores and on sidewalk vendors' tables, there were the murals, the books, the posters of Garvey and Haile Selassie, the bolts of "Kinte cloth" that turned out, as often as not, to have been made in South Korea.

The message was both hopeful and destructive: that this borough, and this hemisphere, was not Home, that it was a place of captivity and exile, and that a true rebirth was possible only through a spiritual, if not a physical, transplantation to the mother continent. So the word "African-American" was in vogue as an affirmation of roots, and rootlessness. But here, this was not new.

The first African-Americans of Flatbush village were slaves who danced on Pinkster Day and took their orders in Dutch. They were in Flatbush by 1660, and in 1698 there were 71 captives on the census rolls to serve 405 freemen. It was claimed that the Hollanders were lenient taskmasters and that the Africans were worse off after the British achieved their one-shot conquest in 1664 and began to settle New York. Certainly, even the *white* servants who came to the British colony under formal documents of indenture were treated like dogs.

By 1750, blacks made up nearly a third of New York's and Kings County's population, the largest concentration north of Charleston, South Carolina. They peopled Francis Guy's *Winter Scene in Brooklyn*, driving horses, hauling wood, slipping and falling on the ice at Front and Main. By then, they had tried two times to break their chains. The first New York revolt came in 1712. Fires were set and eight whites were killed. Posses set out and destroyed six blacks. Then came the trials. Fourteen slaves were hanged, two were burned at the stake, one was roasted alive, one was starved to death, and one was broken on the wheel.

In 1742, the cry went up again: "The Negroes are rising!" It was called The Great Slave Plot. This time, thirteen were burned, twelve hanged, and seventy-two banished. That was the last rebellion. But during the Revolutionary War, fear that the blacks would revolt in their absence kept many slaveholders from taking up arms. After their success in the Battle of Brooklyn, the British exploited the hostility. They billeted black Loyalist troops in the homes of the Brooklyn gentry, placing the erstwhile masters under the boot of those they had possessed.

The war ended and the Loyalists sailed for Canada, my wife's Huguenot progenitors from the Hudson Valley among them. New York's first Act for the Gradual Abolition of Slavery was passed in 1799. It provided that "any child born of a slave within this State after the fourth day of July next, shall be deemed and adjudged to be born free." But there was a catch. Such children had to work as servants of their mother's "proprietor" until the age of twenty-five for a woman, twenty-eight for a male.

And still the Negroes danced. In the parlor of the Lefferts Homestead in Prospect Park, a document dated 1803 hailed "Carolus Africanus,

Rex – Captain-General and Commander-in-Chief of the Pinkster Boys." A couplet eulogized his glee: "When you know him, then you'll see / A slave whose soul was always free."

By the 1820s, almost all the slaves of Brooklyn had been released. They seemed to have just melted away. The Gazetteer of 1835 reported fewer than two thousand Blacks among a population of 32,057. (There were 238 Paupers, 8 Deaf and Dumb, 8 Blind, 7 Idiots, 3 Lunatics, 894 Swine, 81 Sheep and 38 Black Voters.) In 1863, targeted by Irish mobs in the anti-draft riots of the Civil War, many blacks took refuge in the Vanderveer windmill on Flatbush Avenue, sheltered by villagers whose grandfathers had held human beings as property.

Decades before Marcus Garvey, a group of whites had set out to do his work. In 1830, the Brooklyn Colonization Society announced its proposal to ship the city's Negroes back to Africa. But the descendants of chained Africans demurred. At a protest meeting at "African Hall," a manifesto was issued:

> We know of no other country that we can justly claim, or demand our rights as citizens, whether civil or political, but in these United States of America, our native soil. . . .
>
> We shall be active in our endeavor to convince the members of the Colonization Society, and the public generally, that we are *men*, that we are *brethren*, that we are *countrymen* and *fellow-citizens*. . . .
>
> It is a strange theory to us, how these gentlemen can promise to honor, and respect us in Africa, when they are using every effort to exclude us from all rights and privileges at home. . . .

The borough's schools would not be desegregated until 1893. European immigration then swept the Negroes from sight. By 1910, blacks made up only 1.4 per cent of Brooklyn's inhabitants, the lowest ratio since the dawn of foreign settlement, back when the Canarsees sold their land to the Dutch for brandy and bars of lead.

Then the pendulum swung again. A new influx from Manhattan followed the Fulton Street subway as it was extended deeper into Brooklyn, swinging end-to-end on the A Train. By the end of the Second World War, there were a quarter of a million blacks in the borough, most of them in the neighborhood called Bedford–Stuyvesant, "Brooklyn's Harlem." It was a place, an author found in 1946, where "poverty and squalor are emphasized by parkless, shadeless streets crowded with ramshackle tenements. Packed in this dismal district are sights that arouse pity, terror, and anger."

But Brooklyn's citizens of color were generally invisible; only Jackie Robinson's batting average was of any concern to the outside world. Growing up in Flatbush in the fifties, I had the acquaintance of exactly three black souls. One was our postman. One washed our windows. One was a classmate in my earliest grades named Carlton Brown. Everyone else was Jewish, Italian, Irish, Polish, or the fellow we crudely dismissed as "Mister Gold Teeth" from the Chinese Hand Laundry. As it turned out, all these were merely sojourners. Their edition of the Village of Flatbush lasted barely sixty years.

How had Flatbush become overwhelmingly black in the span of less than two decades? The process was a combination of panic, stigmatization, economics, rapacious mortgage and real-estate practices, and the lure of the Long Island suburbs. The word "blockbusting" entered the vocabulary.

This was what the Bride of Flatbush Avenue had watched from her vantage point at Martense Street – the complete reconstitution of a neighborhood, a study in white and black. The transfer of populations had been almost total; it recapitulated in miniature the partition of India and Pakistan; it was the Greeks and the Turks abandoning their villages and changing countries in 1923. In Flatbush, neither those who fled nor those who flooded in were of one class or country. But people like me were not ethnologists. We all saw color first, and culture second.

An older man like Eddie Babb of the PLEGNA Civilian Patrol could remember boarding the subway to Flatbush around 1960 and being the only black face on the IRT: "Nobody pointed, nobody stared, no one said anything. But you always felt it. You always knew."

Now I had come to know the opposite, to ride The Beast or the B41 or to walk solo through the boisterous barrage of teens under the scaffolding at Erasmus Hall High, a pink face as conspicuous as Eddie Babb once had been on the Number 2 train. Nobody pointed, nobody stared. I assumed that everyone assumed that I was a lunatic, or a cop.

Only the buildings were unmoved, and the occasional bewildered holdover like the ice-cream man, Henry J. Bahnsen, or Neil Telsey of Discount

Liquors, or the historical Chobans, or my mother. From the pews of the Reformed Protestant Dutch Church to INFINITY Indigenous, this little world had tilted on its axis. The Japanese had Japan and the Jews had Palestine, as Marcus Garvey had proclaimed. And now, 350 years out of Africa, the Africans held the Wooded Flat.

I wondered what Carlton Brown would say.

&

I also wondered what actual Africans would think of the Afri-centric renaissance. On Flatbush near the PLEGNA office was an establishment called "Akwaaba, The African Restaurant in Brooklyn." It had been reviewed in the *New York Times*. Under the category "Best dishes," the article listed *omo tuo, watche, kenkey, egushie* and *jollof,* none of which rang a bell in my culinary consciousness equal to, say, corned beef on rye. But I was ravenous after a long walk up the avenue, and I was famous for eating absolutely anything, so I strolled in to have some lunch.

What I found was a brightly-lit room with a dozen tables and, behind a glass partition, the kitchen. Above this was a sign that listed the various offerings with English explanations. I learned that *omo tuo* was "rice balls," and *kenkey* was a corn-meal paste. And there were additional selections: *fufu* and *banku* and *nkrakra*, which was a hot-pepper soup. Junior's, this wasn't.

The *Times* had noted that the staff's command of English was "at times uncertain," and this was substantiated when a server approached me, set down a tumbler of water as big as a Grecian urn, smiled uncomprehendingly at every question I asked, and then sat down on a chair by the kitchen window to watch "All My Children" on a TV mounted over the door. An in-depth interview here seemed increasingly unlikely.

When a commercial came on, I waved for the woman to return and pointed on the menu to *jollof* with fish, comfortable in the knowledge that, according to the *Times*, this would be a rice dish flavored with soy oil and peppers for "a nutty flavor." One could never go wrong with rice.

There were no other customers. The presence of recent African immigrants in Flatbush had been a surprise to me at first, though the popularity of Kinte cloth had made it difficult to distinguish fashion plates from Lefferts Gardens from Liberians just off the plane. But I had passed several sidewalk incense-vendors in fabulous flowing robes and a couple of Ghanaian groceries and one shop that sold authentic fabrics from the Gold Coast and Côte d'Ivoire. Once a month, an African congregation convened at the Reformed Dutch Church. And on a counter at Akwaaba – the word means "welcome" in Ashanti, according to the *Times* – was an issue of *Ghana Newsweek* whose headline read: "IS GHANA BROKE? Finance Minister Paints Gloomy Picture of National Penury."

Eventually, while I awaited my lunch, two well-dressed African-American men came in and sat down side by side with their backs to me. They were followed, a few minutes later, by two Arabs, who plunked down a heavy duffel bag filled with counterfeit Karl Kani-Jeans and Reebok-logo T-shirts and proceeded to sell most of them, at $4.50 each, to the two other diners and the server and the chef.

What about the *jollof* and fish? It was delicious – a small, whole, crispy-skinned pomfret with snowy flesh, reposing atop a drumlin of rice and covered in a very thick, very smoky (burned, actually), red tomato sauce. Seven dollars. Next time, *fufu*.

∾

I went back to see Anthony Stone at his clothing store, full of facts and figures concerning the history of slavery in Brooklyn. I had made copies of pages of history books and encyclopedias, and he studied them with great interest, intrigued that his race had existed so long in a place where he felt so new.

On Flatbush Avenue, Anthony Stone went on some more about moving "back" to Africa, and about how much he had loved the Philippines during his hitch as an Air Force mechanic, and how the indigenous Negritos, not MacArthur or the Marines, had wrested that archipelago from the Japanese through sabotage and cunning.

"They treat you like a king over there," he said, an islander's son, marooned on an American boulevard, yearning for the far Pacific.

Like Serge Pierrelouis, the Haitian transit cop, Anthony Stone was full of schemes. He had written a couple of rap lyrics, one of them a takeoff on the Malcolm X frenzy, and had sent them to the Library of Congress for copyright. He kept ordering new merchandise, trying to stay ahead of the breakneck pace of street fashion, but complained that business had been indifferent, even over Easter. A few customers drifted in and out, checking the prices on the Asian-made African styles, but the only item he sold while I was around was a ten-dollar belt.

Then we got on the subject of religion. I told him about my visit to the Watchtower and the Lubavitchers' circus parade, and how the Jehovah's Witnesses awaited the Kingdom of God, while the Hasidim kept their eye out for the First Coming.

"Everybody's searching for the Messiah," I said sagely.

"Messiah *in* us," replied Anthony Stone.

9

"In the United States," I had read in a fascinating book about the religion, "the word *voodoo* is used in a casual and derogatory way to indicate anything on a spectrum from the deceptive to the downright evil." And this was true – "voodoo economics" was the term given to the fiscal policies of Ronald Reagan by those few critics whom the policies had somehow failed to make rich.

The book was called *Mama Lola: A Vodou Priestess in Brooklyn,* and it made it clear that voodoo (the more common American spelling) was a stream that ran deeply through the enormous Haitian community that had supplanted the predominant Hebrews and Hibernians of my mother's neighborhood. Most Haitians, even practicing Catholics, sipped from this brook in times of distress. The outside world knew little of this. To the rest of us, "voodoo" connoted stiff-legged zombies with Little Orphan Annie eyes, rising from their jungly graves to kill and kill and kill.

Way back at the Midnight Star in Prospect–Lefferts Gardens, I had learned in a few minutes with the hyperactive Julio that voodoo could be more of a healing art than a midnight parade of bloodless corpses. (Assisted by Ézili Freda, his Sorrowful Virgin, Julio had been able, he said, to cure a sickly woman the very first time he tried.) But the Midnight Star apparently had gone out of business, and now I was much farther down Flatbush Avenue, in a district of Botaniques crammed with emollients and altarpieces, and of Haitian groceries, law firms, real-estate brokerages, shipping agents, music stores, radio stations, dentists, lunch counters, storefront churches, and travel offices. In other words, I was nearly home.

One of the largest of the Haitian-owned businesses was La France Travel, and its proprietor was a man named Jerome Herold. (The biggest of all was A and B Furniture on Church Avenue, the store whose owner had been shot dead by the teenaged assailant while getting into his Mercedes at closing time.) According to the office manager at the newspaper *Haiti Progres* – "*Le journal qui offre une alternative*" – M. Herold would be an excellent source of information about the Haitians, a nation about which I was even more ignorant than usual, having never been sent down there during all my years as a far-from-intrepid foreign correspondent. If I was going to learn anything about the spirit world, this would be the place to make a start.

Jerome Herold sat behind a desk in a back room of La France Travel. His ticket agents were encased in a bulletproof cabin in the main part of the office, like subway token clerks or Off-Track Betting cashiers. The door from the street to the agency was kept locked at all times. Supplicants with sincere faces (like mine) were admitted with a loud buzz.

Jerome Herold had come to Brooklyn in 1973 with three hundred dollars, which was more than many other Haitians could muster, but still not much of a grubstake to get started in the Most Important City in the World. He had driven a gypsy cab, then a limousine. He had bought impounded cars at police auctions and resold them at a profit. Now he was a successful baron of the ethnic travel industry and he was planning to buy into a charter airline to ply the under-served route between Flatbush and Port-au-Prince. There were six hundred thousand Haitians in Greater New York, he said, and all of them wanted to go home, at least for Christmas.

"My dream is to help my country take its share of the Caribbean," Jerome Herold told me. We were sitting face to face at his desk, which was covered with a thick sheet of glass that held in place currency notes from the many countries he had visited. M. Herold, who wore a gold watch and a Masonic ring, was just back from Benin in West Africa, where he had taken part in a conference, the theme of which was how to dispel "Afri-pessimism."

"Haiti don't get nothing," he was saying. "Santo Domingo gets billions and billions, right next door. Saint Martin and Antigua get eighty thousand tourists. Haiti don't get nothing."

In Flatbush, at first, Jerome Herold had got plenty of nothing himself. It was twenty years ago, and the blockbusting was at its peak. He remembered the psychic landscape as the neighborhood changed.

"You could see the anger on the people's faces," he said. "You could see the white women make way as you walked by. You could see how frightened they were. Yes, you could see the fear."

Now, when the door to his office was open, he could squint through the layers of crime-resistent plastic and see the sidling youths and the village wives and the hurtling vans, hustling for one-dollar fares, that the Haitians called "tap-taps." It was his people's city now, this stretch of this long thoroughfare.

"Flatbush Avenue," said Jerome Herold. "A place for those who have hope, who like to dream, to become somebody. And a place for those who are lost, who don't know who they are, to go back and forth without doing nothing."

I thought that pretty well summed it up.

He paused.

"It's good versus evil here," the travel agent said.

"Could good lose?" I asked.

"It could," he replied. "Unless we get organized. One block from here, it is a war zone. It is dead. In three years, it will be here."

Exactly a block away, exactly three years before, a twelve-year-old boy named David Opont, recently arrived from Haiti, had been doused with fuel and set on fire by a fourteen-year-old, ostensibly because he refused to take drugs. The facts of the incident were a bit muddled – there was no physical evidence that drugs were involved – but David Opont had survived his burns, and he had become a symbol of Brooklyn's capacity for horror and heroism. Creole songs were written about him: "*You are a link in the chain, the chain that will never be broken.*" The child who attacked David Opont was convicted of attempted murder, kidnapping, robbery, and assault and was sentenced to the juvenile maximum. Three years. He would be out of detention in a couple of months and back on the avenue.

We were talking about the burned boy and his terrible ordeal when two *enfants* not much older than David Opont came into the office of Jerome Herold and kissed him gently on the left cheek, then bowed to me and shook my hand. These were Herold's sons, students at the parochial school of Our Lady of Refuge, dressed in uniforms and ties, two more links in the chain. Momentarily, they excused themselves, saying they had to return to the church for study hour. The older boy, the father said, was already looking at pre-pre-medical courses offered by a nearby high school. That was noble Midwood, the school that made me and Woody Allen what we are today.

When the boys left, I made my pitch. I had been to the big Église de Dieu in the old Rialto Theater. I had been to Catholic churches and I had stood outside the Clarté Céleste and heard the guitars play. Now, I said, I wished to learn more about the spiritual world.

"I will call Sò Ann," said Jerome Herold.

∾

Sò Ann – born Annette Auguste – was the Haitian Streisand, though with a somewhat less dynamic voice and about fifty fewer platinum albums. She was a singer, a political activist, a talk-show host, and, since the moment of her First Communion back in Haiti, when as a seven-year-old she astounded everyone by suddenly trembling uncontrollably and speaking with the voice of an old woman, she had been possessed by a powerful *lwa* that enabled her to heal anyone who was not fated to die.

She lived in a wonderfully dark and cluttered Victorian house on a quiet side street just east of Flatbush Avenue, in an area that had been Irish Catholic until the great sea change. Much too early for my date with her, I lingered under the flagpole at the St. Vincent Ferrer elementary school on Glenwood Road, a half-block from Sò Ann's house, watching two workers who were placing marigolds around a small granite marker. It was a memorial to a U.S. Marine, Major Eugene McCarthy, St. Vincent Ferrer Class of '69, killed twenty-two years later in the Gulf War. I wondered how many McCarthys were left around here to mourn him.

At the hour of the appointment Jerome Herold had arranged for me, I appeared at the designated big green house and was shown into a formal drawing room containing a plastic-covered three-piece sofa set, a bookcase stuffed with texts on sociology and marketing, various Haitian wood carvings, prayer plants, silk flowers, Greek vases, delicate statues of Mandarin scholars, matching lamps with pottery bases, and a wall hanging of the Last Supper. The man who had admitted me went into the dining room and began to softly strum a guitar.

Sò Ann appeared presently, a sizable woman in a loose-fitting green dress with a red flower pattern, her hair brushed to obedient straightness and her age, I guessed, close to fifty. Looking for an opening, as mesmerized as Ronald Colman in Shangri-La, I mentioned that I had read the book about Mama Lola, and Sò Ann snapped back that "voodoo don't come in books. Voodoo inside you."

I nodded in complete agreement.

"Spirit not in bottle of something," Sò Ann said. "Spirit not in picture of something. Spirit always with you. Spirit *in* you. When the spirit let you alone, *you can do nothing.*"

But the spirit was not happy with Sò Ann. In recent years, she had let her devotions slide while laboring full-time for the restoration of democracy in her poor and fearful homeland. Her passion took many forms. Yawning, she explained that she had been up all night as a featured commentator on a phone-in program called "*Haiti en Ondes*" – "Haiti on the Air." Then she rose, went to the hallway, and, after burrowing for several minutes in Fibber McGee's closet, handed me an audio cassette with her picture on the yellow label and the title *Sò Ann – Libète*. The word was Creole for "liberty" and this was what the Haitians and the Jews of my grandparents' time had never known until they came to Brooklyn.

Annette Auguste did not consider herself especially fortunate to have been chosen to be "ridden," as it was described, by her *lwa*. The burden of her blessing was a soul-wrenching conflict between curse and cure, power and futility. One morning, she had awakened in a sweat and had felt compelled to warn one of her five sons not to go to school that day. She had dreamed that harm would come to him en route.

"My son said, 'You always dreaming, dreaming, dreaming,'" she recalled. "I go back to bed. He go out, he get hit by a car. I don't go to any lawyer, because spirit knew it was going to happen.

"Some people don't want everybody to know they are possess," Sò Ann said. "But I'm not ashamed about it. It's my culture. It's real African culture. In Haiti, the French people wanted us to get *their* religion. When you children, the priests don't want you to go voodoo. But we have *eyes*. We have *ears*. We *know*. You don't have to go to church to pray to God.

"I'm not ashamed about it. So many people in the world *want* to have a spirit but they can't. Spirit always with you, always protect you. Other people, they *jealous*."

The potentialities of possession were enormous. Sò Ann cupped her hands in front of her lips, made a quick puffing sound, and said, "If I come in your house, have a little powder, I can put a curse on you. Not just any kind of powder. Sometime you take the skin of the snake or the frog, make a powder, put it in the skin of a person and their skin turn just like a frog. Yeah!"

There were limits. A Chinese proverb held that there was medicine for sickness, but none for fate. Sò Ann turned this upside-down. She said, "If you have a curse, I can cure. If I see nothing that my spirit can do, I tell them to go to hospital."

She invited me to come with her to Haiti when her country finally was free. In Flatbush, she admitted, devoting her full energies to politics had left her "a little cold with the spirit." She was planning a feast for her *lwa* to try to recover his approbation, but there were always limits to what voodoo could achieve at this remove from Haitian water and soil.

Back home, her full power would manifest itself and she would be as fresh and fervent as a seven-year-old girl at First Communion. Awaiting that hour, she sang her patriotic lyrics and worked long night-hours on the radio, rallying her partisans. In Haiti, all would be well. All would be revealed.

"In my country," Sò Ann declaimed, "we have a powder, you can *kill* people with that powder."

"There is a powder killing people in Brooklyn," I said, thinking myself clever. "Cocaine."

Sò Ann had five sons. Two were at Midwood High School. The others were at colleges downtown. (That explained the marketing textbooks.) We talked for a minute about drugs and crime. There was no way, in Flatbush, not to.

"My boys not doing drugs," the priestess said. "They do good things. They good children so far. *So far*. We don't know tomorrow."

∾

I went out of the big Victorian house and headed home to listen to Sò Ann's cassette. Walking past St. Vincent Ferrer, looking up into the bright midday sky, I was startled to notice that one patch of high, wispy cloud had turned distinctly and impossibly pink, and another portion was a weird lime green. I blinked a few times, trying to make the mirage disappear.

It wouldn't go. It wasn't a rainbow; it hadn't rained in twelve days. It wasn't dawn or sunset's rosy-fingered glow, not at 1:32 in the afternoon. Perhaps someone had fired a couple of paintballs at the moon. Maybe it was Sò Ann, just showing off.

I swear this happened.

∾

Sò Ann was just an amateur, other Haitians said. The manager at *Haiti Progres* gave me numbers to call and names like "Ninaj" and "Moumousse." Serge Pierrelouis, the transit patrolman, took me around to meet people. I went into a music shop on Flatbush Avenue called Digital Records, whose overhead sign had been riddled by BB shot. The clerk told me to go to Church Avenue and look for a certain botanica.

"Ask for the priest," he advised.

The botanica was La Clavicule du Roi Salomon – King Solomon's Collarbone. It stood on the south side of Church Avenue, east of the Reformed Dutch Church and four short blocks from A and B Furniture, where the Haitian community's most successful businessman had been killed by a teenaged boy.

"The priest, please," I requested, once inside King Solomon's, leaning casually on the counter and trying to make it seem as if asking to see a practitioner of spirit possession was something I did every day.

"Upstairs," a young woman said, pointing to a side door.

At the top of the linoleum-covered stairway was a hot, dark waiting room, with seven red chairs and a fourteen-inch television that was featuring a rerun of "Home Improvement." There was nobody in sight. I took a seat. Through a doorway, I could see a small chamber fitted out as an altar to Danbala, the snake spirit, with a statue of a coiled cobra and a large painting of the Garden of Eden with a serpent prominent in the scene. Also, for reasons I was not about to guess at, there were two loaves of twisted challah egg bread, two two-liter jugs of generic cola, an egg positioned atop a small mound of powdered sulfur, one bottle of Smirnoff's, and another jar of Hennessey cognac.

While I was making note of these rather eclectic furnishings, a woman padded up to me silently from behind and, scaring me half to death, formally announced, "Priest see you now."

I was ushered into another room that contained more challah bread, various lacquered crucifixes and Last Suppers, a diploma certifying someone to be a licentiate in "Magie Yogi Indien," a fruit cake, a lot more booze, a plastic falcon with a handkerchief of red satin draped over its head, various candles, two small obsidian (or plastic) pyramids, and an effigy of Ézili Dantò, the black Madonna.

Sitting in a red chair with a plastic cover, wearing wire-rimmed glasses and a leather skullcap, shuffling a deck of Tarot cards, and positioned in front of a large American flag, sat Similhomme Louis, the man I had come to see.

"Voodoo?" he said, repeating my inquiry. "Come with me to Haiti. We initiate you and wash your hair and you learn voodoo."

The story of Similhomme Louis was one that had become familiar. He had migrated to Brooklyn in 1970. He had labored in a factory, learning English from his co-workers and amassing sufficient funds to establish what he claimed had been the first religious-goods store in Haitian New York. There now were dozens of others, of course – Botanica Santa Philomena, for one, was kitty-corner from the Clavicule – but those he dismissed as "parasites." He had just signed the papers that made him a citizen of the U.S.A.

"People in Haiti talk like we got money in the streets up here," he said. "You get here, man, you have to *work*. You have to pay *tax*. People say, 'The government will give me money. The government will give me things.'"

He said the word in the Gallic manner – goo-vern-mont.

"Well, the government is *me*."

He moaned about a lack of business downstairs and how the embargo slapped on his old country by his new country to punish the generals was making it impossible to import statues and certain other necessities. He complained that when he tried to make a big party for his *lwa* in the cafeteria of Erasmus Hall High School and invited students to attend, parents protested that he was evil and satanic and was going to turn their children into zombies.

But he wasn't, he insisted. The only time he ever got into the *zonbi* thing was November 1, All Saints' Day, and that was a small, private affair.

"I invite you," he announced. "First November. If I have space for only four people, you be five."

Unfortunately, First November I would be in Canada, trying to make sense of ten weeks on Flatbush Avenue. It was just my luck.

"Anyway," said Similhomme Louis, "I can't do anything really spiritual in New York. When I have to make sacrifice, I have to go to Haiti. The *racine* is not here. It is only in Haiti."

He was wounded by the fact that the Erasmus parents thought he was a harbinger of ill.

"But what about Danbala?" I said, a sudden expert. "Isn't the serpent potentially evil?"

"You have to have Lucifer," said the high priest of King Solomon's Collarbone. "If there's no evil, how do you know what is good?"

⌀

Full of ideas, chasing opportunity like a foxhound, Serge Pierrelouis hustled me hither and yon. One minute, the uniformed subway constable and I were at the offices of "*Haiti en Ondes*"; the next, we were squeezing down an alley and through a side door into the basement headquarters of HEAR – Haitian Enforcement Against Racism – a group that sold sponsorship of destitute children back in Haiti to comparatively affluent Americans at a cost of eighty-two cents a day. It sounded like a pittance, but to a child of a beggared, brutal nation, pocket change could mean the difference between stamina and starvation. At HEAR, I accepted a flyer, stuffed it in my pocket, and then the amply padded Serge and I went down to lunch at a place called Ling Ling Chinese, with him facing the door, as cops were always trained to do.

I had lists of people to see and leads to follow, until I was knocked cold by a woman behind a desk at a community service center, who asked, "Would you like to meet a Haitian Jew?"

This was like asking Cecil Fielder, "Would you like me to throw the next pitch underhand?"

"Well, maybe," I replied, biting my tongue.

I thought they were putting me on. I was given the address of a storefront called the Arcane Business Agency, and the name of one Lucien Delly.

Good joke, I thought – a Kosher Delly.

Early one evening, just after dinner, I walked toward the address the woman had given me. It was 1372 Flatbush Avenue, halfway between La France Travel and the offices of *Haiti Progres*. But number 1372 had to be a hoax. It was a battered storefront with a sliding grille that had been ripped and shredded, so that long spines of metal hung down at angles like the spokes of an umbrella after Hurricane Andrew. There was no sign or decal to indicate what the place was used for. It looked like just another abandoned Flatbush wreck. Out front, the metalwork and plaster had been spray-painted by someone named ANIMAL, an escapee from "Sesame Street."

But there were lights on inside. Sitting in the rear, at a desk piled high with paperwork, was a small, white-bearded, dark-skinned man, dressed in the black suit and white shirt and black tie and topper of an Orthodox, but not Hasidic, Jew. This, I aver, was as true as pink and green sky.

I walked in and slalomed my way around a dozen scattered armchairs and television consoles and writing tables and said, with ceremony, "Mister Delly, I presume?"

I presumed correctly. Above the various desks were fourteen different certificates asserting that one Lucien Delly had completed assorted university courses in Paralegal and Business Studies. And this was the matriculant himself, shaking my hand and asking me, "Why have you come?"

"To meet you," I said.

He had been born a Roman Catholic, he was now a practicing Jew, and between Haiti and the Congregation Young Israel of Vanderveer Park he had been, he said, a Free and Accepted Mason, an Episcopal bishop in Yonkers, New York, and a follower of Eckankar, Religion of the Light and Sound of God.

"I studied everything," he said, "and I decided to observe Judaism. So far, I feel much comfortable there. It is like a family. No discrimination. Believe in one God. Shma Yisroel. One God. It's a whole God."

"What do other Haitians think of you?" I asked.

"I'm not interested in knowing what they think," said the Jew. "If you talk with them about denomination, they think Jews very bad people. They think Jews killed Jesus. They say, 'You against *God*. You kill *God*.' But they talking about something they don't know about. The question is: Is Jesus God?"

"Are you waiting for Moshiach?" I inquired. Expecting their Messiah to arrive at any moment, the Lubavitchers were beating drums and flying blimps.

"I don't go that far," Lucien Delly replied. "I don't care if Moshiach come or don't come. It's not important to me. What is important is to live now, to do your best."

Lucien Delly's nine-year-old son was in Catholic school. (Jewishness, by tradition, was matrilineal, and Mr. Delly's wife had not converted.) Anyway, the father said, denomination mattered less than devotion. This was a practical, philosophical man.

He had been working out of this office since 1978, and the piles of paperwork on the multiple desks made it appear likely that he hadn't filed or thrown away a form or a letter in any of those fifteen years. On Friday nights, he slept here, as it was not permissible for him to take a dollar cab home after the Sabbath-eve service. And, like everyone else on Flatbush Avenue, this unlikely character in the suspenders and horn-rimmed glasses had seen his share of woe.

"The crime goes door to door to door," he said. "Everything going from bad to worse to worse and worse. You drive a taxi, they kill you for *nothing*. This afternoon, I was here by myself and four or five boys, sixteen or seventeen years old, pulled my gate down and locked me in. For them, that was their fun."

We were conversing like this when a man and woman walked in to discuss some immigration matter, as if sent to demonstrate to me that Lucien Delly really was a paralegal problem solver and not some actor put up to this by Serge Pierrelouis and the nice folks at HEAR.

"People are not really happy here," the man who had walked in said, after a time. "Haiti was such a good country. My grandmother told me that Haiti was great, it was the goodest island. Even in 1970, you go there, you want to stay there. So tropical. The gardens . . ."

"Do you miss it?" I asked the man, whose mellifluous name was Clervil Mézamour and whose wife's was the equally musical Edlyne Playsir.

"Day after day after day," he replied.

Clervil Mézamour was a big, handsome man who worked as a cook down at Sheepshead Bay, where the fluke and bluefish boats put to sea. (Ms. Playsir was a home-care attendant.) Yet he was afraid to walk the streets, afraid to ride the buses, afraid to sit on his porch under a summer sky.

"We need strong laws," he said. "We don't have strong laws. A criminal kill four or five guys, you might not see him for four or five months, and then you see him on the street again. You blow up a house and kill everybody, I see you again, three months later."

He lowered his voice.

"When I first came here," said the big, handsome man, "I saw the white fear and it made me sad. In the beginning, it made me angry, too. I thought, 'I know who I am. Why are they afraid of me?' But now, I've learned why, and it makes me sad. I'm scared, too. It's not fair, to be scared, every day, even to go next door. I told my wife when I saw the first leaves on the trees, 'Oh, no. It's summer in Brooklyn.' Summer is the terrible time. The kids are free and everywhere."

What a strange and tangled place my little Dutch village had become. Here I was sitting at the unmarked Arcane Business Agency, Inc., talking to a man who, when I was being bar-mitzvahed around the corner in 1963, was a Catholic in Haiti, but who now, at a time when I did not attend synagogue, was a Jew in Flatbush. A year from now, I thought, the way things were going, he would be a monk at a Taoist temple and I would be Archbishop of Canterbury.

It was growing late, nearly 7:30. "Where are you parked?" asked Clervil Mézamour.

"I don't have a car," I answered. "I walked."

"You *walked*?" everybody gasped in unison.

"Sure," I said.

"Go now," said Lucien Delly anxiously, wishing me godspeed. "Go now. It is getting dark." And so I went.

10

After the Haitian Jew, it surprised me not at all when I went into a tiny stall next door to a Palestinian bodega and met an Afghan tax consultant who was married to a Dominican lab technician. By this point, having wandered through the Byzantine realm of the Bride of Flatbush for week after week after week, I would not have been shocked to meet Barbra Streisand herself, carrying a bag of Chinese take-out from the Ling Ling and a forty-ouncer of Midnight Dragon. But this never happened.

Instead, I was walking past the corner of Flatbush and Newkirk Avenue one morning when my eye was caught by a small overhead sign that said, "KHYBER TRAVEL AGENCY." This immediately brought back fond memories of my days in Pakistan – about eight days, actually – and an afternoon spent watching military men play polo on a field in Rawalpindi with the mountains of the Khyber looming behind them. That was as close as I had got to the border. Coverage of the Afghan war itself I left to Arthur Kent.

The Khyber Travel Agency turned out to be an office so narrow that I could stand on the checkerboard tile floor and touch both walls with my fingertips. Its proprietor was a young, exceedingly friendly fellow named Taj Akbar – "Great Crown" – who, with his tousled black hair and a mustache, looked very much like Robert Downey, Jr., trying to look like Charlie Chaplin, the Great Clown. Immediately upon my arrival, Taj Akbar dashed next door into the Palestinian grocery for hot tea, which I added to my account of Flatbush freebies that already included one banana and one bath in magic cologne.

"Special Haj Airfare – $1,226," said a sign on the wall, a Seat Sale bargain for anyone who happened to be strolling down Flatbush Avenue on his way to Mecca. Taj Akbar was new at this travel game. So far, he posed no threat to Jerome Herold at La France. He was renting this tiny space from a Pakistani friend who was not charging him any rent, which was only fitting, since Taj Akbar wasn't selling any tickets. This may have been why, when I walked in, he was sitting at his desk and reading *101 Best Businesses to Start*. I doubted that an Afghan travel agency in a Haitian neighborhood was listed among the 101.

I told him where I came from and what I was about.

"If God grants you long life," Taj Akbar said, "you will come back and sell me a book and I'll sell you a ticket to Toronto."

This wasn't the young man's first enterprise since his arrival in the Land of the Free. He had worked in a medical laboratory on Flatbush Avenue, which was where he had met his wife, a Spanish-speaking Dominicana. A certificate on the wall attested to the fact that he had completed the H and R Block course in Basic Income-Tax Preparation, but hardly anyone came to him to have his or her taxes done, either. Still, he was a lot more joyful than I would have been in his shoes and his shirt and tie.

"We just got married and I'm still happy," Taj Akbar said. (I told him it was the same with me and my Canadian, even after nineteen years.) People, he said, had been afraid for the couple's prospects. (Us, too.) You couldn't find two cultures more disparate, nay-sayers cried. (Ditto.) But Taj Akbar's mother had given her clear sanction. (End of comparison.) When she came over from Peshawar to inspect the bride, she wound up staying for seven months.

That was nothing – the wife's mother moved in *permanently*. Hispanic, Moslem, Jewish, African – it didn't matter to Taj. His *lwa* was the old spirit of Brooklyn.

"Everybody same," he said.

Taj Akbar had grown up just outside his parents' native land in the relative placidity of Pakistan. His flight from Peshawar to Kennedy Airport in 1984 – the same year I was in Pakistan to cover the Islamification campaign of President Zia ul-Haq – had been his first trip to the West. Nine years later, he could avow, as few others in Flatbush could, "I keep my door locked, but I'm not afraid. I am not frightened. I believe in God."

He rose each morning at six, put on his shirt and tie, and drove in from Ozone Park, Queens, to sit in Flatbush and read *101 Best Businesses*. The Dominicana had given him two sons, Kamal and Bilal. Married to a Moslem, she nevertheless maintained her Catholicism.

"My wife has her Bible," Taj Akbar allowed. "I'm not like World Trade Center, blow people up for being different religion."

I wondered about the two little boys. I said, "In Judaism, the children take the mother's faith."

"In Islam," proclaimed Taj Akbar, beaming like the lovesick Tramp in *City Lights*, "it's the father's!"

∽

On Friday afternoons, Taj Akbar locked the rarely crossed portal of his little business and went to pray to Allah in a converted mansion on the most beautiful street in New York.

This was Albemarle Road, in the section of Flatbush called Prospect Park South. Separated from the rampage of Flatbush Avenue by the open cut of the Brighton Beach subway and by a Grand Canyon of economic disparity, the Queen Anne and neo-Tudor monster homes of this mature urban suburb were Brooklyn's palaces of the Loire. They had been built at the turn of the century by a developer named Dean Alvord, who aimed "to create a rural park within the limitations of the conventional city block" and to make it "acceptable to people of culture with means equal to some of the luxuries as well as the necessities of life."

From the beginning, it was clear that Prospect Park South would be a place apart. Brick gateposts at each intersection were decorated with the entwined initials of the subdivision. As the trees grew and gardens were planted, the verdancy of the area insulated it even more from the stridency of polyglot, middle-class Flatbush. By 1917, the separation was as total as today. West of the subway tracks was Alvord's refuge of the upper classes. East of the open cut, the new apartment buildings and the walk-ups over the storefronts were filling with the parents of the future Wallachs and Streisands and Malamuds, the Haywards and Kilgallens and Kazans. And that was the year that P. G. Wodehouse and Guy Bolton set the old Dutch village to song:

> When it's nesting time in Flatbush,
> We will take a little flat,
> With Welcome on the mat,
> Where there's room to swing a cat,
> I'll hang up my hat.
> Life will be so sweet with you –
> When it's nesting time in Flatbush, in Flatbush Avenue.
>
> Our little home may have de-fects,
> Like all the flats in town.
> It's wise not to lean on the walls,
> Because they might fall down.
> It's rather badly lighted, which makes it hard to see.
> The neighbors play the Gram-o-phone each night till after three.
> But it will be a paradise if shared, my love, with thee . . .

On a Friday noon at nesting time in 1993, I walked toward the Albanian Mosque on Albemarle Road – formerly the residence of the chairman of the Fruit of the Loom undergarment company – in complete awe of my surroundings. The mammoth homes and pyrotechnic gardens in full spring blossom made the proximity of the frantic Flatbush strip, with its schlock stores and bricked-up apartments, seem surreal. I walked past the incredible Japanese house. It was as if the Heian Shrine of imperial Kyoto had been swept up by a tornado and set down gently in New Netherland. Across the street was the Italian palazzo. This wasn't Brooklyn, it was a World's Fair.

I stepped up my pace and walked on to the house of worship, which was a heavy brown-brick building with double castle doors in front of which men in white lace skullcaps were standing around in small groups, waiting for the call of the muezzin. I had reached the *Qendra Islame Shqiptaro-Amerikane New York dhe New Jersey*, otherwise known as the Albanian Mosque. I stepped onto the porch and someone handed me a pamphlet that read:

Muslimanizimi ka shardet e veta, të cilat janë 33. Këto sharde janë detryë a domosdoshme për t'i mësue, besue dhe zbatue në veprim për çdo musliman dhe muslimane të mënçem.

This explained everything. The men outside, numbering no more than thirty, represented the expatriate Albanian community that had outfitted this splendid old home for their religious purposes. They didn't live in Prospect Park South; the men with whom I chatted were cooks and barbers and clerks from Sheepshead Bay and Flatlands, who somehow had escaped what had been the poorest and most oppressive communist state in Europe. Once a week, and on holy days with names like *Nisfu Shaban* and *Lejletul Kadr*, they assembled here, removed their shoes, and went inside to worship. Joining them were several Arabs in Aladdin's robes, a few Pakistanis, the odd Indonesian, and, after the service had already started, Taj Akbar the Afghan, waving to me as he genuflected toward the Eastern wall and tried to make up for lost time.

We were in a large, bright parlor with light-green walls and a red Oriental carpet. (I sat quietly against the back wall, and no one made me feel unwelcome.) At the southeast corner of the room was a small booth, painted Islamic green, and standing in it was the imam, looking benign and professorial in a black robe and white headgear, reading from the Holy Koran.

Presently, the holy man set down his prayer book and began a long expostulation in one of the most obscure and difficult languages in the world, a stemwinder from which I caught exactly two words – "Islamismy" and "cultura" – while glancing over at Taj Akbar, who was as lost as I was.

When the prayer service concluded, I said my goodbyes to Taj Akbar and commenced the long trek home. The luxuriant homesteads of Prospect Park South dissolved into the Ditmas Park Historic District, another elegant subdivision from the turn of the century, and then the streets grew less and less leafy and tranquil, until I was back on Flatbush Avenue near Lucien Delly's office, walking past the stores with uninhabited apartments above them and the apartments with no living stores below.

But Prospect Park South stayed with me. I never had known that such majesty still existed in old Flatbush town, replacing the demolished manor houses of the Zabriskies and the Vanderveers. A few days later, I located a book that listed some of the tycoons who had once lived along Albemarle and Buckingham and Rugby.

Reading off a list of them, I came to the founder of the company that manufactured Hellmann's Mayonnaise. My mother fashioned the gigantic smile that warned me that one of her *bon mots* was forthcoming.

"Hellmann?" she asked. "He must have had quite a spread."

~

From the first moment I saw her, I was afraid that someone would decide to paint over the Bride of Flatbush Avenue and that no one ever would believe that she had lived. Already, the advertising sign from Two Brothers Electronics covered most of her gown and train, and it was obvious that, if the tenant in the apartment above the store were to decide that he needed another window, the portrait would be dismembered beyond repair.

So I began the process of preparing my mother for the fact that she would have to get on the B41 bus with me to see my painted lady. My mother had been known to board the Flatbush Avenue bus *by herself* – one time, she had even met an acquaintance of hers who claimed to be the grandmother of the actress Winona Ryder – but that was heading south from East 31st Street, toward the ocean, not north, toward notorious Church Avenue and the ever-smiling Bride.

Then fortune intervened. One weekday, my mother prevailed upon a friend to drive her out to the mammoth mall at Westbury, Long Island, for a shopping spree. She returned, seven hundred dollars lighter, with ten silk, rayon, and knit blouses and six summer-weight skirts from Abraham and Strauss. Then, laying them out on every piece of furniture in the little apartment, she began the torturous process of trying to decide which two or three she actually wanted to keep.

When Little Debbie was consulted on this matter, her advice was predictable – keep everything and buy more – but for my mother, seven hundred dollars was two months' Social Security, so a lot of the stuff would have to go back.

"How much does it cost to rent a car?" my mother asked me, trying to get me to schlep her out to Westbury for the refunds.

"In Florida," I said, "Ninety-nine dollars a week. In New York, ninety-nine dollars a day."

I made this sound like a king's ransom, and that's how I got my mother on the B41 bus, bound for the A & S store on Fulton Street in Downtown Brooklyn. Clutched in several shopping bags were all the blouses and skirts she was going to return. Debbie was aboard as well; she had to be, for it was her A & S credit card to which everything had been charged in Westbury. This was far from the first expedition of its kind. We were the only family I knew that carried more stuff *to* a department store than we took away.

I pointed out the landmarks as we traveled – the Loew's Kings, of course, and the Lugo Hair Center and the Arcane Business Agency and Khyber Travel. As the bus passed Erasmus Hall and the Reformed Protestant Dutch Church and we approached Martense Street, I instructed my mother to move to the left side of the bus and to squat down low enough to be able to take in the Bride and her sweet, sweet smile. And so she saw the painting.

A few hours later, she had sent my sister off to hand back the clothing and complete the paperwork for the credit-card refunds, and we were sitting, just the two of us, in the little snack bar on the ground floor of Abraham and Strauss.

"Why did you want to show me that painting of the bride?" my mother asked.

"She's so evocative," I replied. "She summarizes everything. She's been there so long. She's seen all the changes."

"Have you stood on the sidewalk and looked up at her?"

"Yes," I said.

"She appeals to you?"

"Yes."

We paused and she sipped at her coffee and I drank my orange juice.

"Do you know why?" I asked my mother.

"Why?"

"Because she is you," I said, and she began softly to cry, and I heard her whispering into her coffee cup, "Oh, Allen . . . oh, Allen . . . oh . . ."

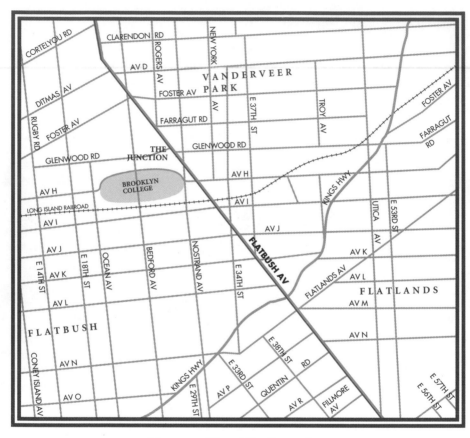

Chapter Five: The Junction

The Junction

1

Back at the hacienda, my mother decided to cook her famous Two Kinds of Meatballs.

Everyone was relaxed and relieved. My mother's temporary wardrobe had gone back to A & S. Little Debbie had enjoyed a couple of days' work substitute-teaching at a nice school on the Lower East Side. And I had completed my exploration of central Flatbush without being tied up in the back room at Sybil's or followed home by armed bandits. Hearing all those stories of mayhem and murder had put the fear of God in me, but after the Albanian Mosque and the Reformed Dutch Church and Sò Ann with her frog-skin powder, I wasn't sure which God it was.

Preparatory to her Caligulan orgy of cooking, my mother had arranged on the metal sink-basin cover that doubled as her only kitchen counter:

> tomato paste
> garlic powder
> Wesson corn oil
> 1 egg
> 1 lemon
> a box of matzoh meal
> salt and pepper
> 1 Bermuda onion
> 2 pkgs ground beef

Then she began to arm-wrestle from the overhead closet various implements that looked as if they had been lifted from Donald Lipski's *Pieces of String Too Small to Save* in the entrance hall of the Brooklyn Museum.

There was a metal grater that she carried towards me for examination, saying "Forty years. Forty years," and there was a strange spiked tube, a lemon-juice extractor of some sort, that she had acquired just before the Korean War.

The recipes (as if she needed to look them up) were contained in a small notebook that my mother had wrapped protectively in aluminum foil in this very kitchen in the year 1950 AD because, I suspected, baby Allen had taken to teething on it. The pages of this Dead Sea Scroll contained the earnest engineering of the young bride of Flatbush – Stuffed Fish, Potato Pancakes for Two People, Roast Beef – but across the instructions for the preparation of Salmon Croquettes, my father had scrawled, in capital letters, "BEN DON'T LIKE."

Occasionally, however, the novitiate had triumphed. Once, she made a roast of beef according to a recipe given to her by Ella Fishman, my father's cousin. The guests that night were Ella herself and her husband, Jack. When the meal was done, Jack Fishman lowered himself into a chair in the living room and, snarling accusatorily at his spouse, asked Ella, "Why can't *you* cook like that?"

Now it was forty years later, and my mother, dressed down in white slacks, a sleeveless yellow linen top, and a pink shower cap, was folding the egg and the diced Bermuda into the ground beef while the radio played Dinah Shore, Frank Sinatra, Nat King Cole, and Ella Fitzgerald, the same songs by the same people whose voices would have filled the same room forty years earlier.

Then we heard a couple of notes from the introduction to a tune I didn't recognize, and my mother gasped and said, "Don't tell me that's 'If'!"

It was, indeed, Perry Como singing "If."

"It's 'If,'" I said. "Should I turn it off?"

"No," my mother replied. "I won't succumb."

"If I were a king . . . ," Perry Como sang, subjunctively.

"If I start crying," my mother said, "I can always blame the onion."

The Two Kinds of Meatballs were Italian and Sweet and Sour. The former was a legacy of Fred Lucci, and the latter was what my mother would take to the hospital in old Hellmann's Mayonnaise jars when her father was dying of a liver tumor. It was customary, she said, to make the Italian balls jumbo and the candied ones petite. (Little Debbie loved little meatballs.) Some of my mother's friends acquired the vast amounts of sugar required for their own sweet-and-sour sauces by heisting packets from the condiment rack at McDonald's, but my mother was not the kind of woman who would walk into McDonald's and steal.

Instead, she pilfered her sugar from a diner on Flatbush Avenue called the Oasis.

As the cooking marathon progressed, I realized that some of the pots my mother was womanhandling on the gas range were older than I was. Every day and evening here was a voyage back in time. Little Debbie's first scribblings were intact in the recipe book. A dog-eared copy of Doctor Spock still held tabs my mother had inserted at "Rashes and Fevers." A tiny brass Indian chief on a keychain that hung on a nail in the kitchen door-frame had been hers since her wartime working days.

In a fit, she now decided that Two Kinds Of Meatballs were not enough and commenced to make Hungarian Goulash, hacking defenceless carrots to slivers and blinding Argus-eyed potatoes with the enthusiasm of the Lord High Executioner.

On the radio, Judy Garland sang "Rockabye Your Baby with a Dixie Melody."

The phone rang. It was my eighty-one-year-old father in Florida with his daily news broadcast, advising us how many miles he had bicycled, whether or not he needed to turn on his air conditioner to sleep, the state of a pain in his left leg below the knee, and the market price of cantaloupes.

He had fled Brooklyn, alone, in 1980, following two of his brothers to the Sunshine State, and thirteen years later, he was thirteen years younger than when he left. He lived alone, worked part-time in a succession of small tobacco stores and newsstands, rode his bike at least twenty miles each day around and around the perimeter of his enormous campus of whitewashed condominiums, and passed his evenings watching "Headline News" and taping children's television programs for his daughter, Baby Doll (a.k.a. Little Debbie) to use in her classrooms. Currently, he was employed as a stock boy at an outlet called the Party Supermarket, making sure the shelves were never empty of noisemakers and funny hats.

"It's definitely a blockage," he said, as soon as I came on the line. The sore leg was making it impossible for him to achieve the five daily miles of hiking with which he complemented his twenty-mile bike ride. Now, after a couple of hundred yards of walking, he had to stop and rest and wait for the tightness to abate before he could plod on. His own doctor was noncommittal. He was being referred to a specialist. The problem appeared to be vascular.

We scattered into separate rooms and listened in on all three phones at once. My father was unusually distressed. One physician had left him sitting on an examination table for twenty minutes while he took care of someone else. Someone had warned him that, if he didn't have the blockage unjammed, gangrene could set in. There was an intimation that he might need angioplastic surgery.

"Angioplasty," Baby Doll said on the phone in the living room that was watched over by the Modigliani. "That's the balloon shit."

"Yeah," said her father. "That's in and out."

He was going to send his X-rays to the son of the brother of the widow of his late brother David. This man was a radiologist. More important, he was family.

"Can you still ride your bike?" I asked.

"No pain at all when I ride," he reported. I pictured the small, determined traveler, white-haired and nut-brown, pumping around Century Village, waving to every Sadie and Sid.

"Then it can't be serious," I pronounced, wishing the crisis away.

In Brooklyn, now, we devoured the meatballs and froze the goulash and Debbie took a Russian gypsy cab back to seaside Canarsie. When the dishes had been done and I had taken a slender 86-to-13 lead after two turns (HEINOUS, DROVER) at Scrabble, my mother suddenly grew serious and said:

"I feel like I have to make an appointment to talk to you."

This was after four hours together on one of the best days of all.

"Sometimes you're warm," she went on. "Sometimes you're cold. I never know how you're going to be."

I threw down SUCCEED for another fifty-point bonus, and the Mills Brothers sang "Paper Doll."

"This is not a complaint," my mother said. "Just an analysis."

"We're the same as any two people living together since Adam and Eve," I replied. I thought the acknowledgement that we were housemates would mollify her.

"No!" she rejected. "Your father and I were always consistent."

I wasn't going to touch that one with a ten-foot juice extractor. Ever the diplomat, I went to bed. The final score was 358 to 213.

∾

The intersection of Flatbush and Nostrand avenues, the Piccadilly of my first known world, was called the Junction. This had been a muddy X of rutted roads and truck farms until 1920, when the IRT subway arrived, bringing with it the European Catholics and Ashkenazi Jews whose hold on the neighborhood had now expired, with a few paralyzed exceptions, such as us. Surrounded by hundreds of apartment blocks and handsome one-family homes, lined with banks and businesses, the Junction was the terminus of the Number 2 train from Manhattan, an end and a beginning, a crossroads without a colonial history, and a sizable town in itself. My mother's apartment was a block away, on the other side of the tracks.

All the buildings and many of the stores here were exactly as they had been in 1960 and even before. As far as I could tell, there had been no construction and no demolition at or near the Junction for at least thirty years. The College Theater had been remade into Consumers Distributing, and an old-fashioned ice-cream parlor called Jentz's was now a Kentucky Fried Chicken franchise, but Lord's Bakery was unchanged, and so were the Campus Sugar Bowl and the Aegean Isles restaurant and the newsstands and the Boston Fish Market. The interchange was sociological as well as physical; here, Caribbean Flatbush began to slide into Caucasian Flatlands. Brooklyn grew whiter as you went southward towards the briny sea.

Every square of Junction pavement was familiar to my stride. (It was only the people who were strange.) It was here in 1964, in front of Jentz's, that I tossed a football to Robert Kennedy, who was campaigning for the U.S. Senate, and he autographed it and flipped it back. It was here that the other East 31st Street Bombers and I, on our screeching metal roller skates, raised our hockey sticks in salute as President Johnson cruised down Flatbush in a bulletproof car. It was here that I walked hand-in-hand with a debutante named Sheila after our junior-high-school prom, an experience that put me off girls and back on hockey for the next eight years.

Gaining the Junction, southbound drivers accelerated madly, sensing a wide, straight path to the coast. Pedestrians crossed the broad boulevards at risk of death (the "WALK" signals were a satanic trap; they changed to red after a couple of seconds and left you stranded in midstream, dodging Dodges). The sidewalks were twice as wide as the crowded pavements of the old Dutch village a mile to the north. There was some street-market activity, but nothing like the frenzy of Flatbush and Church or Flatbush and Fulton. There might be a crowd of beery layabouts spilling from the OTB parlor, or some Haitian women squatting beside blankets full of spices and wooden utensils, but the general atmosphere was, by Flatbush Avenue standards, purposeful and orderly.

Brooklyn College students and commuting office workers climbed in and out of The Beast and on and off city buses and freelance vans. A man and a woman in white smocks set up a table and invited me to have my blood pressure checked, charging a dollar that would be given, they swore, "to charity." A Russian immigrant sold children's books of estimable quality for the impossible price of fifty cents.

In front of the former Flatbush Savings Bank, now The Greater New York Savings Bank (or simply, "The Greater"), a young woman stood over a collection of trinkets and garments, like a statue of a Catholic saint, arms down, palms out, hardly moving, saying nothing as the borough bustled by. Her folding table was neatly arranged with wooden key-charms, cloth bracelets woven with various given names and zodiacal signs, and carefully folded frilly shirts and dresses. From her navy-blue skirt and white blouse and thick strands of gold necklaces, and from her tiny stature and pure black hair and walnut-colored skin, I knew her to be an Otavaleña from the cream-tipped Andes of Ecuador.

The Saturday-morning market at Otavalo was a secret that every tourist to South America knew. Linda and I had once been there on an April morning, rising before dawn to join the vendors setting out their shawls and blankets and rough wool sweaters, while the waking sun burnished the snow on the sleeping volcanos.

Now, Otavalo had come to the Junction. In fact, there were thousands of Ecuadorian vendors and musicians in the city, and one of them was this small, silent woman on the curb in front of the bank. I went up to her, pretended to browse through the merchandise, and then inaugurated a conversation in my junior-high-school Español.

"*¿Qué piensa usted de Brooklyn?*" I began, using the polite conjugation. What did she think of the place?

"*Brooklyn no es buen sitio,*" she replied. Not a good spot. But she added: "Manhattan worse."

"*¿Tiene miedo?*" Was she afraid?

"*Tengo miedo de los ladrones y la policía.*"

Her name was Lucila. She was worried about thieves who could slice her open and cops who could shut down her unlicensed commerce and send her back to latitude zero. As we spoke, a few women came up and fingered the bracelets and clothing, and Lucila recited their prices in the only English she knew. Behind her, one of her countrymen, handsome and muscular, with a long, braided queue, sat in a small white Honda, keeping his eye on everything, marking me. I felt his gaze and shied away. Twenty more times I walked this block, but I never saw him, or Lucila, again.

I went into The Greater and sat on a bench against the wall and watched the tellers minister behind their glass-and-brass enclosures. Like Junior's and the Loew's Kings, the old Flatbush Savings Bank at the Junction was perfectly unchanged. The bank was dim and cool, pronouncing the seriousness of its purpose without recourse to the bas-relief beavers of the Williamsburgh tower or the aphorisms of the Dime at Albee Square. Here, I was eight again, adding another couple of dimes to the contents of my School Savings Plan; I was thirteen, depositing the bounty of my coming of age.

While I was swooning, a woman sat down next to me. She was a Jew of extreme age, hunchbacked and barely able to walk, her pink overcoat clasped at the bust with a safety pin and her black stockings not rising as high as the hem of her skirt. Her hair was gathered in a net, and I thought: she will be trailed home from the bank and bludgeoned. I watched her move to the cashier's cage and take money and fold it into her purse. She departed, and I followed her through the double doors and down the sidewalk to the corner of Hillel Place, staying far enough behind to not rattle her, and then I voicelessly wished her luck and cast her loose.

I wandered a while, looking for landmarks, and found that the Flatbush Terrace banquet hall, where my bar-mitzvah festivities had been held in

1963, had been turned into a cut-rate furniture store, and that it, in turn, had gone broke. Now the place – Bus Stop Discount – was sealed like a Mason jar in graffiti and metal grating, never to re-open, one more cancer on a node of neighborhood life.

But across the street, another hall called the Farragut Manor was open. The Manor was a big, mirrored room, in which a couple of hundred tables could be set up for luncheon or dinner while an orchestra played lilting airs. In place of Hebrews doing the *hora*, there were Haitian wedding receptions and Trinidadian calypso shows. Back in prehistoric times, Lou Jacobson, my mother's only brother, had installed the air-conditioning system here. And now, every day, the Farragut Manor was where a number of seniors, mostly women, gathered for a subsidized meal and the companionship of a vanishing sorority.

There was a woman at a long table near the entrance collecting fifty cents from each diner, greeting everyone warmly and clasping hands, though her own hands were knotted and gnarled, just like my Linda's. Her name was Laura Geffen, and she had lived her seventy years on Flatbush Avenue, the daughter of a man who had owned a candy store across the street from the old Farragut Theater that was now a YMCA. At the Seniors' Center that convened daily at the Manor, Laura Geffen was the chief executive of the Sunshine Committee, deputized to confer felicitations to the general membership, sing encouragements to the ailing, and whisper to the inconsolably bereaved.

In the room were about a hundred people, chatting and knitting and playing cards and watching "Donahue" under the heavy crystal chandeliers and Uncle Louie's smoothly purring air ducts. Some of the seniors were black and some were white, and when I mentioned this to Laura Geffen, she said, "I've always lived in a mixed neighborhood. I don't notice the color."

"But they notice you," I told her.

"My friend had a baby," she said by way of retort. "Someone asked me, 'Is it very black?' I said, 'I don't know. I don't see the color. I see a *baby*.'"

Laura Geffen was a survivor. She had seizures and diabetic blackouts. Her right knee was in a brace because the cartilage had given out. One day, she was coming down the stairs in her building when she was tripped by a couple of men, and she fractured her pelvis on both sides and all the bones in her left leg.

"I *have* to think it was an accident," she said, and maybe it was.

"Do you go out at night?" I asked her.

"I go home after lunch," she answered, "and that's *it*. I'm *in*."

"And this is your life," I said softly.

"It's not a life," the sunshine lady replied.

∾

Between the Junction and my mother's apartment, there was nothing but the old Long Island Rail Road freight route and the rhomboidal parking lot where her former boss at the medical-supply warehouse had been shot but somehow not killed. Crossing the rail line, Flatbush Avenue crested a small rise, and it was at this rather humble summit that I had taken the "Cry to God for Pardon!" pamphlet from the elderly Chinese evangelist and turned to watch the Concorde lift into space.

There were honeysuckles here, along the fence, in summer, and in winter it was possible to look through the naked boughs and up to the fourth-floor kitchen where Hennie Jacobson Abel Lucci had been kneading meatballs for more than forty years. Walking home this way each noon from Midwood High, I'd wave to her, and she would put my Beefaroni on the stove to boil.

The rail line in the steep, weedy cut had been a fixture of my childhood, sending its slow and clamorous serpents beneath our window at the least opportune of times: the climax of Perry Mason's cross-examination, or the roundelay of "Sing Along with Mitch." I had no idea where the trains came from or where they were headed, but they entranced me, and I would peer between the safety bars of the bedroom window and count the coal hoppers and boxcars until they concluded in a grown-up Lionel caboose.

A cinder-block wall had been erected along the Flatbush Avenue sidewalk to keep miscreants from dumping refuse or entering the embankment, but this being Brooklyn, the wall acted as an incentive, not a bar. Now, when I looked down toward the tracks, I saw that one set of rails was intact, but the ties had been ripped up and the whole right-of-way was covered in a midden of old automobile tires, jettisoned appliances, scrap metal, and household garbage. There was so much trash in this narrow little valley that it seemed inevitable that it would eventually be filled to the level of the surrounding streets and could be paved over for parking. Someday, archeologists would burrow into this dunghill and find multifarious artifacts of the golden age of creative littering.

But the trains still ran! Showering one morning, alternately scalded and pelted with sleet by our building's antique plumbing, I was certain that I heard the unmistakable rumble, but by the time I scrambled out and raised the window, it had passed, whatever it was.

A couple of weeks later, it happened again. This time, my mother dashed to the kitchen window and I headed for the living room, but the trees had come into leaf, and it was impossible to see down into the cut. Still, we knew we had heard a train.

I looked up the number of the Long Island Rail Road freight office and talked to a man named George Burns. It was true. A couple of times a month, a few cars were sent down the Bay Ridge line towards the terminus at the harbor piers.

"They're not any hundred-car deals any more," George Burns said, but that didn't matter. It was enough that something in Brooklyn still worked.

∾

Parallel to the railway and even closer to the apartment was the wreck of the Flatbush Car Wash. Once, this narrow strip between our building and the tracks had been a turning loop for streetcars, but the Flatbush Avenue trolley route had been replaced by the B41 buses a few months after I was born. Later, the car wash opened under a colorful neon sign that was still in place on a pole in the sidewalk, and from our window we could watch exuberant Puerto Rican ranch-hands wiping down the vehicles as they were extruded from the noisy sudsing hall.

It was unclear why the place had closed – there were more cars on East 31st Street than ever before – but under the sign now was another heap of balding tires, plus filing cabinets and a washing machine and mufflers and fenders and knots of filthy clothing, and though the gates at each end of the wash-house had been pulled down and locked, someone had managed to pry open one corner of the barricade and was probably living inside. Sometimes, I saw my Midwood successors sneaking down the hillside behind the car wash, but whether they were mainlining heroin under the honeysuckles or merely doing their math homework, I could not discern through all the foliage.

Next to the defunct car wash was an abandoned service station, with its gas pumps ripped out and still more garbage windblown into repulsive piles along its fence. Barely a hundred yards from home, at the corner of little Aurelia Court, I had come to the very worst of Flatbush Avenue. Even parts of the fence had been stolen – the supporting poles were here one day, gone the next, leaving a flimsy filament of chain-link to billow like the sails of a shipwrecked barque.

Walking past this blighted garage one morning, I noticed that every car parked along the west side of Flatbush Avenue had been broken into. I counted them: five, six, seven vehicles in a row, with their windows smashed and radios ripped out. (The thieves were rapacious but not heartless; they left children's toys untouched on the back seats.) Heaps of powdered green safety glass lay like beach sand on the road. Two days later, the cars were gone but the glass remained. And that was when I saw the dead dog.

She was a red mongrel bitch, a big, ugly animal, lying on the sidewalk at the corner of the abandoned gas bar, her nipples hard, her dark eyes still open, casting my soul to hell. When I came upon her, walking home in the golden afternoon from one of my peregrinations, her moment of death had been very recent. There was still the sheen of life to her fur. But no breath brought her to.

∾

I didn't want to go upstairs and tell my mother about the carcass. I had vowed not to denigrate her neighborhood. I was a transient, but this was her home and likely would be until she died. We had agreed that the question I asked everyone else along Flatbush Avenue – "Why do you stay here?" – I would never broach at home. Because there was no answer.

I walked down Aurelia Court to East 31st Street. In yellow numerals on the exterior wall of the abandoned garage, I could read the outfield dimensions of our old stickball court – "*105* FT." to straightaway center. But the painted pentagon of home plate had vanished, and so had the measured red and blue lines of our fantasy hockey rink. Of all the boys who had run here and skated and sledded to the railroad tracks, only one had come back. I was alone.

Between our building and the apartment block next door was a narrow alleyway that led to a cement "back yard." That area was now fenced off as a deterrent to burglars and drug fiends, but the alley itself was open. Along one wall ran the concrete ledge where we used to race our Dinky cars and pee in the dirt for mud pies. Here we played "Giant Steps" and "Red Light, Green Light," and Brucie, my best friend, would bring out his toy soldiers and commit them to battle along this miniature Burma Road.

I sat on the ledge and basked in the setting sun, warm on my right arm and cheek. In a painted heart above my head that had been there when I was a child, two sets of initials were still entwined "4 EVER," but the letters had faded and I couldn't tell what post-war pairing, what Hen and Ben, they might have been.

Dreamily, I looked down, and on the cement beside me, as green as broken glass, was a toy soldier. I picked him up and blew the dust away. He was a British rifleman in a pith helmet and khakis, aiming his Enfield at some Zulu or Zanzibari in the name of Imperial majesty. At his waist hung a canteen and ammunition pouches, and his calves were wrapped in puttees.

I put him in my pocket as treasure. Later, I placed him on my dresser with me in his sights, and I wanted so much to believe that he was Brucie's.

2

On East 31st Street, trash flowed like lava and car alarms cried rape, but inside, the building where I had grown up and where my mother still lived was spotless, shiny, and (we thought) safe. Its care had been entrusted to a South American accountant named Roberto, who somehow, through one of life's little accidents, had gone from being a respected professional in Montevideo, Uruguay, to a thankless job as a tenement superintendent in Brooklyn, America.

The "super," handy and hungry for tips, had been a part of Brooklyn folklore for decades. Grease-stained and a mechanical magician, invariably the father of dozens and the husband of a venomous shrew, the superintendent was exemplified, when I was young, by an ogre named O——, who would follow me into the elevator, press "B" before I could hit "4," and then stalk after me in the labyrinthine basement. Wild-eyed and drunk, he would moan "Aaaa–belll, Aaaa–belll," his arms held out in front of him as he clopped along like Frankenstein's Munster.

But Roberto wasn't like that. He was a large man, part Spanish, part Italian, a sensitive soul, whose most urgent repair was to his own broken dignity. Brooklyn appalled him. When I met him one day in the gleaming lobby, he asked me if it was true, as he had heard, that in Boston, when a customer went into a store and bought something, the shopkeeper actually said, "Thonk you."

"Yes," I replied. "And in Canada, if somebody steps on your foot, *you* say, 'Excuse me.'"

I'd see him outside, sweeping up the refuse that some of his tenants liked to air-mail from their windows rather than portage ten or fifteen paces to the garbage chute, and he'd say, "I don't think this place for my wife and son."

"We used to pee in the dirt right here to make mud pies," I'd tell him, pointing to the denuded "garden," trying to assuage his consternation with tales of the building in the old, old days.

"Now," he'd say, "ees a public toilet."

He invited me to his flat and said that no one else in the building had ever been allowed inside. I accepted the honor and rang the bell at the designated hour. When the door opened, I nearly went blank.

After twenty-five years, after everything, I was back in Brucie's apartment.

It was magnificent. The parquet floors glistened like melted Parkay. A grandfather clock chimed discreetly in a corner. Shelves of bowling trophies and china figurines competed for attention. In a grey sweatshirt splattered with paint, hiding his dirty hands, my host sat in an armchair in the same corner to which Brucie's father would adjourn each evening with his pipe and the *New York Times* crossword. But Brucie was now a bureaucrat in Washington, his parents had moved to Florida, and there they had died, and now I was in his living room with all the memories and ghosts.

Roberto's wife came in. She was a Cuban-American, wry and clever and cute, and her name was the Spanish word for charity. But East 31st Street suited Caridad no more than it befitted her husband. Each day, she drove their ten-year-old son to distant Queens rather than send him to the ravaged local public school that once had educated me and Little Debbie. Then she drove back out to Queens in the afternoon to bring the boy home.

A few years earlier, she had lost a job in Manhattan because she was too ill too often to suit her boss. What she felt was a lingering malaise, a persistent achy flu that the doctors first suspected might be Lyme disease but that turned out, as I might have told them, to be lupus. Some days, she was unable to get out of bed at all, but once a year, on New Year's **Eve, she** would go out and dance until it almost killed her.

"Does your wife ever lie down and feel dizzy, like she's spinning?" Caridad asked me once.

"She was just in the hospital because of that," I replied. And I told her how Linda had been dependent on steroids since the winter of 1965.

"I'd rather have the pain than take the pills," said the super's wife. "My bed is my medicine."

Coming out of the elevator one morning, I turned to find Roberto bent over in the lobby, picking up hundreds of little foam pellets that one of our neighbors had let fall from a packing crate. The entrance hall was otherwise immaculate: the dummy fireplace, with its carvings of doves in a grape arbor, was as it always had been, and so were the plaster walls with their phony wood-grain and the latticed windows with their ersatz coats of arms. But Roberto was fuming.

"I know who do this," he told me.

"Learn to laugh," I advised the super. "It's May! It's a little late for snowfall."

"Ees late for snow," he repeated, his mouth twisted into a tortured grin. "An' ees early, too."

Satisfied, I opened the first of the two big iron doors. As I went out, I heard him behind me, softly muttering.

"Animals."

∾

In open-mouthed horror I watched one night as two teenagers started to build a basketball court beneath our window. I saw them emerge from the building across the street with a ladder, a hammer, and a hoop. They set to work at the last maple tree shy of the dead end, pounding away at the trunk, setting nails and hanging up the net. Then they took the hammer and blasted at the sidewalk itself until a piece of concrete broke loose, and they used this as chalk to draw a foul line and a three-point arc on the dark asphalt of East 31st.

I called to my mother, who was in the kitchen, smoking and playing solitaire and listening to Patsy Cline, and said, "Forget about sleeping."

We were granted a reprieve from the start of the season by the fact that the boys didn't have a basketball. But this was about to be redressed. A third teen appeared with a can of pop and a new orange ball and, draining his drink and heaving the empty can into the "garden," he inaugurated the spirited whooping that I expected would last all night and all summer.

To anesthetize her senses, my mother moved into the living room and commenced to watch Canadian Prime Minister Brian Mulroney talk about free trade on the "MacNeil–Lehrer NewsHour."

My father called. The distantly related radiologist had made his report. There was a partial blockage in an artery that would require either surgery on the leg or surgery on the neck or no surgery at all. He was continuing to ride his bike and walk his miles, gingerly, stopping frequently to rest, but carrying on through the pain, like Mickey Mantle on his two bad knees.

Sour and beaten, frayed by the noise outside, my mother came into the bedroom and thanked me for not belaboring the issue of her inability to quit this place. She said, "At least you don't tell me, 'It's *your* choice to be here.'"

Of course, it never had been her choice. Ben Abel might have joined the flood tide to Long Island in the fifties, but he didn't drive and he couldn't leave his brothers. Fred Lucci might have bolted when the Caribbeans came, but he didn't have the dough. Now, neither did she. Since she was a long-time tenant, New York's rent-control law maintained her here for $380 a month. (A "de-controlled" apartment of the same size elsewhere in the city would rent for twice as much.) So she had stayed. Forty years. Forty years.

She told me how she had tried to accommodate herself to life among black people, how on a bus in Virginia in 1941 she had offered her seat to an old, lame colored lady who declined it, not believing a white woman's sincerity, and both of them had stood for the entire ride. And how a cousin from Norfolk had come north and had taken her dancing at the Tropicana. Dazzling, in her prime, she had walked right past Duke Ellington's piano, and the maestro had looked up and said, "Hello, honey." The cousin was maddened – "He's *black* and he *talked* to you?" – but my mother proudly rebuked him and said, "Phil, this is *New York*."

Now this was also New York outside the window, a meshed hoop hammered to a maple tree at the dead end of a Brooklyn street. Half a dozen kids had joined the game. I told my mother, "I'm sure we made much more noise than that playing hockey and stickball." But that was on another planet in another time.

∾

The basketball hoop on the maple tree lasted less than twenty-four hours. The pith of the trunk wasn't sturdy enough to endure the Jordanian dunks. The boys moved down to the corner of Aurelia Court and made up a new game that involved slamming the ball against the "Dead End Street" sign. The noise was maddening, but their inventiveness was to be commended.

Summer came early. By mid-May, it was hot enough for some of the people across the street to barbecue and picnic in the "garden," and for the four surviving Jewish grandmothers of our building to bring their folding chairs to the sidewalk. But my mother never joined them. Their chatter was insipid, she said. They reminded her of her condition. They aged her.

I'd come back from my trailblazing in late afternoon, and she would be talking on the phone, or sitting by the fan at the kitchen window, smoking and drinking lukewarm Ovaltine. I would go into the bedroom and sort through my notes and peruse the various papers – *Newsday*, the *Jewish Press*, the *Carib News* – until dinner time. Or I'd write a maudlin postcard to Linda in Toronto, pledging *amour* and counting down the weeks.

On one of those indolent afternoons at about 4:30, a thunderstorm of astonishing ferocity swept down East 31st Street. First, the sky grew so dark so quickly that the orange "anti-crime" streetlight came on. Then dust began to blow in whirlpools at the dead end, and the maple trees, whose implantation I had watched from this same room as a four-year-old, danced around the lampposts in a *pas de deux* of frolic and destruction. The boys at their sign-smashing basketball game ceased shrieking in mock terror and ran for cover with real fear. Branches came down.

Then the rain. First, heavy, pregnant drops, then sheets of shimmering water cascaded against the brick walls of our building and washed the old car wash in revenge. Thunder droned, Mulroney-like, and echoed from the buildings beyond. Lightning flashed like Steven Singer's sculpting torch in his metalworks at Rachman Bag.

Quietly, her footsteps eclipsed by the storm, my mother came into the bedroom and stood beside me. She looked out at the torrent and said one word.

"*Vengeful*," my mother said.

3

There were other survivors at the Junction. Bill was an Irishman and a friend of my mother's, who had worked for twenty-six years as a bartender at a cozy Flatbush Avenue pub called the Chesterfield. He still lived in the neighborhood, but the Chesterfield had become Club Cheetah, a strip joint with a five-dollar cover charge and an exterior painted Hallowe'en orange with big black spots. Vertical blinds at the front window were left slightly open, so that, walking by or passing on the B41 bus, I would occasionally catch a glimpse of a bored feline on a small stage, arching her back and advertising her pudenda to two or three slumped-over drunks.

Bill was a big fellow, bald, chatty, world-wise. He had retired from his mixological career. An abscessed foot had him hobbling on one padded sandal and one New Balance sneaker. His apartment was in a building whose lobby featured a mural of the nearby Brooklyn College campus drawn in black and white, except for the dome of the school's trademark bell tower, which gleamed a brilliant gold.

A sign in the building said, "In Case of Fire, Use Stairs," but someone had crossed out the word "Stairs" and had substituted: "SCREAM!"

My mother and I were schmoozing one afternoon in Bill's living room, which had been decorated rather delicately for a man his size. He had excavated three tiny black-and-white photographs that he thought might find a place in this book. They showed: Midwood, my high school, under construction, circa 1941; a Memorial Day parade on Ocean Avenue, of comparable antiquity; and, in their pool at Prospect Park Zoo, sea lions that later, Bill said angrily, died from eating cubes of bread in which someone had inserted razor blades.

He talked of saloons past: Christie's, the Moonbeam, Eddie's Cavern. I wanted Bill to come with me to Club Cheetah, but this was beneath him; he wouldn't be caught dead in a bottomless bar. Across Flatbush Avenue, right below his window, was another little tavern called the Vanderveer, where he had worked for a while after the Chesterfield went bad. But now the Vanderveer's mock-Tudor facade was boarded up and the stucco was spray-painted and the owner, like the old Dutch Vanderveers themselves, was gone, gone, gone.

My mother admired Bill deeply. He was a rare lode of wisdom and stability amid the panic. The Junction had fallen right out from under his aching feet. He said, "I get on a bus, I'm the only white guy on the bus. But it doesn't bother me; I just sit down. I notice, but it's not a problem. It's just unbelievable that it happened so fast."

Bill was also entertaining a fellow named George. They were old, old pals. After a lengthy disputation on the subject of the proper accompaniment for roast beef – brown gravy or natural juices – they commenced to spin tales of Flatbush Avenue in the thirties, of riding in a twelve-cylinder Buick to the end of the paved road at Avenue U and then taking a ferry across the inlet to the beaches of Rockaway, Queens.

How had the path to the ferry dock been marked in those bygone boyhood days?

"Dey had erl drums," George said.

"Oil drums?" I asked excitedly. It wasn't the history that set me aquiver; it was hearing pedigreed Brooklynese.

"Yeah," he repeated. "Dat's what I said. Erl drums."

∾

"A pack of louts, oafs, dimwits and dunces, all talking an unearthly gibberish," John Richmond and Abril Lamarque wrote of the popular conception of the borough's elocutionists in 1946. "The weird impression has been established that the average Brooklynite can talk only out of the corner of his mouth, while delivering raffish slang and colorful colloquialisms."

This may not have held true in 1993 – the average Brooklynite I met spoke Creole or Yoruba – but finally, in my mother's friend's friend, I had dug to the linguistic bedrock.

Hearing this man speak, I squirmed with delight. Or, as Chimmie Fadden would cry, "Say, yer otter seen me!"

Chimmie Fadden, a wildly popular fictional character of the 1890s, was one reason some people in Brooklyn a century later still said goil for girl and erl for oil. He was the creation of a New York *Sun* writer named Edward Townsend and was given to such phrases as "Dat's de trouble wid everyting" or "Wot de yer tink dat mug done?" On the subject of females, Chimmie opined: "I learned one ting sure; if dere's er woman in de game yuse wanter keep yer eye peeled all de time, fer if yer snooze – why when yer wakes up yer ain't in it. Dat's right."

Townsend didn't invent the dialect – he hoid it all around him. It had erupted, modern scholars believed, in the 1830s, when a group of American authors and playwrights, influenced by Dickens and Thackeray, turned for their subject matter to the immigrant, mostly Irish, slums of lower Manhattan. The characterizations were epitomized in Ben Baker's play "Mose, the Bowery Boy" – "unique compound of east-side swell, gutter bum, and volunteer fire laddie" – and the language that the hero spoke sprang from the streets and returned to the streets to be imitated and affected by the mob.

The lingo was *Boweryese*. It flourished long before talking pictures served up the Three Stooges ("Soitainly!") or Leo Gorcey and the Dead End Kids ("Dis is duh pineapple uh yer career"). It was the mother tongue of newsboy Chimmie Fadden, at the turn of the century one of the most famous literary characters in America, and of Stephen Crane's novel *Maggie: A Girl of the Streets*: "Dat Johnson goil is a putty good looker. Maggie, I'll tell yeh dis! Yeh've edder got teh go teh Hell or go to woik."

As far back as 1881, a survey of New York train conductors found that four out of five, approaching the station one block north of 80th Street, called out, "Eighty-foist!"

(As late as 1964, a study of Manhattan department-store clerks found that those who worked at fashionable Saks Fifth Avenue sent shoppers to the "fourth floor," while those at S. Klein's, a discount house, directed them to the "fawth flaw.")

How had my borough become saddled with the title of Dimwit Capital of duh Woild? Professor Geoffrey D. Needler of Pace University ascribed it to the utterances of the dying Dodger fan played by William Bendix in the 1946 movie *Lifeboat*. The war had made Brooklyn a universal symbol of what Professor Needler called "tough inarticulateness," and had transformed the erstwhile City of Churches into "a surly wasteland of incivility and mindless baseball boosterism."

Thomas Wolfe hadn't helped, either, with *Only the Dead Know Brooklyn* and its famous "I can tell you t'ings about dis town you neveh hoid of."

What Wolfe and William Bendix wrought, Ed Norton perfected. By the time I came along, although distinguished linguists were loudly insisting there was no such thing as a distinct Brooklyn accent, the East Toity-Foist Street Bombers and I sincerely believed that we were the inheritors of a noble syntax as different from the impure argots of the Bronx or New Jersey as Danish was from Vietnamese.

My generation learned from "The Honeymooners" and "The Life of Riley." Surviving tapes of my first play-by-play hockey broadcasts, circa 1972, reminded me that I was prone to occasionally lose my composure and scream, "De're fightin' faw duh puck in duh kawner!"

Twenty years later, Little Debbie, though ostensibly an educator of youth, never settled for just one syllable when two or more would do, as in show-wuh for sure and hee-yuh for here. Brooklynese was a badge of street-wisdom; it conferred membership in the tribe. I even heard traces of it from the super's wife, Caridad: "I came from Cuber," she would say, "when I was fawteen yee-yuhs old."

The *Times* saw Brooklynese, or whatever it was, fading to extinction, doomed by heterophone immigration, confined in its death throes to the city's "few white enclaves," such as Canarsie and Bensonhoist and the lunch counter at Junior's on Flatbush Avenue.

"The pungent dialect . . . seems to be fading into history," the newspaper declared. But the *Times* never interviewed Bill's friend George on the subject of barrels of petroleum.

∾

Not everyone had successfully shaken the glottal ghosts of the past. Those who were unable to find work as network news anchors because of oafish diction were thrown a life preserver by Brooklyn College and a course called Correcting Your Accent. This originally was offered as an undergraduate seminar, with a passing grade awarded to those who could, after weeks of instruction, correctly pronounce the following sentence: "There is a flaw in the floor."

This was more difficult than it looked. University students aside, there were still thousands of people in the borough who, if they could speak English at all, would prescribe that one repair "a flaw in duh flaw" by squoiting erl on it. For those post-graduate Bendixes, the college's Adult Education branch offered Correcting Your Accent two evenings a week.

I was so eager to attend, I nearly volunteered to *pay* the seventy-five-dollar tuition fee. But then I got a grip on myself and called the public-relations officers and told them I was a reporter, and they let me in for free. It was a close call.

At seven o'clock on the first Monday of evening sessions, I found myself pacing a corridor at Whitehead Hall, on the Brooklyn College campus, waiting for the instructor to arrive. With me were my classmates: a junior-high-school mathematics teacher from the Indian Punjab, by way of Nigeria; a dental-office clerk who had fled St. Petersburg, Russia, when it was still Leningrad, USSR; a tiny, shy Shanghainese girl; a huge, outgoing Jamaican woman; two Israelis; and a Jewish attorney from the Bronx, who specialized in the cases of older adults, and who did not, she declared, want to be known as a "seen-yuh law-yuh."

As the clock ticked past the advertised hour, we found ourselves coagulating in a corner of the hallway, making small talk about ourselves and our countries. The Punjabi said that he was having trouble making himself understood to his Russian, Cantonese, and Puerto Rican pupils. The Chinese said nothing at all. The enormous Jamaican woman said she was hoping for personal instruction. But in order for her to enjoy this kind of attention, the instructor would have to show up.

By 7:45, it was beginning to seem that this was not going to happen. Volunteers were chosen to hunt down an agent of campus security to find out what was going on. As they departed, I took the only course of action I could imagine.

I decided to teach the class myself.

"Isn't it wonderful," I announced for openers, "that there exists a language that enables people from Russia and China and Israel and India to talk to each other?"

A few heads nodded.

"Esperanto!" I cried. The joke went over everybody's heads, ricocheted off the gilded bell-tower, and crash-landed in the Quadrangle. I abandoned humor as a vehicle of instruction.

Of course, I retreated, I was talking about English, as spoken on my travels down Flatbush Avenue by Sò Ann the voodoo priestess and Roberto the Uruguayan super. I told them about Yisroel Francis, the Jewish black man, and Lucien Delly, the black Jew.

"Where I work," said the dental-office clerk from Petrograd, warming to the subject, "we have one black man who is a Chinese priest and a Buddhist monk!"

I described my wanderings up and down Flatbush Avenue. I elaborated on the Sterling Place plane crash and the sixty-five cents of little Stephen Baltz, on the Malbone Wreck and the Prison Ship Martyrs. I noted that the building in which we were now assembled – indeed, the entire Brooklyn College campus – had been built upon a site that formerly held the Big Top and Menagerie of the Ringling Brothers circus. An aerial photograph in the college library showed the huge lot beside the Long Island Rail Road tracks in the late 1920s, spotted with circus tents that bulged like cocoons, white and oval and plump.

The lawyer from the Bronx cut me down. She testified that one-third of the people who worked in her building carried guns. She wondered how I could be so upbeat about Brooklyn, could find it so fascinating.

"No other street in the world could hold the diversity of Flatbush Avenue," I said.

"Only an outsider could see it," the lawyer replied.

We quieted down, frustrated by the real teacher's absence. (Everyone else had paid seventy-five bucks and received no benefit but my inanities.) I leaned back against the wall and listened to the others chatter in the common tongue of the educated world. I looked at their faces and remembered the Golden Temple in Amritsar, the riverside Bund in Shanghai, the Hermitage in Leningrad. I thought: I went from here to see their worlds and now they've come from their worlds to mine.

The instructor never showed up. The search party returned with instructions for everyone to come back on Wednesday. As we were walking down the stairs to return to our individual solitudes, a small woman I'd hardly noticed hurried to link step with me. In the bubbling cadence of Trinidad, the most lovely accent of all, she turned to me and said, "You know, I don't think you *need* this course."

4

My mother met Doris at Brooklyn College at a night-school course called Philosophy of Everyday Living. After class, they went out for coffee and Doris said, "I don't know if I can be your friend, because you'll hurt me."

"I'll never hurt you," my mother vowed. Doris, who was employed as a court stenographer in Downtown Brooklyn, gave my mother her business card. It was 1951.

Together, through the years, the typist and the Bride of Flatbush studied square dancing and oil painting, folk music and entry-level ceramics. One semester, my mother created and brought home a clay head of the young Allen Abel that she later had to discard because the dampness of a Brooklyn winter got into it and it became infested with small white bugs. But she did keep her calipers, using them at home to judge the thickness of her husband's hamburgers to a tolerance of millimeters, lest he take a pencil to her recipe book and mark it "BEN DON'T LIKE."

Doris, meanwhile, continued to live alone, served many decades in the halls of justice, played Scrabble with the intensity of a Boris Spassky, traveled all over the world, and purchased the first color television set I ever saw – and very little else. This made her famous with her friend Hennie, who was the last of the big-time spenders by comparison, at least until it was time to take the stuff back to Abraham and Strauss.

"Her purse was snatched," my mother told me one evening when I asked about security near the apartment building where Doris lived. "They only got her change purse, with *forty-five cents* in it. She even found the purse! They threw it away at the corner. She was mad because the strap was broken."

Doris's windows overlooked the corner of Aurelia Court where I had seen the dead red dog. It was rumored that the victims of five separate homicides had been dumped on the Flatbush Avenue pavement right outside the building in recent months, but I could not verify this statistic with eyewitness testimony. Still, since my mother estimated Doris's accumulated worth to be in the hundreds of millions of dollars (minus forty-five cents), it was something of a surprise that she, like Bill and like Hennie, had stuck it out around here.

Most days, Doris took her lunch at a seniors' social that was held in the B'nai Jacob synagogue on Glenwood Road at the north end of the Junction. When this club announced its gala Spring Party, my mother and I were invited to attend as Doris's guests – as long as we paid for our own lunches. So, on the special day, we set out, me in my Dockers, my mother in black slacks and a blue floral-print blouse studded with faux pearls, three rings, several gold chains, beaten-silver earrings shaped like tiny owls and studded with turquoise, a slick black slicker, and the sunglasses she always wore when it rained.

Slowly, we walked the long block, past Lord's unchanging bakery and the new ninety-nine-cent stores, toward the old *shul*, fighting a tide of prancing youngsters with Jansport backpacks and Charlotte Hornet caps, two bleach-faced tourists just off the cruise ship for a day in Montego Bay. When we reached Glenwood Road, my mother paused and breathed concertedly, several times, accumulating the oxygen she would need when she made her grand entrance at B'nai Jacob.

But the front doors of the synagogue were locked, and a side entrance brought us unexpectedly to a classroom where Lilliputian chairs awaited preschoolers named Andrena, Develyn, Jakaiah, Kaila, and Suede. It was recess, and these new Sons of Jacob were outside in a narrow alley, riding tricycles, playing Ring Around the Rosy, and pounding each other with fists.

My mother found the elevator and headed up to the banquet room to find Doris, while I went prowling, for this was the synagogue where I had recited my bar-mitzvah prayers and screeched my *haftorah* on the ninth day of February, 5723. The party at the Flatbush Terrace, now Bus Stop Discount, had been held the next afternoon.

I made my way to the entrance to the prayer hall, but it, too, was locked. Through a small window, I could see the red dot of the (electric) eternal flame above the ark of the Torah, and daylight illuminating the stained-glass panels in the eastern wall. Behind me, in the main lobby, some of the colored windows had been smashed and broken, and the whole place gave off an eerie aroma of abandonment and age.

I hadn't been in this building since the last Monday of November 1963 – nine months after my bar mitzvah – when I attended a memorial service for

John F. Kennedy, shot dead the Friday before. Above the doorway, "A Tree of Life" had been endowed by the parents of my peers and successors, each gilded leaf marking a donation in the name of some thirteen-year-old boy or girl. I looked for an Abel, but golden tokens had been beyond our means.

The old names remained, but the benefactors had long since fled to Long Island or Florida. On Glenwood Road, there had been a sea change in tribes and traditions. In a room rented to a Haitian kindergarten on the mezzanine of a Jewish house of prayer, a poster said "Happy Easter." I wondered how long it would be before B'nai Jacob was sold off and converted to an Église de Dieu.

Upstairs was the classroom where I had "studied" Hebrew, and, much more avidly, listened to World Series games on a transistor radio concealed in my book bag, with a cable to a tiny earphone running up inside my shirt. The room was derelict, and chairs were piled up. Covered in dust were histories of the Chosen People and biographies of Ben-Gurion and Herzl.

Wandering down long-forgotten hallways, I found the small side chapel where they would bait us boys with bagels and lox to come on Sunday mornings and bind the prayer-filled leather cubes called *tefillin* around our heads and arms. I came upon a pile of prayer books and indexed *haftorahs*, which were the portions of the Holy Scriptures a boy would have to memorize, then chant for the congregation on the Sabbath of his coming of age. I had learned mine by mimicking a rabbi's recording, and now, for the first time, I opened a bilingual reference book that told me what those dimly remembered cadences had meant, so long ago. My chapter had been from the Book of Judges: "THEN sang Deborah and Barak the son of Abinoam on that day, saying, / When men let grow their hair in Israel, / When the people offer themselves willingly, / Bless ye the LORD. / Hear, O ye kings; give ear, O ye princes; I, unto the / LORD will I sing; I will sing *praise* to the LORD, the / God of Israel . . ."

The gala Spring Party was about to begin in the auditorium. I walked in and was amazed. About a hundred and fifty senior citizens had made their way past the roti palaces and the check-cashing fronts, the incense sellers and dollar-cab touts, and now they were taking their seats at long tables set with purple cloths and bright pink napkins and bowls of peanuts and chocolate nonpareils. Most of the gents wore suits and ties. A couple of the ladies sported jewelry it would take two men to lift.

We sat down to bean-and-barley soup, my favorite. I was at the end of one table, and my mother was to my right. My soup tasted burnt, and there was a chicken neck floating in it like an overturned canoe. Then came a breast of chicken stuffed with sawdust, some de-flavored rice, and broccoli reduced to the consistency of tapioca. All this for only $3.50.

Celebrities were introduced. A woman named Jacobs, our state assemblymember – this was the politically correct term – stood at a dead microphone, hollering about funding for in-home nursing care. She was followed by a plump state senator named Markowitz, who, aping Little Debbie's accent, told us how delighted he was to be hee-yuh this yea-yuh. I liked Markowitz immediately. He had the chutzpah to get up there and praise the meal upon which his audience was choking.

A woman named Weiss, director of the Junction Senior Citizens, had been told that I was writing a book. (*Hennie*: "This is my son. He's writing a book.") She came over and started to regale me with tales of Erasmus Hall High.

"I remember walking up and down Flatbush Avenue," she said.

"You still can walk it," I told her. "I've been walking it every day."

"I know," said Mrs. Weiss. "I'm not afraid."

She paused.

"I lied," she said. "I *am* afraid. It's *good* to be afraid."

She pointed to Markowitz, who was encouraging everyone to get out and vote in elections to the local school bo-wawd.

"They shot at him," said Mrs. Weiss. "Right outside his office." I did not see how they could have missed.

It was time for entertainment. Eight choristers, two of them men, moved to the front of the auditorium and, squinting at songsheets, made enthusiastic attempts at "Edelweiss" and "The Battle Hymn of the Republic." These were followed by a rousing approximation of "When the Saints Go Marching In."

The audience loved it. Some sang along. Those who still could, clapped.

A man in a leisure suit the color of peas stood up and appealed for everyone to join a bus trip to the twenty-five-cent slot machines of Atlantic City. He said, "Think of those who *can't* get out of the house and how much they *wish* they could go." But there were few takers.

The President of the Borough of Brooklyn, Howard Golden, was called on to say a few words. Mr. Golden, a tall, lean man, who looked like the horrific actor Vincent Price, had held his office for sixteen years and had become, of necessity, a pragmatist. He talked about Brooklyn being "always the land of the immigrant."

"It would be wonderful if everyone could love one another," he said. "But it's not true that we do."

The culinary segment of the affair having concluded – sing *praise* to the LORD – the featured performers set up their equipment. These were professional musicians named Bien and Gellers, the latter on Yamaha keyboard and the former on tambourine and maracas, and in a succession of silly hats.

Bien and Gellers launched into "Bye, Bye, Blackbird" and the joint started rocking like the Brooklyn Paramount.

Women grabbed women and began to fox-trot like fiends on Benzedrine. Someone started a conga line.

Then they played "When You're Smiling," and all hell broke loose.

I went over to talk to Doris. I had not seen her in a long time. Recently, she and my mother had suffered one of their occasional fallings-out, but, like most of the others, this had not lasted longer than six or seven years. She was wearing glasses and a paisley blouse. She smiled, and the first thing she said to me was, "Am I shrinking?"

She had never been a big woman. I remembered her in my bar-mitzvah year at the controls of her brand-new '63 Valiant with its incredible push-button transmission, trying to stretch herself to see over the steering wheel. She had held on to the Plymouth longer than most car-owners; actually, about twenty years longer. When she finally sold it in 1988 and donated the proceeds to charity – in exchange for a tax receipt – she had put only fifty-one thousand miles on it in a quarter of a century.

At the auditorium on the upper floor of Congregation B'nai Jacob, my mother had gone off to a far corner to smoke, and the two-man orchestra was trying to get everyone to do the merengue, with success.

I motioned toward the gyrating, geriatric mass and said to Doris, "People my age don't know whether to be cheered or terrified by this."

"I know," my mother's classmate replied. "But it encourages *me*. I see these people and I think, 'I still have twenty years.'"

My mother came back and sat down. Organized merriment was not her style. She danced with no women.

Bien and Gellers played an old Yiddish standard called "Tum Balalaika." It was hypnotic and mournful. I didn't know the words. I looked over at my mother, who was crying behind her sunglasses and singing along.

It was time to go. We said goodbye to Doris and Mrs. Weiss. Outside, the sun had come shining through. We made our way down a side street where, in 5723, Catholic kids had thrown pebbles at us and chanted "Christ killers! Christ killers!" as we passed their yards on our way to B'nai Jacob. Now these Papists were grown and gone to the suburbs, educating children of their own.

Back home, my mother began her daily round of phone calls to friends. A man named Rudy had been at the dance, she reported. Rudy was sixty-eight. He had gestured toward the fox-trotters and disdainfully told my mother, "Look at them – they're so *old*."

"No, Rudy," she had replied as the blackbirds fluttered and flew. "Don't you understand? They're *us*, and we're *they*."

∽

Most days, if she ate at all, my mother took her lunch at a coffee shop on Avenue I that was owned by a pacifistic Serb, assisted by a rebellious Greek and two indentured Mexicans. This establishment, successor to a luncheonette my father and his twin had operated here in 1949, stood at the crossroads of continents. To the west was a splendid district of large private homes and snooker-table lawns, maintained by Orthodox Jews and patrolled by their private police. To the north and east were the Caribbeans, to the south was an ethnic bouillabaisse, and across the street were the premises of "G. Gina Do Bong, African Reader and Adviser."

The cooking at the coffee shop was an improvement on Congregation B'nai Jacob, but that hardly meant three Michelin stars. It was the clientele that made the place so wonderful – every nation, every stripe. Also, the decor, which featured several antique soda-fountain implements, assorted New York Mets memorabilia, and a large mounted photograph of Moe Howard and Larry Fine, the patron saints of short-order cooking, pouring maple syrup all over Curly's neanderthal skull.

It was the kind of place where Connie, the Greek, would be slamming soup pots around in the sink like Spike Jones's percussion section, while Don, the Serb, winner of the Josef Stalin look-alike contest, would be heckling her, saying, "How come every time you get mad, you take it out on the equipment?"

Ignoring him, Connie would offer up a chicken-salad sandwich and ask a diner, "You wanna piss of peekle with that?"

There were fifteen stools at the counter and five small free-standing tables. Customarily, my mother commandeered the table at the rear, and sat there behind her sunglasses, nibbling at a toasted Bialystok roll and sipping half a cup of light, light, light coffee, while I took advantage of the Serb's geniality to peruse every newspaper and magazine in stock without paying for them. A chart on the wall advertised vanishing Brooklyn pleasures: cream-cheese and jelly sandwiches, egg creams, even the occult combination of syrups known as a cherry-lime rickey.

The drink was a relic of the forties. At Abel Brothers in my soda-jerking prime, we almost never served one. Looking up at the sign, I wrote in my notebook, "When was the last time somebody ordered a cherry-lime rickey?"

Five minutes later, an Hispanic gentleman sat down at the counter and ordered a cherry-lime rickey. Why did this keep happening to me?

Morose and sullen in the mornings at home, glumly smoking by the kitchen window until her intestines debouched, my mother came alive at the polyglot luncheonette on Avenue I. Half the customers seemed to know her; the other half had just dropped in from Madagascar or Peru. She held court, bantered with the Serb and the Greek and Victor and Eusebio the Mexicans, dazzled working-class men with her wardrobe and wit.

"Where do you live?" they would ask her, entranced by this gem in a Formica setting.

"Over there," she would reply, pointing toward the east like Babe Ruth calling his shot in the 1932 World Series. "In the slums."

At the coffee shop, she would greet a neighbor who had been an usher at the Loew's Kings, and an unhappy fellow from Bensonhurst she described as a "millionaire roofer," who wore unlaced Avia sneakers and jeans with a hole in the hip pocket, through which his wallet was eyeing its escape. Another regular was an African-American in a bright-red beret, who worked at one of the area's most hazardous occupations – installing cable-TV wiring in apartment buildings near the intersection of Flatbush and Church. It wasn't the roof-climbing that was dangerous; it was the neighborhood.

"I thought the Bronx and Harlem was bad," the man in the red beret told us one lunchtime, "But on Dorchester Road, man, the bullets fly *all the time*. The other day, my men and I were installing cable behind a building, when here comes a guy running, carrying a *cash register*, with the police right behind him. They lined up all my men against the wall, too. Yes, that's what he was carrying. A cash register and a toy gun.

"The next day, I saw three guys shooting at an armored car on Church Avenue. *That* one made the TV news."

ॐ

When their shift behind the counter at the coffee shop ended, the Mexicans left the Serb and the Greek behind and repaired to a cantina operated by men from their own country. This was the new El Rodeo, a taste of home. For Victor and Eusebio, the journey from workplace to barstool took about forty-five seconds, depending on the traffic light. The coffee shop was right across the street.

El Rodeo was managed by a fellow named Chalow from the state of Puebla, where all the best cooks came from. Chalow had been in the United States for ten years, and in Brooklyn, New York, for six months. I told him I thought he had chosen an odd site for a Mexican restaurant, wedged as it was between thousands of Haitians and the community of kosher-keeping Hebrews.

"We got about twenty-two kinds of black people here," Chalow replied, looking out through the big front window. "Sometimes they even come in and eat."

My mother had never sampled Mexican cuisine, but to get an hour out with me alone, she would try anything. Arriving at El Rodeo early enough to ensure that we'd be able to walk the two hundred yards home before dark, we chose a table, and she ordered *pollo a la milanesa*, while I went for the beef fajitas. Above us was a painting on black velvet of an Aztec warrior carrying off a melon-breasted queen. We decided to share a single bottle of Corona, not wanting to get too tight.

Victor, in his Mets baseball jacket, and Eusebio, wearing his name on a gold necklace, were at the bar, drinking a beer called Clara Pacifica. Eusebio, I knew, could imbibe all he liked; he lived in a room above the coffee shop, a mere wobble away. (My mother called him "Serve-io," because he served her coffee every day.) Only one other table was occupied. Against the rear wall, five men were watching a television news program about schoolboy crime, headlined, as I translated it from the Spanish for my mother, "Studying to Kill."

The *pollo*, when it arrived, was uninspired, a pair of breaded chicken cutlets afloat in yellow cornstarchy sauce. But my fajitas were first-rate, and, although she would touch neither the rice nor the beans that accompanied them, my mother accepted the sampling of meat and onions I forked over and made goo-goo eyes for more. That, the Corona, and some corn chips with salsa was the sum of our Mexican dinner. We thanked the server and paid our bill and were making our way to the door, when Victor from the coffee shop rose from his seat and begged us not to leave.

Grinning and beckoning, he held up a video cassette and invited us to stay and watch it. "Studying to Kill" was switched off, and the tape was inserted in Chalow's VCR. My mother settled in a chair and beamed. Quietly, she said to me, "You don't know how I crave anything *different*."

The tape had just come in from the state of Morelos, whence Victor and Eusebio had migrated. It was semi-professional footage of a small-town rodeo, entitled "El Niño Maravilla" – the Boy Wonder. Glancing up at the monitor, then at the men in their loneliness, I saw the Flatbush Mexicanos with moist eyes fly away home.

The Boy Wonder rode Brahma bulls like a feather floating on the ocean. We saw him first in a rough-hewn corral, with other *vaqueros*, sitting on fence rails, cheering and heckling, and then in a real arena in a small Morelos town, where village youths teased and taunted the animals by waving hats and bedsheets. On tape, the bulls were introduced respectfully by name – Silver, Elf, The Destroyer – but none could dislodge the Boy Wonder, though he wore spurs on his sneakers as he kicked his mounts, demanding still more fury.

Between the bursts of action, as he watched the screen and sipped his Pacifica, I asked Victor how he had come to this place. I had read that the Mexican population of New York had risen from five thousand to nearly a quarter-million since 1980, and that most of these were solitary men from the deep southern states, who now were working at Korean groceries and fish markets for two hundred dollars a week, or delivering pizza for a dollar a call plus tips, or, if they were lucky, staffing the counter at a luncheonette for a decent guy like Don the Serb.

"I came to stay only a few days," Victor said. That was two years ago.

"Did you walk across the border?" I asked.

"No," he said firmly. He held up his hand as if presenting a document. "Passport."

He quieted and looked back up at the Boy Wonder of the state of Morelos.

"All my family is there," he said.

The men at the table at the back paid no attention. One talked on a cellular phone. Up front, there were the six of us: Eusebio, Victor, Chalow, the waitress, my mother, and me. On the television, the Boy Wonder beamed triumphantly as The Destroyer gave up bucking and knelt down to rest.

"This man make a lot of money," Victor said, contemplating the screen.

"On the bulls?" I asked.

"No," he replied. "On the video."

5

Two blocks beyond the coffee shop and El Rodeo, at the corner of Nostrand Avenue and Avenue K, stood the large brick building where I learned Spanish, algebra, biology, and how to sneak onto the catwalk above the ceiling of the auditorium during the film the eighth-grade girls had to watch about human reproduction. This was Andries Hudde Junior High School, named for a Dutch surveyor, brewer, and colonial secretary, who, in 1636, had been one of the wealthiest men in New Netherlands.

Had he held on to his property, and had he lived to the age of 390, Hudde – pronounced HUD-ee – would have found himself owning the Hotel Nevins where Israel Abolafia lived and the OTB parlor on Montague Street where the old man played the ponies; the Watchtower of the Jehovah's Witnesses; the big hole in the ground at Flatbush and Atlantic avenues; Gleason's Gym; all of DUMBO; and enough Junior's cheesecake to buy off a British invasion. This, however, was not to be. By 1638, Hudde had sold off his lands to pay accumulated debts, and he soon disappeared. It was rumored, when I was at his school, that he later had become a pirate, despite the fact that Pittsburgh had yet to be discovered.

It was one of my priorities to pay a return visit to Hudde J.H.S., where I had been chosen as salutatorian of the Class of 1964 as the achiever of the second-highest scholastic average of the year. I wanted to see if my name was still posted on a wall of honor in the school lobby, and, if possible, I wanted to meet the 1993 salutatorian.

Unannounced and uninvited, I showed up at the front doors of the school one morning and ran into another of those security officers who seemed to have been a late training-camp cut of the Minnesota Vikings. (New York City's uniformed school guards constituted the ninth-largest police force in the United States.) Feigning an appointment with the principal, whose name I did not even know, I bluffed my way into a corridor that led to the main office. Here, in a display panel just outside the doors of the auditorium, was the little brass plaque with my name on it that I had come to see.

"Reader, if you seek my monument," I said to myself, "look about you!"

But I was the only seeker. In the quiet lobby, I stood for a moment and studied the names on the wall of fame. In my era, they had been Glasser, Cohen, Goldstein, Nadel, Shalom. Recent times had brought Chin, Cabrera, Punyasena, Tran, Ahmad. Along the corridor, there were signs in Haitian Creole.

Something clicked. It was the spring of '64 again and I was standing here, in front of the honor board, and Principal Weiss was announcing my name on the public-address system as the academic First Runner-Up. I was fourteen years old and four-foot-measly, weighed less than a watermelon, and could name all the World Series winners since 1903. Beside me for the induction ceremony stood the valedictorian, Glasser, my intellectual superior by a point or two. But finishing second inspired little jealousy; Glasser was even punier than I was, and, where knowledge really counted, he didn't know Duke Snider from the Duke of Earl.

I dissolved back to the present. Alone, out of sight of the guard, I ventured down the hallway and up the stairs to the second floor, looking for my old homeroom. The corridors were lined with grey tiles and the walls were painted yellow, which seemed vaguely familiar, but the water fountains were bone-dry and all the clocks were frozen at 7:48, which made them three hours slow or nine hours fast.

As I followed the yellow stripe down the center of the corridor, I soon realized that I was completely lost. The school was laid out like a giant letter H, and I didn't even know what wing my room was in. I couldn't find Mr. Berman's earth-science lab, or the math class to which, one autumn Friday, my cohorts and I had returned after lunch to find Miss Banks sobbing as she wrote on the blackboard: "President Kennedy is dead."

Backtracking feverishly, lest I be discovered by a security patrol and sentenced to repeat the ninth grade, I gained the main office, handed my Radio-Canada business card to a secretary, and awaited the royal treatment – or the bum's rush. On a bulletin board behind me as I sat and waited was a photograph of a member of the class of 1970 named Martin J. Fettman in full NASA astronaut regalia, and since everyone in the office was talking about Marisa Tomei (class of '83) winning an Academy Award for talking Brooklynese in *My Cousin Vinnie*, I had reason to believe that I was probably ranked no higher than third now in the category of Most Famous Hudde Alumnus of All Time.

Presently, I was informed that the principal was not available, and anyhow, with Commencement still several weeks away, the salutatorian for 1993 had not yet been selected. When the choice had been made, I was informed, I would be informed. Until then, it was adios, alumno.

I gave the secretary my mother's address, then realized that I didn't have to. They'd had it on file at Andries Hudde since I showed up there, tiny and twitchy, just after Labor Day of 1961. The Abels may have been only number two for brains, but nobody beat us for permanence.

∽

When classes at Hudde broke for the day, or on Sunday mornings, winter and summer, I would flash my student transit pass and board the Nostrand Avenue bus, pass through the Junction, and change at Newkirk, bound for my father's candy store. The distance was only about a mile to the northeast, but it seemed like a journey to a separate galaxy of trees and parks and big private houses full of Irish and Italian sons. Near home, our streets were coldly lettered and numbered, but surrounding the store there were avenues named for cities that, to a young Brooklyn boy, seemed as exotic as Constantinople. There were Albany, Schenectady, Utica; and, though I could not yet know its portent, two blocks from the store was Troy Avenue.

The soda fountain my father and his brother owned was virtually identical to the Serbo-Grecian coffee shop where my mother, decades later, would be a late-morning habitué. There was a cigar humidor and racks of newspapers and magazines at the front, a long counter with swiveling stools that squealed like piglets, and a few small tables, where sundaes and sandwiches would be cordially served, usually by me, for a nickel tip. Display cases held greeting cards and model airplanes, there were racks of neatly arranged candies and gum, and sequestered in dozens of drawers and cabinets was an assortment of sundries that ranged from shoelaces to mourning crepe to Granny Clampett corncob pipes.

One of my life's few regrets was that Linda never got to see me tread the slatted boards behind the long, smooth counter of the candy store, scooping double-dip cones and mixing malteds, in my oversized white apron. She never came by for coffee and marble cake, or helped me sweep the sidewalk at sunrise on one of those most special mornings, when my father would gently rouse me at twenty past five, and we'd walk to the store like Cold War conspirators through the darkness of the unborn day. The brothers had sold out, at a substantial loss, three years before I met her, and now there was not even a photograph surviving of Abel Brothers, and Son.

Abel Brothers had been sold in 1970 to a couple of Poles, who soon foisted it off on Koreans. There had been an attempt at beautification at Avenue D and Albany Avenue in the intervening decades, including the installation of new streetlamps and a wide, ornamented brick pavement. In front of our store now was a wooden bench that would have been a lovely place to lap at a vanilla-fudge cone in the old days. But these were the new days, and the bench had been torn apart with such animal ferocity that only one splintered slat was left in place.

The Koreans had moved on in turn. A sign over the entrance said, "WING HING LOON CANDY STORE," and those words, I knew, were Cantonese. (*Wing Hing* means "Eternal Prosperity.") Expectant and anxious, I moved inside.

Almost everything was precisely as it had been. The magazine shelves were the walnut-brown that we had painted them. The candy counter was the one I had kept stocked with Almond Joys and Tootsie Rolls and Goldenberg Peanut Chews. The newspaper rack featured *El Diario* and the *Carib News*, but the Irish *Echo* and the Italian *Oggi* were right alongside. A few of our old customers, the Quigleys or the Rizzos or the Glynns, must have stuck it out.

Two Chinese women were standing idly behind the long counter of the soda fountain. As I looked around, they stared at me with bewilderment and suspicion; they couldn't tell if I was thinking of buying the place, or robbing it. I made a big smile and approached the older woman, saying, "This store my father's long time ago."

It got me nowhere. I asked to see the back rooms where my father and I had bunked in the awful summer weeks of 1968, after his marriage fractured. I wanted to go down to the basement and search for the cartons of old *Sport* magazines and *Hockey Digests* that had been left there when the brothers pulled out. But the Chinese would have no part of this. My fluency in broken Mandarin was of no avail. It was the wrong dialect.

I went out onto the sidewalk again and studied the front display windows, then moved along. Next door had been a German delicatessen, where the Behrens family made the world's best rice pudding, but now it was a Chinese takeout called Number 1 Kitchen, its denuded waiting room separated from the cooking area by a shield of bulletproof plastic. Nearby was a small pizza parlor, and I stopped in for a couple of slices, but the cook had been on Avenue D only since 1971, and the Abel brothers had fled a few months before.

There was one more landmark to visit. In front of a row house on East 42nd Street, just north of Avenue D, was a shrub that was barely visible, at this time of year, behind a bloodbath of brilliant azaleas. No one in the neighborhood knew this now, and I doubted that anyone would care, but this block had been the home of a genuine Brooklyn Dodger, and the bush had come from holy Ebbets Field.

It was safe to say that "Chink" Zachary was not going to be elected to the Baseball Hall of Fame. He was a big, bald, beefy guy – real name, Albert Myron Zarski – who had pitched a total of seven and one-third innings in the National League in 1944. He never won a game and, in his three at-bats, he never got a hit.

But Zarski–Zachary had made friends in baseball – it was the irrepressible Casey Stengel who had drawn attention to his slant-eyed appearance, calling out to him one day, "Hey, ya Chink, whatcha doin'?" – and if he couldn't get major-league sluggers out in games, he was superb at throwing batting practice. For years, he worked for the Yankees, Indians, and Braves, tossing soft ones for Mantle and Maris and Colavito and Mathews to belt into the seats at Yankee Stadium or the Polo Grounds. Then he'd come into Abel Brothers for a soda and bring me scorecards and anecdotes, a consort of living gods.

When the wreckers came to Ebbets Field to tear the heart out of Brooklyn, one of the groundskeepers called Al Zarski to ask him if he wanted any of the greenery that had grown up around the shrine. (He may have been the only ex-Bum still living in the borough.) Ten years later, in 1970, Zarski moved, not to Utica Avenue but to Utica, New York, leaving the plant behind in his front yard. His batting-practice career had ended when one of the Milwaukee Braves felled him with a line drive to the skull.

"Was it Hank Aaron?" I asked him on the phone one night, calling Utica to report that the shrub on East 42nd Street was still alive and well.

"Nah," Chink Zachary replied. "Aaron couldn't hit *me*."

∾

The selections had been made. The valedictory address at the Forty-Second Annual Commencement of Andries Hudde Junior High School would be delivered by a girl named Jane Chong, whose parents operated a Carvel ice-cream store. My successor as salutatorian, twenty-nine years removed, would be Justin Yagerman, son of the librarian at Canarsie High School and a Manhattan matrimonial lawyer.

I was invited to meet the two fourteen-year-olds. Both lived outside the immediate district, but had been attracted by Hudde's "magnet" program in math and the sciences. The Jewish boy rode a yellow bus to school, and the Korean was driven by her mother every day on her way to the family sweetshop. The gifted children studied in separate classrooms, pushed ahead of the masses academically, and ate lunch by themselves. As Justin put it when I asked about the rest of the student body, "there's a lot of kids you wouldn't want to meet."

The school was now, in the newspeak of the times, "80 per cent minority." Bilingual classes were offered to help the disadvantaged Haitians keep pace. A poster in a hallway recorded the nationalities of pupils studying English as a Second Language: 35 per cent were Russian; the rest, a League of Nations of Polish, Nigerian, Albanian, Yemeni, Lithuanian, Korean, and Chinese. The principal, Mel Brand, told me that, in addition to the magnet programs for the gifted, Hudde could boast of "the quietest hallways in the district." But on my way up to meet the academic kingpins, I passed one room where a teacher was screaming as loud as he could, "SIT DOWN! EXCUSE ME! QUIET, PLEASE!" I assumed that his rebellious inmates were not the magnetized whiz kids.

Congratulating Miss Chong on her achievement, I explained apologetically that it was Justin, my exact counterpart, whom I had come to see. She was obviously relieved to be excused. Being interviewed by me, she could sense, would be no walk in the park.

I met one-on-one with Salutatorian Yagerman, who was twice the size I had been when Principal Weiss read out my name in 1964. He was tall and lean and had feet the size of skateboards, wore a pink button-down Oxford shirt, and cracked his knuckles as we talked. He had just taken a "mock" Regents exam, a statewide test usually given to much older students. His score was 96 per cent.

He liked Hudde as much as could be expected. His special courses were stimulating and challenging. He said, "You're not scared of getting jumped when you walk out of here. But a couple of blocks down, over by the Junction, it's not so good." He waved in the direction of my mother's apartment.

Justin Yagerman was as close to my teenaged reflection as I was likely to find within fifty blocks of home. He watched "Seinfeld" every week and wondered how people who didn't live in New York could possibly understand it. He had been, he said, to "millions of ball games" and a lot of Broadway shows. He thought of himself as a City Kid and, thirty years ago, so did I. But his parents' house in beautiful Ditmas Park had been listed for sale, and it looked as if they were going to move to Long Island. Though there were now more than a million kids in the city's public schools, the city was no place for kids.

"When I was your age," I told Justin, "my friends and I used to take the subway to Yankee Stadium by ourselves and nobody thought anything of it."

"My parents would *never* let me go to the Bronx by myself," he yelped. "You can get *shot* at Yankee Stadium."

Pending relocation to safer precincts, the librarian and the lawyer had slapped a six p.m. curfew on their well-bred and talented son. He said he had been "mugged" twice, but these were minor crimes: his bike was stolen out from under him when he was seven, and once he was walking to a bus stop when an older boy demanded a dollar. So he gave him a dollar. End of mugging.

He showed me a computer printout of the address he would deliver on graduation night at the Walt Whitman Auditorium at Brooklyn College. It was commendably literate, and there were even a couple of laugh lines.

"My mother cried when I gave my speech," I told him.

Justin said, "*My* mother better not."

∾

I had entered Brooklyn College at a very young age: one and a half. In a section of the campus that was tranquil and quiet – except when a freight train roared by on the Long Island Rail Road tracks – was an ornamental goldfish pond about fifteen feet wide and fifty feet long. It was here that my mother would bring me on fine afternoons to toddle around the perimeter of the pool and throw crusts of body-building Wonder Bread to the Velveeta-colored fishies.

Forty years later, to enter the same university grounds, you needed two pieces of identification and a damned good reason. Uniformed guards had been posted at all entrances, and visitors were channeled through a checkpoint in Whitehead Hall. Arriving there, I told the sheriff that I had an appointment with the public-relations director. Then, having been admitted, I poked around to see if such a person actually existed.

Soon, I was in the office of a fellow named Coniglione, and I was asking him about courses at the school that might be germane to my project, in addition to the phantom called Correcting Your Accent.

"How about the Archeological Dig?" he asked me, leafing through the summer-school calendar.

"Sounds good," I replied.

"Yes, it is good," said Coniglione, a slim, stressed, energetic, overworked man. Then he noticed something and looked up from the catalogue.

"Oh," he said. "The dig is in Bulgaria."

I went out and roamed the grassy quad that had replaced the ancient circus grounds. The air smelled sweetly of mown grass and honeysuckle. Behind me, on a small bronze tablet, was embossed the Ephebic Oath of the Ancient Athenians: "We will strive to transmit this city not only not less, but greater, better and more beautiful than it was transmitted to us."

From a bench in the shade, I admired the female students who were reposing on the greensward in very little clothing, while trios of shirtless, athletic males tossed footballs around and made exaggeratedly dangerous catches. Then, fidgety as always, I moved on.

There had been times on this journey when I felt as lost as a comet in a foreign firmament, and other times when reborn memories enfolded me in warmth and wonder. It had been like that at the Loew's Kings, the display case at Hudde, my father's store. Now it was happening again. Blundering around Brooklyn College, I had found the goldfish pond.

It was just where I had left it in the album of my oldest recollections, at the edge of the campus, near the railway tracks, and although the water was a bilious billiard-table green, the pool was full of life. A pair of mallards puddled around in the slime, and a big turtle worked on his tan on the only rock in the lagoon. White and magenta water lilies exposed themselves unashamedly, and a couple of hand-holding Chinese students were throwing Wise potato chips into the murky consommé.

This lush and lovely campus, where my sister had gained her degree in Elementary Education, where my mother and Doris had studied Philosophy of Everyday Living, and where I had taught one session of Correcting Your Accent without thought of compensation, was a blessed sanctuary of scholarly repose in the middle of a besieged borough. It had turned out tens of thousands of schoolteachers and professionals, and it offered a first-rate calendar of films and concerts and theater to Brooklynites brave enough to attempt nocturnal travel. Yet there had been those who did not want a college here at all. During the hearings in 1926 that led to the selection of this site, one speaker had referred to the Junction as being "at the end of the world."

A man named Browne from a local real-estate association was adamant in his opposition.

"Why buy and maintain," he demanded of the Mayor of New York, "at the taxpayers' expense, several acres of land to be used for nothing better than football, cane rushes and moonlight necking?"

"You forget, Mister Browne," said the Mayor, Jimmy Walker. "That couldn't happen in Brooklyn."

The mayor got his way. The circus was evicted and the civic-owned college was built. (There had also been a small golf course on the site.) The Junction became the focus of a vibrant new community of learning and social activism. Booksellers and stationers thrived. One block from the campus was Public School 152. Right across the street was Midwood High. For a time, before Hudde was built down at Avenue K, it was possible to go all the way from kindergarten to graduate school at the corner of Bedford Avenue and Campus Road, then to leave here to try to make the new Athens greater, better, and more beautiful.

The passage of time was marked by the march of graduates from the three contiguous academies. At P.S. 152, we square-danced in the playground and drank our two-cent half-pints of milk, and lay our heads on our desks to sleep. At Midwood, we read Cervantes in Castilian, and blew up test-tubes of magnesium, and wore Soupy Sales polka-dot bow ties. Many of us moved on to Brooklyn College: Brucie and his two older sisters, and Little Debbie, and our cousins, and dozens more. Breaking the chain, I went off to Rensselaer and marriage and newspapers, and never looked back until now.

High above the classrooms, the bells of the college carillon kept the hours and the years. They were rung out from the golden dome atop La Guardia Tower, and we could still hear them, when the air was calm and the neighbors quiet, over on East 31st Street.

The Keeper of the Belfry at Brooklyn College was a man named Frank Angel, a generously sized fellow with a diamond in his ear and long curls that hung back in horror from a hairline in full retreat. Frank Angel was the director of the cinema program at the Brooklyn Center for the Performing

Arts and a computer expert, but his real passion was the carillon. It was a job, I suggested when we met, with a-peal.

I wanted to know who made the bells ring, and it was something of a disappointment when Frank Angel informed me that, well, nobody did. The tolling of the hours and the regular concerts of Beethoven and Bach and Wagner were controlled by a machine in the sub-sub-basement of the Whitman Auditorium. He walked me down there and unlocked the door to a windowless closet to show me a control console and a small brown metal box.

Inside this cabinet were several miniature tuning forks, a "Digital Chronobell," whose hourly pings were amplified electronically and broadcast from loudspeakers in the tower with the gilded dome. (The speakers were shaped like bells to make the sound more authentic.) Concert melodies were nothing more than cassette recordings of a real carillon in Philadelphia. I was crushed. So, I sensed, was Frank Angel.

"The company puts out a list of melodies," he admitted. "They have classical, patriotic, and what they call 'Popular Music.' Except what they call 'Popular Music' is stuff like 'The Farmer in the Dell' and 'Pop! Goes the Weasel.'

"To me," he went on, "you want music to be something that *integrates* itself into the daily life of the university. It shouldn't intrude when you stroll through the Quadrangle. 'Pop! Goes the Weasel' does seem to call your attention."

The Digital Chronobell had been programmed to tinkle unobtrusively between classes, strike the hours with traditional Big Ben chiming, and terrify moonlight neckers with one booming De Profundis at exactly eleven p.m. In a monograph on the carillon, Frank Angel noted that this single note "was used to announce the beginning of the Grand Silence in monastic Europe." But to the jackals of the new Brooklyn, De Profundis was a wake-up call.

"I get many nice notes, and I've only had two complaints in ten years," said the Keeper of the electronic Belfry. "And one time a professor of French sent me the sheet music to 'Frère Jacques.' He thought it was a real carillon."

Where Frank Angel spent his own college years, there had been real bells. He remembered days in South Bend, Indiana, when he would sit contentedly, suffused with the glorious sound. He even found a way during interludes in his lessons to sneak up into the carillon itself. He'd sit with his back to the beams and *feel* the bells stirring his soul. It was only natural: the passion that the Keeper maintained in Brooklyn had begun with the lunch break of Notre Dame.

6

Walking the street from the Manhattan Bridge to the Junction, I had passed at least twenty small Chinese restaurants with names that ranged from the hopeful – Taste China Taste, Golden Profit – to the self-parodying Ling Ling and Wong's Wong. Down near the moldering Hotel Nevins was a putatively kosher place called the No Pork. There was a Jane Fond – not Fonda – at Avenue H, and two different shops labelled King Kong. I would walk in, try to start a conversation, gain only silence.

Despite two years' residence in Beijing, my grasp of written Chinese was rudimentary. I could read off a couple of simple characters, and I recognized immediately that the pictograph for "gold" above the doorway of a restaurant at Lefferts Gardens had been mounted upside-down, but that was about it. I knew only enough spoken Mandarin to leave the false impression that I might know a lot more.

In Manhattan was a young man who could assist me, a gray-flannel Canadian corporate lawyer, named Nico, whom I had known in China when I was an underqualified correspondent with a generous expense account and he was a pitiable student, padding around unheated dormitories in corduroy slippers and lining up for the people's commissars' inedible commissary food.

In China, we went off on an expedition together, and Nico, who had mastered Chinese at Williams College, translated interviews for me. A subject would declare, "Who *is* this round-eyed idiot?", and Nico would smile and tell me the man was saying, "Welcome to Jiangxi Province."

Nico's days on Broadway were numbered; his firm was sending him back to Beijing to upgrade the China office. He wanted me to come to "the city" for a farewell at some posh Parisian café. Refusing to leave Brooklyn – why would anyone ever want to? – I managed to transmute this into an invitation for coffee with me and my mother at the Campus Sugar Bowl, beneath Frank Angel's artificial bells.

It was a great, windy, sunny Sunday morning. I waited for Nico at the Flatbush Avenue terminus of the Number 2 subway, while my mother moved on to the Sugar Bowl on Hillel Place to grab a table and get a head start on her cigarettes. When his train pulled in, and we walked over to join my mother at the restaurant, the first thing she did was snatch Nico's shoulder bag and stare at him in abject horror, just as the people of Jiangxi Province had gawked in astonishment at me. Nico was gorgeous, but that wasn't why.

"You brought a *camera* to Brooklyn?" she cried. "Nico, *nobody* brings a camera to Brooklyn."

It was love at first sight. Nico had already met Ben Abel in Shanghai – my father was blanketed on a roll-away cot in a room at the Peace Hotel, burning with fever, at the time – and he had taken Little Debbie to dinner in London, but this had inexplicably failed to blossom into romance. Now, he peppered my mother with questions about her sisters and Fred Lucci and the old neighborhood and what Little Allen had been like as a child.

"One day, he cried," my mother told him. "He said, 'I'm the only kid whose father doesn't have a car.' And I told him, 'No, Allen. You're the only kid whose father owns a candy store.'"

We got up to begin a hike along my avenue, while my mother took the bag with the camera in it and carried it back to the apartment. I led Nico all the way to Church Avenue and showed him the old Erasmus Hall Academy and the cemetery where the Dutchmen were buried and where Irving Choban got mugged. We stopped in at Khyber Travel, and Taj Akbar, working a seven-day week, flashed his Chaplinesque smile and said that he had actually sold some airline tickets to Pakistan. Moving along, I pointed out the Beth Rivka school for Lubavitcher girls and the boyhood home of Eli Wallach.

I showed off some representative sights: boys in Phillies Blunt sweatshirts; a police and fire call box with all the copper wiring ripped out; the sign at Digital Records that someone had riddled with buckshot, just for kicks. ("Avoid being judgmental," Nico cautioned me.) At Henry's ice-cream parlor, the considerable Henry J. Bahnsen was stuffed into the same booth we'd shared a few weeks before. He said that his wife had wondered if he had been too honest in our interview. He rejected the notion. He said, "I'm the kind of guy, I'll call you a sonofabitch right to your face."

We left before he could. But then, back at the Junction, we ran smack into the fervid black chauvinist I had first met on Fulton Street, the zealot with the Ancient Egyptian get-up and the chart that showed the imagined disposition of the Twelve Tribes of Israel. (Levi = Haitians, Manasseh = Cubans, etc.) The orator and a couple of his henchmen were set up at the triangle of Nostrand and Flatbush avenues, preaching over a portable loudspeaker and handing out flyers that said "THE REAL JEWS ARE BLACK" and "THE MOST HIGH SAID THAT HE WOULD BRING THE SWORD AGAINST ESAU, THE SO-CALLED WHITE MAN."

As we were the only white men in sight, the speaker attempted to engage us in argument, and as he was the only Canadian present, Nico politely accepted.

"Look at your arms! What color are you?" the Egyptian demanded, as I attempted to lower myself into a sewer.

"Pink, I guess," Nico replied. A few Levites stopped to listen in.

"THEN WHY DO YOU CALL YOURSELF A WHITE MAN?"

"Let's go, Esau," I whispered.

"Wait," Nico said. "I want you to ask him where the Chinese fit in."

But by this time, I was across the street.

We went into a storefront called the Peony Kitchen. Many of Brooklyn's Chinese take-aways kept no furniture at all between their front doors and the bulletproof shields that protected the cookery staff, but the Peony offered a few desultory tables. Here, one could sit and slurp noodles while trying to peer through the peekaboo blinds of the Club Cheetah strip joint directly across the street. Next door to the Peony was the bankrupt Bus Stop Discount that had once been the Flatbush Terrace, and right out front was, strangely enough, a bus stop where passengers waited for the crawling B41 or the supersonic vans that were stealing half the avenue's riders. So it was a busy location.

In vertical columns along both sides of the kitchen window were the four pairs of characters that made up a traditional Chinese gateway blessing. (I recognized three of them, which was about as useful as trying to sing the musical scale knowing only Do, Mi, and La.) Nico translated the poem: May business prosper and riches increase.

"Of course," I said. "I knew that."

We went up to the shield and tried to establish contact with the young woman behind it. She was tiny, with a voice to match, wearing glasses, pale-skinned. Nico inserted a few sentences of Mandarin through the cash drawer and, wide-eyed, she took it in.

She unlocked a metal-grated door and suddenly we were inside the Peony Kitchen's kitchen. Her name was Zheng Minzhou, which means "sensitive." She was twenty years old. She and her parents lived upstairs, and a back stairway enabled them to come and go from the inner sanctum without having to enter public space. Not that the threat was that great. The restaurant had been held up only twice in six years.

"Ask her if they ever broke in through the roof," I told my translator.

"One time through the roof," Miss Zheng responded, in English, before Nico could speak. Eight years in America, Miss Zheng had assumed the English-sounding name Vincy. She worked at the Peony from noon until early evening, went off to a community college, then returned to the kitchen to work again until 1:30 in the morning, satiating the creatures of the night.

We ordered noodles and fried dumplings, and Vincy made a show of serving us at one of the tables out front. There was only one other customer, and he was a street person, stirring his soup with his fingers. Always the stylist, regardless of the surroundings, Nico asked for chopsticks.

"Just like old times, Allen," he said, lost in the Middle Kingdom, as we began to eat. "You and me again, at the Great Bell Temple."

We cleaned our plates and left. A block away was another restaurant I wanted to see, the bewildering Jane Fond. I could decipher one of the two characters in its Chinese name – the first an easy one, meant "a well" – but the second one was beyond me until Nico explained that it meant "riches," so that the Jane Fond, rather than being the butchered name of a famous actress, was actually the Well of Wealth, transliterated into English.

But this was a euphemism. At the black-hot woks were three young men from Fujian Province on the South China seacoast – Fookien, in their dialect – and these men were hardly taipans up to their elbows in gold. They were, it was likely, as indentured and bound to the service of an unseen proprietor as were the emigrant English women and men of the 1770s who agreed to "covenant, promise and grant" their "Service and Employment . . . in consideration for Passage, Meat, Drink, Apparel and Lodging."

In recent years, Fookienese by the thousands had been sloshing land-ward along both coasts of our gold-paved continent, or deplaning at our open-armed airports with counterfeit papers and innocent brown eyes. A few days after Nico and I hit the Jane Fond and the Peony Kitchen, another several hundred Chinese came abruptly ashore in Rockaway, Queens, after their ship hit a sandbar. Most were from the usual villages of the usual province, and they had paid thirty thousand dollars, a decade's ransom, for their transshipment. (A "village" in China could have ten thousand people.) They were bound for the King Kongs and No Porks of the metropolis, compelled to work off their massive debts under penalty of suffering or even death.

It was a big scandal – a half-dozen of the human cargo of the *Golden Venture* had washed up dead – and a crackdown against the "snakeheads" who organized such cruises was promised. The luckless aliens who survived were going to be dried off, cleaned up, given a hearing, and sent back. But the poverty of China was so oppressive that no law-enforcement effort by either side would ever stop people from trying, and trying again.

At the Well of Wealth, Nico's eruption into flawless Mandarin caused the customary plummeting of lower jaws and fumbling of spatulas. That's why I'd brought him along. A chubby guy with a close-cropped haircut came out of the kitchen and sat with us in complete amazement, as if I had brought in a talking horse, or Rudy the rhino. His name was Lin Hang. Lin was a surname meaning "forest," and Hang was, aptly enough, the character for boating or shipping or navigation.

Thus, as Nico introduced him: Sailing Lin.

Sailing Lin, following a pathfinding older sister, had steamed out of Fuzhou, the provincial capital, two years ago, bound for wherever he wound up. It was, of course, his first and only trip abroad. He said, "I never thought of what a foreign land would be like. I just thought a foreign land must be better than China." He left behind, as so many of them did, his wife and his kid and his parents.

We wished him luck and a reunion with his loved ones, and he smiled, as if this might actually come to pass.

"Ask him what his dreams are," I commanded my aide-de-camp, saccharinely, in closing.

"Dreams?" said Sailing Lin, repeating the question. "We all have dreams. Everyone hopes for higher and better. But dreams must wait for later."

He had never heard of Jane Fonda.

Nico came back with me to our apartment on the fourth floor with the nice view of the ravaged car wash. Almost none of my post-Brooklyn friends had ever seen where I came from.

Nico sat under the ersatz Cassatts in the living room and looked through the photo album of my bar-mitzvah party at the Flatbush Terrace. I hadn't seen the pictures in decades. They showed my father, still dark-haired at fifty one; my mother, radiant at thirty-nine; my sister, an eight-year-old imp. Of the neighborhood cronies at the head table – the East 31st Street Bombers, my best friends in the whole world – the only soul I could locate on the planet today was Brucie down in Washington. Most of the others, I couldn't even name.

The visit was over. My mother gave Nico back his camera, and I walked him toward the subway station, over the freight tracks, past the heaps of trash.

He stopped at the steps that led to the platform, and he asked me, "Allen, is this home?"

"I don't know," I replied. "Brooklyn. Troy. Toronto. China. You don't know how many times I have a *déja vu* of China. Linda and I know we'll never do anything as" – I fought for a word – "*impactful* on our lives again."

I thought that was what he wanted to hear.

"But is this home?" Nico repeated.

I looked around.

"Home," I said.

7

But it wasn't my home. It was my mother's. I had a couple of shirts in the closet and a return plane ticket to Linda. My mother was the one with the forty-year-old grater and the Iron Age pots and pans.

After two months, though the question had neither been asked nor answered, I finally was beginning to understand what had sustained her here for so long, and for so long alone. I saw that security was not carried in an iron pipe, but in the knowledge that others cared and were near. Bill, Doris, Roberto, the coffee shop, the phone calls – "Hullo, is Hennie dere?" – the filaments were stretched so thin that they had nearly broken away. But shakily, the web still held.

In the chain of this community, there were links of nostalgia, rancor, self-pity, sadness, and fear. Each day I spent on East 31st Street, I absorbed a little of each. I felt the web enclosing me. I found myself thinking: If fate sent me back here, I would survive.

One day, we walked over to another apartment building to see a man named Edge. This was short for Educated; during the Second World War, this fellow, now seventy-two, had been the only college graduate in a battalion of a thousand men. He said, "I helped the others to write letters and learn to read before they died."

It would not be prudent to give out Edge's right name or his address. He was a jeweler and expert gemologist and, although overtly retired, he still carried on a business from his home. Yet when my mother and I went up to see him, he didn't even lock the door behind us.

"I got an electronic system," he said. "But who cares? If they know what they're after, they'll come in through the walls and ceiling."

Unlike Bill with his surprisingly dainty furniture, Edge's living room contained almost no furniture at all, only a few display cases of rare minerals and a coffee table upon which was resting an amethyst the size of a bowling ball. His walls were dirty, but the educated man's fingernails were clean.

My mother had come to have some of her gold charms restrung and others sold for cash. She laid the little trinkets on the dining-room table. There was a Betty Boop, a lion's head, a couple of Statues of Liberty, and some banal items that Debbie must have bought for her that said things like "Number 1 Bookkeeper" and "Mothers Are Forever." No bleeding heart, Edge produced an eyepiece from his pocket and examined them and said, "Scrap 'em all."

"But they *mean* something to me," my mother said.

"They mean *nothing* to me," the gemologist retorted. "Take 'em to a scrap dealer, melt 'em down."

He went to the closet and came back with a couple of opals and offered them to her for seven hundred dollars, "wholesale." The opals being rejected, he tried again with some pearls – "Boy, dese are *nifty* pearls!" he Bendixed – and then a magnificent necklace made of several hundred tiny gemstones, strung together to form bands of red and white and blue and purple. No sale.

"Some of these charms are antiques," my mother said, returning to the matter at hand.

"To be an antique, it must be a hundred years old," the expert countered.

"Then we both have twenty-odd years to go," my mother announced.

My mother spread out the charms and tried to decide which ones to keep and which to cast to the crucible. With little remorse, she jettisoned "Number 1 Bookkeeper" and "Mothers Are Forever" and "Number 1 Friend" and a large script *H*. Betty Boop and the Statue of Liberty she would not part with.

Edge turned on an electronic scale and scooped up the four unwanted baubles.

"It comes to three pennyweight," he calculated. In American dollars, that was $21.75. Nobody was going to get rich today.

The gemologist went back to the closet and returned with box after box of gold chains of various thicknesses. He spread them out on the tablecloth, and my mother sifted through them, approving, rejecting, liking, hating.

I watched the pantomime and listened to the banter, and I suddenly understood why we had come. It wasn't the gold charms or the twenty-one dollars. It was the interchange, the affirmation of commonality, the proof that the web was still tensile. This was much more valuable than sapphires, and, in this place, after forty-four years, far rarer.

"Can you put the Liberties on the ends and Betty Boop in the middle?" my mother asked, as Edge began to attach the little gold charms.

"Anything your itty-bitty heart desires," the jeweler agreed.

"What my heart desires," my mother said, "I can't have."

CHAPTER SIX

Across the Flatlands

1

Eighteen thousand years ago, the Laurentide glacier that had crumpled up Prospect Park, creating the "somber-hued wonderland" of Park Slope and giving generations of scabrous muggers ravines in which to hide, melted into an outwash that scoured the rest of the borough as level as a bowling green, all the way to the ocean. Coming upon this terrain in the seventeenth century, the first Dutch settlers gazed at the broad, even, featureless plain and named it Nieuw Amersfoort.

Then the founding fathers woke up one morning and looked around at the landscape and smashed clay pipes over each other's heads and said, "Joops! Make that 'Flatlands.'"

Compared to famous Flatbush, the village to the north, Flatlands was unnoticed and unloved. It was the Manhattan Bridge of neighborhoods. Topographically, it offered little excitement, to be sure. Flatbush Avenue rocketed through it like a dog to a fireplug. The gentle hump that carried the avenue over the Long Island Rail Road tracks was the highest point of land. The skiing was lousy.

But Flatlands had much to offer. At the center of the district was a bustling commercial strip, and at the southern extremity was sparkling salt water and a new National Park. There were lovely homes and treelined avenues. A handsome Dutch church still stood at historic Kings Highway, and a couple of gabled homesteads had been preserved. There was a major shopping mall, an amusement park, two carousels, an eighteen-hole golf course, and a marina. You could play Bingo or buy a Mercedes-Benz. Yet no one sang of nesting time in Flatlands.

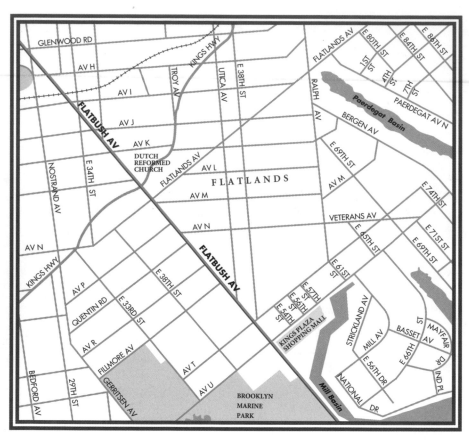

Chapter Six: Across the Flatlands

Walking south along Flatbush Avenue, I shed morbid cares. The street seemed broader, the sky lower and bluer, the sidewalks more inviting of a stroll. A south wind carried the sea. Nobody squatted on the pavement, selling incense or candied nuts. Children rode bicycles and skipped rope. The Zaca Botanica at Avenue I, southernmost of the voodoo-supply houses, could have put out a sign: "Last 'Go Away Evil' Oil Before Turnpike." There seemed to be less evil to evict.

The change of mood was contagious. At Avenue J, the Kam Hong take-out had a bulletproof shield. But at Avenue K, a hundred yards to the south, the Best Wok restaurant did not. A convenience store in the same block left a rack of newspapers *right out on the sidewalk.*

On the jukebox at Coughlin's Grill, you could hear the Rovers or the Clancy Brothers or Erin's Pride, singing "When New York Was Irish." Since the demise of the Vanderveer Tavern, and the surrender of the Chesterfield to the jungle cats, Coughlin's had become either the first Irish bar in Flatlands, or the last, depending on the direction in which you were staggering. It stood on the west side of Flatbush Avenue near Avenue K, identified by a green-and-yellow sign and a door that was usually open by nine o'clock in the morning.

Inside, Coughlin's was a period piece from an era that I thought had ended, period. A beautiful wrought-tin ceiling overarched a long bar, a couple of tables, a portrait of John Fitzgerald Kennedy, and a photo of Jackie Robinson. Drinkers bunched back from the picture window, shunning the insolent daylight. Bobby Gallagher called it "the poor man's country club."

Bobby Gallagher had lived on East 31st Street for twenty-four years, in a "private house," one block from my mother's apartment and two blocks from the little Irish bar that had become his alternative habitation. He was the regular that the other regulars commanded that I meet. "Tawk to Bobby," they said. But the first few times I went into Coughlin's, seeking Bobby Gallagher, he had always just gone out to fetch some guy a hamburger or run a bet to the OTB.

The way they talked about Bobby, I expected he'd be too shamrocked to speak. When I finally met him, on the fourth try, I recoiled: he was thin and pale, white-haired, with thick glasses, a hedgerow of stubbly whiskers, and besieged rows of teeth. But Bobby Gallagher was an educated man, introspective and aware.

He had been around the world seven times, he told me as I nursed a beer – and he a Coke – at one of the private tables. He had worked as a corporate travel consultant in "the city." He had seen Hawaii, New Zealand, Alaska, Tahiti. And he had seen the world come marching down Flatbush Avenue, right towards his house. But he thought the worst was over.

"I think the neighborhood has stabilized," he said, and he pointed north, toward the Junction and my mother's place. "Past Avenue I, it's *gone*. Around here, most of the Irish that were going to leave have already left. The ones still here are probably going to stay. They can't afford to get out. The only ones leaving now are comin' out of McManus."

I caught his punchline. McManus was an Irish funeral home on Flatbush Avenue. Even Fred Lucci, my mother's second husband and a purebred Italian, had left Brooklyn in one of McManus's lower-priced coffins, draped with the flag the government gave free to any deceased veteran. We buried him out in Nassau County, where he couldn't see the dead dogs of his widow's world.

Bobby Gallagher, who was in his fifties, had grown up in a derelict section of northern Flatbush called "Pigtown." The area formerly had been the back lots of the Martense and Vanderbilt and Zabriskie farms, pestilential lowlands where swine rooted and Irish and Italian immigrants were consigned. (Yellow fever was endemic in Pigtown late into the nineteenth century.) But Bobby preferred to remember the blessings of a Brooklyn boyhood: the walks to the daffy Dodger games at Ebbets Field; the priceless gift, free to any child, of an Erasmus education. A classmate at the Hall was Barbara Joan Streisand, but they had not been close. Barbara sang in the girls' cantata. Bobby Gallagher was in the glee club.

"She was a loner," he remembered. "She knew she had a career, and she concentrated on that."

Twice a year, in May and in October, the inhabitants of Coughlin's Grill blundered out into the blinding ether to keep alive one of the great Brooklyn traditions. On a quiet Sunday morning on a dead-end street off Avenue H, they brought out the broomsticks and the little rubber balls called "pinkies" and pitched and swatted and laughed and drank until they had completed nine innings of stickball. Then they all drove back to Coughlin's to relive the glories of the day.

The first game of 1993 was scheduled for a few days hence. Bobby Gallagher invited me to attend and promised to introduce me around.

"We're like a little family," Bobby Gallagher said. "Refugees from the Vanderveer."

ॐ

The little stub of Troy Avenue that lay between Avenue H and the Long Island Rail Road was not exactly Wrigley Field. Along one side of the street ran an eight-foot wire fence that protected a branch office of New York Telephone. On the other side was the warehouse of a firm called Laquila Construction and the perfumed abattoir of Golden Simcha Kosher Poultry. A sewer at the dead end marked home plate. Outfielders had to contend with two dumpsters in the roadway and a couple of trucks parked along the right-field foul line. For box seats, there were some chunks of concrete jettisoned here and there to crumble and rot.

A broken-down old sportswriter was the first one at the park. Two days earlier, my mother had spotted Bobby Gallagher on Flatbush Avenue, running one of his myriad errands. (She knew him through Bill, the ex-Vanderveer bartender.) "Remind him!" Gallagher told my mother. "Make sure he's there at a quarter to ten!"

On Sunday, not wanting to miss anything, I arrived at a quarter to *nine*.

That left me alone for a good forty-five minutes to sit on the cement and wonder if Bobby Gallagher had been pulling my leg. But he hadn't. At 9:30, Jimmy Green pulled in, wearing a T-shirt with the number 16, and in New York that number meant Dwight Gooden of the last-place Mets or Whitey Ford of the old-time Yankees.

Jimmy Green described himself as an "unemployed bah-tendah." He was thirty, and "sorta between houses right now." He had grown up on East 34th Street, but his mother had moved him up to Cape Kahd, which explained his Brooklyn–Boston accent. East 34th, Jimmy said, was now full of Hasidic Jews. He said, "Dey swahmed right in dere."

We each pulled up a slice of curb and waited for the teams to arrive. The others, Jimmy said, were having their pre-game meal at Coughlin's: barley, hops, and water.

"It's a 'heavy-hitter' bah," he said. "Dey staht out early. But *I* should talk? Because I do, too."

A few cars glided down to the dead end and parked on the sidewalk in front of the Golden Simcha. A fat man got out of a Plymouth and shouted, "Let the games begin!" An open-bed Dodge pickup disgorged five more players, and in the back were cases and cases of Budweiser, none of them lite.

"It's official," Jimmy said. "The beer is here."

The players wore T-shirts that said: "HELP! I've fallen and I can't reach MY BEER," or "I like a seven-course meal – A HOT DOG AND A SIX-PACK."

Some of the men, barrel-chested and short-haired, were police officers. Others were retired from the NYPD. They were dividing themselves into teams called the In-Laws and the Out-Laws. It appeared that everyone was either a cop, an ex-cop, or being sought by the cops.

"One guy ain't heah," Jimmy said, pointing to a woman who was video-taping the action, which so far consisted of men walking over to the pickup truck for more nutrition. "He was afraid she'd sell the tape to 'America's Most Wahnted.'"

A woman named Nancy sat down next to Jimmy. She was his companion of recent weeks, a slender blonde in tight jeans, a black T-shirt that said "San Diego," and black pumps. Nancy had lived until recently at the Junction. She had sent three kids to my old Public School 152, and one of her sons was on the football team at Midwood High.

Nancy had made the decision to move to Bensonhurst when someone put a gun to her teenaged daughter's head on Glenwood Road and took her coat and her jewelry.

"It was good for her," she said. "I told her what would happen around there if she wore jewelry."

I thought of my mother in her silver owl earrings and her Statue of Liberty charms.

"Where'd you meet Jimmy?" I asked Nancy.

"In Coughlin's," she replied. "He's a sweet kid."

Jimmy had risen from the slab and was taking furious practice swings. He said, "Last October, we played nine innings and the score was nothing–nothing. I don't know if it was us, or the beer."

"They should play 'The Star-Spangled Banner,'" I said, and then cleverly added, "or 'When Irish Eyes Are Smiling.'"

"They should make a new song," Nancy retorted. "'When Irish Men Are Drinking.'"

Jimmy Green was going to bat leadoff and cover left field for the Out-Laws. He had grown up playing stickball, as I had, between the parked cars of narrow side streets, with a manhole lid for home plate and treetops for foul poles. The game was quintessentially Brooklyn; it was the art form of boys who grew up miles from a patch of grass. Making contact with a rubber ball by swinging a narrow wooden stick looked difficult, but it was even harder than it looked. On East 31st Street, we threw curves and knucklers, climbed on cars for great Willie Mays catches, and fist-fought over fair or foul balls.

Back on Troy Avenue, the semi-annual Coughlin's Grill World Serious began. There was no wind, and the sun burned like acid. Squinting into the glare, Jimmy Green ignored the first two high, bouncing pitches and then lofted an easy fly to left field that the left fielder easily dropped. Jimmy wound up on third, but died there when the next three Out-Laws struck out.

I had nominated myself as official scorer, and had been acclaimed unanimously. But there was no score to keep. For six innings, no one else hit a ball out of the infield. In fact, except for a towering drive by an In-Law named Larry that went over the kosher-chicken building and curved unfortunately foul, almost every man summarily whiffed.

But then, with two out and nobody on base in the top of the sixth, Jimmy Green stepped up and belted a double to left. The next man, of course, struck out. Jimmy slouched back to the bench and retrieved his Budweiser. Disappointed at not being driven home, he turned to me and Nancy as he eased back toward left field and shrugged, "I can't do it all by myself."

"At least I'm going with the best player," Nancy smiled, melting his pain.

The score remained 0–0 until the Out-Law eighth. A kid named Kenny lined a single off the Golden Simcha. Then Big Kevin, an old teammate of Jimmy Green's from East 34th Street, hit a one-hopper to third that went for an error. First and third now, and nobody out.

Two strikeouts followed, and this gave Jimmy Green, who was sorta between houses and cities and careers, a chance to be the hero. As he strode plateward, several of the other Out-Laws began chanting, "MVP, MVP."

Then Jimmy Green slammed a single up the middle for a 1–0 lead, and someone on the bench called out, "Now nobody's gonna criticize the way you train!"

That should have been the ball game, 1–0 for Jimmy's team. The lead held until the bottom of the ninth. Then, with one out and a runner on first, a slugger named John Donahue sent a bullet out toward left field for a hit. Jimmy Green fielded the ball, bobbled it, picked it up again. The tying run was already home, and John Donahue was circling the sewers. Desperately, with the game on the line, Jimmy pegged the ball toward the infield, but the throw was low and wild, and it skipped away as Donahue plated the winning run. Game over.

The final tally:

	1	2	3	4	5	6	7	8	9	T
Out-Laws	0	0	0	0	0	0	0	1	0	1
In-Laws	0	0	0	0	0	0	0	0	2	2

There was no joy in Coughlinville. Jimmy Green sat down next to me and said, "My throw. My throw. It was low. I know, it was low. I feel like the '86 Red Sox..."

Everyone was heading back to the grill to celebrate winning or losing. Nancy put her arm around Jimmy and said, "Let's just go straight home." But he wouldn't raise his head.

I walked away from the agony. Bobby Gallagher never showed up.

2

Flatlands was like the Galápagos Islands: its creatures held no natural fear of Man. They arose each day with the expectation that they would still be alive at nightfall. And many of them were.

Down here, shop clerks lived up to Roberto the Super's legend of Bostonian gratitude. ("I hear they say, 'Thonk you.'") Everyone was more relaxed. In a barber shop on Flatbush Avenue called Mr. Imperial, the welcome was so congenial and the mowing so expert that the customer in the chair next to mine looked at his reflection in the mirror and said, "That was so good, I should get *two* haircuts." But he had only one head, so he paid his eight dollars and left.

Mr. Imperial, located just south of the intersection with Kings Highway that marked the historic heart of Flatlands village, was the first parlor this side of Prospect Park that specialized in removing hair rather than selling "Wet 'n' Wavy" bolts of someone else's. It featured all the traditional trappings: a wall poster of Ebbets Field, a phony hundred-thousand-dollar bill taped to the big front mirror, canisters of arcane tonsorial potions that had not been touched since Garibaldi's last trim, postcards from beach resorts that featured the lunar buttocks of women, and a radio that had been programmed to blow itself up should anything but Sinatra come on.

A barber named Joe had been working at Mr. Imperial for twenty-three years. He threw a towel around me and declared war on my rampant foliage.

"You been here before?" he asked me.

"Yeah," I said. "In 1964."

That was the year I saw *A Hard Day's Night* at the Marine Theater next door to Mr. Imperial and couldn't understand what all the girls were screaming about. Now the Marine Theater had been knocked down and a big Korean fruit store had taken its place. And the Brook Theater, around the corner on Avenue M, was gone as well.

"How's my wife been doing cutting my hair?" I asked Joe the barber.

"Not too good," he replied, snipping disdainfully.

I mentioned that I was planning to write a book about Flatbush Avenue. This was met with a few minutes' silence. Then Joe said:

"You're a writer?"

"Yeah," I admitted.

"A writer," he repeated. "How long you been out of work?"

"I'm working," I said.

"Doin' what?"

"Writing."

"You get paid for dat?"

"I hope so."

"You write any udder books?" Joe asked.

"One on sports and one about the Middle East."

"Dey sell?"

"Not many," I said. On the radio, Frank was singing "You and the Night and the Music."

∾

Starting out from my mother's apartment on a jaunt towards the welcoming sea, the first notable sight I would come to was a house described in the American Institute of Architects' guide as "a well-dressed neighbor in a *tacky* neighborhood, like a Harris tweed jacket among polyester leisure suits."

The Coe House was a Dutch homestead from the 1790s that had been moved from its original site and now stood barely thirty yards off Flatbush Avenue on East 34th Street. It was, from the outside, a rare and beautiful thing, with its distinctive ski-jump roof, its towering birch trees, and its flamboyant magnolia, shedding pinkish petals that lay like lingerie on a flagstone walk.

Once, the house had been part of a seventy-five-acre farm, but now it was the centerpiece of a fifty-two-week headache. I was leaning on the white picket fence one morning to admire it, when a man and a boy walked out of the front door. I thought they had come to shoo me from their property, but the boy was merely being sent off to school. The man, it seemed, was being sent off his rocker. He gave his name as David and admitted, unenthusiastically, that he was the new owner of the old, old house. The price, he said, had been in "the mid two hundreds."

"Why did we buy it?" David said, and again: "Why did we buy it? Why did we buy it?"

"Why *did* you buy it?" I asked, getting into the spirit of the game. "Why did you buy it? Why did you buy it?"

There was no answer.

David explained that the house was closed to the public, but that this was not a great loss because there was nothing remarkable about the interior. Outside, he sighed, the Harris tweed badly needed patching. Every time Brooklyn was hit by a "Storm of the Century" – there had been three in five months over the winter – birch boughs went crashing into the two-hundred-year-old Dutch roof, forcing David to call for a two-hundred-

year-old Dutch roofer. When such damage occurred at the Lefferts Homestead at Prospect Park, the city paid Arne Israel to fix it, but at Coe House,
David said, "it's a constant struggle to stay just a little bit behind."

Graceful Coe House quickly surrendered to its polyester inferiors, lost in
the arriviste architecture that lined this stretch of Flatbush Avenue in low-
rise apartment buildings, homely storefronts, garages, and restaurants. The
glacial outwash, though agriculturally fertile, had never been a populous or
popular area. The farther down the avenue I went, the more discontinuous
and haphazard the arrangement of buildings seemed to be. The IRT subway,
with its cargo of immigrants, had halted in 1920 at the Junction. In Brooklyn
terms, I was out on the frontier.

(Historically, even tiny Flatbush village had dwarfed Flatlands in population, 3,500 to 1,600 when the Civil War began, 12,000 to 4,000 in 1890. Flatlands was the last of the independent towns to be consumed by Brooklyn's
voracious expansion. On January 1, 1896, it capitulated, "shaking off the
drowsy slumbers of Dutch antiquity," in the words of one account, "for the
newer life of a progressive present . . . the rights, the privileges and the digni-
ties of cityhood.")

Directly across the road from a gravestone store was the veterinary
clinic to which I had brought Caesar, my first parakeet, when he contracted
some kind of fungal infection in the spring of 1963. An ointment was prescribed – it cost as much as the budgie had – and in my enthusiasm to have
Caesar healthy again, fluttering around our little apartment and shitting on
the curtain rods, I applied the preparation so liberally that it gummed up
the poor bird's pores and he croaked. Still, it was nice to see that the animal
hospital was functioning, thirty years after I wrapped my lifeless pet in
paper towels and shot him down the incinerator chute on my way to
another day at Hudde.

The infirmary was announced by the continuous barking and bellowing
of dogs in a pound at the rear and by a mural on the southern wall depicting a
yellow-eyed panther, its coat a midnight indigo, its whiskers thick as stickball bats. The noise from the kennel was hardly soothing – it sounded like a
Gleason's Gym for four-legged boxers – but the fence was sturdy, and I
walked past without being torn to shreds.

I was in a jumble of narrow lanes that led to the jewel of old Flatlands, the
Dutch Reformed Church. Unlike its counterpart at the nucleus of the Village

of Flatbush, the Flatlands church did not find itself aswirl in a cyclone of street markets and gunfire. There was a hum of traffic from Kings Highway and the persistent barking from the canine sanatorium, but when I found an open gate and wandered into the cemetery beside the perfect pure-white clapboard church, I couldn't see or hear another person. If Flatlands itself was an oasis within the crumbling country of Brooklyn, then this church-yard was the wellspring of its calm.

It was the first time since the Botanic Garden that I'd been alone in a large public space without feeling afraid. London plane sycamores and white oaks fanned me like the slaves of an Indian rajah. I looked at the moldering tombstones of the Dutch Flatlanders – Rapelje, Wyckoff, Voorhies, Stryker, Funck – a last glimpse before their deep-etched lettering faded forever in the acid of our industrial atmosphere. And I saw the same transformation I had noticed at Flatbush: a family named Sprung, whose headstones had been inscribed in the eighteenth century in Dutch, had changed by 1850 to Sprong, with memorials in English.

I moved to the far corner of the yard – it was closest to the dog pound and its furious dingo barking – and saw that someone had painted the "satanic" numerals 666 on the gravestone of a man named Garrison (d. 1878) along with the cordial message, "MAY HE BURN IN HELL."

The church itself was locked against invasion by the satanists. I had to content myself with an exterior view of this most simple and elegant Greek Revival building, consecrated in 1848 as the third house of prayer on the site, and I backed up and backed up until I could just see the golden weathervane that crowned the spire. In February 1977, some defect in the chimney touched off a fire that burned the roof off and scorched the interior right down to the fretwork, but this had been repaired without a visible scar. An oxidized copper plaque affixed to a boulder near the front gate traced the origins of "the King's Highway" to the founding of Nieuw Amersfoort in 1636, although it had, of course, been a pathway of the Canarsee Indians for centuries before that.

"Over it," the plaque read, "the Indian Braves and Captain John Underhill with his colonial soldiers passed." And here, on August 26, 1776, Lord Cornwallis and his men "silently marched in the night," bound for the rout of Washington's new army in the folded vales of Prospect Park.

Fourteen years later, George Washington would drive past this churchyard as president, having accepted the surrender of Cornwallis himself at York-town, thus taking Kings Highway from its king.

Kings Highway was now a multi-lane Daytona speedway with treed medians that curved around Brooklyn from Bensonhurst to Brownsville, bearing huge amounts of traffic, its course as lazy and serpentine as Flatbush Avenue's was arrow-straight. Both streets played havoc with the symmetry of the borough's gridlines, so that travelers on Kings Highway at one point leapt suddenly from East 59th Street to East 91st Street in a single block, and Avenue P found itself crossing Flatbush Avenue *between* Avenue M and Ave-nue N. Visitors who sought the intersection of Kings Highway and Quentin Road were directed to two such locations a mile apart. No wonder it had taken so long to settle Flatlands.

Paying homage to those who had made the heroic effort to overcome the isolation and cartographic confusion, the Emigrant Savings Bank at the cor-ner of Kings Highway and Flatbush Avenue offered a russet-colored frieze: "a tribute to the thousands of mothers who, throughout the history of this community, have taught their children the habit of thrift." Depicted were a Canarsee squaw, who tended her papoose, while a guileful Dutchman attempted to trade a few blankets for title to Indian land. There was a sailing ship and a twin-engined airplane, which was how the pioneers had come to Flatlands, and how their distant descendants had fled it.

The main commercial district of Flatlands began south of Kings High-way. It included Mr. Imperial the barber and the Korean market with its inevitable Mexican stock boys that had replaced the Marine Theater. There were more saloons of the rump Brooklyn Irish – Greenfield's; the Cuckoo's Nest – and a big McDonald's with a drive-thru lane. At Lenny & John's Pizza, an ambitious but amateurish mural of an Alpine lakeside villa wrapped around three sides of the hot, narrow restaurant. The pizza, crisp and cheesy, leaking oil like the Exxon Valdez, was superb.

Only one Flatlander had been murdered that I heard of: the clerk in the Four Aces Pawn Shop, shot quite dead by thieves. But this was an isolated incident and, as always, I carried nothing worth pawning or stealing. I was relaxed, but I was still in Brooklyn.

"Flatlands residents have the last laugh," a publication of the Borough

President's office stated, praising the district's "quiet, small-town feeling" and "very ordinariness of life." It was the natural location in which to fulfill a family imperative, and the imperative was Mother's Day.

∾

As I came out of my pre-imperative shower, my mother was singing "Don't It Make My Brown Eyes Blue" with appreciable enthusiasm, completely off-key. It was five o'clock in the afternoon, and, as usual, the Crystal Gayle cassette was playing. In an hour or so, we would head for the very ordinariness of Flatlands for dinner.

Between songs on the tape, I could hear Frank Angel's computerized Brooklyn College carillon tolling the hour. A fire engine tore down Flatbush Avenue, siren screaming. Sirens were a fixture of the soundscape; at night, I heard one every five minutes or so. But I had to agree with the restaurateur Henry J. Bahnsen, who had said, back at his failing ice-cream parlor, "The sirens are bad, but the worst thing is when they stop outside your window." Outside our window, now, six boys were playfully slamming their basketball against the "Dead End Street" sign.

Aping Crystal, my mother sang, "It's been a too-long time with no peace of mind, and I'm ready for the times to get better."

I couldn't remember the last time I had been with my mother on Mother's Day. We had spent few holidays of any kind together in recent years, with the exception of Thanksgiving in Troy last autumn, when Linda broke the heart-flipping news of my impending Brooklyn sojourn. My visits were usually scheduled to coincide with TV assignments in the Center of the Universe: Jesse Jackson campaigning for the presidency; the election of Mayor Dinkins; a profile of Spike Lee. But this year we could go out together like mother and son, and she could make Ava Gardner eyes at me.

From Florida, my father had sent his ex a greeting that said, "Think of this little card . . . as a great big hug!" I bought a baby boy's card with a picture of a teddy bear, and left it on the kitchen table to save postage. (Mommy had preserved my own forty-three-year-old Teddy and sometimes propped him in a chair in the living room to keep Little Allen home by proxy.) And my sister's card said: "I know I keep you busy / but you keep me busy, too . . . / While you're busy / taking care of me, / I'm busy loving you!"

This was the sentimental side of our Little Debbie. But she also possessed a devilish facet. In April, she had sent Linda and me an anniversary card that read: "You could search the wide world over / And never ever see – / A finer pair than you two / On any family tree!"

Between the words "any" and "family" she had inserted "dysfunctional."

∾

At 5:30, my mother down-shifted into her glamour mode. She emerged from behind the broken, sliding, slatted door of the apartment's only bedroom in slacks and a Japanese robe Debbie had bought for her on one of their Westbury binges. But the robe didn't *go* – she looked like a tanned, gray-haired, swordless Yiddish samurai – and so she retreated into the bedroom and closed the sliding door.

On the second try, she came out in a royal-blue knee-length skirt, a short-sleeved blouse in a pattern of yellow, red, purple, and blue flowers, pendulous earrings, and a long, knotted, double-strand necklace of rhine stones. I assented wordlessly. She stuffed an extra pair of pantyhose into her purse, checked that the windows in the kitchen and living room that led to the fire escape were locked, muted Patsy in mid-number, pulled down the shades, extinguished the lights, double-bolted the door, rang for the windowless elevator, and we were off.

Our destination was Nell Flaherty's, a big, popular restaurant-bar with an Irish theme on Flatbush Avenue near Avenue R in central Flatlands. Debbie was there to meet us when we disembarked from the B41, bearing her customary steamer trunk of paraphernalia and a single yellow rose for Mom. When we entered the eatery and saw that it was packed to the rafters with boisterous families, our mother brightened – she always came alive in crowds – and announced, "This is where the Irish bring their kids, so they'll know what a bar is."

But Nell Flaherty's was no Coughlin's, dim and defeated. Here, at long tables, Mother's Day honorees in corsages and cardigans were being toasted by their husbands and heirs. In another group, an older gentleman was standing with a glass in his hand and belting out the First World War anthem, "Over There," while his relatives labored with embarrassed futility to get him to sit down and shut up.

"Don't I look well?" our mother asked, and, like members of the Canadian Senate, her children nodded ritual approval. She looked *good*, too.

We were shown to a table on a small platform near the back of the room, and a server hauled up a blackboard of specials: swordfish, salmon, scampi, clams, mussels, tomato bisque, sole Francese. Debbie ordered a Tom Collins and I took a light beer. Our mother requested a Whisky Sour, "straight up, big head," that she expected, after decades of similar requests, to arrive on the rocks and headless. And it did.

"I love your Southern Fried Chicken," she told the server.

"We don't have it on the menu any more," the woman said.

"How are the pork chips?"

"*Pork chips*?" I hiccuped.

"Sorry," my mother said. "It's my cataract."

She settled for chicken wings and a side order of roast "Irish" potatoes. I went for the swordfish, and Debbie chose Chicken Dijon, which arrived afloat in a Gowanus Canal of tawny sauce. The food was good, the honoree content.

I looked around. Young women in strapless black dresses were teetering on skyscraper heels like Melanie Griffith in *Working Girl*. Photographs of Dublin invoked a Hibernian flavor, but banners announced weekly barrages of karaoke and country line-dancing, dragging Nell Flaherty's squarely into the American mainstream. It felt like Boca Raton, Florida, on Father's Day, not Flatlands, Brooklyn, on Mother's. *Everyone* was white. A Ghanaian stumbling in here, I thought, would feel as small and separate as I had at Akwaaba back in Lefferts Gardens, eating *jollof* rice and sweet, creamy fish. Yet it was the same city, the same borough, the same avenue.

"It'll never come back," Henry J. Bahnsen had snarled, far up Flatbush. But at Nell Flaherty's, "it" had never left.

Debbie the Jobless, compelled by generosity she could not suppress to spend money she did not have, had bought a gift. (She was as defectively addicted to shopping as Rudy the Rhino had been to Betsey the Hippo.) From her voluminous swag, my sister produced a vibrant blue vest embroidered with a large rendering of the Pink Panther and handed it to one of the few sixty-nine-year-old women in the United States who would wear such a thing in public. The recipient was delighted.

The room was pulsating with festivity. Every stool at the long bar was taken. That older gentleman had risen again and was warbling either "Rose of Tralee" or "The Most Beautiful Girl in the World" in either English or Gaelic. It was so noisy at Nell's on Mother's Day, and the crooning was so lugubrious, that it was impossible to tell.

"Do you want to come back here for your birthday?" I asked my mother, shouting over the din.

"Not if he's still singing," she answered.

3

"Let's walk home!" my mother clucked, when her chicken wings had been reduced to a heaping ossuary. This being "quiet, small-town" Flatlands, we did walk, with purpose but not panic, traversing a dozen long, lettered avenues, passing the McManus Funeral Home and the Mr. Imperial barber shop and Coughlin's Grill and finally the Zaca Botanica that marked our re-entry into the spirit world in which we resided.

We even met Doris along the way. She had been taken to dinner by friends and, when we happened by, she was waiting at Kings Highway for the B41 to carry her back along Flatbush Avenue to her apartment. Yoo-hooing us mad musketeers, she made it a foursome and pocketed the senior citizen's half-price bus fare. My hulking presence made everyone feel safe.

"We saved you fifty-five cents," Little Debbie said, greeting our mother's classmate from Philosophy of Everyday Living.

"*Sixty* cents," Doris countered. "They raised it."

Walking had been my preferred method of travel along Flatbush Avenue ever since the B41 had broken down at Grand Army Plaza on the very first morning, and Debbie and I had had to reconnoiter a hiking route to the fog-bound East River shoreline. The Abels' predilection for pedestrianism was deeply ingrained, dating back to Grandpa Abelowitz's days, when not taking the bus meant saving a nickel. Now that the fare was a dollar and a quarter, I covered more ground on foot than Phidippides of Marathon.

On Flatbush, the alternatives to walking were the blue B41 buses, the marauding gypsy vans, with their little Haitian or Trinidadian or Jamaican flags dangling from their rear-view mirrors, the licensed Italian and Russian livery services, whose cars could be ordered only by telephone, and the rampant "dollar cabs" that raced the vans that raced the big blue buses. Metered yellow taxis, in Manhattan as common as street-sleepers, were unknown here. From the Junction northward, of course, the rude, rattling Number 2 subway completed the range of options.

Brooklyn had long been in love with speed. In 1668, a six-gulden fine was levied for "very dangerous and harmful driving and racing with wagons, principally by young people." The elder Dutchmen who founded the somnolent villages were in no hurry to go anywhere, but their successors were frantic commuters, and their world was measured in traveling time, transfers, and tolls. First came the stagecoaches, then the horse-drawn rail cars, reaching across the glacial moraine to Flatbush village in 1860, with stables and garages where the Loew's Kings theater now stood frozen and forlorn.

Later, the electric trolleys; by 1895, it was estimated that they were killing an average of one Brooklynite per week. "The country rang with horror at the holocaust of victims sacrificed to the reign of electricity in Brooklyn," said the *Standard-Union*. A minister named A. W. Mills urged the transport companies to honor the commandment "Thou shalt not kill." Soon, a new nickname for Brooklyn's baseball team, formerly the Superbas, was derived from "trolley dodgers," emblematic of a borough of dashing fools.

As the streets became impossibly chaotic – when it got so bad that an innkeeper at Yellowstone Park claimed to have fled Brooklyn after the trolleys killed off his entire family – the era of the elevated steam trains was also reaching its peak. Downtown Brooklyn became a many-headed Hydra of Els – York Street, Myrtle Avenue, Fulton Street, Fifth Avenue – all leading to Brooklyn Bridge. And beneath the tracks, in the dappled shadows of streets in perpetual eclipse, pedestrians were under constant threat of a rain of terror from the skies, as the *Daily Eagle* noted in 1891:

> When the evening shades are falling,
> Or the morning sun is high
> Comes a hot and blazing cinder
> Straight into your upcast eye.
>
> When your sweetheart shopward wanders,
> Mingling deep in fashion's stream,

Overhead the fireman ponders
And lets off a cloud of steam.

Then the jovial iron worker,
While your fears you fondly lull,
Swiftly drops a ton of metal
Down upon your hapless skull. . . .

But we must have rapid transit
In this town at any cost.
Take a walk – but if you chance it
Count yourself among the lost.

Rapid transit came rapidly to central Flatbush along the Brighton Beach line, the infamous Franklin Shuttle, and, in 1920, the Nostrand Avenue IRT, which terminated at the factories, garages, coal pockets, gas stations, and circus tents of the Junction. Outer Flatlands, a sparsely settled Siberia of truck farms, fishing boats, rendering plants, and erl drums, received no subway service then, and it had none now. It had been nearly three-quarters of a century since any new rapid-transit lines had been pushed through the Wooded Flat, and in that time the number of cars and vans and trucks and buses had multiplied like fruit flies, begetting the same kind of vehicular chaos that had picked off Brooklyn's poor trolley dodgers, a hundred years before.

Aware of the anarchy, I hugged the storefronts, watched for curb-jumpers, crossed carefully at the lights, and stayed out of the predatory vans and dollar cabs that weaved and feinted like the young Muhammad Ali. I walked when I could, took the city bus when it was raining, and came to look forward to travels underground on The Beast, where the motorman, most of the time, was licensed and sober. But I was lucky. The only thing worse than being a pedestrian on Flatbush Avenue was having to get behind the wheel and drive.

Driving for a living in Brooklyn was a task for the desperate. Gaye Gionlee was typical, a refugee from the violent hell of Liberia, who had landed at Kennedy Airport with some clothes in a duffel bag and the phone number of a distant cousin who lived above a restaurant on Flatbush

Avenue. Speaking almost no English, Gionlee found day work at a car wash and spent his nights taking a dollar cab up and down Church Avenue. Even at the bottom of the ladder, there was competition; some of the cabs were charging only ninety-nine cents.

Gaye Gionlee, three months in the New World, was shot dead in his borrowed Oldsmobile early one April morning on historic Church Avenue, one block east of the Lubavitcher school and the White Castle hamburgery and grand old Erasmus High. The robber, or robbers, got $250. In death, the refugee got his photograph in "New York's Picture Newspaper"; the headline in the *Daily News* called him "18th cabby slay of '93." This was a record pace. In 1992, the article said, forty-six drivers had been murdered in The Greatest City in the World. The *Post* took note that only eleven Americans were killed by enemy fire in Operation Desert Storm.

And the cousin of the Liberian, who lived above the restaurant on Flatbush Avenue, said, "I've been here two years and I haven't seen anything good about America. All I see is killing people and robbing."

∾

The city buses slept in a hangar in deepest Flatlands, across the street from a children's fairyland called Fairyland. The Flatbush Bus Depot on Fillmore Avenue, low-ceilinged and dimly lit, took up the entire block. If all its buses were brought out on Flatbush Avenue at the same time and parked end to end, it would be a normal rush hour.

Upstairs was a locker room with a billiard table, where the drivers hung out between runs. From the start, I had wanted to meet the men and women who wrestled the buses up and down the avenue, but my interest hadn't really peaked until I spent one morning at the downtown end of the line, on Tillary Street by Borough Hall. Drivers idled there for a few moments before beginning the long run back to Avenue U. One of them, a man named Will, told me, "It's not a job, it's an adventure."

Will also told me, "Go to the drivers' lounge and meet the guys." So I did. The drivers' lounge at Fillmore Avenue was reached by a long stairway at the west end of the depot. On a weekday afternoon, I climbed up nervously – I did everything nervously – in the expectation that, since this was city property, I'd get the immediate boot. Instead, I found a nest of

Ralph Kramdens: boisterous, blustery, Brooklynite. Even the dispatchers were cordial. "Go tawk ta dem," they bade me, when I asked for permission to conduct an interview or two.

I went into a small room that was an office of the Transit Workers Union. A fellow named Smitty was there; also, Swan, Von, two women, a man from Grenada; a dozen drivers carrying seat cushions, wads of blue and orange transfers, timesheets, route maps, schedules. Some of them had been working the Flatbush Avenue run for more than twenty years, north to south, south to north, as worlds collided and changed. They called themselves blueshirts, operators, "Ops." It could not have been an easy occupation. A bulletin board solicited charity for an Op named Willie Hooks, "critically shot in the face by a passenger aboard his bus." There was a memorial plaque to a driver named Harvey Shields: "Appointed August 20th, 1971 – Slain October 10th, 1981."

Clifford Swan was the dean of the blueshirts in the room. He was thirty-nine when he started, and that was twenty-two years ago. Before that, he had worked in a toothpaste factory. Swan was a gracious, steady man, who wore a ring that signified ten consecutive years of unblemished operating. He said, "The first few years, it got to me. It took a bit of doing to become comfortable. It wasn't the driving – that was the easy part. I wasn't quite used to people behaving the way they did. The little names they called you. The adults with kids, coming in the back door. That got to me somewhat. It was just plain stealing.

"Then I learned to look at it another way. I was transporting about three hundred people every day. I figured, if ten gave me a hard time, that wasn't bad, ten out of three hundred."

The economics of the big blue buses were such that a man or woman might work a fifteen-hour day, but only get paid for eleven hours, yet still be happy. It was called the bingo system: work the morning and evening crushes, take three unpaid hours off in between, and receive the maximum salary. It meant starting at 6:50 in the morning and finishing at seven o'clock at night, with a dead zone at midday, but by booking enough bingos, an Op might make fifty thousand dollars in a year. So they pored over schedules months in advance, wielding their seniority, claiming their bingo runs.

But the long hours and the fare evaders and the traffic took their toll. One of the drivers whispered to me, "We have a lot of problems. We have some alcoholics. Some drivers go home and beat up their wives. *Nobody's* sane here. You *can't* stay sane."

"If you don't like driving, and you don't like people," Smitty said, "it'll drive you up the wall."

"How do you stay sane?" I asked Von, who was a skinny man in rose-colored sunglasses, wearing a Casey Jones engineer's bandanna.

"I *don't* stay sane," he replied. "It's easier that way."

"We got ourselves a character," Smitty announced.

"Soon, I can *retire*," Von said, pointing to Smitty. "And he can *retire*. And the rest of them are the Children of the Damned."

Smitty said that once he had earned sixty-one thousand dollars in a year by working sixteen- and seventeen-hour days. Von had peaked at fifty-four thousand, including five hundred hours of overtime. On that kind of money, you could raise a family. Many had. The father of Al Roker, Jr., the television weatherman, had been a Flatbush Avenue Op.

Steering the B41 was hard enough, but it was the gypsy vans that were driving the drivers berserk. As soon as I mentioned them, the room filled with snarls and imprecations.

"Those drivers make a thousand dollars a day!" someone shouted.

"No," said the Grenadian, calmly. "On a good holiday, maybe eight hundred. Average day, four-fifty or five."

"They caught a guy one day," a man yelled. "He made twenty-two trips in one hour, five people a trip, a dollar a person!"

I tried to do the arithmetic in my head, but it was impossible because everybody was screaming at once.

"They put the bus lines out of business in Panama!"

"They cut you off like crazy!"

"The Transit Authority caused the problem by cutting service," said Von the Insane. "People were standing there and waiting hours for a bus. A van would stop at a light, and the people at the bus stop would say, 'I'll give you a dollar if you give me a lift.' That's what started it."

"You know what they call it?" asked the man from Grenada. " 'The dollar and the dream.' "

The man from Grenada was big, thoughtful and round-faced behind wire-rimmed glasses, and he spoke with a slight stutter. He had studied the gypsy vans and he understood their appeal. He said, "People from the islands are used to being picked up and let off where they want. It's fighting the Man, that's what it is. People feel they're helping a brother out."

Smitty said, "Fifteen years ago, if a van went down the street with its door open, nobody would get in."

"In Toronto," I said, "there are thousands of people from the islands, but there aren't any gypsy vans."

"In Toronto," said the Grenadian, who had lived in Ontario for a couple of years, "the police enforce the law."

"In New York," said someone else, "it's almost total breakdown."

"I wish I could say the breakdown's leveling off," sighed Clifford Swan. "But it's still falling."

Against the vans, the city had two weapons. One was a new "Limited" service on the B41, which skipped all but a few major stops between Avenue U and Borough Hall, eight miles up the line. The gypsies nipped up so many riders that the Limiteds were often half-empty, making for a swift, comfortable journey. But just as often, the Limited got stuck in an infarction of Flatbush Avenue traffic and sat fuming at Parkside or Church or Glenwood, while the vans went screaming through red lights in their lustful hunt for fares. And even the Limited was owned and operated by the Man.

The other weapon, of course, was the Transit Police. The penalty for conveying passengers for profit along an established bus route was three hundred dollars on the first conviction and a thousand thereafter. At Avenue U one day, I saw a TA squad car marked "Surface Enforcement" head off a van like an English sheepdog and pin it between two blue buses while the summonses were written out. But, as the *Carib News* noted, "the need to work and support themselves forces them to consider such fines and penalties trivial."

The gypsies were fighting back. Most vans were now equipped to notify the others of the proximity of Surface Enforcement by citizens-band radio, even if they weren't citizens. Or a driver would be selected as "bait" and offered sacrificially to tie up the police in paperwork for a couple of hours, while the rest of the fleet cruised like sharks. Then they all chipped in to pay the fine.

While the cops chased the vans and the vans fled the cops, the blueshirts of the Flatbush Bus Depot bid for their bingos and sat on their cushions and set out for Borough Hall. Then they came back to base at Fillmore and thence home to count the days until the last Last Stop.

Some weekends, Smitty would take a second job, driving a chartered inter-city bus for extra pay. I pictured him cruising down to the Atlantic City casinos at sixty-five miles an hour, carrying my mother and Doris and the seniors from Congregation B'nai Jacob with their pea-colored pants and their handbags full of quarters.

"It must be quite a change," I suggested, in the little office above the big garage.

"After the experience of the city streets," Smitty said, "when you get out on that highway – oh, man, it's *beautiful*."

4

On a blustery, gray Tuesday in April, Fairyland was the saddest place on earth. My mother and I were taking an outing along Flatbush Avenue when we came upon it; she had always loved walking in the wind. The small compound of kiddie rides across the street from the bus depot had been opened the year after I was born, as if specially commissioned to delight a royal prince. Now the park was the same, but the prince had grown and, at Fairyland today, there were no children.

The gates were open. There was no damage, no graffiti. Painted figures of storybook characters lined the outer fence. Tiny red fire trucks stood ready on a circle of track. Little boats bobbed helplessly in a spinach-colored pond. There were bottle-nosed airplanes, the "Whip," the carousel. All empty and still.

Two teenaged boys were lounging by the tame roller-coaster for tots. One of them, wearing a Yankees baseball cap turned backwards, called to me, "Ya wanna buy tickets?" I walked closer to him and took off my Orioles hat and pointed to my mother and said, "She used to bring me here when I was a child, forty years ago."

I felt ridiculous and expected that he'd "dis" me and laugh. Instead, the young man in the Yankees cap fairly burst with pride. His name was Ricky Marrero, age eighteen. He was the full-time ridemaster and amateur historian of the Flatlands Fairyland.

"Isn't it amazing," Ricky said, "these rides are the same as when we were kids."

When Ricky Marrero was driving the tiny red fire trucks, I was covering the Toronto Blue Jays and had been married for four whole years. When I steered them and clanged their bells, there was not yet a little Ricky. But he was right; the little Fairyland at Fillmore Avenue encompassed all our childhoods. I smiled, and together we marveled at the fine condition of the antique rides.

Inwardly, I was reeling again. The goldfish pond at Brooklyn College, the toy soldier on the ledge, and now this.

When I came to, Ricky was asking my mother, "What was the surface like back then?" The Bride of Flatbush Avenue cogitated for a moment and recollected running after her first-born in sandy sandals. Someone must have trucked in a load of Brighton Beach when Fairyland was new.

"I thought so!" the young archivist cried. "Sand!"

Now it was asphalt, and the adjacent snack bar had become a Burger King, but otherwise, time had not touched Fairyland, though the baby boy was forty and the beautiful, barelegged young wife in sandals would soon be seventy. My mother went off to admire the horses on the carousel. I thought: If we don't leave this place, maybe we will grow no older.

But it was too chilly to linger. The outwash plain of the last Ice Age offered no barrier to an onshore gale that felt like the harbinger of the next one. We were down near the end of inhabited Brooklyn, almost to the salt marshes, in a district of scattered stores and body shops, just north of the big Kings Plaza mall. The sea air was over us, and the roar of the big planes coming down to Kennedy with their Uruguayan superintendents and Afghan travel agents and doomed Liberians carrying duffel bags of clothes.

On the west side of Flatbush Avenue was a showroom, possibly a former automobile dealership, with bright red walls, abandoned and locked up. On the east was a garage that had sold and installed car alarms. It also was vacant, now that every licensed and unlicensed driver in the borough had bought an alarm and set it screaming. There were lumber yards down here, vending cedar fencing and tongue-and-groove doghouses to the homeowners on the handsome side streets. And more veterinary hospitals, funeral homes, bedding and carpet warehouses, fast-food joints, lighting stores, discount clothiers, newsstands, diners, electronics dealers, Irish saloons. The sky was big here, the stores low and roomy, the avenues broad. Manhattan seemed as remote as Mars.

Pushed by the wind, we walked all the way home, a long two miles, stopping only at the Flatlands library. My mother had a quotation tickling inside her head and wanted to set it right. It was a verse from *Hamlet*, Polonius's advice to Laertes, the long admonition that concluded with: "To thine own self be true."

Longhand, on a sheet torn from my notebook, she copied it out: "This above all . . ." It was her motto. Most of the time, these past few years, her own self was all she had.

∾

Flatlanders were just starting to get the hang of urban devastation. At one empty store, some novice vandals had spray-painted, "Fick you." Another building had once been a Bohack's supermarket. Now it was splattered with graffiti and the display windows were plugged up with cinder blocks. A big sign said "BI GO"; the "N" had fallen off or had been stolen. From the outside, the place looked like a landlocked shipwreck, but it was still operational. This was real bingo, not a bus driver's bonus run.

Just down the block was a stately brick mansion with a columned portico: the Torregrossa Funeral Home. A few days earlier, I had seen big crowds milling around the building, television cameras, police cars. Now Ralph, the security guard at the Bingo hall, explained why. It was, he said, "that Hayzhian businessman."

It was the funeral of Wilner Bourcicault, the prosperous owner of the furniture store on Church Avenue, who had been shot dead at the wheel of his Mercedes-Benz by the calm teenaged boy. Searching for a motive, the newspapers whispered of extortion rings within the Haitian business community. The alternative – sheer randomness – was too awful to consider. It was the new Brooklyn, violent and blurry: boys killed men; the Irish buried Fred Lucci; Italians laid out Haitians, Catholics all.

"Big crowds over there the other day," said Ralph at the bingo hall. "They broke the record at Torregrossa's."

He recalled a Brooklyn Dodger idol, dead of a heart attack, who had lain in state at the same chapel.

"That Hay-zhian," Ralph said, amazed. "He outdrew Gil Hodges."

∾

Further up Flatbush Avenue at Avenue N, a mural covered the western wall of the Ryder Station Post Office with blowups of commemorative postage stamps: Kennedy, Eisenhower, Martin Luther King, First Man on the Moon, Hope for the Disabled. And there were portraits, not taken from stamps, of the usual Brooklyn icons – Jackie, the Duke, Gil, Pee Wee, Campy, Carl, and Barbra (but not Woody, Mary Tyler, or Shemp).

I walked into Ryder Station and asked a clerk about the mural. I said, "Does the artist work here?" The artist didn't. The clerk said, "Her name and number's on the painting." I went out again and looked and looked. Around the corner on Avenue N was an even more elaborate scene – fireworks over the Brooklyn Bridge and the illuminated skyline of Gotham. In the foreground, there were characters dressed as American Revolutionaries. A couple of Dallas Cowboy cheerleader types carried a banner that identified the artist as a woman named Bonnie Siracusa from Great Neck, Long Island.

I called Bonnie Siracusa and she agreed to drive all the way to Flatlands to meet me at Ryder Station. A few days later, she did. The muralist was a petite, brown-haired, hazel-eyed woman, who had studied Fine Arts at Carnegie–Mellon and who now specialized in turning private rooms and doctors' offices into mock Roman villas and illusory Arabian palaces.

Bonnie Siracusa and a team of assistants had spent three months on the paintings at Ryder Station, doing their part, Bonnie said, "to build pride, prevent graffiti, and bring about positive feelings." (Back at Empire Boulevard, others had done the same with their portraits of Booker T. Washington and Roberto Clemente and Sitting Bull.) Bonnie was the Diego Rivera of the glacial outwash. The mural at Nobody Beats the Wiz, an electronics store on Avenue U, was hers as well. She had painted herself as Dorothy, with Toto wearing a Walkdog.

At Ryder Station, Bonnie stopped passers-by with interesting faces and cast them in her pyrotechnic East River scene. She said, "The people of

Brooklyn are so friendly, so open. You go in a laundromat and people tell you their life story. They take out pictures. They invite you to their homes. This is like the Ancient Rome of New York. All New York started with Brooklyn."

The muralist's Medici was the station manager, a middle-aged man named Thomas G. Roma. We went into his office. It was a shrine to the Dodgers.

"How did you feel when they moved to Los Angeles?" I asked Tommy Roma.

"Apotomy died," he said.

A part of him had perished.

Tommy Roma had lived the Dodgers. He had been a member of the television Knothole Gang. He still had his souvenir bat, ball, and glove. He had met Carl Furillo, the Italian outfielder, and Snider, the Duke of Flatbush.

I asked Tommy Roma if Ryder Station was a safe place for his letter carriers to work.

"It's nice around here," he replied. "It's an affuential area."

But the rest of Brooklyn was going to hell. It had started when O'Malley moved the Dodgers. This was a fact of history, as certain as Gettysburg or the Alamo.

"When I was growing up," the station manager said, "my mother and my sister could walk down the street *nude* and nobody would bother them. We were always protected by organized crime. But now, my mother, eighty-five years old, got mugged."

The hazel-eyed muralist and I clucked in condemnation.

"Eighty-five years old," Tommy Roma said. "It's almost *sacrilegious*."

∾

On a warmer, sunnier Saturday, a few weeks after my mother and I were there, I went back alone to the saddest place on earth. Fairyland had been transformed by the change of seasons. The rides were whirring, children were gamboling and pleading and giggling, balloons were exploding, music was everywhere. I sat down on a bench and watched the pageant, as my mother must have sat, forty years earlier, on the same bench, watching me.

Now the mothers were Dominican, Russian, Haitian, Chinese, but their children laughed in one language.

My bench was freshly blue. I picked at the paint with my fingernail and revealed green, and beneath that, yellow, and under the yellow there was red, the primary colors of my primary years. Around and around went the five little boats, as the baby Ahabs rang their bells and spun their wheels, helmsmen on a tide of fantasy.

Ricky Marrero, the teenaged ridemaster, recognized me and beamed. He said, "We got every ride startin' up every two minutes! Days like this, it gets *packed* here so's you can't *move*." Ricky had painted the fire engines and retouched the carousel horses, and he had placed crisp new American flags at the stern of each of the little bobbing boats. The season was new but the sound was eternal.

Lilliputian airplanes swooped and dived. Machine guns, mounted front and rear, attacked Serbs, Somalis, Saddam.

"Somebody wanted to buy the figures on the fence," Ricky Marrero said. He pointed to Snow White, Pinocchio, garish clowns, a couple of astronauts. "He wanted them for his daughter's bedroom."

Ricky turned serious.

"He didn't understand," he said. "We'll *never* sell those paintings. Without them, this wouldn't be *Fairyland*."

5

Kings Plaza was as still as a forest pond. It was just before ten o'clock in the morning. The outside doors opened before any of the stores did, so I walked in and sat on a wooden bench in front of a jewelry store called Malson's, which was protected by heavy metal gates, even though it was inside the enclosed mall. In Brooklyn, there was no such thing as being too secure.

No one questioned me as I reposed. This taking of pleasure in sitting quietly, watching the parade, was uncommon in a son of a frantic city. As a child, I had been as fidgety as any of my tribe, but later, I had learned the art of anesthetic indolence from baseball coaches in the lobbies of American League hotels. Practicing it now, a shiftless sphinx at Kings Plaza, I wrote in my spiral pad: "I'm the first misfit of the day."

But I wasn't to be the last. As the clerks in the shoe stores and knickknack boutiques unlocked doors and turned on lights, old men in soiled caps shuffled in to begin their long days of public solitariness. Then came an old lady in bedroom slippers and a mink hat, and two women made up like gypsies.

At 10:02, the first recorded anti-smoking announcement came over the loudspeakers, but the young saleswoman behind me – her booth sold baseball caps with emblems of marijuana leaves and the code word "BLUNT" – ignored it and lit up. Miffed, I rose from my station and walked along the corridor, following a couple of security guards in black state-trooper hats and clean white uniform shirts. Each guard carried a billy club and two pairs of handcuffs, ready for whatever the day might bring.

Kings Plaza had changed everything. Its inauguration twenty years earlier had brought right to the edge of the Flatlands tidewater an institution that was as alien to Brooklyn as palm trees. It was a full-sized suburban mall, with two department stores – Macy's and Alexander's – and scores of smaller shops, restaurants, and services on two levels. Huge parking lots and a marina on Mill Basin were included in the complex. There was an indoor carousel. Instead of a collection of prosperous knots spaced along an eight-mile cord, Flatbush Avenue had become an economic barbell, with the Fulton Street pedestrian zone at one end and Kings Plaza at the other. The big blue buses and their illicit competitors fed the extremities and bled the center.

At Kings Plaza in mid-morning, several boys with severe emotional problems were being led along by three men. One child, as thin as a cattail, was an Orthodox Jew; the fringes of his prayer shawl hung beneath his jacket, and he grabbed them and pressed them to his forehead as he loped unsteadily down the hall. Another boy, African, in a shocking-orange ski coat, was panting and hooting, as a tall, blond attendant put his arm around his shoulder and said, soothingly, "Let's go up to the toy store." They climbed a stairway and disappeared, but later, I could hear the child bellowing from the far end of the mall.

I found myself alone at a table at Nathan's Famous, ready for an early lunch. This was a branch of a Coney Island landmark, founded by a man named Nathan Handwerker, who purportedly had introduced the hot dog to Brooklyn in 1916. In recent years, Coney Island had turned from a salt-water fairyland into a shooting gallery with real bullets, but the original

Nathan's remained in business amid the wreckage of abandoned roller coasters and the burned-out bath houses of the Gilded Age.

The Nathan's counter in the Kings Plaza mall served the familiar delicacies without the jeopardy of a Coney Island junket. I ordered a frankfurter, a lemonade, and a knish – pronounced kuh-NISH – which was a pastry shell filled with peppery mashed potatoes, and I sat in one of Nathan's booths and ingested this classic Brooklyn meal, full of nostalgia, while children in wheelchairs were being fed crinkle-cut French fries by patient women in nurses' shoes.

Looking around, I spotted a woman in a nearby booth who had a snowstorm of papers scattered on the table in front of her. She was deep in concentration, writing something in a notebook, sipping coffee, and smoking discount-brand cigarettes.

I moved closer and studied her. She appeared to be about my age, with bushy, blackened hair and fingernails painted alternately red, white, red, white, red. She wore a green silk scarf, a black leather vest, a twisted headband, six rings, silver bracelets that jingled like the bells of an ice-cream truck, and a scarab-beetle pendant. Her lipstick had been applied with errant aim, and her teeth were in disrepair.

"Are you a writer?" I asked the woman.

"I can't talk now," she replied. "I'm working on stories."

But she did talk, for a moment. Her name was Linda Levine, an unemployed bookkeeper and unpublished poet. She told me that she sat here, at Nathan's in Kings Plaza, every Wednesday and Friday at noon, writing, collecting her thoughts. I could return another day, and she would speak.

She gave me her telephone number and immediately asked me not to call. She lived with her mother, an Austrian Jew. The woman had been through a lot. She was hostile to strangers.

"She might snap at you," Linda Levine said. "New York mothers can be difficult."

"Can they?" I smiled.

~

I was an hour early for the date. I sat at Nathan's and drank lemonade and waited. Next door was a pet shop; chirping and growling filled the air. The

store was having a special on rottweilers: a hundred dollars off, while supplies lasted. A sign invoked a seven-day warranty on parakeets and finches.
In case of avian catastrophe, it said, "the body must be accompanied by
receipt."

I felt a tug at my right arm, and it was a tiny boy in an oversized Philadelphia Phillies cap, smiling like an angel and offering me a folded plastic straw.

A bearded and disheveled man was wheeled into Nathan's Famous on a
hospital gurney by an attendant with a ring in her nose. The man was wearing a blue dress shirt and lying face down on the cart, his lower parts
wrapped tightly in a thick khaki blanket. It appeared that he had no legs. His
right elbow was in a splint, and he seemed to be only semiconscious.

But he was just resting. As soon as he was pushed within hailing distance
of the restaurant counter, he reached beneath the khaki blanket and pulled
out a discount coupon that entitled him to two franks for the price of one.

At noon, Linda Levine arrived, as I knew she would. She wore the same
leather vest, the same scarab. Her eyebrows were painted as raggedly as seis-
mographic charts. She unfolded her papers and said, "You can't make
money in poetry."

Her life story unwound. She had studied at Brooklyn College for a few
terms without graduating. She had worked at a library in Los Angeles for five
years. But the library – all libraries – frightened her. So much had already
been written. Why should she even try?

Fighting the current, she laid everything out like surgeon's tools. Pens,
erasers, paper, a pack of cigarettes in a decorated Punjabi leather case, a
Swingline Tot stapler. She numbered each line of each fresh page, as if poetry
were a baseball box score, and penciled in her batting order: "Idea / Précis /
Plot / Conflict / Development / Proof / Finis." She handed me a blue index
card that was labeled "The 10 Categorical Situations":

1. Man and the World
2. Man and Man
3. Man and Family
4. Man and Good
5. Man and Wrong
6. Man and the Established Norm
7. Man and a New-Situation previously inexperienced.

8. Man learns a lesson.
9. Man imparts a lesson.
10. Man and Mystery & Täbû.

She said that she had written fifty books of poetry.

"Who has seen them?" I asked.

"Nobody since college," she replied. She saw the way I was looking at her.

Linda Levine said, "Everybody has to be a little crazy to become famous after they're dead."

She retrieved a sheaf of lined pages. The first poem I came to was "The Motto."

> To bolt the door
> And break the rules;
> To drape the Mat outdoors
> And draw the curtain-rope
> The Motto is as ever: Beware!

"I like to write when I'm high," Linda Levine said.

∾

For our third encounter, I brought my mother, the retired bookkeeper. Linda Levine was at her usual table at Nathan's, immersed in concentration. We sat quietly for a while, showering in bottled music and the hellish screams of caged parrots from the pet shop next door.

"I come here to get away from my mother," Linda Levine said by way of explaining herself. There wasn't much else to say. We made some small talk, and then left her alone with her work.

I ordered some fried chicken, and my mother had a hot dog with sauerkraut. We sat down out of Linda Levine's earshot.

"It didn't take her *one minute* to complain about her mother," my mother said.

"How long do you think it took *me*?" I responded.

∾

Little Debbie came with me on my fourth visit. She sat on a bench outside Nathan's Famous while I went in to see Linda Levine. Now the poet was working on a prose composition, an analysis of Mary Shelley's *Frankenstein*. She copied out passages that excited her, longhand, and took page after page after page of notes. Just like me.

"Welcome to my office," she said, sweeping the ashes and the butts and the coffee-creamers aside.

She said she had been sitting in a park recently and someone had seen her scribbling and asked, "Can you write a poem about me?" But she refused.

"Why didn't you try it?" I probed. "Why not write about your *real* world? Why does it always have to be 'Man and the Established Norm'?"

"I guess I'm just a metaphysicist," Linda Levine said, smiling.

I collected my sister and we went over to Sbarro for pizza and a pasta salad. Not far away, slouching alone at a table for four, was a woman with dirt on her face and in her hair, a silk blouse with a tie knotted at the neck, and a man's sport coat much too long in the sleeves. She was raving, "You got to have permission from the bunny rabbit to go to Nathan's."

Two security guards in white shirts and black hats stood nearby. After a few minutes, they walked away. The woman called after them, "You're not supposed to work. This is the year two thousand!"

CHAPTER SEVEN

To the Ocean

1

Out on Mill Basin, just south of the Linda Levine Mall, there were a couple of harebrained jet-skiers, racing up and down the turgid slough as if it were Lake Buena Vista, and, lolling at anchor, dozens of handsome pleasure craft with names like *Rocky* and *Bonnie Babes*. Across the channel, I could see a row of million-dollar homes with satellite dishes and private piers, to which were tied magnificent yachts. Cormorants flew by, and there were a couple of ducks tilted arse-up as they nibbled. I was back in maritime Brooklyn, eight miles from Walt Whitman's East River flood tide, his "numberless masts of ships."

Down here, the scow that caught my eye was a big brown houseboat at the far end of the wooden dock. If my calculations were correct, and if the houseboat was inhabited, it had to be the last Flatbush Avenue residence before the ocean. Southward from here, my *Geographia* map showed an abandoned airport, the nature trails of the Gateway National Recreation Area, a Coast Guard station, a body of water unappealingly named Dead Horse Bay, and a toll bridge to the narrow spit of Rockaway, Queens, the final sliver that stood between Flatlands and Venezuela.

I walked down onto the boardwalk and tried to enter the dock that led to the houseboat, but it was fenced off, and the gate was locked. Attached to Kings Plaza was a marine-supply store. A clerk told me that, yes, someone did live in the brown houseboat and the someone – he pointed to another row of slips – was *that* man.

"Just ask for George," I was told. And the clerk started laughing.

George was helping a fellow sailor paint a speedboat with fresh stripes of red. He was a hefty, full-bellied man, with arms like construction cranes, no

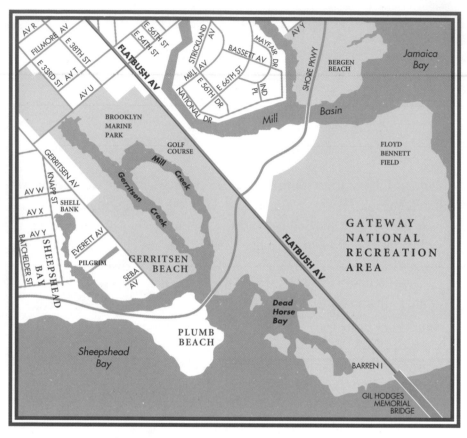

Chapter Seven: To the Ocean

shoes, a Fu Manchu mustache, and multiple tattoos – a spider on his left hand, a dragon on one calf, a cigar-smoking skull on the other. He gave his last name as Grivas and said that it was Cypriot Greek.

We looked from a distance at George's home. It was a flat-bottomed barge with rough brown siding, forty feet long and fifteen feet wide, that held two bedrooms, a bath, a living room, a kitchen, and a den on two levels. There was a television and a phone. George said that he paid three hundred dollars a month for dockage rights, and that he had started to heat the home with wood, because the price of propane had gone too high.

The houseboat had survived repeated Storms of the Century with minimal need of repair. It wasn't motorized; moving out of Marina del George, if it came to that, would require a tow. Still, it looked like a fine place to live, out on the water at the edge of old Nieuw Amersfoort, with Nathan's Famous just up the plank and Sovereign Motor Cars directly across the street, in case George Grivas ever felt the sudden urge to buy a new Mercedes.

"It's beautiful," he said. "Desolate. No neighbors."

George took advantage of his surroundings. Recently, he had deep-sixed an old microwave oven, adding to an artificial reef that attracted delicious blackfish.

"Is it beautiful even in the winter?" I asked.

"In the winter," George said, "I do skeet shootin' off the roof."

Yet even in winter he was not completely alone. A retired couple lived full-time on a fifty-foot Richardson yacht nearby. Another houseboat was used as an office by the family that owned the marine-supply store. And George Grivas had just won custody of his seven-year-old son.

The boy's name was Demosthenes. He was now calling out from the deck of the houseboat, waving and begging for lunch. Leaping and yelping behind him were two black dogs no smaller than George.

It was a long story, and not a pretty one, George said, as he unlocked the gate to his pier and we walked over to fix Demos and the puppies some chow. His own childhood had been rough: an abusive father; seven years in a group home on Staten Island; incomplete terms in the Army and the Air Force and the National Guard. Now his marriage had broken up and Demos was his. He wanted to get the boy out of Brooklyn, move to Virginia where they had relatives, give his son trees and space to grow.

He offered to sell the houseboat to me for forty thousand dollars. But as we got closer, I could see that it was not exactly Cleopatra's royal barge. George opened the door and one of the dogs – Rommel, a pit bull the color of ripe olives – burst out with such ferocity that I thought he was going to knock us all off the pier and into the muck of Mill Basin, at which point Bigfoot, his partner, would leap in and hold us under.

The place had not been decorated by a gentle hand. Mattresses were strewn on the floor, above and below, and there was weightlifting equipment scattered around, and clothing, and the child's toys. Rommel came back from relieving himself on the poop deck, smiling, and nuzzled me like a petting-zoo lamb.

The boat rocked just enough to make me queasy, so I made an excuse about having a luncheon date at the mall. George wanted to show me his aquarium tank before I left. He said, "I just run some intake in there from under the boat and a couple of months later – crabs, shrimp, and sponges!"

I shook his hand and thanked him.

"I do it for the kid," George said.

∾

The ground on which I was standing, when I disembarked from the Grivas family home, was sea-swamp, filled in as part of an overblown plan to turn useless outer Flatlands into the greatest saltwater harbor in the world. In 1910, the New York Times was full of it: "That vast tract, half land and half water, just back of Rockaway Beach, which is now given over exclusively to the oysterman and the holiday fisherman, is to be dredged into a harbor where a great fleet of future Mauretanias may comfortably dock."

A full-page rendering showed Manhattan as a remote, marginal hamlet – the immemorial Brooklyn fantasy – while Jamaica Bay, "this great expanse of water and marshland," teemed with docks, factories, wharves, warehouses, merchant and passenger steamers, and gigantic commercial piers. By 1950, the Times predicted, this new port would be the throbbing node of a city of ten million people, not a mere addendum to New York, but its new capital and the fount of its millennial wealth.

It was rather a lofty proposal for an area previously dedicated to pressing the oil out of rank little fishes and turning horses' corpses into glue. The upland hummocks and tidal flats of Jamaica Bay had long been used by the city's most loathsome industries. When the southerlies blew, the stench of the fertilizer factories and guano plants was said to drive Flatlanders to suicide.

The largest of the reedy clumps of land, now reshaped and widened and attached to the elongated spine of Flatbush Avenue, had been known for about three hundred years as Barren Island. It didn't take a Columbus to discover that the old name still fit. It was open, unwanted country. Past Avenue U, the avenue zoomed southward through sedge and poison ivy toward the tollbooths of the Rockaway Bridge. The great port city on Jamaica Bay had never been built. The *Mauretania*, "Grand Old Lady of the Atlantic," had been broken into scrap in 1935.

The Canarsees had called the island Equendito and harvested oysters and clams there. Later, the Dutch grazed a few horses on the salty hay and the English dredged a little sand. By 1800, there was a tavern on the island for the pleasure of fishermen, and this watery watering hole was still active thirty years later when one of the most exciting, least-known episodes in Brooklyn history occurred right in front of its doors.

In March of 1831, a ship named *Vineyard* left New Orleans with a cargo of molasses, sugar, and cotton and more than fifty thousand Mexican dollars in coin. The destination was Philadelphia, but, somewhere off Cape Hatteras, the crew got the idea of heaving the captain and his mate overboard and making off with the cash. So they did.

Fifteen miles off Long Island, the mutineers set fire to *Vineyard*, split the money, and divided into two small boats. One of the boats sank, taking four of the men and twenty-three thousand dollars with it. The other boat was swamping so badly from all the specie that all but five thousand dollars had to be jettisoned. Still, that wasn't a bad haul for 1831.

The four survivors – seamen Charles Gibbs and John Brownrigg, cabin boy Robert Dawes, and a black cook named Wansley – came ashore at Barren Island. The owners of the tavern, brothers named John and Will Johnson, thinking the men innocent victims of shipwreck, fed them and let them go. On the mainland, Brownrigg confessed, blaming everything on Gibbs and Wansley. The former was the ringleader, he said, and the latter had kayoed the captain with an iron pump. So Wansley and Gibbs were taken to the jail in Flatbush village and promptly hanged.

The treasure was never found. By 1860, the Johnson brothers, who may or may not have recovered it, had vanished or died, and the island was being turned over to larger and ever-more-noxious enterprises that reconfigured the shoreline beyond any mutineer's recognition. Two industries were paramount. One was the pressing of menhaden, a small and abundant fish, into an oil used in the manufacture of paints and leathers. The other was the skinning, sawing, grinding, and boiling of animal bones and flesh into fertilizer and mucilage. Hence, the name of the body of water on the western side of the island, Dead Horse Bay. In 1878, a visiting writer from *Harper's Monthly* described the facilities as "disgusting."

There was a time when as many as fifteen hundred people lived here, when Barren Island had its own stores and churches, a police detachment, and a public school. German and Irish immigrants worked in the fertilizer plants, blacks from Virginia in the fish-oil works. When the population of menhaden crashed in the 1890s, the Virginians departed. Later, the advent of the automobile and the subway reduced the supply of dead draft horses, and that nullified the glue factories. But Barren Island changed with the times. It became a garbage dump.

In 1936, the Parks Department served notice on the few remaining families to get off Barren Island. Airport and bridge development, complaints about the odious smell, and the extension of Flatbush Avenue had doomed the settlement. In 1938, the omnipotent Parks Commissioner, Robert Moses, wrote a memorandum entitled "The Future of Jamaica Bay." It said: "Here lies the opportunity for a place within the limits of the city where the strain of our city life can be relieved, where the nerves of tired workers may be soothed, where the old may rest and the young may play."

The grandiose plans of 1910 were as forgotten as the menhaden works and the Mexican treasure in the shifting dunes. Today, Barren Island was a houseboat, a highway, a National Park. I steered myself south. Somewhere under my feet, I dreamed, were bags of silver.

∾

A twentieth-century guano heap covered the next half-mile. Once I passed the Kings Plaza janitorial jurisdiction, my waterfront stroll across landfilled Barren Island quickly turned into a repulsive tiptoe through a great wall of broken china, plastic, mufflers, beer cans, tailpipes, newspapers, soda bottles, and Prestone antifreeze jugs. Rats scratched in the pile.

The trepidation I had felt during my solo traverse of Prospect Park had returned. I kept looking over my shoulder. No one in his right mind went walking down here. My presence was proof of that.

Suddenly, the sidewalk widened into an unpaved parking lot, and a rampway sloped down to the water. Tied up at the sea wall, its bow pointing toward South America, was a large, rusted, beaten-up fishing boat, its spars and winches bent from heavy use and its yardarm black from spouted exhaust. The name on her prow was "J M HUNTER."

It was odd to think of a borough of tenements, messiahs, and car alarms as the headquarters of a commercial deep-water fishery, but it was true. Sheepshead Bay, a couple of miles to the west, had been sending its sailors out for flatfish and blues since long before the mutineer John Brownrigg turned pigeon on a tavern stool. Several dozen boats still sailed from Sheepshead each morning – the *Parable*, the *Dorothy B*, the *Irish Mist* – and in the late afternoon, young men in bright yellow hip-waders would stand on the dock, crying, "Porgy here! Flounder here! Squid! Squid!"

The Mill Basin fleet was considerably less numerous; as far as I could tell, the *J M Hunter* was the only full-sized fishing vessel on the pier. Still, she was hardly an excursion boat to be chartered by day-trippers with rods from Sears-Roebuck and buckets of wriggly bait. She was an eighty-five-foot oceangoing "dragger," with room in her holds for a hundred thousand pounds of whiting, mackerel, and fluke. Out on the water for days or weeks, working the rich banks off Gloucester, Massachusetts, or scraping the Long Island shelf, the *J M Hunter* was the Flatbush flagship, the *Mauretania* of Mill Basin.

I walked down the ramp towards her. Some young men, and several older ones, were at work in a warehouse beside the dock. The older men, leather-skinned, sat in chairs on the wharf, chatting in Italian, while their fingers worried strands of knotted green net. Expertly, they untangled the mesh, and it lay across their laps like the billows of a nylon sea.

Other men were coming from a walk-in freezer with boxes of crushed ice, and were packing fish in the crystals. The lettering on the cartons said "Fresh Long Island Seafood." Technically, this was true, of course; the borough was the butt-end of Long Island. And it was likely that the rest of America would have thought "Fresh Brooklyn Seafood" some kind of a joke, just as it laughed in the sixties when Mayor John Lindsay dubbed New York "Fun City."

The Flatbush flagship was under the command of a Sicilian named Vincent Marinello, who somehow – I could not get this story straight no matter how many times he told it – had become known in the Fresh Brooklyn Seafood industry as "Mister Jimmy Hunter." Vincent, or Jimmy, had been born to sail. His mother descended from a long line of fishermen, and his father was in the Merchant Marine. As Jimmy, or Vincent, put it, "I never was work on land all my life."

Though he now spent most of his time here on the dock at the Hunter Fish Company, overseeing, he still put to sea often enough to be able to claim, as he did, "I spend fifty-five years on the ocean. You got to love the ocean. It's my life."

"Why do you love it?" I asked him. He was instantly engaging and eloquent, except when trying to explain how he got the name Jimmy Hunter.

"Free," the old salt said. "Away from everybody."

Vincent Jimmy Hunter Marinello – short, heavy-armed, weathered – walked over to his car and came back with a page from an Italian community newspaper. He wanted me to see a photograph of a banquet at which he had been awarded a plaque in recognition of his years on the bounding blue.

Deep water was one thing, but this basin of bilge off Flatbush Avenue seemed a less-than-ideal setting for the imbibing of the romance of the sea. Still, salt water was in Jimmy Hunter's veins. In 1951, he had been in the crew of an Italian ship that hit a rock and sank. He kept sailing. In 1953, he was third mate on a Norwegian tanker when he jumped ship in America. Ten years later, at the helm of his own Boston trawler, he lost electrical power and all his navigational gear in a ferocious storm, and he nearly ran her up the beach. He remembered the exact date: February 17, 1963. A week after my bar mitzvah.

"When you in charge on a ship," Jimmy said, "you can't show the crew you scared. When you bring her back in, you proud of yourself. You think, 'I did it!'"

He thought for a moment.

"Sometimes, you really *are* scared," he said. "But you come through everything and you go out again. You like a seagull. You just come through."

ॐ

Jimmy Hunter pulled no punches when I asked about the career path his son would take. He said, "My father don't want me to be seaman. I don't want Frankie to be seaman."

Frankie was seaman.

Frankie was a big, big bruiser in his early thirties, standing on the dock in the sunlight, wearing the baby-blue uniform of a softball team called the Brooklyn Bombers, with the sleeves cut loose to contain his Samson's arms. Self-confident, sharp, and outgoing, Frankie Marinello was a street-wise sandlot kid, like I was, and a stout sailor, like I wasn't. He lived in Bensonhurst, handled the business end of Hunter Fish, went to sea when the crew was shorthanded, and could not imagine doing anything else.

"You don't wake up in the morning and decide to be a commercial fisherman," Frankie said. "You're born into it. You don't retire, either. You do it till you die."

We were standing next to the *J M Hunter*, and Frankie was describing the twin-screw propeller and the dual generators and the nine-hundred-horsepower engine and the fish-finding gear in the wheelhouse that cost a hundred thousand dollars.

"When she was built," Frankie said, admiringly, "she was the queen of the fleet."

Now she was a fourteen-year-old dowager in need of paint and trim. Cosmetic surgery was routine; it was economics that battered a fishing boat as roughly as a nor'east gale. At sea, the *J M Hunter* followed the schools of whiting, squid, and porgy, but never had she found enough – even with all her electronics – to fill her fifty-ton hold. Sometimes the shadows on the sonar screen were thick with fish, and sometimes they were chimeras.

"Fish means money," Frankie said. "You've got to put meat over the dock. You go up as far as Boston if you have to. You hear that a storm is coming. You ignore the weather report. You just *go*."

We looked out in the channel and watched a pair of racing shells from

Kingsborough Community College glide by like insects from a Cronenberg film. They were women's fours, the young scullers straining, chant of the coxswain sharp and urgent. It was the a beautiful day to be on the water. Even this water.

"When you're in the middle of the ocean," said Frankie Marinello, "you're in a different world. You see whales, and tunafish jumping clear out of the water. But you're not by yourself out there. Sometimes, there's fifty or sixty boats, some of them bigger and better than ours."

"What do you see when you come back here?" I asked, turning around to face the other way.

"Flatbush Avenue," Frankie said. "Flatbush Avenue goes from million-dollar homes to crackheads."

I received permission to go on board and look around the queen. On her deck, two Polish crewmen – unlikely brothers, tall and short – were tinkering with the machinery, while a couple of Mexicans and a Russian labored with the cartons of iced fish. The Poles were even more mismatched than they appeared: Mutt had been a plumber in Madrid and spoke Spanish; Jeff was a coalminer in France.

"Poland, French, America, French, Poland, America, French," the smaller brother said, an autobiography in seven words.

In the wheelhouse, I was studying the Furuno Color Video Sounder (and a *Playboy* centerfold) when I met a man who introduced himself as "Bob, the deck boss." Bob was wearing a blue T-shirt with a picture of a fishing boat and the motto: "America's First Industry – An Endangered Species."

The message was no joke. In Newfoundland and Nova Scotia, draggers like the *J M Hunter* were being blamed for the decimation of the cod. It was alleged that their heavy nets were scraping the bottom raw and taking up far too many young fish that would never grow to spawn. Thousands were unemployed in Witless Bay and Ecum Secum and Seldom-Come-By. The equation, there and here and everywhere, was relentless: too many fishermen; too few fish.

I asked about life at sea, and the deck boss recited the Marinellos' strictly enforced trinity: "No women, no alcohol, no drugs." Living without those three for a few days, he could handle. It was ice that tortured him.

"That's the worst nightmare," Bob said. "In the wintertime, she can ice up, and the weight will knock you right over."

"What do you do if that happens?" I asked.

"I pray," the deck boss replied.

∞

Just south of the berth of the *J M Hunter* was a maritime restaurant called Nick's. It was an attractive, pine-paneled room, where you could order a clam roll and watch "Magnum P.I." while you lunched. There were more tables outside on a sun-kissed patio, making Nick's a sort of Mill Basin Malibu. A retail section offered an assortment of Fresh Brooklyn Seafood, and there was a tank of live lobsters with a hand-lettered sign behind it apologizing for high prices. Behind the counter, mounted on the wall, was a plastic hammerhead shark.

I walked in and, employing my two decades of finely honed reportorial skills, asked for Nick.

"Nick's not here," the counter clerk said.

I sat down at a table to ponder my next move.

Back at the counter, I asked if anyone else could tell me about the establishment and how it came to be here on the bonny banks of Barren Island.

"I can," a man said. He introduced himself. Cleverly, I had gained an interview with Frank Rosa, son of Nick.

Frank Rosa was thirty-one, handsome and green-eyed. Like Frankie Marinello, he had grown up on these waters, the son of an Italian immigrant fisherman. It was the same story – the Old Man and the Seafood. Frank and Frankie, Nick and Jimmy, were partners, competitors, neighbors, and comrades in a disappearing trade. The bonds in this miniature Cannery Row were as tight as a sailor's knots.

"This town isn't full of fishermen," Frank Rosa said. "It's not like Rhode Island, where everyone's a fisherman. Here, you tell somebody what you are and they say, 'You're a *what?*'

"We know what we are," Frank Rosa went on. "We're commercial fishermen. There's no glory in it; there's nothing but a lot of work. You work *very* hard to make an average living. You start really young and you don't need a great education. But it's the *uniqueness.* You're different from everybody else."

("My friends think I'm crazy," Frankie Marinello had said. And perhaps he was. A couple of weeks earlier, the crew of a small trawler on Long Island Sound found themselves being shot at from a passing speedboat in what appeared to be a dispute over lobster territory. One man dived into the sound and escaped, but another was plugged four times. If the trend continued, the *J M Hunter* might have to be fitted with cannon.)

Frank Rosa's mother had passed away, and his father had suffered two heart attacks. Frank's brother couldn't go on the water; he got seasick. (So he built the restaurant.) In the mid-eighties, the Rosas almost gave up. The cost of the gear, the electronics, and the labor was getting excessive. But the emotional toll of walking away would have been greater. So they sent their boat – it was smaller than the *J M Hunter* – out at four o'clock in the morning with whomever they could employ for whatever they could catch and clean and sell. The rest came in by truck.

It was hard to see the Flatbush fishery lasting much longer. The commercial piers were being squeezed, with Kings Plaza and its marina to the north and a huge new Toys "R" Us store to the south. It was getting more and more difficult to find experienced hands; not many of Brooklyn's immigrants and refugees had been deep-water fishermen back home.

Frank Rosa was worried that the history of his people and the Marinellos and all their struggles might be lost. He said, "I've axed Jimmy so many times to write it down." But nothing had been written down. Some day, Frank promised, he was going to take a video camera to sea. Then the tape would prove that once there was a time when waves washed foam around his boots, and the gulls shrieked overhead.

2

Across Flatbush Avenue from the marina and the mice and the Marinellos was a full-sized, eighteen-hole golf course. Out here on the broad, green links of Marine Park, with the Russian olive trees displaying their pungent yellow blossoms, and with terns and herons patrolling the still waters of Gerritsen Creek beyond a stand of tall sedge, you could easily forget that you were in Brooklyn. That, of course, was the whole idea.

A decorous and seemly game, golf seemed as alien to the borough as fox hunting, polo, or proper grammar, but it had a long history here. When we were teenagers, Brucie and I used to frequent another Flatlands course, brandishing an ancient set of wooden-shafted mashies and niblicks that we had found in a closet in a back room of Abel Brothers. I was a short-but-accurate driver and a skillful putter, but my golfing career, and my friend's, ended the day that Brucie wound up and launched a tee shot over the boundary fence and into the back of a moving dump truck. Having vested our bus fare in a deposit on the ball, we were bankrupted. It was a very long walk home.

At Marine Park, on a bright and breezy morning, I entered the clubhouse, passed the equipment shop and the Linkside Cafe, with its framed photograph of the Three Stooges in plus fours, and exited onto the course without being apprehended. I made my way toward what turned out to be the eighth tee, which lay just above the shallow creek and its abundant avian fauna. When I arrived, four gentlemen were disembarking from motorized carts, having completed their journey from the seventh green, which must have been at least ten yards away.

"Good morning," I offered, giving nothing away.

"Are you fishing down there?" asked one of the men. (He had sensed instantly that, since I didn't have clubs, cleats, or a cart, I probably wasn't the new course professional.)

"No," I replied. "I'm your gallery."

The duffer in the cart was Jack O'Leary, a retired pressman from the *New York Times*, sporting white shorts, a white golf shirt, and a handicap of seven strokes, which was not bad for a seventy-five-year-old amateur.

Golf was the great restorative. Harry MacDonald, another member of the foursome, had owned a small computer-service business that perished in the last recession. He had turned to bartending in Bay Ridge, Brooklyn. Harry MacDonald said, "I've seen too many senior citizens who drink all day and then go home to watch "The Price Is Right." I won't do that. I've been active all my life."

Bob Nevin had been a colonel in the Army Reserves. (He wasn't the former National Hockey League player of the same name.) Trying to impress the golfers, as I had dazzled the Correcting Your Accent class at Brooklyn College, I was reciting my litany of Flatbush Avenue lore – the Malbone Wreck, the Prison Ship Martyrs, the circus at the Junction. But when I came to the terrible Sterling Place plane crash of 1960, Bob Nevin cut me short.

"That plane hit where I lived," he said evenly. Of course. It was his relatives – the barefoot Mrs. Nevin and her two small children – who had come through unhurt when the DC-8 from Chicago sheared off the roof of their house. I didn't have to tell the rest of the story. It was a small borough.

The foursome moved off in their carts again, and I sat crosslegged under a tree and waited for them to swing back around to where I was resting. It was cool in the shade, and when the wind gusted I couldn't hear the traffic from Flatbush Avenue, which was only a few yards away.

I was daydreaming, watching a ladybug roam around my shoetop, when they returned from the outer holes. They were moving toward the eighteenth, the final challenge, 530 yards, the longest of all. I walked along.

After a nice drive to the fairway, Bob Nevin sliced his iron shot towards the bulrushes at the edge of Gerritsen Creek. The ball rolled into the tall grass and flushed a black-crowned night heron, which let out a raucous *kwawk* and flew right over our heads. The other men were hunting for Bob Nevin's ball, but I just stood and watched the beautiful bird flap and dip and disappear.

"What was that?" Jack O'Leary asked me, when they had given up the search.

"Heron," I replied. I took it as an omen. In Brooklyn, not even the night herons went about at night.

~

But my mother did, Fridays and Sundays.

On Fridays, it was to a dance in an old streetcar barn at Sheepshead Bay called Trolley's. Two nights later, at the Marine Park Jewish Center a few blocks north of the golf course, it was to Parents Without Partners. The dances kept my mother going, and she liked to think that the reverse was true as well.

Week after week, she would return by Russian taxi at 1:40 in the morning and, after the unlatching and relatching of the two deadbolts had roused me from my hard-earned slumber, she would come into the bedroom and inform me that "everybody" at the dance had been asking to meet her son, the Morley Safer of Canada. I didn't doubt this – to not know me was to love me – but I resisted firmly, until the night she burst in and said, "Guess what! Someone expired!"

"Like, dropped dead?" I asked, fully awake.

"I didn't look," she replied. "I *don't* look in those situations. All I know is they were administering to him on the dance floor. The music stopped. And people were saying, 'Move back! Give him air!'"

She paused to let this sink in.

"And everybody was asking to meet you," she said.

I relented, and we made a date for Sunday. When the evening arrived, I didn't even have a sports coat to put on, just another denim shirt. My mother, on the other hand, put on brown culottes, a floral-print blouse in rose, black, and olive, mock-lizard shoes, a brown jacket, gold hoop earrings, a beaded faux-bronze choker, and a metallic woman's-head pendant I had bought for her in Johannesburg, South Africa. She had her sunglasses on, an elegant pair, studded with mother-of-pearl.

We took the B41 down to old Dutch Flatlands and dined at the New China Inn. The Marine Theater was gone, the Brook Theater was gone, but the deep, dark Cantonese restaurant remained exactly as it had been thirty years before. The New China Inn was not one of those new take-out counters operated by New York's new Chinese. Even the menu recognized the Inn's status as a Flatbush Avenue landmark: the chop suey–chow mein section was labeled, unabashedly, "The Classics."

I ordered a combination plate with "subgum" chicken chow mein, and my mother went for the regular chow mein, fried rice, and egg roll. Nico, the Sinophile, would have fainted – these dishes were about as Chinese as Buddy Hackett – but we didn't care.

My mother looked out the window to the spot where another Chinese restaurant, called Honam's, had stood when she was a girl in second-hand clothes.

"When we came from Bay Ridge to eat at Honam's on Flatbush Avenue," she said, "I thought I'd gone to heaven."

Nirvana for her now was dipping noodles in plum sauce with her first-born across the booth. When I wasn't looking, she reached into her purse and pulled out a black-and-white photograph no larger than a postage stamp that showed me in a corduroy sailor suit at the goldfish pond at Brooklyn College, age one and a half. I looked around, trying to avoid her moony gaze, and saw a big room half-filled with white and Caribbean families, and decorated with silk flowers and wallpaper chrysanthemums.

The food arrived.

"Different cook tonight," my companion announced, after the very first mouthful.

"Oniony," she critiqued.

But to me it was an exact replication of 1963; only Aunt Cel and Uncle Dave were absent. Speakers above our heads emitted Petula Clark and Mantovani. When we finished eating, my mother went off to sit by the front window and smoke, and I went to talk to a woman at the cash register whose name was Nancy Lum, which was another way the southern Chinese pronounced the word for "forest." The Lums had been operating the New China Inn for half a century, which sounded like an awfully long time, until I realized that I had been eating here, in and out of sailor suits, for more than 80 per cent of it.

"Business is not like it used to be," Nancy Lum said. She pointed north on Flatbush Avenue, toward my mother's apartment. "Further up, bad. Around here, not so bad." That seemed to summarize everything.

"How long will your family stay here?" I asked her.

"We stay as long as we make it," she replied.

I paid the bill and collected my date. It had been a wonderful dinner. The fortune in my cookie said: "You have an ambitious nature and may make a name for yourself."

∽

"Look! There's B——!" my mother cried at the Marine Park Jewish Center. "He's the one who said he wanted to go to bed with me. I said I'd never be able to keep up to him."

"Which one is he?" I asked, squinting into the crowd.

"There," my mother said. "The one with the cane."

We were sitting at a table with our backs to the wall, which pretty well described the Parents Without Partners. My mother was swizzling her screwdriver, and I was counting the bubbles in my beer. What an evening this promised to be.

"You're gonna see a different mother tonight," my date predicted.

She waved for Fay. This was a woman in black spandex on the bottom and orange fishnet on the top, spike heels, blonde-streaked hair like Dyan Cannon.

"How was Trolley's on Friday?" Fay asked my mother.

"Someone expired," my mother replied.

Fay sat down beside me and waited for my questions like a cabinet minister in a formal interview.

"I used to walk home from Sheepshead Bay at two o'clock in the morning with no shoes on," Fay said, describing anterior Flatlands. But that was a long time ago. Now her brother-in-law had been knifed, and there had been a killing at a garage around the corner.

"Why don't you move to Florida?" I asked.

"I tried that, for a year," Fay replied. "I got tired of people saying I had a New York attitude."

Fay got up and Jack sat down; it was like a chair at Mr. Imperial the barber. Jack was a taxi driver in Manhattan, which meant a legal, yellow cab. Jack came here, week after week, but he always departed as alone as he arrived.

"I bet if my mother came here, *she'd* walk out with a man," he said.

"What would your father say?" my mother interposed. She always knew how to cheer him up.

"Why do you come here?" I asked the taxi driver.

"That's the best question you asked in a year and a half," he replied softly. "To meet somebody, I guess."

He fixed me in his eyes.

"I think my situation might be impossible," Jack said, as he got up.

I thought: what if I was in this lifeboat with them, pressed against the sea at the bottom of Brooklyn, with no one to caress me and cut my hair for free?

Yet there were possibilities. Barely moving, locked eye to eye, a couple danced to Vicki Carr's "Let It Please Be Him." She was in a red top and blue jogging pants, chunky, a Peggy Cass. He was taller, bald, with thick glasses, a Richard Deacon.

"They met here," my mother reported. (She was the Walter Winchell of the PWP.) "We don't know how it happened, but it did."

I met George. George claimed to have been a mercenary in Korea, Vietnam, and three African civil wars he was not at liberty to identify. And Al.

Al said he grew up running errands for Jewish gangsters in the Brooklyn neighborhood of Brownsville. (So did Phil Silvers.) He said he had known a man who had committed toity-eight moiduhs.

Next came Harry. In a well-tailored olive-green suit, Harry was the best-dressed man at Parents Without Partners. But he wasn't long for Flatlands. His plan, he told me, was to build an underground house somewhere in the mountains of Virginia or North Carolina, because everywhere else in the country was going to be unlivable due to sonic booms.

"Sonic booms," he asserted. "As we go faster and faster, there's going to be more and more."

"Hmm," I agreed.

Harry had found companionship as well, at least temporarily. An amateur singer, he had taken up with a woman who claimed to be an operatic professional from Austria. Somewhat dubious – this was Brooklyn, after all – he asked her to warble a few semiquavers.

She did.

"I thought she'd break every glass in the house," he said. Then it was his turn. "I did some singing," Harry said. "She told me twenty ways I stink." So he was back at Parents Without Partners, just a few yards from the softball fields of Marine Park that ran down to Gerritsen Creek.

After about an hour, I told my mother that I'd had enough and asked her to find me a ride back to East 31st Street. She scouted around and located a volunteer.

"It's a shame," she said as I was leaving. "The fellow who *really* wanted to meet you isn't here."

3

Gerritsen Creek, named for the Dutchman who built the first tide-powered grist mill in North America on its shore in 1645, flowed south from the Jewish Center, drained the Marine Park golf course, and emptied into a repugnant quagmire of garbage, scrap wood, and flotsam. This fetid marsh, where the inlet met a sandy strip of coastline called Plum (or Plumb) Beach, was not an easily accessible spot, yet about fifty of us had made our way down here on a cool, threatening afternoon, and now we were waiting for the tide to come in.

The pestilential fens in which we were sloshing held every conceivable artifact that humanity could manufacture – pink insulation, auto parts, smashed-up boats. But none of us had made his way to the bottom of the borough just to view an assortment of trash; we could see that on our own home streets, or in the lobby of the Brooklyn Museum. Quite the opposite – we had come for nature study. We had come to see the mating of the horseshoe crabs.

It was billed as one of the most wondrous spectacles of the maritime world. Each May and June, at new and full moon, responding to some innate compulsion, these lumbering, military, nine-eyed, sword-tailed relics came ashore at high tide, up and down the edge of Atlantic America, to breed and lay their eggs. Then, as they had for two hundred million years, the horseshoe crabs returned to the sea and disappeared.

In their wake would come birds by the thousands to feast on the clusters of eggs. The symbiosis was critical to the birds' survival, yet the crabs were older than birds; older than mammals; older than dinosaurs. In fact, they were not crabs at all, but a separate order, incomprehensibly ancient yet physically unchanged, a beacon illuminating zoological prehistory, ugly, frightening, harmless, fascinating, and little understood.

The walking tour of Plum Beach was organized by the National Park Service, which now had responsibility for this fraction of Brooklyn's sixty-five miles of coastline. Gateway National Recreation Area, which was bisected by Flatbush Avenue as it neared its final rendezvous with the bridge to Queens, was possibly the most bizarre outpost of a vast park system that stretched from Alaska to the Everglades. A collection of scattered sites in New York and New Jersey, Gateway included old military bases and ammunition dumps, popular beaches and bays, wilderness and wildlife, campgrounds, jazz concerts, vegetable gardens, ethnic fairs, grand opera, volleyball tournaments, and the ghost runways of New York's first airport, where, as if to demonstrate the incongruity of the whole operation, a student driver had recently run over and killed a peregrine falcon with an ambulance.

The assembly point for the nature walk was a vandalized concession stand in a rest area on the south side of the Belt Parkway. Carless, I took the Nostrand Avenue bus to the end of the line and walked about a mile in the mist. At the parking lot, rangers gathered us together, gave out leaflets describing the natural history of *Limulus polyphemus*, and prepared to march us down toward the dump in which we would await the rising of the tide. We made a strange sight, with our Gore-Tex jackets and our field guides, complacently standing right on the shoulder of the highway, which was inch-worming ahead with rush-hour traffic, the drivers cursing and blasting their horns.

We were students and teachers, mostly, and we hadn't gone far into the salt marsh before two boys from Stuyvesant High School were given a seine net and hip-waders and instructed to go out into the middle of the creek and stretch the mesh between them. This they did – the water was swirling and burbling and painfully cold – and when they came back to shore we saw that they had collected dozens of tiny shrimp, some hermit and green crabs, and a few snails.

The haul was placed in buckets, and we crowded close and stared, just as another group of urbanites had been mesmerized when Ranger Joe Spano ripped open the bark of a wild black cherry tree in Prospect Park and exposed a nest of termites. The awakening of the city to the presence of nature was always a wonder in itself.

"Does anyone have any questions?" asked one of the guides, a retired high-school biology teacher named Mickey Maxwell Cohen, as we walked along.

"Yes," I said, looking around at the heaps of garbage. "Will anybody ever come down here and clean this place up?"

The reply was squelched by a shout from the boys in the water. They had spotted the first of the horseshoe crabs, a dark, unearthly disk, much larger than I had imagined, a brown-black Darth Vader helmet nearly two feet long, floating a few yards off the beach. Everyone rushed to the shoreline to see it.

"It won't hurt you," the boys were promised, and so the beast was lifted from the water and Mickey Cohen held it up. Its top was as smooth as a Frisbee, but underneath – ventrally, to the biologists – it kicked the air with its eight "walking legs" and flexed its movable spine. The eyes, all nine of them, were little more than tiny bumps in the shell. There may have been additional, even-more-primitive light-receptors in the median ridge that science had not yet discovered.

The shell was hinged, and attached to the rearward portion was a long, thin, sharp tail, called the telson, that the Canarsees had utilized as the tips of their fishing spears. Three centuries later, researchers were extracting blood from horseshoe crabs and using it in tests to detect potentially fatal impurities in medicines.

"It's a small one," said Mickey Cohen on the Brooklyn shore. "A male."

In the water now, as the tidal rip came rushing into the mouth of Gerritsen Creek with such force that the high-school boys could no longer keep their balance against it, were more and more of the animals. They were all males, cruising the strip, awaiting the arrival of the larger females, whom they would follow up onto the sand. Sometimes, our leaflet noted, several males would surround a single egg-laying female, bumping and shoving, until one of the Fabios would succeed in attaching himself to the female with his hooked pedipalps. After she had deposited four thousand of her caviar in a small hole, he would fertilize them. Then all would return to the ebbing waters.

A hundred miles to the south, on the shores of Delaware Bay, the scene would be enacted on the scale of a De Mille extravaganza: miles of beach, paved as if by cobblestone with two million mating, digging crabs; and nearby, gulls and turnstones and sandpipers and dowitchers in their respective multitudes, waiting to scratch open the shallow caches and feast on the eggs within. Perhaps one egg in 130,000 would survive this onslaught and grow to adulthood, yet this equation had allowed both bird and crab to coexist and flourish for a thousand thousand centuries.

At Plum Beach, it would be a lesser cavalcade, but no less miraculous for the small numbers. I wandered away from the group and stood on the beach for a few moments and watched the dark shapes straining toward shore. There were five crabs, ten, then twenty.

It was a powerful message. Even in this battered place, the mandate had been carried out, the ageless appointment accepted. Breathless, I marched back to my bus stop through the wet, heavy sand.

∾

In the morning, Mickey Maxwell Cohen met me at the office at Gateway, where he coordinated natural-history programs for the pupils of the scoured city. He was an energetic, passionate man, who had attended, and taught at, Erasmus Hall High School in the years when, he said, "it was like getting a private-school education at a city school." Those days were done, but at Plum Beach and Gerritsen Creek, Cohen hoped to awaken an awareness of the natural world in children whose own worlds were often dreadful and scarred. Respect for all living creatures, he believed, could begin with tiny crabs in a seine net.

We set out, just the two of us, along a trail to Dead Horse Bay that began near the tollbooths at the base of Flatbush Avenue, ten and a half miles from the Rice–Mohawk reconstruction yard under the Manhattan Bridge. The trailhead wasn't easy to find – it was partially blocked by a stand of poison ivy that had grown as big as a subway car – but Mickey had laid out the route himself, so there was little danger of us getting lost in the reeds and having to signal to incoming aircraft by flashing s-o-s with our belt buckles.

We were walking on the landfill that had reshaped and anchored Barren Island in the only National Park I knew of that was built largely on urban detritus. Gingerly edging past the toxic hedge, we came to a spot where three paths diverged in a waving forest of *Phragmites*. This tall, useless, rampant reedgrass was the plant that most quickly colonized such denuded areas, growing so densely that smaller grasses and wildflowers had no chance to take hold. Only where the park trails had been hacked out could sunlight reach the fringes, and it was at these margins that Mickey pointed out saplings of huckleberry ("tastes like heaven") and bayberry and the tender shoots of the edible pokeweed, once a Canarsee Indian staple. There was even a young ailanthus, three feet high, the southernmost Tree that Grows in Brooklyn.

We followed the left tine of the trident and, about fifty yards in, Cohen showed me a large stone disk lying on its side in the sand. It was a millstone, a remnant of the outer Flatlands settlements in the age of the menhaden works and the mutiny on the *Vineyard*. Cohen knelt beside it, took my hand, and guided my fingers like a Braille reader along the worried smoothnesses of the stone. An eighteenth-century artifact, it was too new to be Hugh Gerritsen's, too old to be part of the landfill. But it would have taken two such stones to grind grain into flour. A search for the mate was being conducted by twenty-first-century sonar. It could not be far away.

Cohen stood up and pointed out some nests of an insect I knew well – tent caterpillars, the pests that we used to blow up with firecrackers on East 31st Street. Then, with his fingernail, he sliced open a bright red gall on the branch of a wild black cherry. Inside, to my amazement, was the egg mass of a delicate wasp, a Barbasol of pure white foam.

"When it matures, the wasp will live only one day," the teacher said to his only pupil. "It will mate, and then it will die."

The trail rose slightly, crested a dizzying fifteen feet above sea level, and then descended again, through more of the head-high *Phragmites*, until we reached the beach. On the last surviving splintered pylons of the dock of the old Rockaway ferry, the boat that my mother's friends Bill and George ("erl drums") had taken as kids before it was discontinued in 1937, Mickey Cohen knelt down and gathered up fronds of an aquatic plant called rockweed. He showed me its organs of reproduction, which were bulging bubbles of goo.

Rockaway, so beautifully named, was directly across the channel, a half-mile away. It was a beach resort and summer colony, where, when I was ten, my mother and her sisters had taken a small bungalow. With my eyes closed now, I could see screen doors, sand castles, a boardwalk, a penny arcade; I could hear "Sink the Bismarck" and "Save the Last Dance for Me." I had not been to Rockaway for so long that I did not know if a return visit would bring me to an unchanged idyll or a seething slum. But this wasn't the time. I looked out across the water and recalled how little I had known of my own Brooklyn, back at the East River shore, a few weeks ago.

Suddenly, I heard voices, turned, and saw that we were surrounded. Twenty-five children from Public School 194 were combing the rocks and sand, bending over, gathering objects, dashing back to their teachers to exhibit them and learn their worth. One little boy came running to Mickey Cohen and held up a small, dark, shiny cylinder that I took to be driftwood, hollowed by the tides. But I was wrong. It was a fragment of bone from a horse, with the marrow long removed.

Of course: Dead Horse Bay. More of the children came running up now, with portions of legs and ribs and toe splints that, a century before, had been chopped up at factories called Barren Island Bone and the New York Sanitary Utilization Company. Cut up, boiled, and cast into the trash heaps to be churned and uncovered and washed away by a century of storms and waves, the bones were returning to Barren Island. We could read the trails of the teeth of the saws.

The class from P.S. 194 headed back toward their bus, leaving behind their treasures for the next beachcombers – this was a National Park, after all – and Mickey Cohen and I kept walking. At the point where Dead Horse Bay merged with the main inlet, he showed me boulders of glittery Manhattan mica and identified them as the products of the excavation of the earliest subway tunnels. The recent Storms of the Century had changed everything here, he said. Entire layers of landfill had been blown away, peeling back a window to the past.

He knelt at the base of a bank of sand, four feet high, that had been exposed by the gales. Reaching and digging and scratching like a badger, he tugged and yanked and finally pulled a knotted nest of ladies' nylon stockings out of the escarpment. Rising with them in his hand, he broadcast, "Here is nineteen-fifty-three!"

He was right. The beach was strewn with bottles from the Eisenhower years. We knew them immediately by their shapes: Log Cabin syrup, ribbed like a beehive; Vicks VapoRub, blue and squat. Further along, the shoreline *was* bottles – Clorox, Rose-X, Bromo Seltzer, Pepto Bismol, Philips' Milk of Magnesia. Kinsey's – "The Unhurried Whiskey." Noxzema. Seagram's. Mum.

Many were shattered, yet thousands were unbroken, sea-washed and whole, a brown and green and crystal pavement of memories. But there were no Coca-Cola or Pepsi bottles. Those had carried a two-cent deposit. And no milk bottles. The milkman took those away.

"This is what survives," Mickey Cohen said, as awestruck as if he had come upon a nest of Stegosaurus. "It's the pre-plastic era. Everything came in glass."

He bent down and picked up a small, dark slab.

"Baby-shoe sole," the teacher said.

"It might have been mine," I sighed.

We moved north into an incipient peat bog, where the roots of the *Phragmites* were beginning to turn to soil, an entire cycle of colonization, death, and decomposition played out on a scale of years, not millennia. We were turning off the beach to return to the trailhead, when I spotted something in the sand.

It was a silvery package that looked from a distance like a football. But, we soon saw, it wasn't. It was a chicken, headless but still white-feathered, its body wrapped carefully in strips of thick gray tape and placed here, where the waters met.

We stepped back, but we couldn't take our eyes off the bundle.

"A ritual of some sort?" Mickey Cohen suggested, after we had been silent for a while.

"Voodoo," I said, as if I knew. In the voices of the swooping gulls, I thought I heard Sò Ann, laughing.

4

Every Saturday afternoon, if the weather was fine, a delivery truck would rumble down Flatbush Avenue and turn onto a side road just short of the tollbooths of the Rockaway bridge. After passing an unmanned military gatehouse, the truck would turn again and pull up in front of a series of large, disused buildings.

Men would jump from the cab of the truck and others, who had arrived separately in their own cars, would hurry over to join them. From the cargo bed, grunting and shouting, they would remove a huge, heavy coil of artificial grass about thirty yards long, and they would unroll this on a giant patch of weathered, blistered concrete. Then they would get out their flat-sided bats and their bamboo leg-pads and the Indo-Pakistani Cricket League would be ready for another day of action at the National Park.

Gateway National Recreation Area was now consecrated to crab-mating and athletic recreation, but its location was a haunting relic of an age of courage and romance. A hundred years after the inscrutable sands of Barren Island entombed a cache of bloodstained Mexican silver, this pariah-land of fish oil and horse's bones had been remade into one of America's first major airports. Finally, the featureless topography of Flatlands had become an asset; there wasn't a mountain for miles. The complex was christened Floyd Bennett Field, after a hero flier, and it became a departure point for Europe, for California, for fame, for war, for death in a mangled wreck.

Sixty years later, everything was still intact: the hangars, the runways, the Art Deco terminal building, the control tower, the offices and oil tanks and light-beacons and waiting rooms. This had been Amelia Earhart's airport, Howard Hughes's, one-eyed Wiley Post's. It had sent Whirlwinds to the sky,

Lockheed Vegas and Gee Bee Racers – and a young John Glenn, coast to coast in three hours in a supersonic "Project Bullet" F-8 rocket-plane. But now the only fixed-wing aircraft that lifted from Brooklyn tarmac were hobby models, droning like enraged metallic wasps.

During the week, Floyd Bennett Field came to life as a training station for police helicopters, squad-car drivers, and Emergency Medical Service vans. Its runways, once the longest in the world, now cracked and weedy like the Roman streets of Ephesus, were turned into obstacle courses, marked with orange plastic cones (in a National Park!). Endangered falcons transited at their peril. But on weekends, only the cricketers, flailing and yelping, broke the silence of the vast, empty field. Hangar Row fell quiet and became the best kind of museum: a gallery of the imagination.

I went exploring. Departing passengers and pioneers must once have entered the field by a walkway from the Flatbush Avenue side. A fence now blocked the path, but two ornate streetlamps survived as sentinels. One of the glass globes was intact, but the other had been smashed or lost or stolen, and the area between the building and the avenue had been turned into a picnic area, where park visitors, if there ever were any, could listen to the traffic while they ate. Nearby was a rusted metal tower, loud with perching crows, topped by white and green searchlight lenses that I could have reached, were I the type to scale a hand-over-hand ladder a hundred feet straight up. I wasn't, so I stood and craned and gawked for a while, and gave myself kudos for prudence.

The hangars, great and gray-blue, were arranged in a row like chessmen, north and south of the control tower. They held machinery, snow-removal equipment, portable toilets, temporary grandstands, and a big stage on wheels that would be rolled out in a couple of weeks for Irish Fest '93. A couple of them had been taken over by the Police Department, and in front of one hangar was an incredible armored amphibious duck, painted in NYPD colors, with fore- and aft-mounted machine guns, big spongy tires for use on land, and a huge propeller and rudder for nautical deployment. This was the weapon, I reckoned, that the forces of law and order would dispatch should New York be attacked by Libyan frogmen, or the Little Mermaid gone berserk.

Above the entrance doors to the terminal building was an insignia: green copper wings, extending from a map of the Americas, heralding this patch of

Laurentide outwash as the gateway to the world. This it never had become. Built before the high-speed parkways could feed it passengers, Floyd Bennett Field proved to be too remote from Manhattan to be a commercial success, leaving it largely to experimental or military purposes throughout most of its history. Newark had preceded it, and had claimed the valuable U.S. Mail and much of the early passenger traffic. La Guardia and Kennedy (formerly Idlewild) International had followed as the foci of the frequent-flyer era.

Floyd Bennett Field had been, for a time, it is true, one of the busiest Naval Air Stations on the East Coast, the point of departure for tens of thousands of crewmen and women toward Germany, Korea, Vietnam. But the last Navy plane – the last plane of any kind – had long since departed, and for the past few decades, a civilian could fly to Floyd Bennett only by car, truck, or the Rockaway bus. Now it was a National Recreation Area, and it struck me as ironic that I had touched down at a thousand airports on six continents, but never had I, and never would I, land at my Flatbush Avenue home field.

On the opposite, eastern, side of the building, a small display had been erected. A photo of Howard Hughes showed him in a hat and business suit at the controls of an aircraft, perhaps the Northrop Gamma in which he flew, in April of 1936, from Floyd Bennett Field to Miami in four hours, twenty-one minutes, the fastest flight ever made. And there was Wiley Post, a white patch over his lost left eye, posing beside the *Winnie Mae*, in which he – and Will Rogers – would be killed.

Another panel gave a brief biography of Floyd Bennett himself. A young aeronaut from upstate New York, fearless, leather-helmeted, he had piloted Commander Richard E. Byrd to the North Pole in 1926 and was waiting to accompany the first aerial expedition across Antarctica when he volunteered to lead a rescue mission to Labrador in 1928. Fellow fliers – the German and Irish crew of a transatlantic Junkers – were down and marooned in the wilderness.

Bennett volunteered to go for them. Halfway to Labrador, he contracted pneumonia. He was taken to a hospital in Quebec, where he died, even as the great Lindbergh himself was flying north with a vial of life-saving serum. He was thirty-eight.

Near the historical photos, attached to the terminal itself, was a weathered brass plaque that long predated the National Park Service's occupation and the Indo–Pakistani bowlers. It was a pilot's prayer, dated 1938 and addressed to Our Lady of Loretto, Patron Saint of Aviation. In a single sentence, it crystallized all the daring and the danger of the Floyd Bennett years: "We beseech thee thy blessing upon these aircraft, so that those who entrust themselves to them in aerial journeys . . . may find happy landings and return safely to their own."

I turned around to see the planes but they all had flown away.

∾

Whatever its commercial failings, the flying roster of Floyd Bennett Field equaled the pantheon of the skies. The great airfield opened four years too late for "Lucky" Lindbergh, who took off for Paris from a bumpy strip in Westbury, Long Island, which was now occupied by the shopping plaza where my mother, when she could wangle a ride, would buy the multiple skirts and blouses that she would return a few days later in Downtown Brooklyn. But as soon as they were ready, in 1931, the mile-long runways of Barren Island flung aloft the serious and the stunt-makers, hurling them toward Newfoundland, Wales, Russia, and the rest of the world.

From here took off the longest nonstop flight ever made – to Istanbul, 5,011 miles – and the speediest – to Los Angeles, ten hours and change. Laura Ingalls dashed to Burbank and back, setting women's records on both legs of her trip. Major Jimmy Doolittle piloted an American Airlines prototype out of Los Angeles and touched it down on Brooklyn, seven years before his lightning Tokyo raid. Wiley Post flew around the world, solo, in seven days, nineteen hours. Five years later, Howard Hughes and four companions shaved four full days off the time.

In July 1933, two thousand spectators gathered on the future cricket oval to watch Amelia Earhart take off for California in the Bendix Trophy race. (The previous summer, she had flown the Atlantic alone, from Newfoundland, cementing her immortality.) Six pilots competed: two dropped out; one crashed and died. Earhart completed the race, finishing third of three, and lived to fly again. Four summers later, she waved goodbye from Miami and disappeared.

It could get silly. In 1931, crews of Germans and Hungarians inaugurated what became known as the "Goin' Home" flights from Floyd Bennett Field, publicity stunts that often turned to tragedy. The Germans and Hungarians, however, were fortunate. They landed, respectively, in Newfoundland and New Jersey.

A year later, an aircraft sponsored by a Norwegian shoe manufacturer went down in Newfoundland, but the pilots lived. The *City of Warsaw* made it as far as France. The *Leonardo da Vinci* landed in County Tyrone, Ireland. Two Portuguese, whom the newspapers referred to as "noblemen" with blood as blue as horseshoe crabs, got *Magellan* off the ground at Floyd Bennett Field, then immediately crashed. The aristocrats survived and returned home . . . to Cincinnati.

Lituanica left Brooklyn for Vilnius in 1933, crashed in Germany, and all hands perished. *The American Nurse,* a Bellanca Skyrocket, was supposed to conduct a "scientific expedition." A woman named Edna Newcomber was going to parachute into Florence, Italy, to honor Florence Nightingale. A woodchuck was carried as a test of the effects of high altitude on rodents. Somewhere between Flatlands and the Azores, *The American Nurse* and all aboard her vanished at sea.

Then there was "Wrong-Way" Corrigan, a leprechaun from Texas by way of California, and his second hand single-seater, *Sunshine.* A restless, guileless, sky-mad barnstormer, who had worked in Lindbergh's pit crew, Douglas Corrigan was itching to put his own name in the books when he either committed or counterfeited the great mistake that won him his undying fame.

It was July 1938, and Corrigan had just quit his job as an aircraft welder in a dispute over a five-cent raise. *Sunshine,* which he had purchased for $325, was a boxy little monoplane of questionable airworthiness, but he had registered it as an "experimental" plane, and proceeded to fly it to New York from California. Itching for trans-oceanic adventure a year after Earhart's disappearance, he ran into a bureaucracy not eager to sanction another dead young American pilot.

The plane was on the ground at Floyd Bennett Field. Stymied, Corrigan asked permission to return to California. This was granted, along with a warning from the station manager not to take off in a westerly direction. If *Sunshine* was going to crash with a full tank of fuel, as everyone expected, it would be preferable if it went down in Jamaica Bay and killed a few gulls, rather than plow into the terminal building and scorch the bright new plaque to the Patron Saint of Aviation.

Taking off eastbound, Corrigan climbed to five hundred feet, disappeared into haze and fog, and then, he claimed, misread his compass for the next twenty-eight hours. At that point, he noticed that there was water beneath his wings. This might have been a problem, had he actually overshot California, since he had already eaten all his chocolate bars and Fig Newtons, he was low on fuel, and he spoke no Japanese. A short while later, however, Wrong-Way was relieved to discover that he had unerringly miscalculated his way east, not west, and now he was in Ireland. His first words upon landing at Baldonnel were, reputedly, "Where am I?"

He was a hero in a darkening age. He was hailed wildly in Dublin, then in London. The New York *Post* printed its headline of his exploit backwards. His pilot's license was duly suspended, but only until the day he was scheduled to return to New York, by ship. In motorcades and ticker-tape parades, he was seated in cars that were driven in reverse. In Texas, he was awarded a watch that ran the wrong way.

Fifty years later, Wrong-Way Corrigan still wore the same leather jacket. In 1988, *People* magazine found him in California, not far from the orange grove he had purchased with the money he earned when he starred as himself in a movie called *The Flying Irishman*. Cast into celebrity by devilishness and pluck, he had known the darker side of life as well, losing the youngest of his three sons to a plane crash in 1972. For the golden anniversary of his famous flight, he returned to Dublin in a four-hundred-seat jet.

He had outlived Hughes, Post, Earhart, and Lindbergh. Of his spurned application to fly the ocean legally, he told *People*, "They told me to get lost, so I did."

∾

The terminal building had now been named the Congressman William F. Ryan Visitor Center. The ground floor had been renovated, and there were meeting rooms for Park Service functions and an accordion panel of big color photos that advertised Gateway as a multi-purpose resource. Above the lobby was a stained-glass skylight. A white dove spread her wings in a halo of celestial blue.

The building seemed not to be open. Scouting around, I found one of the doors at the Flatbush Avenue side unlocked. So I walked in. It was hot, dry, and silent. Flies buzzed against windows, trying to escape.

From the lobby, a stairway led toward the control tower I had seen from outside. I tiptoed up, slid a sawhorse aside, and got to the second landing. The refurbishing had not progressed beyond the ground floor. Up here, among denuded offices and empty, unlit halls, I was walking on paint chips and fallen plaster in the Loew's Kings of the air age.

A narrow staircase full of wasps led to the tower itself. I climbed up, two steps at a time, my heart thumping, and reached the top. All the dials and gizmos had been stripped from the console, but otherwise it was as if the airfield was ripe for rebirth. The view was fabulous: the pattern of runways, shimmering with heat, clear and hungry for traffic; beyond them, the glistening waters of the bay. To the right was the bridge to Rockaway. To the left was the World Trade Center, twelve miles distant, and between the tower and the Towers lay all the territory of my three-month escapade.

It was too hot and airless to linger. I descended to the second floor, and then, suddenly, I heard footsteps. Thinking I was about to be apprehended for trespassing, I was preparing my response – "Where am I?" – when a panting Coast Guardsman in blue fatigues came sprinting up the stairs.

Rushing right at me, he barked a question: "Are you working on the microwaves?" But before I could answer, he had run off.

I went back down to the sanitized lobby and looked at the photo display. I had made an appointment to meet the park's "cultural historian," but the fellow had not appeared. Outside, more men in blue were worrying over a van full of electronic gear.

Finally, the historian arrived. Brian Feeney had worked for eight years on the preparation of Ellis Island for public viewing, and now he was assigned to Floyd Bennett Field. He talked about acquiring a surplus collection of old planes from the Smithsonian Institution and turning the empty hangars of deepest Flatlands into a fabulous reliquary of the air age. But he was working for an administration that could not yet afford to repaint the second floor of the old terminal.

I told Brian Feeney that I had already made my way up to the control tower, without his permission. But he didn't complain. Instead, he led me toward a door and asked, "Have you seen the tunnels?"

"The *tunnels?*"

Yes, the tunnels. Under the tarmac where the Indo–Pakistani Cricket League clattered each sunny Saturday, a network of passageways led from the terminal to what would have been the anchor bays of whirring, waiting planes. These pre-jet jetways had been sealed during the Second World War – as defense against saboteurs? – and they had been forgotten until Gateway maintenance workers rediscovered them and strung up a few lights.

A door led to the basement and more big, bare rooms. Brian Feeney found a panel of electrical switches, and we entered the main tunnel, which was lined with blue and yellow tiles, much like the birth-certificate vaults beneath the Board of Health. Some of the original iron handrail was intact, and the flooring of blue and white blocks had retained some color through all the years of dampness and neglect. But the tunnels dead-ended in stairways blocked by piles of sandbags, and we could go no further. The exit holes, of course, had been paved over many years before.

Turning back, I wondered who else had walked this way – Doolittle? Earhart? Citizen Hughes, with Ava Gardner on his arm?

5

Brian Feeney gave me a lift along runway 6 to the far end of the field. We drove north-east – "heading zero-six-zero" – as had the ambulance that followed Wrong-Way Corrigan as the tiny plane called *Sunshine* shuddered into the mist. The runway concluded at the edge of a section of Jamaica Bay called Big Channel, so we turned right on an old taxiway and came to a huge hangar, once a Navy seaplane base, now filled with Park Service equipment and personnel. Next to it was another old Navy hangar from the days of the U-boat patrols, empty now but not too rampantly vandalized. As if to reinforce the dereliction, a single search-and-rescue plane had been left to decay outdoors, at the north side of the hangar. The plane's propellers had been removed, and its wings sheared off, leaving only the fuselage, balanced on three flat tires. A stepladder led to a cockpit whose windows had been smashed. Weeds poked up through the pavement, and a herring gull lay freshly dead on the ground, its eyes open and its plumage still clean and white and storm-cloud gray.

I thanked the historian for his time and walked south along the main road of the old military installation. In a grassy field to my left were three glossy ibises, probing the ground with scimitar bills, quickly waddling a couple of steps, then stopping to poke again. ("Uncommon," said the *Golden Field Guide*, "but extending its range.") I crossed runway 12, freshly repaved and still used by Coast Guard helicopters, the last vestige of powered flight at lonely Floyd Bennett Field.

Further along was the Coast Guard base itself – Air Station Brooklyn – and then a complex of dormitories, classrooms, a cafeteria, and a gymnasium left vacant when the Navy ran out of wars to fight. This campus was now being used by the Job Corps, a federal government agency set up in the 1960s as part of a combat that showed no signs of being honorably concluded, the much-advertised War on Poverty.

The Gateway Job Corps Civilian Conservation Center, as it was formally titled, had enrolled 203 young people of both sexes and all races for its current session, but twenty-three of them were AWOL on the day I showed up to look around. Courses were given in construction trades, apartment maintenance, and culinary arts, and it was possible to study to become a park ranger. Requirements for admission included being under twenty-two, economically disadvantaged, and "unable to benefit from continuation in a regular school."

In exchange for as much as two years of their time, the Job Corps hard core received vocational instruction, a dorm room and roommate, three meals daily, medical and dental check-ups, ten taxable dollars a week in allowances, and what was called, in Corpspeak, "normative training."

According to a brochure I received at the main office, this meant becoming "comfortable with mainstream social behavior."

According to a secretary in the director's office, this meant, simply, "You don't hit me; I don't hit you."

The director of the Gateway Job Corps Civilian Conservation Center was a barrel-chested *Stand and Deliver* type named José Rosario. In his office, invited to take a seat beneath numerous congratulatory plaques and citations, I asked Rosario where the kids came from.

"We get them on the way," he replied. "On the way to the hospitals, the jails, and the cemeteries."

It was late afternoon, school was out, and most of the student body of this university of last resort was hanging around the gym. Lounging on the steps was a young man named Dwayne Meighan, who had gone to Public School 152, as I had, and Hudde Junior High, as I had. Then he had become a drug dealer a couple of blocks from the Junction, working Flatbush Avenue near Newkirk Avenue, which, he said, everybody now referred to as New Crack.

"Me and my five brothers grew up on Flatbush," he said as I sat down next to him and told him of my ten-mile journey. "I'm glad to say that we're all still alive."

Dwayne Meighan had no trouble meeting the entrance requirements for Job Corps. He was twenty-one, his hair in tight dread curls, his legs in baggy blue shorts, his feet in unlaced black Adidas. He described himself as a "street hustler" who had gone through the criminal-justice system – "sittin' there, caged" – often enough to decide on a different career. He had been here for ten months. Dwayne Meighan was taking courses in cement masonry, but, like most of the others, he was majoring in Second Chance.

"I stayed away from the drug scene when I was young," he said, beginning his story. "I didn't want to get in and get hurt."

"How did you stay out of it?" I asked.

"I didn't say I stayed out of it forever," he smiled. "I'd sell enough to make six hundred dollars, spend two hundred, make another six hundred. I was making *crazy* money. I got to where I could buy nice clothes, but I didn't get no Maxima. To get a Maxima, you got to be killing people."

The Nissan Maxima, fitted with gold-colored wheel covers and flashing colored lights around the license plates, was the vehicle of choice at the current moment at the corner of Flatbush and New Crack.

"Why'd you stop?" I wondered. It was an unusual circumstance, to be sitting here in the late afternoon in a National Park with a former drug dealer on my right hand and a glorious, distant view of Manhattan's startling, jagged skyline before me.

"Ain't got no friends when you're selling drugs," Dwayne said precisely. "Your only friend is your gun. The money comes in so fast, people change. They switch on you – turn on you – do you something wrong.

"The money was good, but it can't last too long. If you can stand it five years, you're gonna be dead or in jail. I didn't like jail. 'Get up. Move. Don't move. Do this. Do that.' And I was worried about my Moms. They could come get me and hurt my Moms."

Dwayne Meighan had grown up on the block where the Haitian boy, David Opont, had been set on fire for refusing to take drugs, or so the story went. Dwayne had an uncle who had earned, he said, "a million a week," but this uncle now was in the penitentiary. Dwayne had come to realize that he was probably heading for one hell or the other himself. Then his Moms suggested trying to get into Lyndon B. Johnson's Job Corps.

"I said, 'I'll go try it,'" Dwayne recalled. "I came for orientation, three weeks. I liked it. It was better than being out on the corner. You didn't have to worry about people rolling by, shooting at you.

"The first six months, I lived in the dorm. A gay person was my roommate. It was a challenge to me, to sleep in the same room as a gay person without getting hyped up if he looked at me funny."

"What did you learn here?" I asked.

"I learned that I can wait. I want to have kids and live long enough to play with them. I want to walk down the street and not worry that somebody's gonna shoot me 'cause I stole their kilo. I want to live someplace that's not violent, someplace my kids can play in the schoolyard and not pick up bullets on the ground."

A Job Corps brochure said, "Let's face it, in the real world of work, you have to be able to read, write, speak intelligently, and do basic math in order to stay on the job." But Brooklyn's reality required skills more difficult to instill; the "normative" conditions were violence, poverty, aimlessness. I had walked through the worst of the Wooded Flat and come out the other side to reedgrass and ibises, but Dwayne Meighan and his classmates would have to re-enter, and endure.

In a few minutes, a bus was due to take the corpsman in the baggy blue shorts back to Newkirk for the weekend. He was a day-student now, home most evenings, drinking Crazy Horse and smoking Blunts, he said, but never, ever, touching a vial of crack. Crack, he said, made you crazy.

In front of the gymnasium was a flagpole that was surrounded by a newly laid sidewalk and some benches. Dwayne Meighan, apprentice mason, had helped to install the sidewalk. It was his Maxima.

"Look at it," he invited me. "You work on something, and it looks good, you can stand back and say, 'I *did* that.'"

"It must be a good feeling," I said.

"You know what we call that feeling?" Dwayne Meighan asked. "We call it 'gettin' paid.'"

∾

I walked back up beside Big Channel and came again to the Coast Guard base. Expecting uniformed sentinels with brush cuts and M-16s, or at the very least a 10,000-volt Jurassic Park fence, I glided past the entrance gate, noticed that it seemed to be standing open with not a soul guarding it, reversed engines, and ducked inside Air Station Brooklyn without so much as a "Friend or foe?".

Surprised at my luck, I found myself in a quadrangle of buildings at whose center was a swimming pool, a beach-sand volleyball court, and a whitewashed structure that I took, correctly, to be the enlisted man's saloon. The cars in the parking lot wore license plates from Oregon, Arkansas, Alaska.

Behind me was a cinder-block structure called Building 90, built by the Job Corps. It turned out to be a P X, with a female barber, a dry-cleaning service, and a grocery where anyone who just happened to be detouring a mile off Flatbush Avenue could pick up a hero sandwich and a Snapple. Suds and smokes were unavailable, but only to me. A sign advised, "No Beer or Cigarettes Without Military ID." My draft card, circa 1968, probably wasn't good enough.

There were some barracks on the east side of the quad, and a formal headquarters building that I entered with increasing bravado. In the foyer was a series of oil paintings – "Rescue" and "Vigil" were two – that showed outstretched hands in the storm-stirred brine being clutched by brave Coast Guardsmen. These scenes were not fiction. In a trophy case was a thank-you plaque donated by the owners of a Norwegian tanker that went down in 1964 with no lives lost.

I wandered down the hallways, this way and that, and, when someone finally questioned me, I said that I was looking for the public-relations office. This got me steered towards a good-looking young Texan named Mark Fisher, a lieutenant, junior grade, who had been posted to Air Station Brooklyn directly from Hickam Field, Hawaii.

I explained what I was about, the Texan nodded, and within moments I had been whisked into a cavernous hangar, in which four gleaming, red-orange Aerospatiale HH-65A "Dolphin" helicopters – 49 per cent French, 51 per cent American-made to secure the government contract – were being picked over by mechanics like the carcass of a Christmas goose. A fifth chopper was noisily revving its rotors outside, next to the softball field.

A red-haired, freckled, round-faced man came over to shake my hand as if I belonged here. He turned out to be no less than the commanding officer, Captain James J. Rao, out of Bensonhurst by way of Canarsie High. The camaraderie and informality was delightful; for a moment, it made me happy to be a taxpayer. Then I realized that all my taxes went to Ottawa.

The United States Coast Guard had been sending rescue missions aloft from Floyd Bennett Field since 1938. The development of a helicopter pickup harness had been carried out at Air Station Brooklyn, and over the decades it had been put to frequent, life-saving use, here and around the globe. A pamphlet Lieutenant Fisher gave me told of heroic rescues and occasional tragedies. In 1939, three drowned when a Coast Guard float plane, sent to retrieve a seaman with pneumonia from the ketch *Atlantis*, disintegrated as it tried to take off. In 1957, four Coast Guardsmen died when a Grumman Albatross crashed and burned at the end of runway 6. But all the officers and men I met were jolly and unconcerned.

One was Aviation Electrician's Mate First Class Tony Santo of New Utrecht, Brooklyn. Tony Santo had been stationed in Puerto Rico, Hawaii, and California. Then he actually *requested* assignment to Barren Island.

"I remember growing up and never knowing *anything* about dere being a Coast Guard base in Brooklyn," he said, a brown-eyed, wavy-haired man with big, tattooed arms and a genuine William Bendix accent. "In fact, I never knew dere was a Coast Guard base here until I was *in* the Coast Guard for a year! When I got into aviation school, I hoid about Air Station Brooklyn. I said, '*Dat's* where I wanna go.'

"The udder guys said, 'Why you wanna go *home*?' And I said, 'I'm goin' back to da Mom.'"

Tony Santo now lived with da Wife. He was thirty-three, with fourteen years in the battalion and six more to go to his pension. It had been a good career and an amazing year. He had been down at Guantanamo, Cuba, plucking Haitian refugees off their sad, sinking ships. Later, when the

Golden Venture jettisoned three hundred Fukienese off Rockaway to drown or make their way to shore, they called him in at three a.m., and he worked all night, refueling the Dolphins as they hurried back and forth to the panicked emigrants.

Most of the men slept in barracks at Floyd Bennett Field or at an old Army bivouac near Sheepshead Bay. Some "lived on the economy" off base. It seemed a rewarding vocation, demanding of skill and full of purpose, with a salary measured in lives saved.

All of a sudden, a loud beeping noise came over the loudspeakers. Then, a woman's voice: "Possible vessel taking on water . . . Possible vessel taking on water . . . rescue swimmer . . . rescue swimmer . . ."

There was more beeping and I heard men running along the corridors and shouts from the hangar. The Dolphin on the tarmac snarled and roared. A lieutenant named Mike Houtz poked his head into the machine shop where I was sitting with Santo, grinning from ear to ear.

"Listen!" Lieutenant Houtz said, beaming. "*This* is what we do!"

∽

On September 6, a few weeks after I had returned to Toronto, the following item would appear in the *New York Times*:

CO-PILOT DIES IN COAST GUARD COPTER CRASH

A Coast Guard helicopter on a routine trip outside New York harbor plunged into the Atlantic Ocean while trying to land, killing the co-pilot and critically injuring the pilot yesterday morning, the authorities said. . . .

. . . there had been no distress signal before the 9 a.m. crash of the helicopter, which was carrying a crew of three and two maintenance workers to the Ambrose Light off the Jersey Shore.

The three-ton HH-65A Dolphin helicopter had flown to the floating lighthouse with its 200-foot tower a short time earlier, dropping off two members of the Coast Guard at the light. . . .

The accident occurred about seven miles east of Sandy Hook in a 50-foot-deep shipping channel.

The co-pilot, Mark Fisher, 29, drowned following the accident. . . .

Five days later, the pilot, Lieutenant Marc C. Perkins, was taken off life-support.

6

The last lap began at dawn on a Saturday morning with sparrows, turtles, and an incompetent dog named Gus. My intention was to get a look at the "wilderness" areas of Floyd Bennett Field, and then, if I could find a way to do it without getting run over, to walk up the roadway of the Rockaway bridge to the Queens border. At that point, having touched every inch of Flatbush Avenue, I would turn around and gladly call it quits.

My sister had been with me for the first step at DUMBO and she was determined not to miss the conclusion of the misadventure. Awakening at six o'clock on a Saturday was not Little Debbie's preference, but since she still didn't have a job from Monday to Friday, her weekends were perpetual, and she could call every one of the next forty days "Sunday" if she wanted to. So she got up with me.

Our early-morning appointment was with a devoted conservationist named Ron Bourque who, with his wife, Jean, had personally scythed dozens of acres of the weedy wastes that had sprung up among the old run-ways to create suitable habitat for nesting birds. The Bourques' project was called the Grassland Restoration and Management Program, and it was yet another of the multifarious and often contradictory enterprises going on down here in the barrens. What with the Job Corps, the Coast Guard, the ambulance trainees, the police choppers, and the barber shop, it was all the Bourques could do to get permission to mow, chop, clear, and burn a few small parcels for their wee feathered wards.

At eight o'clock, I had Ron Bourque in my binoculars when he still was a half-mile away. Debbie and I were standing by the little orientation hut near the Flatbush Avenue entrance to the park, when I spotted him coming through the pinelands. I consulted my field guide: Beige windbreaker with L. L. Bean label. Battered Tilley safari hat. Body bent slightly forward from hours of staring through spotting scope.

The species was unmistakable: an American birder. Uncommon, but extending its range.

Ron Bourque greeted us and led us immediately into the interior. Jean, he said, was off in another zone of the airfield, conducting a census of nesting birds. His own quarry, and ours, was a rare brown and buffy-streaked seed-eater called *Ammodramus savannarum*, the grasshopper sparrow.

"My wife and I are not 'listers,' trying to just tick off as many different species as we can find," Bourque said. He was a self-taught amateur, originally from the Bronx, who had lived for the past twenty years at Sheepshead Bay, Brooklyn. "We want to observe birds and bird behavior, and changes in population."

"And this is important?" I asked him.

"It's important to those who care," he replied.

The function of the National Park Service, I imagined, was to teach all of us to care. But on the runways at Gateway, this purpose seemed to have been overwhelmed by the orange-cone obstacle courses and Irish Fest '93. So we moved along, Ron Bourque grumbling about misplaced priorities and all of us searching the meadow margins for our sparrow, with his thin, buzzy song.

Floyd Bennett Field was not quite the forest primeval. It had been built up from the marshy mess of Barren Island with tons and tons of Jamaica Bay sand, and this had been colonized by a few aggressive species of fast-growing flora: wild black cherry, *Phragmites*, Japanese knotweed, poison ivy. The Bourques were slashing and burning to create and maintain a sort of Indiana prairie where the horse-bone mills had once stood. Then the sparrows and kingbirds and longspurs might be able to co-exist with the HH-65A Dolphins.

"Do you consider yourself eccentric," I asked our guide. "wandering around an old airport, chopping down weeds?"

"No," he answered. "Keeping an area as a respite from the noise and pollution of the inner city is very important. Compared to the city's other problems, in a city with limited money, of course, other things have to come first. We understand that.

"But drive along the Belt Parkway. There are people with blankets spread out under every little tree, trying to have a picnic. This is a place where inner-city kids can wake up in a campground and hear birds singing. It may be the only National Park they'll ever visit. Why do they want to make it Disneyland?"

On the eastern horizon, over Big Channel, a long line of cormorants was heading off to work. I heard a song sparrow's calliope, and picked out more sounds from a nearby hedgerow. Brown thrasher. Cardinal. Mourning dove. I thought of the Barbadian carpenter at Genesis 1:29 who dreamed of the crickets of home. I should go back and tell him: he had only to catch the Rockaway bus and get off before the tollbooths.

"Look around you," Ron Bourque said. We were in a small grassy area that had been set aside as a camping zone for school groups. "It's hard to believe you're in Brooklyn."

A few steps away was the Grassland Restoration area, and at an equal distance on the other side of the campground was a reservoir of unbroken concrete, formerly the tarmac of the Naval Air Station, which was being used this morning by a school that taught people how to ride motorcycles. The Concorde took off from Kennedy and banked right over us, and the ground began to shake.

"Quick! There he is!" Ron Bourque announced a moment later, peering off into the field. I grabbed for my binoculars. Bourque pointed, and I saw it also – a tiny, tawny bird perched on a stalk of broomsedge, throwing his head back and letting go the insect-like buzz that gave the grasshopper sparrow its name. Then it flew a few feet and dropped down into the vegetation as if shot.

"Descends suddenly to the ground and disappears," the *Golden Field Guide* agreed.

"I see it!" Little Debbie trilled when I passed her the binoculars.

"That's a speck of dirt on the lens," I explained.

∽

We were standing with Ron Bourque and shaking our fists at the Concorde when Bob Cook drove up in a Park Service van to say good-morning. Cook was not an amateur lark-lover looking for rarities; he was a full-time employee of Gateway's ominously named Office of Resource Management and Compliance. This, however, turned out to be mere bureaucratese. What Bob Cook really did for a living was crash through the Barren Island underbrush and shove temperature probes up the tradesmen's entrances of noncompliant reptiles.

Introductions were made. Immediately, Cook invited my sister and me to come along on an expedition to the wildest part of the park – the North Forty. This was the kind of unhesitant hospitality that was as much a fixture of Brooklyn life as egg creams and crack cocaine. We accepted, and in a couple of moments we had left Ron Bourque to his sparrows and we were off, just the five of us: the dog, the park ranger, the reporter, the Little Debbie, and the Little Debbie's suitcase full of trail mix, nature books, spring water, and organic apples.

The ranger was blue-eyed, with long, light-brown hair and wire-rimmed glasses that made him look like the young John Denver. Gus, the dog, was black-furred, sixteen months old, and extremely affectionate. We were a merry group, but there was serious business ahead of us. The mission to the North Forty would require Gus's skills as a retriever, and as a retriever, Gus was an absolute dork.

"He's a slow learner," Bob Cook said as we bounced along the runway. "He's having trouble adjusting. He was expelled from field-trial school. His father was a national champion, and Gus couldn't cope with the burden of being his father's son. It's not likely he'll go back for his class reunions. He wouldn't have anything to brag about."

"Where did you get him?" the reporter asked.

"I ordered him from Maine," the ranger replied. "I needed a turtle hound, so I mailed them a live turtle. Instead of throwing a pheasant for him to retrieve, they'd throw Gus a turtle."

"*Throw?*" I squawked.

"Figuratively," Bob Cook said.

The North Forty trail started from runway 6 and wound through grassland and young forest to a freshwater pond that had been created to attract and retain birds, amphibians, and reptiles such as the turtles Gus had been trained to sniff and fetch. Except for the model airplanes that were torturing the silence like aerial dentist's drills, it was quiet here, and remote from Hangar Row and Air Station Brooklyn.

"Take your time and enjoy it," said a Park Service brochure.

At trailheads in the National Parks, it was common for a clipboard to be posted to encourage birders to list any unusual species they had seen as a guide to those who followed. This practice had been followed here, but when I checked the roster it included: Dodo bird, Big Bird, Kangaroo, Lions and tigers and bears – Oh, My!, Ducks, ducks, ducks, and schmucks."

Thus informed, we set out, armed for dodo, searching for any of the three hundred Eastern box turtles that Bob Cook had brought here from suburban Long Island in an attempt to reintroduce the species. To locate the animals, which spent most of their time hidden under piles of leaves, Bob Cook had glued radio transmitters to the shells of some of the turtles. He could home in on them in the event that his hound was unable to find them by smell.

Bob Cook was carrying some electronic gear and a flimsy antenna, held together with tape, that would pick up the signals. We were whacking through the *Phragmites*, merrily destroying habitat, while the ranger attenuated his receiver and mentioned, in passing, that it would be a good idea when we got home to check each other carefully for the ticks that might or might not carry Lyme disease. Great, I thought. I could look forward to seeing my sister in her underwear.

The life expectancy of the Eastern box was the same as ours: eighty to a hundred years, God willing. Bob Cook had rescued his specimens from the projected sites of shopping malls and subdivisions, but he didn't know if they would like Brooklyn any better than the other immigrants I had met along Flatbush Avenue. *Terrapene carolina* was a homing turtle, compelled to return to its birthplace. But, like so many of the immigrants, the turtles of the North Forty could never go home.

"On Long Island," Cook said, "they would come out of hibernation and find themselves in the middle of a brand-new four-lane highway."

In the laboratory of our childhoods, I was the boy with the stickball bat, and Bob Cook was the one who kept a jar full of tadpoles. His father worked at a perfume factory in Queens, but there were relatives in Pennsylvania who fished and hunted and taught a city kid to value nature's treasures before killing them. Then the Earth Day movement of the late sixties stabbed him like a pin and awakened a concerned biologist.

"We're fighting two myths," he said as we paused in a clearing. "One is that people think there is no wildlife in New York City. The other is that people think there is nobody in New York City who knows anything *about* wildlife. The fact is, with the university community here, we have some of the world's greatest naturalists. Of course, they're usually on expeditions in New Guinea."

Gus the hound came back from one of his random sorties with no new information. It looked as if we were going to have to rely on the radio. And, right on cue, it began to emit a soft, steady chip. Cook pointed the antenna this way and that, and we moved toward the source of the sound.

The dog was right beside us, but we saw the turtle before he did. It was a beautiful creature, as big as a man's hand, its upper shell – technically, its plastron – adorned with irregular shapes of gold and brown like a medieval map of the world. It was minding its own business in a dappled copse of sumac when the dog stepped right over it, completely oblivious.

"Gus, you can only get by for so long on good looks alone," his master said, dismayed.

The find was Eastern box turtle number 271, and it had Bob Cook's telephone number on a sticker on its shell. The ranger had circulated flyers: "WANTED DEAD OR ALIVE. ANY AND ALL TURTLES FOUND ON OR NEAR FLOYD BENNETT FIELD."

But the Eastern box was so secretive, and the underbrush so difficult of travel, it was unlikely that any would be spotted unless they crawled up onto the Belt Parkway to hitch a ride back home. Sixteen-month-old dogs, obviously, were no help. It was going to take a lot of electronic bushwhacking over a lot of years to find out whether the transplants had taken up residence in the North Forty.

Bob Cook knelt down next to the turtle and removed some instruments from his knapsack, which was a tenth of the size of Little Debbie's. He changed the battery in the transmitter glued to its shell, and noted the direction it was facing, the amount of shade and sunlight, and the temperature of the ground. He held it up for us to examine – five claws on the front feet, four on the back. He gave Gus a good, long sniff.

There were fifteen dark rings around the perimeter of the plastron, one for each year of the turtle's life. The shell was hinged, and could be closed as tight as the door of a Mercedes roadster. There was a concavity in the under-shell that identified number 271 as a male.

In mating, Eastern box turtles stacked themselves like inverted soup bowls, with the male always on top. In areas of low species density, Cook said, the females could store viable sperm for as long as four years, extracting just enough to fertilize each clutch of her eggs, conserving the rest in case she did not come across another male in the underpopulated undergrowth.

Then, while Debbie and I were nodding in awe of this man's knowledge and his deep respect for the animal kingdom, he took out a thermometer and shoved it up the reptile's rectum, and the poor thing opened its copper-toned eyes and popped out its legs and began to thrash the air like an Olympic swimmer on steroids.

Concluding an examination number 271 would never forget, Bob Cook packed up his stuff and turned on his receiver again, and we marched off to look for more turtles. We climbed out of the thicket and up a steep rise that turned out to be an abandoned ammunition bunker, a heavy concrete loaf from Navy days, now coated in bushes and weeds. It was rough country. Branches snapped in our faces and there were thorns and bristles and sudden, treacherous pits.

"I'm surprised how little vandalism there seems to be in the park," I said as we struggled along. "I expected that it would be full of homeless people, and that these bunkers would have been turned into crackhouses."

"Those people are afraid of nature," Bob Cook reasoned. "As soon as they step off the cement, they're traumatized."

We stood on top of the bunker and looked around at the cherry trees and the waving reeds. In the sixties, there had been a proposal to relocate 180,000 people from Bedford–Stuyvesant to a billion-dollar housing project on the tarmac of Floyd Bennett Field. All of this would have been schools, hospitals, shops, offices.

It had not happened. One corner of the borough had been set aside, a small victory for nature in a mad, unnatural place. Safe and unsuspected, the North Forty enfolded us. I dreamed we were four days up the Limpopo, lost in the trackless veldt.

"Wilderness," I sighed. "This must be what attracted you to your work."

"No," said Bob Cook. "It was the ten-thousand-dollar reward for finding Jimmy Hoffa."

∾

Flatbush Avenue ended as it began, in a tall, blue bridge to another borough. To the west of the toll plaza, there was a pedestrian and bicycle path, and we walked along this until it began to rise onto the span itself. The Manhattan

Bridge had been free, but not the Rockaway; it cost you nothing to enter Brooklyn, and a dollar fifty to depart.

The bridge had been dedicated to the memory of Gil Hodges, and a gray-metal plaque on the administration building honored the Dodger first-baseman. Once, during a World Series against the exalted Yankees, the Catholic churches of humble Brooklyn had rung with prayers that Gil Hodges would break a hitting slump. Now his team was gone and his bridge led from Brooklyn over to Queens, and Queens had the godawful Mets.

Debbie and I climbed up, flushed with import and ceremony, and found our way blocked by about two dozen fishermen, who were casting for flounder in the inlet. The plentitude of fish was astounding. Some men – they were all men – had forty or more stacked up in plastic drums, like tortillas. I hoped that Jimmy Hunter was out today.

A Trinidadian said he had been coming to this bridge for twenty-seven years; "mussels is the bait," he confided. Two Italians were using worms and catching so many fish that they were offering them, three for five dollars, to less-lucky anglers who were afraid to go home empty-handed to their wives. I inspected the catch, and one of the Italians made a fist and said, "We're *killin*' 'em today!"

Another man reeled in his line. Tangled in it was a nightmarish creature, two feet across, its squirming legs caked with sand and mud. Spider crab.

"Scavenger," the man spat, and he sent the beast spinning like a pinwheel, sixty feet to the blue water below.

I leaned on the railing and watched the planes descending to land at Kennedy, ignoring the runways of Floyd Bennett Field. Air France; Lufthansa; TWA. Pakistan International lowered its wheels, bringing, perhaps, Taj Akbar's mother for another seven-month visit. I looked down at the rippling channel and thought of the Puerto Rican fisherman under the Manhattan Bridge: "Is the same water."

There was no point in going any further. We retreated down the bike path and found a trail that led to the water's edge. Now we were UGH, Under Gil Hodges. Three men were down here on a narrow beach, surfcasting, catching nothing. Two others had acrobatically climbed out onto the understructure of the bridge itself to fish from the foundation pilings.

Debbie wandered off while I sat on a storm sewer and glowed with accomplishment and sunburn. A few minutes later, she came back with the empty shell of a horseshoe crab that had molted here, or died, as light and brittle as spun sugar. She pulled a plastic bag from her rucksack and gently wrapped the shell, to be shown to her beloved schoolchildren – if she ever found work. Then I got up and we went off together to stick a toe each in the water and complete the transcontinental trek. Others might have hugged, but we weren't like that.

The sand was soft and springy, littered with shoes and bottles and clam-shells. There were brant in the water, and cormorants in the air. Poking from the ground were pilings that spoke of the villagers of Barren Island. One shred of rope was still attached to an eyelet on a splinter of wood. I ran my hand along the strands.

Who had tied it, I wondered, and where did he lie?

Epilogue

My mother told Roberto the Super that I would be leaving in a few days, and Roberto cried.

She left a small brown envelope on my bed that said, "I AM YOUR MAID, *Hennie.* THANK YOU."

The seventieth birthday was at hand. My father flew in from Boca Raton, dark-brown and gimpy-legged, but not urgently operable, or so the son of the brother of the wife of his own late brother had advised him. Linda arrived from Toronto, and we rented a car a block from Fairyland and took my mother shopping on Long Island. My mother bought only one skirt. Linda bought three.

Little Debbie sent a card that noted that Henry Kissinger and Charlton Heston were also born in 1923. "Who's Sorry Now" was a popular song. Lon Chaney was the Hunchback of Notre Dame.

There were other cards on top of the refrigerator from her friends at Parents Without Partners, and a gem from my father that read: "They said you were getting older, but I didn't buy it! They said you were slowing down, but I didn't buy it! They said you wanted a gift, but I didn't buy it!"

On my arrival, she had commanded that there be no celebration, but I didn't buy that, either. As I had suspected all along, when we finally got around to discussing our plans the night before the birthday, she proposed that we all go to the River Cafe under the Brooklyn Bridge for a spectacular meal and general blowout.

"But that's a hundred dollars a person!" I screamed, finally matching apartment C4 for volume after ten weeks on East 31st Street.

"What about Peter Luger's?" Debbie chipped in helpfully, naming another ritzy Brooklyn beanery. "That's only eighty dollars each."

We decided on a rib joint in Flatlands called Jerry's.

"Do me a favor," my mother said. "If Debbie ordered a cake, tell her to cancel it."

(It was Marie Antoinette gone upside-down: Let 'em *not* eat cake.)

"And no flowers."

She paused.

"'No flowers, please.' Sounds like a funeral."

∾

At 7:30 on the morning of her seventieth birthday, my mother was sitting by the window in the living room, smoking. Linda tiptoed in and congratulated her and handed her a coffee mug that said, "World's Greatest Mom."

"That's for putting up with Al for ten weeks," my wife said. Then she came back into the bedroom and whispered to me: "So far, so good."

It was time for my move. I walked down the long corridor and met my mother just as she was staggering from the living room towards the kitchen to make her Ovaltine.

"Happy Birthday," I said, and I moved to kiss her, but she was turning, and I caught only her left ear.

My mother took a step back and smiled.

"Allen," she said, shaking her head. "Don't overdo it."

Down Under Manhattan Bridge Overpass

p. 13 "the heave'e'yo of the stevedores" – Whitman, *Song of Myself,* verse 26; all Whitman poetic quotations taken from *The Essential Whitman,* selected by Galway Kinnell, Galahad Books, New York, 1992.

p. 14 "refreshed by the gladness" – Whitman, "Crossing Brooklyn Ferry," verse 3.

p. 15 opening of the Manhattan Bridge – *Brooklyn Eagle,* December 31, 1909.

p. 15 death of McGillis – *New York Times,* July 17, 1909.

pp. 15-16 "not half a dozen men" – Kingsley E. Martin, Chief Engineer, quoted in *New York Times,* December 5, 1909.

p. 16 "pedestrian" – Le Corbusier quoted in *American Institute of Architects Guide to New York City,* 3rd edition, Harcourt Brace Jovanovich, New York, 1988.

p. 21 Paul Theroux, "Subway Odyssey," *The New York Times Magazine,* January 31, 1982.

p. 24 "myself effusing and fluid" – Whitman, "Sparkles From the Wheel"; a poem considered by Kinnell to be "idiosyncratic." I sensed my own journey in the opening lines: "Where the city's ceaseless crowd moves on the livelong day,/ Withdrawn I join a group of children watching – I pause aside with them. . . ."

p. 33 "startling jagged skyline" – in "History Gives Way to Progress Along Boro Path Trod by Washington, Whitman," *Brooklyn Eagle,* February 21, 1954. ("Who needs another park?" complained a resident of the waterside district in the same article. "For more muggings?")

p. 40 "kanatarok and o-nen-tso" – *New Yorker,* September 17, 1949.

p. 40 History of the Mohawk ironworkers – *National Geographic,* July, 1952.

p. 42 "10 fathoms of black wampum" – *The History of the Town of Flatbush, in Kings County, Long-Island,* by Thomas M. Strong, D.D., Pastor of the Reformed Dutch Church, of Flatbush, T. Mercein Printer, New York, 1842, p. 32; reprinted 1908 by Frederick Loeser & Co., Brooklyn; reprint purchased by Little Debbie for thirty dollars, year unknown.

p. 43 *Within Two Worlds,* David Munroe Cory, Friendship Press, 1955.

Downtown Nowhere

p. 55 "utter derangement" – letter from Thomas Andros, quoted in "Flatbush in the American Revolution," pamphlet, Flatbush Historical Society archives.

p. 56 "Damn'd Yankee rebels" – *The Prisoner in the American Revolution*, Charles H. Metzger, S.J., Loyola University Press, Chicago, 1971. Metzger wrote that the customary figure of twelve thousand deaths aboard the Prison Ships was "gross exaggeration . . . unadulterated propaganda."

p. 56 "strange, rickety, mildewed" – Whitman, quoted in *Walt Whitman's New York: From Manhattan to Montauk*, Henry M. Christman, ed., Macmillan, New York, 1963.

p. 59 Larry King's return to Howard Avenue, Brooklyn – *When You're from Brooklyn, Everything Else Is Tokyo*, Little, Brown, New York, 1993.

p. 59 "good garbage breaks down" – the song "Good Garbage" by Tom Chapin and John Forster is available on Chapin's *Mother Earth* CD, issued 1990 by A & M, reissued 1993 by Sony Wonder.

p. 62 "cookies and milk" – "Cheap High Lures Youths to Malt Liquor '40s,'" *New York Times*, April 16, 1993.

p. 66 transit riders' survey in *Newsday*, June 22, 1993.

p. 78 casualties on Eastern Parkway – "E. Pkwy Cross Examination," *Newsday*, May 2, 1993.

p. 79 "King Moshiach will arise" – a condensed history of the Rebbe's sermons on the subject of Moshiach is included in the *Lag B'Omer Parade & Outing Souvenir Journal*, distributed at the festival, May 9, 1993.

p. 80 Rebbe Schneerson died in 1994.

p. 86 "the lowest crime rate" – precinct by precinct crime map of Brooklyn in *Newsday*, May 6, 1993.

p. 87 "Brooklyn of ample hills" – Whitman, "Crossing Brooklyn Ferry," verse 5.

p. 87 "somber-hued wonderland" – *AIA Guide*.

p. 89 "Man, Wife, Killed by Robbers" – the *New York Times*, August 9, 1992.

The Green Heart of Brooklyn

p. 107 the death of Juan Perez was widely covered; e.g., *Newsday*, May 21, 1987, "Park Officials Meet to Improve Security at Zoo"; *Daily News*, May 21, 1987, "Into the bears' lair . . ."

p. 109 "a deep rocky glen" – *AIA Guide*.

p. 109 "immoral and criminal purposes" – Olmsted and Vaux, quoted in *Prospect Park Handbook*, Clay Lancaster and Marianne Moore, New York Greensward Foundation, 1991.

p. 110 "disorder, destructiveness and defiance" speech by Robert Moses at Prospect Park centennial, June 2, 1966, quoted on page 116, *Prospect Park Handbook*, by Clay Lancaster, foreword by Marianne Moore, published for Greensward Foundation Inc. by Walton H. Rawls, New York, 1967.

p. 112 "warm the homesick heart" – *Brooklyn, U.S.A.*, John Richmond and Abril Lamarque, Creative Age Press, New York, 1946, p. 10.

p. 113 "wistfully while away the day" – "Through a Grand Gateway, a Classic Urban Oasis," *New York Times*, April 28, 1991.

p. 119 "vaulted breezeway" – *Prospect Park Handbook*, p. 75

p. 125 "tame excitement" – Marianne Moore, quoted in "A Museum Grows in Brooklyn (Painfully)," *New York Times*, November 15, 1992.

p. 127 "George Washington, Esquire," and other insults – Strong, p. 139.

p. 130 "scene of great confusion" – Strong, p. 142.

p. 130 "Good God, what brave men" – quote attributed to Washington in "Flatbush in the American Revolution," pamphlet, James R. Hurley, author, published by Flatbush Historical Society. Of the 400 Marylanders who stormed the house, 290 were killed. By comparison, according to the *Concise Illustrated History of the American Revolution*, by Joseph P. Cullen (Stackpole Books, 1972), 200 Americans were killed at Brandywine, 140 at Bunker Hill. In Brooklyn, 63 of the 19,000 British troops were killed.

p. 131 "We are part of history" – *GAZETTE* broadsheet, distributed by First Battle Revival Alliance, 1715 Newkirk Avenue, Brooklyn, NY 11226.

p. 132 history of the Franklin Shuttle – *Silver Connections – Subway Tales and Biographies*, vol. II, Philip Ashforth Coppola, Four Ocean Press, Maplewood, NJ, 1992.

pp. 135-36 Luciano's problem with the brakes – "The Malbone Street Crash," *Daily News Magazine*, November 6, 1988; "Subway Derailment Recalls '18 Catastrophe," *Sunday News*, December 8, 1974; *New York Notorious*, P. Schwartzman and R. Polner, Crown, New York, 1992; *Cash, Tokens and Transfers*, Brian J. Cudahy, Fordham University Press, New York, 1990.

p. 136 "heads taken right off" – *Brooklyn Eagle*, November 2, 1918.

p. 138 "Nowhere but in Brooklyn" and "all the horrendous overtones" – *Brooklyn, U.S.A.*, pp. 44, 52.

p. 140 "We decided" – James Rubin, "The Brooklyn Dodgers and Ebbets Field – Their Departure," in *Brooklyn, U.S.A: Fourth Largest City in America*, Brooklyn College Studies on Society in Change, vol. 7, Rita Seiden Miller, ed., Brooklyn College Press, 1979.

p. 146 "The citizens of New York" – E. B. White, "Here Is New York," *Harper*. 1949.

The Bride of Flatbush Avenue

p. 151 "This isn't a Caribbean resort" – Ellen Freudenheim, *Brooklyn: Where to Go, What to Do, How to Get There*, St. Martin's Press, New York, 1991.

p. 152 "Flatbush is going" – Pete and Dennis Hamill, *Village Voice*, October 20, 1975. Neil Telsey kept a well-worn copy of the article in his filing cabinet.

p. 152 "Look over your city and weep" – Episcopal Bishop Paul Moore's 1977 Easter Message, quoted by Harold X. Connolly in *Brooklyn College Studies on Society in Change*, p. 360.

p. 156 "the most beautiful of any suburb" – Homer L. Bartlett, M.D., "Flatbush as a Place of Residence," monograph, 1883, Flatbush Historical Society archives.

pp. 156-57 burglar alarms as standard equipment – *New York Times*, March 13, 1910.

p. 159 "bullets flew through their car" – "Police Blotter," *Flatbush Life*, May 24, 1993.

p. 159 "Mexicans worked cheapest" – Joel Millman, "New Mex City," *New York Magazine*, September 7, 1992.

p. 161 "NO REFUGE FROM GUNFIRE" – "Police Blotter," *Flatbush Life*, May 24, 1993.

p. 163 "She is Guyanese-born" – *New York Carib News*, May 11, 1993.

p. 164 Clubbing the Cat – Esther Singleton, *Dutch New York*, Benjamin Bloom, New York, 1968; originally published 1909.

pp. 164-65 "thou noblest spot" – "The Praise of New Netherland," poem by Jacob Steendam, 1661, quoted in *Peter Stuyvesant and His New York*, Henry H. Kessler and Eugene Rachlis, Random House, New York, 1959.

p. 165 "with colors flying" – surrender of Flatbush described in *Peter Stuyvesant and his New York*.

p. 166 "glutting their revenge" – Strong, p. 55.

p. 177 "They sprayed the screen silver" – former usher Lester Binger, quoted in "Talk of the Town," *New Yorker*, April 25, 1988.

p. 181 Houdini's childlessness also noted in *Houdini: A Mind in Chains*, Bernard C. Meyer, M.D., Dutton, New York, 1976.

p. 182 Columbia students meticulously catalogued the architecture of Flatbush Avenue in "Flatbush: Architecture and Urban Development from Dutch Settlement to Commercial Strip," Preservation Working Paper No. 1, Fall 1990, Prof. Daniel Bluestone, Graduate School of Architecture, Planning and Preservation, Columbia University, New York. This study also contains a history of the amalgamation of Flatbush village into the City of Brooklyn.

p. 190 "from thence with a straight line" – Strong, p. 41.

p. 190 "whip or punish" – Strong, p. 58.

p. 190 "mutilating every thing" – Strong, p. 39.

pp. 190-91 "this unfortunate" – "Flatbush, the County Seat," article by John J. Snyder in Flatbush Tercentenary commemorative pamphlet, *Brooklyn Eagle*, May 25, 1952.

p. 191 "it no doubt will appear strange" – Strong, p. 177.

p. 196 "flogged into learning" – "Our Village in Rhyme," poem by John Oakey, John F. Trow Printer, New York, 1863. ('There's a small but quite a famous village,/ Whose inhabitants are chiefly devoted to tillage,/ With occasionally some scamp arrested for pillage . . .' and so on, for twenty-five pages.)

p. 202 slave revolts described in *Dictionary of Afro-American Slavery*, R. Miller and D. Smith, Greenwood Press, Westport, Conn., 1988.

p. 202 *An Act for the Gradual Abolition of Slavery*, enacted by New York State Legislature, March 29, 1799, copy in Brooklyn College Library, Special Collections.

p. 203 "When you know him" – replica of 1803 poster at Lefferts Mansion.

p. 203 *Gazetteer of the State of New York 1836*, published by Thomas F. Gordon, Philadelphia(!).

p. 203 "We know of no other country" – *Long Island Star*, quoted by Ralph Foster Weld in *Brooklyn Village, 1816-1834*, Columbia University Press, New York, 1938.

p. 204 "poverty and squalor" – Richmond and Lamarque, *Brooklyn, U.S.A.*, p. 58.

p. 205 review of Akwaaba – *New York Times*, April 16, 1993.

p. 207 "casual and derogatory" – *Mama Lola*, p. 111.

p. 208 the title translates as "the paper that offers an alternative."

p. 221 "to create a rural park" – "The Visible City," *Metropolis Magazine*, September, 1982.

The Junction

p. 244 "a pack of louts" – Richmond and Lamarque, *Brooklyn, U.S.A.*, p. 2.

p. 245 a selection of Chimmie's exploits, originally published in the New York *Sun*, are contained in "Chimmie Fadden, Major Max and Other Stories," *The American Short Story Series*, vol. 82, Garnett Press, New York, 1969.

pp. 245-46 the origins of Brooklyn's "chimerical" accent are given by Prof. Geoffrey D. Needler in "Kings English, Facts and Folklore of Brooklyn Speech," *Brooklyn College Studies on Society in Change*, p. 173.

p. 246 *Times* article – "Oy Gevalt! New Yawkese an Endangered Dialect?" *New York Times*, February 14, 1993.

p. 251 "The Song of Deborah," Judges 5:1.

p. 258 Hudde's holdings listed in *Keskachauge, or the First White Settlement on Long Island*, Frederick Van Wyck, G.P. Putnam's Sons, New York, 1924.

p. 267   "moonlight necking" – I am indebted to Prof. Anthony M. Cucchiera, Archivist, for allowing me and Little Debbie to graze among the Special Collections department of the Brooklyn College Library.

p. 272   "covenant, promise and grant" – Milton Meltzer, *The American Revolutionaries: A History in Their Own Words 1750-1800*, Thomas Y. Crowell, New York, 1987.

Across the Flatlands

p. 294   "very dangerous and harmful driving" – according to *Brooklyn Eagle*'s "Flatbush Tercentenary Pamphlet," the fine for such behavior in 1668 was six guldens.

p. 294   "the country rang with horror" – *Brooklyn Standard-Union*, October 2, 1893, quoted in *The City of Brooklyn 1865-1898*, Harold C. Syrett, AMS Press, New York, 1968.

pp. 294-95   "When the evening shades are falling" – *Brooklyn Eagle*, July 14, 1892, quoted by Syrett.

p. 296   "18th cabby slay" – *Daily News*, April 26, 1993.

p. 299   "the need to work" – "TA and Police Vendetta Against Gypsy Vans," *New York Carib News*, May 18, 1993.

Down to the Sea

p. 314   "That vast tract" – "Jamaica Bay to be a Great World Harbor," *New York Times*, March 13, 1910.

p. 316   "Here lies the opportunity" – letter from Robert Moses, July 18, 1938, Brooklyn College Library, Special Collections.

pp. 339-40   "Goin' Home" flights and Corrigan's journey described in *Atlantic Fever*, Edward Jablonski, Macmillan, New York, 1972; also, "Notable Flights at Floyd Bennett Field," monograph, National Park Service Historic Structures Report.

p. 340   "get lost" – *People*, August 1, 1988.

SELECTED BIBLIOGRAPHY

"There was another place here once, and it was better than this."

That statement, by the journalist and novelist Pete Hamill in his introduction to *The Brooklyn Reader* (Harmony Books, 1993), a delightful selection of literary glimpses of the Borough of Churches, captures the essence of much of what has been written about Brooklyn by Brooklynites of my generation (and older) in the past twenty years.

In another epoch (these are quoted from *The Brooklyn Reader*), it was possible for James Agee to descend from Manhattan to wallow in Brooklyn's amorphous expanse ("...an exorbitant pulsing mass of scarcely discriminable cellular jellies and tissues; a place where people merely 'live'"). And for Carson McCullers to observe that "Brooklyn, in a dignified way, is a fantastic place."

"It seemed to me that the sun was always shining in Brooklyn," wrote Anatole Broyard in 1954. But that was the Brooklyn of the baseball Dodgers, the Parachute Jump at Coney Island, moonlight necking on the Sea Beach subway. It was not the Brooklyn of Go Away Evil perfume, *Do the Right Thing*, and crack cocaine. (In the Brooklyn I explored in 1993, immigrants recalled their homelands and sighed: "There was another place there once, and it was better than this.")

Now, a harvest of Brooklyn nostalgia permeates the libraries; the Dodgers alone are the subject of a dozen or more recent treatises. In 1986, the official Borough Historian, Elliott Willensky, encapsulated the genre – and the sense of loss – in his book *When Brooklyn Was the World*.

"For Brooklyn, the years 1920 through 1957 represent a kind of golden age," Willensky wrote. (The subways reached the Junction in 1920; the Dodgers bolted for California after the '57 season.) Through this prism, the present disappears.

My own reading before, during, and after my Brooklyn wanderings was largely case-specific, encompassing facts more than feelings. (Horseshoe crabs. The Prison Ship Martyrs.) I spent too much time in New Netherland and too little in Irwin Shaw. ("Yuh don't like Brooklyn, go back to Italy.") Many of the historical reference books I consulted have already been cited in notes. Here is a selection of non-fiction works of more general interest:

The Brooklyn Reader – Thirty Writers Celebrate America's Favorite Borough; edited by Andrea Wyatt Sexton and Alice Leccese Powers, Harmony Books, New York, 1993.

When Brooklyn Was the World 1920-1957; Elliott Willensky, Harmony Books, New York, 1986.

Brooklyn, U.S.A.; John Richmond and Abril Lamarque, Creative Age Press, New York, 1946.

AIA Guide to New York City, 3rd edition; Norval White and Elliott Willensky, Harcourt Brace Jovanovich, New York, 1988.

Guide to New York City Landmarks; New York City Landmarks Preservation Commission, The Preservation Press, Washington, D.C., 1992.

Brooklyn, U.S.A.; Brooklyn College Studies in Social Change, Vol. 7, Ruth Seiden Miller, ed., Brooklyn College Press, 1979.

"Is Anyone Here from Brooklyn?"; Frank Bisogno, Fradon Publishing, 1990.

When You're from Brooklyn, Everything Else Is Tokyo; Larry King, Little, Brown, New York, 1992.

Brooklyn . . . and How It Got That Way; David W. McCullough, The Dial Press, New York, 1983.

Caribbean New York; Philip Kasnitz, Cornell University Press, 1992.

Brooklyn Almanac: Illustrations/Facts/Figures; Margaret Latimer, ed., Brooklyn Educational and Cultural Alliance, 1984.

New York Notorious; P. Schwartzman and R. Polner, Crown Publishing, New York, 1992.

I Remember Brooklyn; Ralph Monti, Birch Lane Press, New York, 1991.

Brooklyn – Where to Go, What to Do, How to Get There; Ellen Freudenheim, St. Martin's Press, New York, 1991.

Silver Connections – Subway Tales and Biographies (3 volumes); Philip Ashforth Coppola, Four Ocean Press, Maplewood, N. J., 1990.

Mama Lola – A Vodou Priestess in Brooklyn; Karen McCarthy Brown, University of California Press, Berkeley, 1991.

Old Brooklyn in Early Photographs; William Younger, Dover Publishing, New York, 1978.

A Ghetto Grows in Brooklyn; Harold X. Connolly, New York University Press, 1977.

Brooklyn Bridge – Fact and Symbol; Alan Trachtenberg, University of Chicago Press, 1965.

Brooklyn Trolleys; J. C. Greller and E. B. Watson, N. J. International Inc., 1986.